Reading Is My Window

Reading Is My Window

BOOKS *and the* ART *of* READING *in* WOMEN'S PRISONS

Megan Sweeney

The UNIVERSITY *of* NORTH CAROLINA PRESS

Chapel Hill

©2010 The University of North Carolina Press
All rights reserved

Designed and set in Whitman by Rebecca Evans
Manufactured in the United States of America

The paper in this book meets the guidelines for permanence
and durability of the Committee on Production Guidelines for
Book Longevity of the Council on Library Resources.

The University of North Carolina Press has been a member
of the Green Press Initiative since 2003.

Library of Congress Cataloging-in-Publication Data

Sweeney, Megan, 1967–
Reading is my window: books and the art of reading
in women's prisons / by Megan Sweeney.
p. cm. Includes bibliographical references and index.
ISBN 978-0-8078-3352-0 (cloth: alk. paper)
ISBN 978-0-8078-7100-3 (pbk: alk. paper)
1. Women prisoners—United States—Books and reading.
2. Books and reading. I. Title.
HV9471.S94 2010
365'.66—dc22   2009032387

Portions of Chapter 1 appeared in a different form in "Beard v. Banks:
Deprivation as Rehabilitation," PMLA 122, no. 3 (May 2007): 779–83. Portions
of Chapter 4 appeared in a different form in "Books as Bombs: Incendiary
Reading Practices in Women's Prisons," PMLA 123, no. 3 (May 2008): 666–72.
Both are reprinted by permission of the copyright owner, The Modern
Language Association of America.

Portions of Chapter 1 and Interlude 1 appeared previously in "Reading and
Reckoning in a Women's Prison," Texas Studies in Literature and Language 50,
no. 3 (2008): 304–28. Copyright ©2008 by the University of Texas Press. All
rights reserved. Reprinted with permission.

Portions of Chapter 3 appeared previously in "Prison Narratives, Narrative
Prisons: Incarcerated Women Reading Gayl Jones's Eva's Man," Feminist Studies
30, no. 2 (Summer 2004): 456–82, reprinted by permission of the publisher,
Feminist Studies, Inc.

cloth   14 13 12 11 10   5 4 3 2 1
paper   14 13 12 11 10   5 4 3 2 1

THIS BOOK WAS DIGITALLY PRINTED.

In memory of my mother,
SALLY DIMOND SWEENEY,
who fostered my passions for
reading and social justice

And to my father,
CLAYTON A. SWEENEY,
who has deepened my understanding
of courage and transformation

In this story
there's always the possibility of morning,
a chance
that the screams which drip down at midnight
are not really threatening
but wishing us well,
wishing us a life
in another story.

M. A. JONES, "An Overture"

CONTENTS

ILLUSTRATIONS AND FIGURES

ACKNOWLEDGMENTS

LIKE A QUILT, *Reading Is My Window* represents the work of many minds and hands. I love how quilts transform discarded scraps and torn fragments into resplendent, meaningful wholes. While participating in a women's quilting cooperative in Port Gibson, Mississippi, I witnessed women with different sensibilities and visions work together to create unique forms of beauty and meaning. When my own eye would dart away from nubby scraps of Pepto-Bismol-pink polyester, another eye would envision such pieces as integral to our design. Collectively, we created works of art that none of us could have anticipated or created on our own. Writing this book involved a similar process, with many people lending a hand in its creation. I am indebted to those who shared pieces of their stories; enabled me to see meaning, value, and beauty where I might have overlooked them; helped me to arrange disparate fragments into a coherent design; and provided intellectual, emotional, and material support as I stitched together the contributions and insights of many voices.

My deepest debt is to the ninety-four women prisoners who shared with me their time, stories, and reflections. These women—from the North Carolina Correctional Institution for Women, the Northeast Pre-Release Center, and the State Correctional Institution at Muncy—inspired me with their openness, creativity, resilience, and humor, and I am grateful for the many things they taught me. Some employees at the prisons where I conducted research also deserve special thanks. Ann Mullin, Valerie Aden, Richard Shuler, and Sandy Weisner supervised my research, helped with scheduling interviews and group discussions, and made sure that I had what I needed. I could not have completed this book without their assistance. I am also appreciative of the prison librarians, chaplains, and instructors who answered my endless questions and allowed me to spend time in their libraries. Pam Cass, Lisa Reicheldorfer, Nancy Kopshine, and Lisa Bond deserve special mention in this regard.

Many of my teachers have played a hand in shaping this book. I am thankful to Ellen Messer-Davidow for inspiring me to conduct fieldwork in a women's prison, and to Rich Doyle and Evan Watkins for introducing me to whole new realms of language and ideas. At Duke University, Wahneema Lubiano modeled exciting possibilities for thinking about narrative, and Jan Radway helped me to discover scholarly conversations in which I might feel at home. Kim Curtis and Rom Coles provided intellectual and emotional support in more ways than they may imagine, and I continue to feel inspired by their integrity, centeredness, and passion. Along with Jehanne Gheith, Kim also introduced me to the joys of participating in a writing group. During my time at Duke University, I benefited from the support of a James B. Duke Fellowship, a Graduate Program in Literature Departmental Fellowship, and a Women's Studies Interdisciplinary Research Fellowship. The Woodrow Wilson Foundation also generously supported me with a Charlotte Newcombe Dissertation Year Fellowship in 2001–2.

A few friends from graduate school have been some of my best teachers. Amy Carroll, Amy Frykholm, Jill Petty, and Rebecca Wanzo have inspired me through their work and helped to reinfuse my own work with meaning and value. With amazing faithfulness, Rebecca has repeatedly breathed new life into my project by reminding me of what I know and why it matters, and by offering incredibly insightful feedback. During my two years as an adjunct instructor at Georgetown University, Dana Collins and Ashwini Tambe also enabled me to see my work through their eyes and helped me to reframe my project in crucial ways.

Since I have been at the University of Michigan, I have received myriad forms of support. Generous financial assistance from the Horace H. Rackham School of Graduate Studies and the Institute for Research on Women and Gender (IRWG) enabled me to conduct new research in two prisons and to purchase books for the group discussions. Three graduate research assistants funded by the English Department—Emma Garrett, Molly Hatcher, and Mickenzie Fasteland—offered material and intellectual support at crucial stages of the project. I also received helpful feedback from presenting my work in numerous settings: the Center for Afroamerican and African Studies Brown Bag Series; the Comparative Literature Brown Bag Series; the Series on Women, Law, and Public Policy sponsored by IRWG; the Harold Cruse/Black Studies Conference; and the Women's Studies Colloquium. Most importantly, my colleagues in the English Department and the Center for Afroamerican and African Studies have welcomed me into a vibrant intellectual community. I am thankful for support from Buzz Alexander, Paul Anderson, Sara Blair, Lori Brooks, Amy Carroll, Gregg Crane, Angela Dillard, Jonathan Freedman, Kevin Gaines, Sandra Gunning, Lucy Hartley, Martha Jones, Tiya Miles, Josh Miller, Anita Norich, Adela Pinch, David Porter, Alisse Portnoy, Xiomara Santamarina, Alan Wald, Gillian White, John

Whittier-Ferguson, and Andrea Zemgulys. Michael Awkward and June Howard deserve special thanks for participating in my manuscript workshop; both offered rigorous and insightful feedback that enabled me to reshape my project in fundamental ways. At key moments, Scotti Parrish, Sid Smith, Valerie Traub, and Patsy Yaeger have reminded me of the value of my work and shown me the importance of pursuing one's passions. A few colleagues have played particularly significant roles in shepherding this book to completion. Cathy Sanok and Jennifer Wenzel offered brilliant readings and suggestions during a period when I was reconceptualizing the project. Jennifer continues to offer invaluable feedback, and many pages of this book show traces of her hand; she models a level of generosity and commitment that I hope to emulate. Over the past three years, the members of my writing group—Anne Curzan, Anne Gere, and Mary Schleppegrell—have also read and reread portions of this book. With humor, patience, and exceptional insight, they helped me to separate the wheat from considerable amounts of chaff and made artful contributions to the book's final design.

This work is supported in part by the Radcliffe Institute for Advanced Study at Harvard University. The year that I spent at Radcliffe afforded me time and mental space that were essential for completing my research and writing. I owe special thanks to Judy Vichniac and Melissa Synnott for creating a stimulating and collegial atmosphere. Among the many people who offered me support during that year, the following fellows deserve mention for asking especially probing questions or for taking time to read my work: Elizabeth Alexander, Elizabeth Armstrong, Hilde Heynen, Jackie Malone, Carla Mazzio, Qin Shao, Martin Summers, and Kate Wheeler. Rebecca Baron invited me to participate in a writing group, and she and Lisa Barbash helped me to rethink my book's organization and title. More importantly, Rebecca helped me to feel at home in my work and in my home-away-from-home, and her thoughtful presence and friendship were highlights of my year. My undergraduate research partner at Harvard, Samantha Tejada, provided tremendously helpful assistance in many forms, from reading drafts to organizing data from hundreds of interviews. Linda Meakes also deserves thanks for her careful transcriptions and for the compassionate interest that she took in the women whose words she was transcribing.

As I have circulated my work in journals and at conferences, many other scholars have given me helpful feedback, including Judith Kegan Gardiner, Phil Barrish, Anouk Lang, Ruby Tapia, and Tanya Erzen. Thanks are due to *Feminist Studies*, *Texas Studies in Literature and Language*, and *PMLA* for allowing me to reprint portions of some already published material. Deborah Brandt, Rena

Fraden, and James Reisch read a draft of my manuscript and provided incisive and generous comments. Avery Gordon read a partial draft for my manuscript workshop and a complete draft after I made substantial revisions. My debt to Avery is enormous. She not only offered crucial suggestions for reorganizing and reframing my chapters; she showed me how to be a better reader of my ethnographic material, enabling me to see the many forms of knowledge that lay before me. Avery helped me to find a language and a voice for communicating what I had learned from women prisoners, and this book is far better thanks to her involvement. Sian Hunter, my editor at UNC Press, offered substantive feedback, encouragement, and patient guidance as my manuscript was transformed into a book. Stephanie Wenzel and Beth Lassiter also helped to make the process smooth.

While I was writing this book, family members and friends would periodically ask if I was still working on my "paper." I hope that they will now understand why writing this "paper" took so much time. Throughout the process, Meghan Hvizdak, Laura Anderson, and Jill Petty have sustained me with their friendship and love. Mary Anderson has accompanied me on every step of the journey, sharing her insights about meaning-making, crafting one's story, and stepping onto the rickety bridge. I am profoundly grateful for her wisdom and support. My mother-in-law, Maureen Carlin, has loved and encouraged me in ways too numerous to count. My mother, Sally Dimond Sweeney, died in 2004, but it is she who first inspired my passions for reading and justice. Later in her life, my mom started annotating the title pages of books to remind herself that she had already read them and to let others know whether each book was worth reading. I can only hope that she would write "loved it!" in the margins of this book. My father, Clayton A. Sweeney, has offered me his steady hand, unconditional support, and capacious love. His presence in my life gives me great joy, and he continues to teach me more than he'll ever know. Finally, over the last sixteen years, Michael Carlin has shown me what it means to craft one's life story in partnership with another. He helped this book come to fruition in myriad ways—from reading drafts of various chapters to making me scrumptious meals—and its pages bear traces of his compassion, generosity, and integrity, his humor and zest for life, and his abiding love. To paraphrase Toni Morrison's *Beloved*: The pieces I am, he gathers them and gives them back to me in all the right order. I am so grateful that I have been able to put my story next to his.

Reading Is My Window

Introduction

Ordinary people don't know how much books can
mean to someone who's cooped up.—ANNE FRANK,
The Diary of a Young Girl

Books are a lifeline to people in here. We live life
vicariously through books.—CAESAR, State Correctional Institution at Muncy

"THEY LULL US to sleep with romance! I'm telling you, four shelves of romance!"
So says Solo,[1] a fifty-six-year-old African American woman, in discussing the
library in the prison where she is incarcerated. In Solo's view, the library caters
to imprisoned women's "fantasy" of "being an entrepreneur or falling in love,"
while offering few resources to help women address the issues that bring them
back to prison. "You pack all these people into these compounds and you don't
have the staff nor the time nor the resources to really deal with *why are you an
inmate?*" she explains. Solo then sharply criticizes current reductions in educational opportunities for incarcerated women, concluding, "You cannot beat the
sin out. You have to nurture the sin out. . . . You just want to beat me, beat me,
beat me, punish me, punish me, punish me, and then expect me to come out of
prison reformed! . . . At some point I'm just gonna become what you expect me
to. I'm gonna become that monster."

Solo's critique of the diminished holdings in prison libraries, her insights
about the dehumanizing nature of U.S. penal policy, and her conviction that
reading and education enable prisoners to follow new paths speak to this book's
central concerns. Drawing on extensive individual interviews and group discussions that I conducted with ninety-four women imprisoned in North Carolina,
Ohio, and Pennsylvania, *Reading Is My Window* explores how some women
prisoners use the limited reading materials available to them in creative and
important ways: to come to terms with their pasts, to negotiate their present

experiences, and to reach toward different futures.[2] My chapters focus on the material dimensions of women's reading practices, as well as the modes of reading that women adopt when engaging with three highly popular categories of books: (1) narratives of victimization, (2) African American urban fiction, and (3) self-help and inspirational texts. My book also situates contemporary prisoners' reading practices in relation to the history of reading and education in U.S. penal contexts.

Since the prisoners' rights movement of the 1960s and 1970s gave way to the retributive justice framework of the 1980s and beyond, prisoners' opportunities for reading and education have steadily declined. Prison libraries became a very low priority during the prison-building campaigns of the 1980s, and many were severely depleted or closed due to diminished funding and space. Limited funding for prison libraries remains a pressing problem. As Solo indicates, the decline of prison libraries has been matched by a decline in opportunities for higher education in prisons. In 1994, Congress eliminated Pell Grants for prisoners, effectively defunding all college programs in U.S. prisons and sparking broader cuts in all levels of educational programming. In lobbying to eliminate Pell Grants for prisoners, Tennessee congressman Bart Gordon conveyed his sense of the wastefulness of educating prisoners by comparing them to disabled animals: "Just because one blind hog may occasionally find an acorn doesn't mean many other blind hogs will. We can't afford to throw millions of unaccountable dollars into prisoner Pell Grants in search of a few acorns." Such images of incarcerated people help to justify their treatment as "members of disposable populations," as "nothing but bodies—beyond or unworthy of rehabilitation."[3]

Recent legal precedents indicate a similar dehumanization of prisoners and a concomitant dismissal of the importance of reading in prisons. In its 2006 decision *Beard v. Banks*—a case that I discuss further in Chapter 1—the U.S. Supreme Court deemed it constitutional for a Pennsylvania prison to deny secular newspapers and magazines to prisoners in its long-term segregation unit, on the grounds that this denial serves as an "incentive[e] for inmate growth." Because these prisoners have no access to television, radio, or telephone, they receive no current news. The dissenting opinion argues that access to social, political, aesthetic, and moral ideas is crucial for preserving one's sense of humanity and citizenship; according to the majority opinion, however, such claims are moot when "dealing with especially difficult prisoners."[4]

The increasing curtailment of reading in prisons bespeaks a dehumanization of incarcerated men and women that makes it difficult to regard them as readers, let alone as human beings capable of deep thought, growth, and change. Some critics contend that prisons cannot serve as "genuine instruments of rehabilitation." For instance, Pat Carlen argues that prisons function "as deliberate and calibrated mechanisms of punishment inflicting state-legitimated pain," while Larry Sullivan maintains that "the behavior patterns one learns in a cage teach one how to survive in a cage, not how to live fruitfully in society as a whole." Dylan Rodríguez insists that "the fundamental logic of punitive incarceration is the institutionalized killing of the subject," and he argues that prison creates a "*state of paralysis* (immobilization) and *condition of death* (bodily and subjective disintegration)." Moreover, critics such as Rodríguez and John Edgar Wideman argue that accounts of individual prisoners' transcendence or transformation falsely reassure readers that existing penal arrangements "are not absolutely evil" because they allow some prisoners to "overcome" and to achieve metaphysical freedom.[5]

Although I believe that imprisonment constitutes a "wastefulness of life" and a form of "social revenge" that damages prisoners and the wider society, my research has inspired me to witness to the myriad ways in which women claim their humanity, practice freedom, and transform themselves while in the grip of "a death-generating institution."[6] Angela Davis argues that the antiprison movement should work to "create more humane, habitable environments for people in prison without bolstering the permanence of the prison system." We must perform a "balancing act," Davis argues, "of passionately attending to the needs of prisoners"—including improved physical and mental health care, greater access to drug programs, better educational and work opportunities, and more connections with families and communities—while "call[ing] for alternatives to sentencing altogether, no more prison construction, and abolitionist strategies that question the place of the prison in our future." *Reading Is My Window* dwells in the space of this challenge by exploring some of the strategies that women prisoners adopt for surviving in the here and now. The phrase "reading is my window"—coined by a woman named Denise—underscores how reading can counter forces of isolation, abandonment, and dehumanization by serving as an opening to other people, ideas, and the world outside the prison. Furthermore, reading generates possibilities for prisoners to reenvision and rescript their lives—to view their experiences in relation to broader social and historical contexts and to glimpse different horizons as they engage with others' stories. Imprisoned women's individual experiences also serve as a window onto our society; if we want to stop the flow of people from our communities into our prisons, we must reckon with the structural causes—and consequences—of current punishment trends. While underscoring our pressing need to redress the social conditions that buttress our destructive system of incarceration, *Reading Is My Window* explores how women use reading to counter the "social death" that imprisonment entails, and to achieve critical insight, self-development, and even transformation.[7]

This book offers the first analysis of incarcerated women's reading practices. Most discussions about prisoners implicitly focus on men; as the chief librarian for the Ohio Department of Rehabilitation and Correction said of penal authorities in her state, "Sometimes I think they forget the women." This neglect of women prisoners stems, in part, from the relatively small number of women incarcerated in the United States. At year-end 2006, women made up 7.2 percent of people incarcerated in state and federal prisons, which translates to 112,498 imprisoned women.[8] To put this number in perspective, it is roughly equivalent to the combined enrollments—including undergraduate, graduate, and professional students—at the main campuses of Ohio State University and the Pennsylvania State University, two major public universities in states where I conducted research.[9] If we consider the long-term impact of incarceration on the lives of these women and their families—not to mention the broader social ramifications of current imprisonment trends—this number seems large indeed. The number of women in prison is also increasing; in fact, it rose 757 percent between 1977 and 2004. During 2006 alone, the number of women in state and federal prisons increased by 4.5 percent, or 4,872 women. This rate of increase is larger than that during the previous five years, and it is almost twice the rate of increase for male prisoners during 2006.[10] The needs and experiences of this growing population merit further study. In the words of an African American prisoner named Starr, "Women in prison are pushed aside because there are less of us than men, but our stories are just as important even if men outnumber us."

Reading Is My Window draws particular attention to the experiences of African American women. Although African Americans represent only 12.8 percent of the U.S. population, black women represent 28 percent of all incarcerated women, and they are 3.1 times more likely than white women to be incarcerated.[11] According to a 2007 study from the Pew Center on the States, 1 in 100 black women between the ages of 35 and 39 is behind bars, as opposed to 1 in 355 white women within that age group.[12] In recent years, some scholars and activists have produced groundbreaking work that foregrounds the experiences of women of color, and organizations such as Justice Now, the National Network for Women in Prison, and Incite! Women of Color against Violence have generated crucial awareness of issues affecting imprisoned women of color.[13] As a whole, however, the prison abolition movement has focused primarily on the experiences of African American men. Moreover, although the criminalized figure of the black woman haunts public debate about welfare reform, single-parent families, and the war on drugs, explicit discussions of black women remain relatively scarce in academic narratives about crime. For instance, in a well-known criminology collection called *Crime*, welfare-dependent African American mothers implicitly represent the source—in James Q. Wilson's words—of "thirty thousand more young muggers, killers, and thieves than we have now," yet the collection offers no analysis of African American women's involvement in crime. The figure of the black female criminal often functions as shorthand for "associations that work best when not fully or explicitly articulated."[14]

Scholarship about U.S. prisoners' reading practices is also rare, and the few existing studies focus primarily on men.[15] Eric Cummins's 1994 study, *The Rise and Fall of California's Radical Prison Movement*, analyzes the roles that reading and writing played in men's prisons in California from the 1950s to 1970s. Cummins argues that both California penal authorities and the prisoners' rights movement emphasized the power of reading, but for different ends. Whereas penal authorities sought to cure prisoners' deviance by strictly regulating their individual and group engagements with books, leftist activists championed the revolutionary potential of prisoners' radical reading and writing practices. According to Cummins, both of these emphases on reading were deeply flawed; penal authorities failed to control the effects of prisoners' reading, while leftists lost sight of the need for concrete changes in the justice system and misconstrued prisoners' radical reading practices as proof of their status as revolutionary leaders. Drew Leder's 2000 study, *The Soul Knows No Bars*, adopts a very different perspective in exploring male prisoners' reading practices. Drawing on his experience of teaching a philosophy course in a Maryland prison, Leder analyzes the insights that emerge in some male prisoners' readings of texts by authors such as Friedrich Nietzsche, Michel Foucault, Martin Heidegger, Cornel West, and Martin Buber.

Two other recent studies draw attention to reading in penal contexts. In their 2005 book, *Finding a Voice: The Practice of Changing Lives through Literature*, Jean Trounstine and Robert P. Waxler discuss the history, aims, and methods of the Changing Lives through Literature Program, an alternative sentencing program that requires nonviolent lawbreakers to participate in a literature seminar rather than spending time in jail.[16] Karla Holloway's 2006 study, *BookMarks: Reading in Black and White*, briefly considers the reading practices of four historically prominent black prisoners: Eldridge Cleaver, Malcolm X, Claude Brown, and Angela

Davis. Holloway argues that in constructing their political personas, each of these figures assigns great importance to the books that he or she read while imprisoned. Two monographs published in 2001—Jean Trounstine's *Shakespeare behind Bars: The Power of Drama in a Women's Prison* and Rena Fraden's *Imagining Medea: Rhodessa Jones and Theater for Incarcerated Women*—explore related terrain in addressing how drama and storytelling serve as means for some incarcerated women to make meaning from their experiences.

Building on these scholars' work, *Reading Is My Window* breaks new ground in exploring the reading practices of women prisoners. By incorporating individual interviews and group discussions with incarcerated women—including their own descriptions of their experiences as readers—the book counters women prisoners' frequent positioning as silent objects of cultural and political discourse. As I explore the shifting roles that reading has played throughout U.S. penal history, I discuss the conditions under which reading can enhance critical thinking and social consciousness. Whereas Cummins emphasizes the dangers of yoking reading to disciplinary or naively revolutionary aims, I explore the specific ways in which reading enables some women prisoners to gain self-knowledge, contextualize their experiences in relation to larger frameworks, mediate their histories of victimization and violence, and develop an understanding of the limits and possibilities of individual agency. By foregrounding the reading practices of African American women, this book also addresses the need for more inclusive scholarship about women's reading practices and shared experiences of reading. From Janice Radway's groundbreaking *Reading the Romance: Women, Patriarchy, and Popular Literature* to Elizabeth Long's *Book Clubs: Women and the Uses of Reading in Everyday Life*, existing studies typically feature white, middle-class women in exploring how women negotiate their subject positions through engagement with books. My work responds to Elizabeth McHenry's call—in *Forgotten Readers: Recovering the Lost History of African American Literary Societies*—for scholarship that counters the historical invisibility of black readers and investigates nonacademic venues in which African American literacy practices have flourished.[17]

I use the phrase "cultures of reading" in this book to designate patterns of reading that emerge in response to specific material conditions and institutional regulations, and in response to the frameworks and expectations that available narratives establish. By identifying cultures of reading in women's prisons, I do not mean to suggest that women prisoners engage with texts in a totally homogeneous, unique, natural, or static fashion. Like all other readers, prisoners bring a wide range of experiences and expectations to their acts of reading. At the same time, considerable overlap exists between the reading practices of some imprisoned and nonimprisoned women. Indeed, all of the genres featured in this study—autobiographical and fictional narratives of victimization, urban fiction, and Christian self-help books—have gained popularity among women on both sides of the prison fence. Moreover, for both incarcerated and non-incarcerated women, literature often serves as what Kenneth Burke calls "equip-ment for living": as a tool for framing and making meaning of their experiences, and as raw material for continually fashioning themselves as subjects.[18] Through their engagements with books, readers often become "agents in and of" their own stories and learn to exercise some control over the meaning of their lives. As they pursue their "own dilemmas of selfhood" and make "excursions into personal life" that "leave the book far behind," both imprisoned and nonimpris-oned women engage in reading practices that sometimes resemble therapy and consciousness-raising. For many readers, encountering the characters and situ-ations depicted in books serves as a means to grapple with the complexities of their own lives; as one reader states in Long's *Book Clubs*, "Some people read to escape from life; we read to deal with life."[19]

Despite these overlaps in the reading materials and reading practices of women on both sides of the prison fence, my research illuminates some context-specific patterns evident in prisoners' material engagements with books and in their modes of reading. As my chapters demonstrate, penal environments directly influence the availability and circulation of books, as well as the uses that prisoners make of them. Furthermore, because prisons offer few resources for helping women to come to terms with their pasts and rescript their futures, some prisoners approach the act of reading with a greater sense of urgency than nonincarcerated readers. Women who are reckoning with the weight of par-ticularly difficult experiences can feel a pressing need to engage in what Louise Rosenblatt calls an "efferent transaction" with a book—a search for something useful to "carry away." Identifying with a character featured in a book enables some prisoners—for the first time—to recognize their experiences as legiti-mate and to situate them within a wider context.[20] Moreover, encountering a character who inspires them, serves as a model to emulate, or demonstrates a capacity for change can seem vitally important to women who feel an urgent desire to change but a deep uncertainty about their ability to do so. Even the tactile and aesthetic properties of books can assume great significance in penal environments, where forms of soothing touch, pleasing sensation, and beauty are sorely lacking. In foregrounding the importance that reading assumes for some women, I do not want to suggest that reading—as compared with other activities such as watching television, attending therapy, or creating some form of art—necessarily plays a unique or more transformative role in prisoners' lives. Rather, I want to elucidate the different roles that reading plays in various prisoners' lives, particularly given the dearth of alternative forms of education, recreation, counseling, and support.

While highlighting the specific material and institutional conditions that shape reading in penal contexts, *Reading Is My Window* also underscores how available narratives establish particular frameworks and expectations for their readers. Writing about recent genre theory, John Frow argues that "genres form a horizon of expectations against which any text is read." They function as "information about how to use information" and help to define the possible uses of texts. In other words, genres construct particular "domains of meanings, values, and affects" and provide "instructions for handling them," including criteria for determining the relevance of various kinds of information. In bringing various discursive worlds into being, genres "actively generate and shape knowledge of the [actual] world"; in fact, genres are "performative structures that shape the world in the very process of putting it into speech."[21] As I explore cultures of reading in women's prisons, I analyze the kinds of stories that various genres enable women to tell about themselves and the world around them. I also analyze when readers flout the frameworks that particular genres establish by fashioning categories and reading practices that they find more meaningful. Furthermore, I discuss the extent to which individual readers shuttle back and forth between different reading practices and assume "the role of the bricoleur who takes up bits and pieces of the identities and narrative forms available."[22]

Reading Is My Window foregrounds narratives of victimization, criminality, and healing because such narratives are among the most popular reading materials in women's prisons.[23] I want to emphasize, however, that categories such as "victim" and "criminal" do not fully encompass imprisoned women's subjectivity. Indeed, I hope that my book will foster recognition of prisoners as complex subjects who occupy many of the same roles as nonincarcerated subjects, including parent, friend, sibling, creator, thinker, and reader. Nonetheless, "people assume positions as actors within known scripts,"[24] and many women prisoners find it useful to position themselves in relation to the narratives featured in this book. One of my aims, as the book unfolds, is to illuminate what can and cannot be spoken through these narrative frames.

Research Sites and Subjects

The prisons featured in this book represent a mere fraction of women's prisons in the United States. I did not conduct research in federal prisons because they present particularly difficult barriers to access. Of the ten states in which I sought to conduct research, seven denied me access to their penal facilities: Illinois, Indiana, Maryland, Massachusetts, Michigan, Minnesota, and New York. The three state prisons in my study nonetheless represent a useful cross section in terms of their geographical locations and populations. The North Carolina Correctional Institution for Women (NCCIW) is located in a rural setting in Raleigh, North Carolina. The facility houses women prisoners of all custody levels and control statuses, from minimum security to death row. When I was conducting my research, NCCIW housed approximately 1,200 women, and as of 2007, it housed 1,300 women. The Northeast Pre-Release Center (NEPRC) is a minimum- to medium-security prison located in an urban setting in Cleveland, Ohio. The facility houses women who have been refused parole but have fewer than five years left to serve. The majority of women have been convicted of crimes such as drug selling, drug use, and theft, and 85 percent are from Cleveland. As of January 2008, NEPRC housed 579 women, of whom roughly half are white and half are black. The prison is consistently filled beyond capacity, reflecting the fact that Ohio has one of the fastest-growing incarceration rates in the United States.[25] The State Correctional Institution at Muncy (SCI-M) is a close-security prison located in a rural setting in Muncy, Pennsylvania. Fifty percent of the women in this prison are medium custody or higher; 162 women have life sentences, and 5 women are on death row. As of December 2007, SCI-M housed 1,208 women; 53.6 percent are white, 36.5 percent are black, and 8.4 percent are Latina. The prison is also filled beyond capacity because Pennsylvania, like Ohio, has one of the fastest-growing incarceration rates in the United States.[26]

The 94 women involved in my study range in age from 19 to 77, with the largest number of women falling between the ages of 25 and 40. Seventy-two of the participants have children, and of those women, more than half have three or more children. Just over half of the participants—48 of 94 women—self-identify as African American, and just under half self-identify as white. The Appendix includes a listing of each woman's pseudonym, age, and racial self-identification. Because women frequently underscore the salience of their race in describing their experiences and responses to books, I generally specify

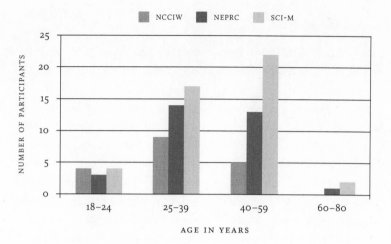

FIGURE 1 Ages of Study Participants

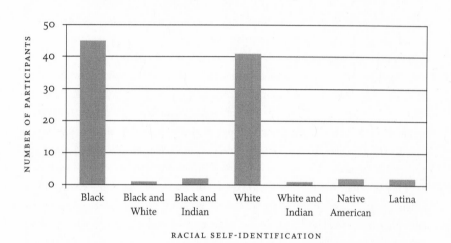

FIGURE 2 Racial Self-Identifications of Study Participants
          (for all three prisons combined)

each woman's racial self-identification when I feature her for the first time in a longer quote or descriptive passage. While signaling the importance of race, I nonetheless want to caution readers not to assume that knowing a woman's racial self-identification provides an easy key to understanding the totality of her experiences.

I did not actively solicit information about participants' crimes, but several women openly discussed their offenses and sentences. They have been con-

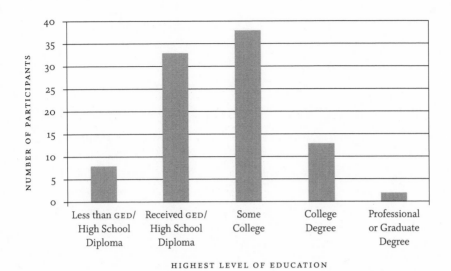

NUMBER OF PARTICIPANTS

HIGHEST LEVEL OF EDUCATION

FIGURE 3 Education Levels Reported by Study Participants
(for all three prisons combined)

victed of a wide range of crimes—including drug possession, drug selling, larceny, armed robbery, embezzlement, assault, child sexual abuse, arson, infanti-
cide, and first- and second-degree murder—and their sentences range from one
year to life imprisonment. At least twenty women with life sentences chose to
participate in my study.

Current statistical information about the average education level of incarcerated women is scarce. Indeed, the 2006 Educational Testing Service Policy
Report, *Locked Up and Locked Out: An Educational Perspective on the U.S. Prison
Population*, focuses exclusively on men. A 2007 publication, *Literacy behind Bars:
Results from the 2003 National Assessment of Adult Literacy Prison Survey*, indicates
that incarcerated women have lower prose, document, and quantitative literacy
levels than women living in households.[27] Women involved in my study may
have a higher level of education than is typical for incarcerated women, given
that some of the participants pursued college-level education prior to their incarceration, while others have taken college-level courses in prison.

"What Do I Want Wanting to Know You or Me?": Methods

I have traveled many miles—literally and figuratively—in the course of developing this book. Prior to conducting this research, I interacted with women

prisoners first as a social worker, then as a volunteer GED tutor, and finally as a volunteer book club facilitator in three different institutions. I decided to investigate cultures of reading in women's prisons while conducting fieldwork—for a graduate seminar on Foucault—at the Minnesota State Correctional Facility for Women. As I was exploring the prison library, I noticed shelves upon shelves of "true crime" books, many of which promised "shocking!" tales of "All-American housewives" whose outward perfection masked their true identity as "psychopathic femme fatales." A prisoner working in the library informed me that women sign up on waiting lists to read and reread the library's true crime collection. After discovering that true crime books were equally popular among women prisoners in Virginia, Washington, D.C., and North Carolina, I decided to write a dissertation that focused, in part, on prisoners' engagements with true crime books. Toward these ends, I conducted individual interviews and group discussions with eighteen women in the North Carolina prison.

During this initial phase of research, which took place from April through July 2001, I began to recognize the varied roles that reading plays in the lives of differently situated readers. Furthermore, I became more aware of how my own desires, assumptions, and practices as a reader are shaped by my position as a white, middle-class literature scholar. My interest in women's readings of true crime books nonetheless caused me to overlook how women were engaging with other genres. In 2006–7, I conducted new research in Ohio and Pennsylvania prisons with the open-ended aim of discovering what kinds of reading materials and practices were prevalent there. I learned a great deal about genres that were largely unfamiliar to me—including inspirational autobiographies, African American urban fiction, and Christian self-help books—and those genres became the foundation of this book.

Each volunteer for my study participated in one life narrative interview, one to two interviews about her reading practices, and four to seven group discussions of particular books.[28] In total, I conducted 245 individual interviews and 51 group conversations. Each individual interview lasted between forty-five minutes and two hours, and each group discussion lasted between ninety minutes and two hours. In an attempt to give participants as much agency as possible, I provided each woman with complete transcripts of the interviews and discussions in which she participated. In reviewing their transcripts, some women merely deleted repetitive phrases such as "you know," while others deleted more substantive statements that they did not wish to have published. I have honored all of these deletions.[29]

In conducting individual interviews with women prisoners, I tried to use open-ended questions that did not suggest a particular narrative trajectory or correct answer. As R. Dingwall argues, interviews are nonetheless shaped by "the role-playing and impression management of both the interviewer and the respondent," and as Deborah Brandt notes, interviewees may tailor their responses to what they believe the interviewer wants to hear.[30] I draw on women's life narratives not as sources of the "truth" about their lives, but as frameworks for understanding how various women embrace and resist existing cultural, literary, and political discourses in constructing stories about themselves. I am especially interested in the explicit connections that women make between their own life stories and the stories that they encounter in books. My analyses also foreground how women prisoners construct themselves as readers and articulate the roles that reading has played in their lives. I do not interpret women's descriptions of their reading practices as transparent truths about what actually happens when they read. As Benwell and Allington argue, "A set of statements describing a reader's experiences in reading a particular book may appear to be a literal *report* of events taking place in a pre-existing reality, but . . . these must be seen as an *account* that (together with other accounts) jointly participates in the construction of that reality."[31] In analyzing women's statements about reading, I have tried to contextualize their constructions of their experiences, and I have tried to parse how my position as a white, middle-class literature professor might have shaped our interactions.

Facilitating group discussions about particular books has enabled me to provide a richer analysis of cultures of reading in women's prisons. My initial motivation for including the group discussions was to learn more about various women's engagements with particular genres and books. I quickly discovered, however, that group discussions introduce several additional layers of complexity. For instance, in discussing true crime books with women in North Carolina, I became aware of differences between women's responses in individual and group settings, which helped me to understand how various discourses assume strategic value in particular rhetorical situations. By attending to the ways in which women positioned themselves vis-à-vis one another and me, I learned to recognize how readers constructed their comments in response to "the implicit on-going evidence of approval or support" from other members of the group, myself included. I also became attuned to readers' "unfolding relationship[s]" to particular books—the ways in which their views about a book shifted during the course of a group discussion.[32]

Including group discussions as part of my study design has also contributed to the productively messy outcome of this study. In the early phase of my research,

I experienced some conceptual and emotional confusion during moments when my role as researcher started to merge with my role as teacher. When women solicited my input about texts, or when I encouraged participants to grapple with contradictions or conundrums that emerged during discussion, the boundary between research and pedagogy became uncomfortably porous. During the later phase of my research in Ohio and Pennsylvania, I was at first unsure whether I should simply facilitate conversations about genres that are popular among women prisoners, play a more interventionist role by fostering women's critical engagement with these genres, or introduce books that were unavailable and perhaps unfamiliar to incarcerated readers. I tempered this uncertainty by involving the readers in the selection process for every book that we discussed. At times, women wanted to discuss books and genres with which they were already familiar, but at other times, they requested that I introduce new books. On several occasions, I therefore brought an array of books to the prison and asked each group to vote for the book that it most wanted to read next. When we were discussing popular or familiar texts, I often played a minimal role in the discussion, asking for each reader's initial thoughts about the book and occasionally posing questions when there was a lull in the conversation. I assumed a more active role, however, when women asked me to share my views about a book or when I asked them to reflect further on a particular passage or issue. When we were discussing less familiar books that I had introduced, the conversation sometimes assumed more of an academic format, with me posing questions and identifying passages for analysis. Yet if the line between researcher and teacher was porous during those sessions, so was the line between learner and teacher. Through our shared engagement with various texts, we were learning from each other about the wide range of desires that readers bring to the act of reading, the limits and blind spots of our own reading practices, and the exchanges and discoveries that collective reading experiences can facilitate. As I discuss further in Chapter 6, the encounters fostered by the group discussions constitute one of the most significant outcomes of my study.

In its final form, this book represents only a small portion of the conversations that I had with prisoners in individual and group settings. After extensive experimentation with the form of the book, I realized that trying to incorporate significant portions of women's life narratives made my chapters unwieldy and interrupted the flow of my arguments. I therefore decided to include two interludes, each of which offers an in-depth portrait of one woman, interspersed among my chapters. The women featured in these interludes construct the links between their life experiences and their reading practices in particularly compelling and distinct ways. Although I deeply regret not being able to incorporate more women's life narratives, I am buoyed by some interviewees' assurance that they will "see [their] presence" and "hear [their] conversations" in my book's overall "spirit."

In reflecting on ethnographic research, Trinh T. Minh-ha argues that the ethnographer must "maintain a self-reflexively critical relationship toward the material, a relationship that defines both the subject written and the writing subject, undoing the I while asking 'what do I want wanting to know you or me?'"[33] In wanting to know incarcerated women as readers, I have wanted many things. I wanted to know something about the thoughts and experiences of women who live outside the frame of daily reference for many Americans. I wanted to understand how women whose needs have been overlooked by family members, social institutions, and the state seek to meet their needs in the midst of further deprivation. I wanted to know not only about some of the struggles that brought these women to prison but also about their imaginative lives and their ways of making sense of their experiences. I wanted to know whether reading and a love of books might help imprisoned women—as it has helped me—to discover their place in the world, to gain insight about their pasts, to experiment with new ways of being, and to conjure worlds and possibilities that do not yet exist. Furthermore, I wanted to bring into relief some of the texture of imprisoned women's lives, to counter our reductive cultural narratives about crime, victimization, agency, responsibility, healing, and justice. I also wanted to bring women to life on the page—through their own words—as readers, thinkers, family members, and friends whose efforts to cultivate rich lives and meaningful relationships continue even when they remain permanently out of public sight. Moreover, I wanted to foster dialogue among readers and thinkers on both sides of the prison fence. And when all was said and done, I wanted to offer imprisoned women an image of themselves that reflects back to them the creativity, strength and tenacity, intelligence, and deep humanity that I witnessed in their engagements with books.

The weight of such wanting is already too heavy for one project to bear, yet the question, "What do I want wanting to know you or me?" pushes me to recognize another layer of wanting that shaped this project from the start and continued to surface throughout its unfolding. In early stages of the project, I wanted imprisoned women to challenge prevailing conceptions of crime and punishment, but I soon learned that—as we all do—women in prison sometimes embrace dominant discourses that seemingly cannot account for their own experiences. At times, I found myself wanting readers to recognize what I saw as the limitations of particular genres. I also found myself wanting some readers to expand their horizons and to want more from the world of reading. I wanted reading to serve not just as fast-paced entertainment but as a path toward expansion, deeper understanding of themselves and the world, and even transformation.

In *BookMarks: Reading in Black and White*, Karla Holloway acknowledges her need to believe that "books could be both an escape and a protection" for her incarcerated son. "Some promise or potential of self-improvement, contemplation, and appreciation of the notion that there were worlds beyond the walls of a prison was what I hoped would be the residue of my son's experience," Holloway writes. "I longed for that assured and informed and thoughtful view of the world and its histories and its mysteries as the consequence of my son's prison reading." Her son's relationship to reading did not mirror her own, however, and Holloway ultimately realized that "there would be no sanctuary for him in books."[34]

Holloway's moving account helps me to name the persistent desires that were at play for me during my interactions with incarcerated readers. In writing *Reading Is My Window*, I have taken pains to make my own desires, expectations, and fantasies "open to critical scrutiny" as "part of the empirical evidence for (or against) the claims advanced."[35] By analyzing moments when a woman's statement or the dynamics of a group discussion made me feel particularly moved, surprised, confused, frustrated, or joyful, I have attempted to parse how my own investments have conditioned my receptivity to women's descriptions of their experiences, thoughts, and feelings. Analyzing the complexity of our encounters has been a humbling and sometimes painful process, but it has enabled me to become a better listener over the course of this study.

During her discussion group's final meeting, a twenty-eight-year-old African American woman named Mocha asked me, "Did you learn anything from us?" This book is my extended response to Mocha's question, my attempt to convey the myriad things that I have learned from women prisoners. In completing this book, I often found myself writing from places of uncertainty, confusion, bafflement, or surprise, and I sometimes felt at a loss for words. My learning curve was steep, in part, because these women's modes of reading were so different from my own, and I initially found it difficult to recognize what various women were seeking through their reading practices. My learning curve was steep, moreover, because I sometimes failed to perceive the importance of what I was seeing; I did not recognize the profound lessons that were unfolding before me.

In learning to understand the wide range of motivations, needs, and desires that women bring to the act of reading, I have returned again and again to

Michael Warner's discussion of "uncritical reading." Warner argues that academics tend to label as uncritical "any style of actual reading that we can observe in the world," and we often presume that so-called uncritical forms of reading—including identification, sentimentality, enthusiasm, literalism, and aversion—are "unsystematic and disorganized." If we jettison the critical/uncritical distinction, Warner suggests, we can better understand how reading practices "are embedded within and organized by ethical projects for cultivating one kind of person or another."[36] Warner's call to acknowledge the different goals of various reading practices and the different kinds of subjectivity that they call into being has enabled me to recognize how women's engagements with books contribute to their particular projects of self-creation. Through such a framework, I have learned to understand how Donald Trump's autobiography, urban fiction, or self-help books about the devil serve as important resources for some women, allowing them to create a space of movement and artistry within the institutional and ideological structures that shape them as subjects.

While getting to know some prisoners as readers, I have also become more attuned to the political significance of reading practices that might seem unremarkable in other contexts. James C. Scott's notion of "infrapolitics" illuminates "the circumspect struggle waged daily by subordinate groups"; like "infrared rays," such struggle is "beyond the visible end of the spectrum," reflecting "a prudent awareness of the balance of power." Given "the conditions of tyranny and persecution in which most historical subjects live," Scott argues, infrapolitics "is political life."[37] Scott's notion of "infrapolitics" has helped me to recognize that it can be a matter of profound political importance when an imprisoned woman insists on the soothing touch of paperback rather than hardback books, develops a deep sense of identification with an inspiring character, or uses a book as a means to witness to her own or another woman's experiences. As I understand it, my task as a cultural critic is to build a bridge between the daily work that imprisoned women perform through their reading practices and the work of transforming the structures and institutions that keep so many women in prison. My hope is that my own development as a reader has been sufficient to do justice to the women and the reading practices that I endeavor to describe.

CHAPTER ONE

Tell Me What You Read;
I Will Tell You What You Are

READING AND EDUCATION IN
U.S. PENAL HISTORY

> What does it mean to have black bodies and books read as
> a single narrative? . . . Whether it was an enslaved African
> who lost life or limb because she dared to read, or laws that
> made literacy illegal, or citizens who staged anti–Jim Crow
> demonstrations in local libraries to protest the back doors or
> the inaccessibility of these facilities, the matter of books and
> reading marks the experience of black folk in America in a
> way that is deeply political and resonantly personal.—KARLA
> HOLLOWAY, *BookMarks: Reading in Black and White*

> I don't think most people should be incarcerated. I think
> they should be educated.—SAKINA, North Carolina
> Correctional Institution for Women

IN ITS 2006 DECISION *Beard v. Banks*, the U.S. Supreme Court deemed it constitutional for a Pennsylvania prison to deny secular newspapers and magazines
to forty of its "most incorrigible" prisoners.[1] According to the 6-2 majority opinion, denying these reading materials serves as an "incentiv[e] for inmate growth"
because it encourages compliance with prison rules.[2] The prisoners referenced
in this case are incarcerated in a long-term segregation unit, where they spend
at least ninety days confined to a cell for twenty-three hours a day. They have no
access to television, radio, or telephone, and they can receive only one visit per
month, from an immediate family member. Because they may not read secular

newspapers or magazines—including a clipping—the prisoners have no access to current news or news commentary. They are, however, permitted religious and legal materials, two library books, and writing paper.

The majority opinion in *Beard v. Banks* constructs reading as a privilege that best serves the interests of the penal system when it is denied to uncooperative prisoners. In his concurring opinion, Justice Clarence Thomas argues that the current ruling is justified because it is consistent with eighteenth-century Pennsylvania punishment practices, which isolated prisoners from the outside world by allowing no reading materials except the Bible and by denying prisoners contact with their families. The majority opinion dismisses legal cases that have found increased contact with the world conducive to rehabilitation, arguing that such findings are moot when "dealing with especially difficult prisoners." Although the Pennsylvania prison deputy describes the policy as designed to make prisoners "productive citizen[s]," the Court's majority opinion thus conveys little faith in the possibility that these prisoners may actually become productive citizens or that reading may facilitate such a process. The deputy's reference to citizenship sounds even more hollow given that only about 25 percent of those confined to the highest level have been moved to a lower level or out of the unit.[3]

In their dissenting opinions, Justices John Paul Stevens and Ruth Bader Ginsburg vehemently critique the "deprivation theory of rehabilitation" evident in *Beard v. Banks*, which justifies any deprivation of a constitutional right as long as a prisoner can theoretically regain that right by modifying his or her behavior. Justice Stevens argues that the ruling "comes perilously close to a state-sponsored effort at mind control" in preventing prisoners from "'receiv[ing] suitable access to social, political, esthetic, moral, and other ideas,' which are central to the development and preservation of individual identity."[4] Indeed, as the American Civil Liberties Union states in its amicus brief, the ruling threatens "to deny [prisoners'] very citizenship" in suggesting that "their knowledge and understanding on matters of public affairs no longer matter." The fact that African Americans and Latinos/Latinas are vastly overrepresented in supermaximum prisons makes this denial of citizenship even more troubling.[5]

Beard v. Banks brings us full circle to the kinds of questions that shaped eighteenth- and nineteenth-century U.S. penal policy: What is the relationship between reading and reform, and which reading materials are most conducive to modifying prisoners' behavior? To what extent are various prisoners capable of reform; indeed, to what extent can they be considered human? To what extent should the penal system control prisoners' reading? Is reading in the penal context a right or a privilege? Finally, what is the relationship between reading and citizenship, and between reading and human subjectivity? Because contemporary prisons are haunted by these historical questions, understanding the history of reading and education in U.S. penal contexts is crucial for grasping the stakes of current debate about reading in women's prisons.

In this chapter, I explore the historically shifting ways in which reading and education have been constructed in U.S. penal contexts. My argument follows a roughly chronological progression, but I approach the subject from four different angles. First, I analyze how racial and gender ideologies have shaped penal attitudes about reading and education since the birth of the penitentiary. Second, I explore periods in which penal authorities have adopted a therapeutic model of reading, constructing reading as a tool for correcting prisoners' alleged moral weaknesses, personality flaws, and failures to comply with social norms. From a third perspective, I discuss the disciplinary model of reading that largely superseded the therapeutic model when penal authorities began to adopt more draconian punishment practices in the 1970s. Within this disciplinary framework, which predominates today, penal objectives dictate library policies and frequently override prisoners' right to read. Fourth and finally, I explore the divergent ways in which penal officials and prisoners have defined the purposes and parameters of penal education. Focusing on the radical tradition of reading adopted by political prisoners as well as some ordinary prisoners, I discuss how prisoners have used reading as a vehicle for self-education, peer education, politicization, and empowerment. The chapter concludes with some brief reflections about the therapeutic, disciplinary, and radical dimensions of reading in contemporary women's prisons. Lest we become wedded to the way things are, understanding this history may help us to recognize the contingency of our taken-for-granted present.

Literacy as White (Male) Property

Since the establishment of the penitentiary system in the early 1800s, racial and gender ideologies have shaped prisoners' opportunities for reading and education. Before the penitentiary, physical punishment or death were the primary means of punishing lawbreakers. By making incarceration the punishment for a crime, the penitentiary provided lawbreakers "with the conditions for reflecting on their crimes and, through penitence, for reshaping their habits and even their souls." As discussed below, penal officials emphasized reading in their efforts to reform penitentiary inhabitants. In constructing prisoners as readers, however, penal officials had a distinct group in mind: white men were the primary inhabitants of penitentiaries, reflecting Enlightenment assumptions that white men were more capable of progress and reform than white women and African Americans.[6]

As the U.S. penal system developed, penal authorities often abandoned their emphases on reading and education when nonwhite and female prisoners were involved. Indeed, the history of U.S. punishment practices confirms Leah Price's contention that reading has never been "just a neutral medium that whites happened to monopolize, but rather a defining feature of white identity—and one that depended crucially on the illiteracy of blacks." As Catherine Prendergast argues, white Americans have historically claimed literacy as white property to be controlled and disseminated by an empowered majority, and the ideology of literacy has helped to maintain the conception of America as a white nation.[7]

The extent to which racial ideologies dictated which prisoners were deemed capable of reform through reading and education seems particularly apparent in the period just after the Civil War. According to historians, the first National Prison Congress—convened in 1870—catalyzed a renewed commitment to rehabilitate prisoners and educate them in "religion, letters, and industry," and this commitment resulted in "the active development and organization of prison libraries."[8] Wardens' enthusiasm about reading is evident in statements such as the following: "All the prisoners who can read understandingly avail themselves of the privilege. The improvement from it is astonishing. Young men who two years ago were taught their first lesson here are now good readers; and it seems as if they had changed entirely in body and mind. They keep themselves now neat and clean, while they formerly were very filthy in their habits. They have better manners, and look more intelligent, more like human beings. Ignorance makes many convicts; education alone makes the man." Zebulon Brockway, administrator of the Elmira Reformatory in New York, hailed "the refining influence" of culture as a means "to cultivate the criminal out of his criminality, and to constitute him a reformed man." Highlighting the role that reading plays in this process, Brockway claimed, "Tell me what you read; I will tell you what you are."[9]

Yet if 1870 marks a time of renewed attention to prison libraries as tools for prisoners' reformation and education, the year also marks a period in which thousands of African American men and women were caught up in the convict lease system, which flourished in southern states and offered no opportunities for reading or education to the prisoners whose labor it brutally exploited. Prior to Emancipation, white men constituted the vast majority of the southern prison population because African Americans were typically punished by their slave masters, and white women typically received corporal punishment in the domestic sphere.[10] However, the Thirteenth Amendment—which was passed in 1865 after the Emancipation Proclamation—authorized slavery as punishment for a crime: "Neither slavery nor involuntary servitude, except as a punishment for crime whereof the party shall have been duly convicted, shall exist within the United States, or any place subject to their jurisdiction." In conjunction with the Black Codes, a series of laws that criminalized everything from "using profane language" to failing to provide written proof of employment, the Thirteenth Amendment fueled the development of a convict lease system that shunted thousands of former slaves back into an unpaid and captive workforce, and southern prison populations rapidly shifted from majority white to majority black.[11]

Scientific racism helped to legitimize the fact that economic incentives completely trumped efforts to educate prisoners in this southern lease system. Because African Americans were considered "purely animal" and incapable of learning, it was deemed wasteful to provide black prisoners with opportunities for reading or education.[12] If "what you read" tells "what you are," the record of late-nineteenth-century penal practices suggests that African American convicts were considered nothing—totally dispensable—and were therefore given nothing to read. The de jure prohibition of reading by African Americans in the antebellum South was thus succeeded by the penal system's de facto prohibition of reading by thousands of African Americans who were shunted from slavery into the convict lease system.[13]

Members of the black women's club movement—educated, middle-class black women who sponsored activities designed to uplift the African American race—sought to counteract the exploitation of black convicts in the South by treating them as readers and thereby insisting on their humanity and intellectual capabilities. For instance, the Phyllis Wheatley Club of New Orleans states in its 1891 annual report that the philanthropy committee "has been making weekly visits to the prison and distributing reading matter among the inmates." Four years later, this women's club reports that "the Philanthropy Committee devote their time to prisons and houses of correction; they give sympathy, advice and reading matter to the inmates." The Women's Club of Atlanta likewise states in its 1897 yearly report, "Chaingangs are being reached, with periodicals, prayers & admonitions, in the best possible way." In distributing reading material to black prisoners, black clubwomen adopted the role of "literary activists" and countered the profoundly dehumanizing ideologies that legitimized the exploitation of African American prisoners.[14]

Black prisoners' opportunities for education hardly increased with the final eradication of convict leasing in 1928. Most southern states merely reallocated forced labor from the private to the public sector: from leasing to chain gangs and prison farms under state management.[15] By 1931, educational programs were still unavailable in the road camps, prisons farms, and penitentiaries of Alabama, Florida, Georgia, Mississippi, South Carolina, and Tennessee, and educational work was just beginning in penal facilities in Arkansas, North Carolina, and Louisiana.[16]

Gender ideologies worked in tandem with racial ideologies in delimiting prisoners' opportunities for reading and education. Historical records suggest that both prison administrators and reformers badly neglected incarcerated women of all races prior to the Civil War. Female prisoners were often housed together in one large room of men's penitentiaries, and they had few opportunities for reading or employment.[17] Various scholars contend that this neglect of incarcerated women stems, in large part, from the fact that criminal women of all races have been deemed more depraved than criminal men and beyond hope of redemption.[18] Moreover, African American and immigrant women, who could never be restored to the white, middle-class standard of "true womanhood," constituted a disproportionately large percentage of women incarcerated during this period. Although few African American women were imprisoned in the pre–Civil War South—since slave masters typically meted out punishment—black women constituted 43 percent of all female prisoners in the mid-nineteenth-century United States.[19]

Prior to the Civil War, the only period when reading played a significant role in women's imprisonment was from 1844 to 1848, when Eliza Farnham served as matron of Mt. Pleasant Female Prison in Ossining, New York. Farnham organized her reform efforts around reading and the prison library. When she arrived at Mt. Pleasant—the first independent women's prison in the United States—the library contained only seventy-five copies of Richard Baxter's *Call to the Unconverted Sinner*. To expand the library's holdings, Farnham purchased penny magazines, travel and voyage literature, instructional picture books, phrenological texts, and highly popular novels by E. D. E. N. Southworth and Catherine Sedgwick. She also supplied reading materials to be placed in prisoners' cells and gave readings of novels such as Charles Dickens's *Oliver Twist*.[20] In her 1844 annual report, Farnham highlights reading as central to "the reformation" of those who have been "reared in ignorance," complains that the prison library consists entirely of donations, and laments that the chaplain provides no instruction for women. Farnham's treatment of female prisoners as readers and her efforts to turn the prison into "a school" sparked significant opposition, particularly given prevailing cultural anxieties about women's consumption of fiction.[21] Mt. Pleasant's chaplain, John Luckey, disapproved of secular education, and he complained to various newspapers that Farnham had given prisoners books "of the most licentious and demoralizing character" and fostered "a love of novel reading averse to labor." Two prison inspectors ultimately condemned Mt. Pleasant on the grounds that prisons must remain "a terror to the depraved" or they will be "detrimental to law and order." When Farnham resigned under pressure in 1848, the state reduced Mt. Pleasant's funding and cut its programs, and it remained in that condition until it was closed in 1877.[22]

The possibility of educating women prisoners first gained national attention in the late 1860s, when white female reformers advocated building women's reformatories that would offer "intellectual, moral, domestic, and industrial training, under the influence, example and sympathy of refined and virtuous women." Between 1900 and 1935, seventeen states established women's reformatories. African American and immigrant women were typically deemed unsuitable candidates for these facilities, which were designed to reinforce white, middle-class femininity; in fact, most reformatories did not accept African American women.[23]

Although few records exist of reading practices in women's reformatories, the 1932 *Prison Library Handbook*, jointly published by the American Library Association (ALA) and the American Prison Association (APA), recommends that reformatories establish one central library and a small book collection for each residential cottage, designed to address the particular "mentality" or criminal history of women housed there.[24] The authors of the *Handbook* argue that helping women to develop "better reading habits and tastes" will "steady them with new resources" for encountering the "temptations . . . which were too much for them before." Toward these ends, reformatory librarians should schedule evening readings by a matron, teacher, or prisoner, and they should find out the "reading capacity and tastes" of each newcomer and send an appropriate book or magazine to her room as a form of welcome.[25] Records of actual practices in women's reformatories suggest, however, that "academic education" was "regrettably weak." Educational opportunities typically focused on domestic training in laundering, sewing, knitting, cleaning, cooking, and table etiquette, while reading-related activities typically consisted of matrons and guests reading aloud to prisoners.[26]

Custodial prisons—former penitentiaries that no longer focused on rehabilitation—housed far more women than reformatories, and African American women constituted an increasingly disproportionate percentage of women in such facilities as the twentieth century progressed. By 1923, black women represented only 12 percent of women sentenced to U.S. reformatories but 65 percent of women sentenced to custodial prisons. In his 1931 study, *The Education of Adult Prisoners: A Survey and a Program*, Austin MacCormick—head of the Welfare and Education Division of the federal Bureau of Prisons and, later, president of the APA—concludes that "educational work of all sorts" was "practically nonexistent" in such facilities.[27]

A number of manuals for prison libraries published from 1877 to 1939 further illuminate how race and racialized notions of literacy have shaped discussions of reading in penal contexts.[28] At the turn of the twentieth century, public librarians embraced reading as a tool for assimilating immigrants into mainstream American culture. Reflecting this dynamic, early manuals for prison libraries foreground the reading needs and potential interests of immigrant prisoners, recommending reference materials such as *The German Immigrant and His Reading* and books that fall under categories such as "Easy Reading for Foreigners Learning English." In ironic contrast to racialized sentencing trends that contributed to disproportionate conviction rates among immigrants, the authors of the *Prison Library Handbook* invoke romanticized images of naive, "foreign-born" prisoners who may be incarcerated "because they did not know they were breaking laws." The authors also recommend that prison librarians personally distribute books to foreign-born prisoners because they may distrust officials. The manuals for prison libraries thus implicitly protect white national identity by trying to bring idealized immigrant readers into the American fold.[29]

The manuals pay far less attention, however, to the presence, needs, and potential interests of the substantial and steadily growing number of African American prisoners. Indeed, although large numbers of African Americans were migrating to northern cities from 1914 to 1929, the presence of African Americans registers primarily as an absence in these manuals. The authors of the *Prison Library Handbook* argue that "service to racial groups" should be integral to library goals, yet they attend to race only in relation to the "foreign-born," buttressing the notion that books and reading remain the domain of white Americans.[30] Although *2500 Books for the Prison Library*—the 1933 supplement to the *Prison Library Handbook*—was published during the New Negro Renaissance and the flourishing of African American literature, it includes only nine fictional texts that relate in any way to African American issues or characters. Only two of the nine works of fiction are written by African American authors: Charles Chesnutt's *The Conjure Woman* (1899) and W. E. B. DuBois's *Dark Prin-*

cess: A Romance (1928). Five of the texts explore issues of racism and prejudice: Chesnutt's and DuBois's novels, Du Bose Heyward's *Mamba's Daughters* (1929), Thomas Sigismund Stribling's *Backwater* (1930), and Mark Twain's *Pudd'nhead Wilson* (1894). However, the remaining four novels depict black life in the comic and exaggerated manner of the racist minstrel tradition: Charles J. Correll and Freeman F. Gosden's *Here They Are: Amos 'n' Andy* (1931), and Hugh Wiley's *The Wildcat* (1920), "Mister Lady Luck" (1920), and *Fo' Meals a Day* (1927). In *1000 Books for Prison Libraries*, published six years later, *Best Stories of Paul Lawrence Dunbar* (1938) is the only African American fiction listed. African American issues and authors are somewhat better represented in the sociology category of *2500 Books for the Prison Library*, which includes representations of black life by well-known African American authors such as W. E. B. DuBois, James Weldon Johnson, Alain Locke, and Robert Russa Moton. Yet the later volume, *1000 Books for Prison Libraries*, includes only two nonfiction texts by African American authors, both of which are considered accommodationist: Booker T. Washington's *Up from Slavery* and Charles S. Johnson's *A Preface to Racial Understanding*.

Moreover, in their rare references to women prisoners, the manuals for prison libraries focus solely on women's reformatories, which rarely housed black women. In the 1932 *Handbook*, for instance, the authors completely ignore the existence of custodial prisons in claiming that the library in women's institutions is like "a school library" and that women's penal institutions have "the character of schools rather than prisons."[31] Given that public libraries restricted African Americans' access to books well into the 1960s, African American prisoners may have had better access to reading materials through some federal and state prisons than through libraries in the "free" world.[32] Nonetheless, during the first half of the twentieth century, penal authorities largely excluded or ignored African Americans in addressing the needs of imprisoned readers.

The Legacy of Bibliotherapy

Starting with the ancient Greeks, who inscribed "Place of Healing for the Soul" above library entrances, reading has long been touted for its curative and healing powers.[33] In the United States, penal authorities adopted a therapeutic model of reading with the shift to the penitentiary system in the early 1800s. Early penitentiaries were fashioned after two primary models—the Philadelphia system and the Auburn system—both of which permitted prisoners to read only the Bible, prayer books, and religious pamphlets, on the grounds that sacred reading materials would induce moral change.[34] Dr. Benjamin Rush, a member of the

Philadelphia Society for Alleviating the Miseries of Public Prisons, was instrumental in promoting religious reading as central to the rehabilitation of prisoners. In his 1812 publication, *Medical Inquiries and Observations Upon the Diseases of the Mind*, Rush argues that criminality is the product of disordered, overactive sensation, and he contends that criminals can restore their equilibrium by reading sacred texts. The Bible is like "an apothecary's shop," he asserts, "in which is contained remedies for every disease of the body." Although Rush prioritizes reading sacred texts, he also suggests that reading novels can be beneficial for patients who have "no relish for the simple and interesting stories contained in the Bible."[35]

In early penitentiaries, a chaplain or "moral instructor" usually served as librarian and closely supervised prisoners' reading. As the penitentiary system developed, however, penal authorities prioritized the profit-making capacity of prisoners rather than rehabilitation; authorities thus lessened their emphasis on prisoners' reading, and penitentiary libraries began to include nonreligious materials.[36] By 1850, the Pennsylvania Prison library included scientific treatises, travel books, and literary works. San Quentin opened a general library for inmates in 1852, and Sing Sing Prison and the Ohio Penitentiary began including nonreligious materials in 1855.[37] Historical records suggest that prisoners "preferred stories of adventure, crime, and violence" and had little interest in the libraries' collections of "moral literature." As the 1853 annual report of the Eastern Penitentiary states, the library's religious section became "crowded with unused books" upon the inclusion of nonreligious materials.[38]

The therapeutic model of reading nonetheless remained central to penal philosophy until the 1970s. As the rehabilitative ideal evolved "from a moral and religious to a medicalized framework," penal officials continued to construct reading and prison libraries as crucial components of their efforts to rehabilitate prisoners.[39] As we shall see, this therapeutic model of reading often overlapped with a disciplinary model. In adopting reading as a method of treatment, penal officials tried to foster prisoners' conformity to disciplinary and social norms. They not only sought to control what prisoners read; they often sought to control who prisoners would become.

In 1870, when the National Prison Congress underscored the importance of prison libraries and prisoners' education, librarians in the public domain were starting to construct themselves as responsible for fostering the moral health of library patrons. In 1878, for instance, Charles Cutter—president of the ALA—claimed that a public librarian "is to be, in a literary way, the city physician, and must be able to administer from the bibliothecal dispensary just that strengthening draught that will suit each case." By the late 1800s, the public library was routinely credited with helping to defeat delinquency, crime, poverty, and intemperance. In an attempt to guarantee that reading would produce such salutary effects, public librarians published several reading guides for library users, with titles such as *On the Right Use of Books* (1880) and *The Reading of Books: Its Pleasures, Profits, and Perils* (1883). Public librarians expressed particular concern about their patrons reading mass-produced fiction; they feared that novels would encourage sensuality and moral decay, dangerously unleash the emotions, invite sympathy for sinners, produce unrealistic dreams of success and a craving for excitement, and challenge gender norms and standards of sexual conduct.[40] Records indicate, however, that libraries often carried numerous works of "immoral" fiction because it was most requested by readers. The tension between librarians' prescriptions and readers' preferences continued to surface through the 1930s, but the conception of the public library ultimately shifted from a "bibliothecal dispensary" run by literary "physicians" to a "literary shop" that caters to the desires of its patrons.[41]

Efforts to regulate the reading practices of library patrons have been even more pronounced and more persistent in the penal context. At least two dozen articles about prison library services appeared in professional journals between 1907 and 1920, and penal and library organizations began to publish guidelines and recommended book lists for prison libraries.[42] In fact, the ALA and the APA entered a period of formal cooperation that lasted from 1932 until the 1980s; during this time, the two organizations jointly authored four manuals for prison libraries and two supplemental book lists. The early manuals for prison libraries tout the benefits of "the reading habit," describing reading as a useful way for prisoners to occupy their time and thoughts, both during and after imprisonment. According to the authors of the 1932 *Prison Library Handbook*, the prison library can serve as "the right hand of the superintendent in her efforts towards rehabilitation and discipline," and it can foster "a new habit" that will connect incarcerated readers with libraries upon their release from prison. The *Handbook's* yoking of reading, rehabilitation, and discipline draws attention to the intersections between therapeutic and disciplinary models of reading. Indeed, reading frequently served as a means for penal officials to "control without punishment."[43]

As early-twentieth-century public librarians did with their patrons, penal authorities often tried to regulate prisoners' access to popular fiction. Handbooks for prison libraries published in the early part of the twentieth century recommend far more nonfiction than fiction and advocate strictly monitoring prisoners' engagement with fiction. In her 1918 study, "The Libraries of the American State and National Institutions for Defectives, Dependents, and Delinquents," Florence Rising Curtis contends that "no one in the prison has a greater responsibility upon him than the one who buys the books and puts them into the hands of prisoners," and she laments that prison authorities "regard so carelessly the worthless and often immoral books which pass freely through the cells." Arguing that book characters "are, in a real sense, companions to the readers," Curtis insists that the "salacious novel" is "not good mental food for the man who needs to learn self-control." Austin MacCormick contends that "it is the obvious task of the prison as an agency of intellectual as well as moral improvement to improve [prisoners'] reading tastes if it can be done." Prison librarians must therefore encourage prisoners to "climb" up the "inclined plane" of literary taste and convert their "interest in fiction to interest in nonfiction"; a reader who likes Zane Grey westerns, for instance, should develop an interest in Theodore Roosevelt's *Winning of the West*.[44]

A few early manuals for prison libraries suggest that prisoners can benefit from reading fiction, but their endorsement of fiction is always qualified. The 1877 *Catalogue and Rules for Prison Libraries* includes 300 works of fiction among 1,000 books chosen "not only to inspire substantial hopes and good purposes, but to point out the best ways of realizing them." However, the *Catalogue* privileges works of fiction that address issues of moral or social significance, such as Timothy Shay Arthur's temperance novels, Charles Dickens's socially conscious novels, and reformer Charles Reade's chronicles of injustices in the legal system, private lunatic asylums, and trade unions. In the *Prison Library Handbook*, the authors acknowledge that "fiction reading can be as profitable as non-fiction if wisely chosen," since the exploits of a romantic lover or daring adventurer may give a prisoner "the happy picture of that which he might have been but was not and, in a vicarious way, he may see himself in the outstanding characters." In fact, they recommend that popular fiction—including adventures, westerns, detective stories, and romances—comprise at least half of prison libraries' book collections. At the same time, however, the authors argue that book collections should center around novels "that are better written than the ordinary murder-a-minute or mushy" varieties, since a "constant diet of fiction" acts like a "mental drug." Furthermore, they urge librarians to expand imprisoned readers' tastes by providing carefully selected guided reading lists and by pasting reviews of "better" books inside the front and back covers of popular books, with captions such as "Here's another good book. Have you read it?"[45]

The authors of manuals for prison libraries convey particular concern that reading about crime will increase prisoners' desires to commit crimes, teach them better methods for doing so, or foster their identification with criminal protagonists. The 1916 *Manual for Institution Libraries* simply states, "Nothing should be accepted which represents vice attractively, contains sensual suggestions, or deals with crime and punishment." In his 1931 study, Austin Mac-Cormick argues that prison libraries should carry newspapers "in spite of the effect of crime news," yet he contends that "it is undoubtedly wise" to limit crime and mystery stories in prison libraries. Although he believes that prisoners can safely read about sex if they receive adequate reader's guidance, Mac-Cormick seems to regard fictional representations of crime as particularly likely to produce unwanted effects. The authors of the 1932 *Handbook* concede that crime, mystery, and detective novels "cannot tell prisoners any more lurid crime stories than they can hear any day in the prison yard." Nonetheless, they echo MacCormick in asserting that it is "undoubtedly wise" to keep such books to a minimum and to bar those that "deal with the modern gangster and racketeer in whose place the prisoner can easily picture himself."[46]

The manuals and guidelines for prison libraries also illustrate the normalizing impulses evident in penal authorities' embrace of a therapeutic model of reading. For instance, the recommended book lists for male and female prisoners—which appear in manuals published between 1877 and 1939—foster prisoners' compliance with prevailing gender norms. Through their book lists for men, the manuals promote an imperialist, individualist, and implicitly white masculinity, and they construct reading as an activity through which (white) male prisoners can learn about the world, gain power in the world, and assume their rightful role in the national project of Manifest Destiny. As one example among many, the 1916 "List of Books for Prison Libraries" designates 480 fiction titles for men, the majority of which depict U.S. imperialism and war. Numerous books focus on cowboys and Indians, "thrilling encounters with Mexicans and Comanches," Custer's last stand, frontier tales, and the settling of the West. Also prominent are adventure tales about pirates, sailors, and kidnappings as well as stories that revolve around boys' and men's forays into the public sphere. These latter stories foreground men's ability to overcome challenges and assert their dominance, whether at school, in college athletics, on the job, or in exotic encounters with Native Americans, Alaskan natives, wild animals, and nature. Similarly, *1000 Books for Prison Libraries, 1936–1939* recommends books that focus on war, the settling of the West, sports, and adventure, and it includes a new genre of "occupational novels," which feature men's employment in fields such as tunnel building, high power-line work, rodeo horse training, and commercial aviation.[47]

By contrast, the book lists and manuals for prison libraries promote an implicitly white notion of femininity based on domesticity and self-sacrifice. The 1916 list includes several love stories and romances as well as numerous narratives that—according to the annotations—feature dutiful and self-sacrificing female heroines. For instance, the annotations describe a "good story of a plucky girl who, when her father dies and the family is left with little income, sacrifices her college career and stays at home"; a novel in which the eldest daughter, "after a taste of fashionable life, goes back to her humbler home and discovers the beauty of her mother's cheerful self-denying service"; and the story of a widow and four kids who "spread happiness in spite of their poverty."[48] In 1000 Books for Prison Libraries, the fictional texts designated for women emphasize the clash between sanctioned gender roles and the artistic and social ambitions of female characters. The annotations describe plots such as the following: "a wife and mother, with ability as sculptor, struggles to combine these aspects of her life"; "Happy marriage threatened by wife's cheap success as best-seller novelist"; "Woman's devotion to theater means an unhappy end to her marriage"; "havoc brought to author when she writes a truthful story about her village"; and "husband leaves celebrity-hunting wife and finds romance in England."[49]

Furthermore, the guidelines for prison libraries construct reading as an activity that can reaffirm women's position within the domestic sphere. According to Florence Rising Curtis's 1918 study, stories of adventure, hunting, sports, travel, "great men," and U.S. history can help to widen delinquent boys' "very meager experience" and "paucity of mental interests." In sharp contrast, Curtis constructs reading as a tool for keeping delinquent girls within a narrow social sphere. Upon her release from the reformatory, Curtis argues, a delinquent girl

must be slow in making friends, lest inquiry be made into her past. . . .
A love for books now becomes not only a pleasure but a great protection,
[since] reading is almost the only recreation that she can enjoy by herself,
the public library is open during her leisure hours and the books are free
for her to enjoy. Here is a community institution to which she may go,
a reputable place, lighted, well-supervised, where she will be protected
from the advances of undesirable associates, and where her presence
will attract no comment.[50]

The disciplinary impulse evident in early-twentieth-century penal models of reading and education became even more apparent with the adoption of bibliotherapy in U.S. prisons. In simple terms, bibliotherapy is "the treatment of a patient through selective reading." In more complex terms, it is "a discussion process, guided by a facilitator, using literature as a catalyst to promote insight, normal development, or rehabilitation."[51] Bibliotherapy first gained national attention in medical and library circles in the 1930s and in penal circles from the 1950s through the 1970s.[52] Following a nationwide spate of prison violence in the early 1950s, penal experts and prison administrators renewed their commitment to rehabilitate prisoners, and in 1954, the APA changed its name to the American Correctional Association (ACA) and encouraged its members to call their prisons "correctional institutions." In keeping with this renewed emphasis on reform, prison personnel began to adopt bibliotherapy as a central mode of treatment, and prison libraries entered a period of extensive development.

More than any other individual, African American librarian Sara (Sadie) Peterson Delaney helped to develop the practice of bibliotherapy during her tenure, from 1924 through 1958, as chief librarian of the Veterans' Administration Hospital at Tuskegee Normal and Industrial Institute. In her writings, Delaney argues that patients may learn from "the manner in which problems are solved" in literary texts, experience a sense of "identification" and "catharsis" from reading material that "embodies familiar experiences," and reveal "the nature of [their] conflicts" through their responses to various texts. In Delaney's view, librarians working in institutional settings should review each patient's diagnosis and prognosis, attend medical staff meetings, and communicate facts about patients' "progress or reaction to reading." Furthermore, bibliotherapists should carefully select materials for each individual, since a book that is "good for one person might be detrimental to another." At the same time, however, Delaney argues that bibliotherapists should allow each reader "to be himself" and "encourage him to make his own plans and to do his own thinking," and they should "strive to see him as he is and to understand and appreciate him." Delaney encouraged veterans to exercise their freedom to agree and disagree with a range of authorial viewpoints.[53] Furthermore, just as nineteenth- and early-twentieth-century black literary societies "furthered the evolution of a black public sphere and a politically conscious society,"[54] Delaney encouraged veterans to develop their sense of citizenship by reading about history, current events, and racial issues from both national and global perspectives. She also developed a broad range of clubs and group activities in which veterans could participate, including—among others—a Library Press Club, Library Debate Club, Nature

Study Group, Historical Forum, and bookbinding department. Through such reading-based activities, Delaney writes, veterans "are given an outlet for self-expression; self-confidence is stimulated and hopes awakened. Latent creative ability is brought out and exercised. There is, too, a gain in education, and the stirring of a vocational impulse which has made possible a satisfactory community adjustment for many of these patients who have been discharged." At a time when African Americans were marginalized as readers and deemed less capable than whites of intellectual development, Delaney constructed black veterans as intellectuals and regarded the hospital library as "a university" that contributed to their empowerment.[55]

Scholarship about the development of bibliotherapy in U.S. penal contexts has failed to acknowledge the foundational role that Delaney played in shaping the practice of bibliotherapy.[56] Yet her work with veterans, as well as her earlier work with "delinquent boys and girls" at the New York Public Library, deeply influenced subsequent conceptions of reading as integral to rehabilitation and fueled the adoption of bibliotherapy in prisons. In fact, Herman Spector, who became a staunch supporter of bibliotherapy as chief librarian of San Quentin Prison from 1947 to 1968, requested a copy of Delaney's "pamphlet on bibliotherapy" and related "reports, policies and statistics" in 1957.[57] Prison administrators expressed interest in bibliotherapy as early as 1940, and by 1950, national guidelines for prison libraries began to reflect bibliotherapy's growing influence. The APA's 1950 publication *Library Manual for Correctional Institutions* states that the prison library "has a very definite, distinct, and worthy place in the essential rehabilitation program for selected offenders," and it characterizes the prison library as "an instrument of wholesome recreation, of direct and indirect education, and of mental health." According to the manual, prison librarians should conduct interviews with inmates and regularly review their case files in order to design reading plans that meet their particular needs. Indeed, the prison librarian "may be the one person that can be of greatest aid to the inmate through a good guided reading program." A document in the appendix of the *Library Manual* further stipulates that prison librarians should keep a permanent record of patterns and changes evident in each prisoner's reading practices. Given the importance of carefully guiding prisoners' reading, the *Library Manual* also vehemently critiques prison librarians' reliance on book donations and urges them to establish interlibrary loan systems with public and university libraries.[58]

In their zeal to adopt reading as a means of rehabilitation, prison administrators and library personnel implemented bibliotherapy in a manner significantly different from Delaney's. Whereas Delaney used bibliotherapy to help veterans work through traumatic experiences and to develop their agency, political consciousness, and civic engagement, prison personnel used it more as a normalization technique, strictly monitoring prisoners' reading and treating them as passive recipients of literary medicine. Penal authorities' investment in bibliotherapy's disciplinary potential seems abundantly clear in one official's suggested method for measuring the effects of bibliotherapy. He recommended asking prisoners to choose one of nine statements about the church as most representative of their beliefs; those who chose "I believe the church is the greatest institution in America today" would illustrate the effectiveness of bibliotherapy, while those who chose "I think the church is a parasite on society" would illustrate its failure.[59]

An early description of bibliotherapy in the penal context—published in *Wilson Library Journal* in 1952—presages the normalizing role that the practice came to play in U.S. prisons. Author Maurice Floch, a clinical psychologist at the Detroit House of Correction, argues that prison librarians should not only choose the books for group therapy; they should also mark "meaty and significant passages" in the books to "save work for the inmate reader." According to Floch, books that emphasize "the major values of our civilization" and "the philosophy implied in the Ten Commandments" are most useful for the "reconditioning" of prisoners, who "lack the moral habits" necessary for behaving "in the conventionally accepted manner." In a 1958 article, Floch describes the "correctional library of the future" as comparable to a hospital "pharmacy." Like a "pharmaceutical chemist," the librarian will classify books "according to the conditions they might be able to remedy," and the prison library will serve as "the repository of those ideas and words without which the rebuilding of personalities is impossible." Whereas psychotherapy entails "personal influence exerted by one person over another," Floch conceptualizes bibliotherapy as psychotherapy in which books serve as "substitutes for people." Books are the best means for exerting influence over prisoners, he contends, because they provide "a more orderly presentation" of ideas than conversation allows.[60]

As prison personnel implemented bibliotherapy, they frequently enacted the controlling impulses evident in Floch's vision of the correctional library. For instance, in his role as librarian and "reading counselor" at San Quentin Prison, Herman K. Spector required that prisoners seek approval for every book acquisition, and he thoroughly censored their correspondence, books, magazines, and newspapers. He also exercised considerable control in facilitating therapeutic creative writing sessions, group therapy sessions based on the Great Books program, and a self-improvement discussion group called the Seekers.[61] Furthermore, in the hope of quantifying bibliotherapy's effects, Spector kept detailed records of library circulation patterns and of each prisoner's library use.[62]

Whereas Spector believed that exposure to literary classics exerted a moral influence on prisoners, bibliotherapy practitioners increasingly constructed prisoners as unintellectual recipients of the reading cure.[63] According to the 1950 *Library Manual*, prison librarians should avoid recommending the "classics," which "are usually for the intellectual reader—a class that includes few indeed in the prison population," and they should omit "psychiatry, home medical books, and criminology" from their collections because such books "may be definitely harmful." The manual also recommends restricting a much wider array of materials than earlier prison manuals, including books that emphasize antisocial attitudes or disrespect for the law, religion, and government; books about federal and state laws; and confessional and pulp magazines. The depiction of prisoners as passive recipients of literary medicine seems especially evident in *Bibliotherapy Methods and Materials*, published in 1971 by the Association of Hospital and Institution Libraries. Prisoners "may not be aware of their deficiencies, or they may be completely indifferent to or resentful of the idea of change," the authors state, so the librarian must subtly foster the desired "personality changes" among prisoners. Such changes do not occur "through teaching and learning," since "the intellect has little to do with the therapeutic process"; rather, they occur through prisoners' emotional responses to a "person-to-book confrontation." It is therefore of the utmost importance, the authors contend, that librarians select effective materials for these confrontations.[64]

In *Bibliotherapy and Its Widening Applications*, published in 1975, prominent public librarian Eleanor Frances Brown argues that bibliotherapists should not only prescribe particular texts; they should also try to regulate the effects that the texts produce and evaluate whether readers' interpretations are right or wrong. Presuming that one can produce precise outcomes by prescribing certain books, Brown argues that unless the bibliotherapist has "observed the [reader] for some time" and studied his or her records, a book may have a different effect than is desired. Although a murder mystery may "give a would-be murderer a nonviolent vicarious outlet for his murderous compulsion," it may inspire another reader "to commit murder." Bibliotherapy can only succeed, Brown cautions, if the reader is willing "to discuss the material with the bibliotherapist just as he would discuss a physical ailment with his doctor." The bibliotherapist must "clear up any misunderstanding the reader may have gained from the content," since "adverse effects usually result from . . . a wrong understanding of the material by the patient." Furthermore, because prisoners typically think of themselves as "the victor or hero" of books and presume that society "is at fault," bibliotherapists must help each prisoner to realize that "the source of his social failure lies within himself."[65]

Despite such attempts to control the outcome of prisoners' engagements with texts, the centrality of reading in philosophies of rehabilitation led to an important flourishing of reading behind bars. During the 1970s—the "golden years of prison library service"—prison libraries received significant legal and institutional support. In 1971, Congress authorized block grants for prisons and jails to establish service with local libraries, develop law libraries, and acquire materials "to help prisoners prepare themselves for re-entry and for positive use of offender leisure time."[66] The ALA also played an active role in improving library service for prisoners, as did state and local governments.[67] As prisons began to rely more on public libraries to augment their services, some prison librarians advocated making prisoners' access to reading materials "less susceptible to correctional institutions' political and economic fluctuations and administrative whims." Some prison librarians also warned one another about the danger of becoming "institutionalized"—serving "the administration's preconceptions of what is needed, rather than what the inmates see as needs."[68]

Moreover, the flourishing of prison libraries fueled a radical practice of reading among prisoners. An increasing number of prisoners used prison libraries to fulfill their own reading desires, which often focused on developing their racial and class consciousness rather than complying with state-defined rehabilitative goals. For example, in his response to the writing prompt "What My Library Means to Me," San Quentin prisoner B. L. Garrett describes his reading practice as "centered in history, political economy, philosophy, psychology, sociology, and trade unionism," and he explains that reading helps him to understand "the class structure" as well as "the interconnections between the patterns of [his] life and the course of world history." Prisoners also began to demand relevant reading materials and greater access to the outside world. In 1970, for instance, prisoners in New York City's Tombs jail destroyed more than 4,500 volumes in the library as part of a broader protest against the jail's intolerable living conditions; their attack on the library communicated particular frustration with its useless holdings, which included "300 copies of the *Autobiography of King Farouk*, 500 copies of the *Coin Collector's Handbook*, *Dining Out in Any Language*, and assorted books in German, French, and Greek." Prisoners in California's Soledad Prison drafted their own library policy demanding access to the same reading materials available in the free community.[69]

Soledad Brother: The Prison Letters of George Jackson provides a glimpse of the kinds of materials that one Soledad prisoner wanted to read. In a 1965 letter, George Jackson explains that many of the books "that are of interest and value to me cannot be obtained here in the library," and he requests information for ordering books by Mao Zedong and W. E. B. DuBois. In a 1967 letter, Jackson writes, "I have made inroads into political economy, geography, forms of government, anthropology, archeology, and the basics of three languages, and when I can get hold of them some of the works on urban guerrilla warfare," and he requests information about "self-teaching" books on Swahili and Arabic. At times, however, Jackson indicates that penal officials "are purposely making it difficult for me to get what I require." In a letter written in 1970, he reports that officials took "all [his] books" and asks his correspondent to send pocketbook editions of works by Frantz Fanon, Malcolm X, and anthropologists Robert Ardrey, Louis S. B. Leakey, and Ruth Benedict. A few days later, Jackson also requests books by "Lenin, Marx, Mao, Che, Giap, Uncle Ho, Nkrumah, and any Black Marxists."[70]

The clash between penal authorities' and prisoners' conceptions of reading is likewise evident in *The Attica Liberation Faction Manifesto*, written in 1971 by male prisoners in New York's Attica Correctional Facility. The authors of the *Manifesto* write that they have been incarcerated "for the purpose of correcting" their alleged "social errors in behavior," which make them "socially unacceptable until programmed with new values and more thorough understanding" of their "responsibilities as members of the outside community." They contend, however, that "the programs, which we are submitted to under the façade of rehabilitation, are relative to the ancient stupidity of pouring water on a drowning man, inasmuch as we are treated for our hostilities by our program administrators with their hostility as a medication."[71] Like many prisoners across the United States, the authors had come to reject the penal conception of rehabilitation as a sham because "custodial concerns, administrative exigencies and punishment [we]re all disguised as treatment." Moreover, they recognized that the penal model of treatment pathologizes prisoners and fosters their institutionalization; as the American Friends Service Committee argued in its 1971 publication, *Struggle for Justice*, such a model perpetuates the idea of the "sick" offender, "impairs or destroys self reliance," and grants the judicial apparatus power "to treat or change individuals' behavior in a way that protects those in control."[72] In an attempt to preserve their intellectual autonomy, the authors of the *Manifesto* note that they face harsh sanctions for trying to "intellectually expand in keeping with the outside world, through all categories of news media," and they demand an end to "the denial of prisoners' rights to subscribe to political papers, books, or any other educational and current media chronicles that are forwarded through the United States mail."[73]

Ultimately, the shift in the role that reading played in penal contexts—from fostering prisoners' social compliance to fostering their empowerment and resistance—contributed to the end of penal authorities' support for reading-centered rehabilitative efforts. Following an extensive outbreak of prison riots from 1969 to 1971, penal officials in many institutions deliberately retreated from their support for reading and installed televisions as a pacification tool.[74] In "Attica—Thirty Years Later," David Gilbert says of the introduction of televisions into Attica Prison, "TV not only serves as a direct means of pacification but has pretty much extinguished the flame of many prisoners' use of cell time to develop as readers and to grow into critical thinkers." Men who were imprisoned in California's Soledad Prison during the 1960s and 1970s likewise blame television for the depoliticization of current prisoners; they contend that prisoners "read all the time" before televisions entered prisons. Writing from an Administrative Maximum federal prison, where every cell is equipped with a television "compliments of the Bureau of Prisons (BOP) pacification program," Raymond Luc Levasseur sardonically comments, "Feeling rebellious, lonely, angry, miserable, alienated, unskilled, and uneducated? Turn on the face of Amerika [sic]. The administration replaces a broken TV quicker than fixing a toilet."[75]

Penal authorities' diminished support for reading was also part of a broader ideological, political, and economic shift away from rehabilitation and toward the development of what is now called the prison-industrial complex. Although a full analysis of this shift exceeds the scope of this book, highlighting factors that contributed to the development of the prison-industrial complex will help to contextualize the evaporation of penal support for reading-centered forms of rehabilitation. In his 1998 article "The Prison-Industrial Complex," Eric Schlosser argues that the prison-industrial complex began to take form in 1973 with the passage of the Rockefeller drug laws. After New York governor Nelson Rockefeller demanded that every dealer of illegal drugs be punished with a mandatory life sentence, the New York state legislature established a mandatory prison term of fifteen years to life for possession or sale of drugs, and it established a mandatory prison sentence for many second-felony convictions. The Rockefeller drug laws catalyzed a profound shift in American sentencing policy, prompting other states to enact their own mandatory-minimum sentences for drug offenses. The trend was fueled by President Ronald Reagan's War on Drugs and by the passage of the Anti–Drug Abuse Act in 1986, which reinstated federal mandatory minimums. Despite a decline in overall crime rates, politicians and the media helped to justify the new draconian practices by generating fear about crime as an out-of-control problem. A law-and-order sentiment took hold in the United States, leading to the reinstatement of capital punishment and an explicit focus on punishment rather than rehabilitation for prisoners. The United States Sentencing Commission's 1987 guidelines stipulate that rehabilitation of a criminal is of secondary importance compared with protecting the public, and they abolish parole for federal prisoners and curtail provisions for good time.[76]

In the 1980s, this shift toward highly draconian penal practices resulted in a sharp increase in the prison population, a frenzied drive to build more prisons, and a massive investment of capital in the punishment industry. The prison-building boom provided huge infusions of state money to economically depressed regions, and rural towns began competing to attract new prisons. As Eric Schlosser explains, prisons have become a cornerstone of economic development in impoverished rural areas because they offer year-round employment with benefits, and they "are recession-proof, usually expanding in size during hard times." Building more prisons and housing more prisoners has been equally lucrative for architecture and construction firms, investment banks, companies that supply products and services to prisons, companies that employ nonunionized prison laborers, and corporations that operate private prisons. The development of the prison-industrial complex—this web of constituents invested in the expansion and maintenance of the punishment industry—thus reinforced the political and economic centrality of prisons in the United States and fostered a shift from a therapeutic to a disciplinary model of corrections.[77]

As a result of this shift, bibliotherapy became a relic of the penal past. A bibliography on prison librarianship, published in 1987, conveys the extent to which bibliotherapy fell out of favor. Prison librarians cannot perform bibliotherapy, the authors argue, because they lack necessary training in counseling; expecting librarians to treat prisoners' "thought disorders" is as foolish as "permitting the profoundly retarded to design nuclear generating plants." Moreover, the authors contend that efforts to rehabilitate a criminal are futile because "there is no earlier condition of being responsible to which to restore him." By 2007, none of the prison librarians whom I encountered was familiar with the concept or practice of bibliotherapy.[78]

Libraries and Prisons: An "Unhappy Marriage"

In the midst of the prison-building frenzy of the 1980s, prison libraries became a low priority, and severely overcrowded prisons routinely slashed their library budgets and converted library space into prison cells. The overall effect on prison libraries was profound. For instance, San Quentin library had 36,000 volumes in 1974, but by 1990, it had fewer than 9,000. As I discuss in detail in Chapter 2, very limited funding is now available for prison libraries, and economic imperatives threaten to outweigh the commitment to library service in private, for-profit prisons.[79]

Furthermore, whereas libraries were once deemed a central component of prison rehabilitation programs, libraries and prisons came to be viewed as incompatible institutions. In the words of criminologist Elmer H. Johnson, "We find an 'unhappy marriage' of two institutional systems" when library and penal ideologies come into contact. Starting in the 1980s, prison officials began to characterize libraries as "middle class institutions" that are "unsuitable and unappreciated in prisons." Library and penal officials also engaged in heated debate about the proper model for a prison library: should the library be governed by corrections-oriented goals, or should it follow the "multi-service, user-oriented model of the public library," which assumes prisoners' right to library service "regardless of correctional goals"?[80] In fact, an ideological rift developed between the ALA and the ACA, organizations that had jointly published guidelines for prison libraries since the 1930s. According to the 1981 edition of *Library Standards for Adult Correctional Institutions*, jointly published by the ALA and the ACA, the prison library should "encompass the variety of services, materials, and programs available in the free community," and materials should be selected "to meet the educational, informational, legal, cultural, recreational, and self-actualizing needs" of the library's users. In 1982, however, the ALA adopted the "Resolution on Prisoners' Right to Read," which endorses prisoners' right to "purchase, receive, read, and permit other inmates to read any and all legal materials, newspapers, periodicals, and books accepted for distribution by the United States Post Office, except those which describe the making of any weapon, explosive, poison or destructive device." Because the ACA was unwilling to embrace this resolution, it began to publish its own standards for prison libraries and continues to do so today.[81]

The tension between librarians' and prison administrators' objectives came to a head with the 1987 publication of William J. Coyle's *Libraries in Prisons: A Blending of Institutions*. In sharp contrast to the 1981 *Library Standards*, which states that an incarcerated person has "the same innate need for and right to informational resources as the free citizen," Coyle—the correctional library consultant for the Colorado State Library—insists that prisoners have no right to library services; prisons provide library services only because "they advance the state's goals and objectives." Although he acknowledges the "democratic belief" that "the opportunity to pursue one's interests . . . is essential to becoming a responsible, contributing member of society," Coyle argues that many prisoners' interests are "intensely antisocial, pathological, and supportive of criminal life-styles," such that library services "geared to interests of inmate users might well be more detrimental than beneficial to constructive change." In critiquing librar-ies that cater to prisoners' interests, Coyle singles out a Pennsylvania prison's "unabashedly recreational" collection of novels by Donald Goines and Iceberg Slim, two African American authors now considered the fathers of contempo-rary urban fiction. Coyle's particular disdain for these works reflects his assump-tion that such narratives—which foreground rebellious black masculinity and draw on their authors' experiences with racism, ghetto living, drug addiction, and imprisonment—could never promote "constructive change." In his view, appropriate materials for a prison library include newspapers, magazines, trade journals, nonfiction books, career information, and directories. Prison librarians should give "no consideration" to materials that are "essentially recreational," and "virtually all fiction might thus be excluded." Leaving little room for the pos-sibility that fiction can foster change, or that readers can make creative uses of all kinds of materials, Coyle reasons that it is wasteful to fund recreational books that do not "contribut[e] substantively to the change process."[82]

Coyle's provocative argument prompted several defenses of prisoners' free-dom to read, including all of the articles in *Wilson Library Bulletin*'s special issue on prison libraries, published in 1989. In one of those articles, Daniel Suvak—a member of the Library Standards for Adult Correctional Institutions Ad Hoc Subcommittee—first challenges the dichotomy between free and imprisoned readers, insisting that our society is full of people who commit crimes but only a tiny fraction of lawbreakers are ever apprehended. Since many prisoners "are former and future voters and taxpayers," Suvak argues that they should enjoy their citizenship-based right to read. He then argues that Coyle's model "guts the library of its best chance to be effective," since prisoners' capacity for healing and change rests on "being treated like human beings." According to Suvak, when prisoners walk into a "pretense-of-a-library and find the authors they appreciate absent, their requests for information screened by someone who is judging how they might pervert it, and their needs filtered through a test of state-determined goals," any chance "for honest interchanges and rapport will be seriously lim-ited, along with any real hope for change." Brenda Vogel's 1995 volume, *Down for the Count: A Prison Library Handbook*, also defends the public library model for prisons. A "library in a prison is a library," Vogel insists. "It should not be man-aged by prison authorities even if it is located there."[83]

The ALA's most recent manual for prison libraries—*Library Standards for Adult Correctional Institutions* (1992)—likewise counters Coyle's argument and endorses five documents that radically foreground prisoners' right to read. According to the "Freedom to Read Statement," written by the ALA and the Association of American Publishers, librarians and publishers should not "establish their own political, moral or aesthetic views as a standard for determining what books should be published or circulated," and they should not label books or authors as "subversive or dangerous," since "Americans do not need others to do their thinking for them." Indeed, no "single librarian or publisher or government or church" should determine what is "proper" to read. The "Freedom to Read Statement" concludes, "We believe . . . that ideas can be dangerous; but that the suppression of ideas is fatal to a democratic society. Freedom itself is a dangerous way of life, but it is ours."[84]

Despite such defenses of the freedom to read, penal objectives increasingly outweigh prisoners' right to read. A few examples from prisons in South Carolina and Texas illustrate my point. In February 1995, *American Libraries* lauded South Carolina's outstanding prison library program. During that same month, however, a disgruntled prison employee complained to the media that South Carolina prisoners were permitted to read Donald Goines's urban novels. The South Carolina Department of Corrections responded by banning Goines's novels and all other "prison classics," on the grounds that they depict violence and sex. According to the department's director of education, the decision was motivated by the "need to bring in materials and programs to enhance a person's ability to rehabilitate themselves." The South Carolina Department of Corrections then laid off all but one library employee, reduced the library, and disbanded its programs. From that point forward, every book purchase has had to undergo a cumbersome review by the state superintendent of education, the Department of Education's budget director, and the library system's advisory council, and according to one state official, "Many books are rejected for reasons unknown." The curtailment of reading opportunities in South Carolina prisons seems even more troubling given that a majority of the state's prisoners have only a sixth-grade education.[85]

In Texas, penal officials decided to ban Toni Morrison's *Paradise* from all state prisons on the grounds that the novel threatens security. According to a 1998 report issued by the Directors' Review Committee of the Texas Department of Criminal Justice (DCJ), Morrison's novel contains "information of a racial nature" that "a reasonable person would construe as written solely for the purpose of communicating information designed to achieve a breakdown of prisons through inmate disruption, such as strikes or riots." The censorship report cites passages from *Paradise* that contain historical references to "crosses on fire in Negroes' yards"; the deaths of Martin Luther King, Medgar Evers, and Malcolm X; and the civil rights and Black Power movements, including a passage about four young black men arrested during a peaceful demonstration, for whatever charges the prosecution could muster "against black boys who said No or thought about it."[86] This decision to ban Morrison's novel seems to reflect the Texas DCJ's fear that *Paradise* will incite prison riots by highlighting whites' historical oppression of blacks. Such a fear seems all the more ironic given the DCJ's decision, eight years earlier, to permit the Knights of the Ku Klux Klan of Waco to mail publications to the state's more than 13,500 white prisoners. Although the DCJ constructed Morrison's novel as "designed to achieve a breakdown of prisons," it did not believe that Klan publications such as *Negro Watch* and *Jew Watch* would jeopardize its ability to "maintain prison order and security."[87]

As evident in the foregoing examples, racial issues often inform fears that particular books will jeopardize prison security. The lists of books recently banned in Ohio and Pennsylvania are extensive, and they contain a striking number of titles by and about African Americans. In addition to several volumes of contemporary African American urban fiction, the lists include earlier urban fiction by Donald Goines and Iceberg Slim as well as the following African American autobiographies: Maya Angelou's *I Know Why the Caged Bird Sings*, journalist Nathan McCall's *Makes Me Wanna Holler*, former gang member Sanyika Shakur's *Monster: The Autobiography of an L.A. Gang Member*, and lawyer Cupcake Brown's bestseller, *A Piece of Cake*. Also banned are periodicals, pamphlets, and books related to racial and class struggle, including the *Nation*; "Philosophy of Class Struggle"; "Interviews with Assata Shakur"; "Debunking the Panther Mythology"; William Styron's *The Confessions of Nat Turner*, a Pulitzer Prize–winning novel that describes a slave rebellion; and *The Willie Lynch Letter and the Making of a Slave*, a best-selling reprint of a 1712 publication that teaches whites how to maintain blacks in slavery. Like the racialized limitations on prisoners' opportunities for reading in earlier eras, contemporary restrictions on prisoners' access to books seem to contribute to the maintenance of literacy as white property. The question that Holloway poses in this chapter's epigraph—"What does it mean to have black bodies and books read as a single narrative?"—remains relevant today. It still means a great deal, it seems, "to have black bodies and books read as a single narrative" and to have certain black-authored books in prisoners' hands.[88]

One particular incident from my research further illustrates penal officials' efforts to control prisoners' reading. A few women involved in my study told me about their participation in a small reading group run by a member of the prison staff. The group had discussed contemporary novels such as *The Lost Scrolls of King Solomon*, *The Wake of the Wind*, and *The Secret Life of Bees*, as well as passages from older, nonfiction texts such as Machiavelli's *The Prince* and Sun-Tzu's *The Art of War*. They were also discussing subjects such as Constantine the Great, Kenneth Lay, Hezbollah, community housing, the Israeli Palestinian conflict, and the Legendary Ball, and they were learning to use words such as "nocturnal," "incident," and "macrocosm." For one assignment, participants had to ask a staff member about his or her definition of humility and then write their own definition of the term; for another assignment, they had to write a definition of freedom. One of the participants said of the group,

> I'm thankful for it 'cause it keeps me healthy intellectually because that's all we deal with is the intellect. It's not a group where you go and cry or get built up. It's just a group where you go, and you logically talk about something. He sets it out, and then we research, and we come back. . . . And he just throws stuff out there, and he'll say, "What do you think about that?" And he'll wait a moment and he'll say, "You do have an opinion?" And we say, "Of course." So he says, "Well then, what do you think about it?" And before it's over, everybody has said something. And you feel like, "Wow!"

When one of the librarians heard about the group, she said that it "blew [her] away" to discover that prisoners enjoy such "deep reading." Upon the recommendation of this librarian and a few women participating in the group, I requested permission from penal officials to interview the group's organizer. Unbeknownst to me, the administration was not aware of the group until I brought it to their attention, and they promptly shut it down because it was not operating under official approval.

Beard v. Banks, the Supreme Court case that serves as the entry point into this chapter, underscores the extent to which contemporary prisoners are seen as dangerous wards of the state whose reading should be dictated by correctional goals. Although religious reading materials have a protected status in *Beard v. Banks*, post–September 11 fears about Muslim extremism have led to new restrictions on religious materials as well. In the spring of 2007, the federal Bureau of Prisons implemented the Standardized Chapel Library Project, which directed chaplains in federal prisons to remove any books, tapes, CDs, and videos that do not appear on a list of approved resources; the list includes 150 book titles and 150 multimedia resources for each of 20 religions. The directive, which stems from Justice Department recommendations, aims to bar prisoners' access to religious materials that could "discriminate, disparage, advocate violence or radicalize." In accordance with the Standardized Chapel Library Project, chaplains in federal prisons dismantled library collections that took decades to assemble—often leaving their shelves almost bare—and chaplains in state prisons felt pressure to follow suit. However, although Republican lawmakers routinely support curtailment of educational and rehabilitative programming in prisons, the Standardized Chapel Library Project prompted outcry from Republican lawmakers, religious groups, religious scholars, and civil libertarians. As the chairman of the Republican Study Committee said in response to the directive, "Anything that impinges upon the religious liberties of American citizens, be they incarcerated or not, is something that's going to cause House conservatives great concern." The Bureau of Prisons has decided to re-allow formerly purged materials until it completes a review of all materials in chapel libraries, but it has not abandoned the idea of creating such lists. The "unhappy marriage" of libraries and prisons thus continues to generate pressing questions about prisoners' right to read and their status as literate citizens.[89]

"Prisoner-Students": Education and the Radical Tradition

As the preceding sections suggest, penal officials and prisoners have sometimes defined the purposes and parameters of penal education in divergent ways. Debate about educational opportunities for prisoners has revolved around issues of control and access: What is the purpose of penal education, and who should dictate its parameters? How much education, if any, is appropriate for various prisoners? While penal officials have attempted to control the amount and content of prisoners' education, incarcerated men and women have forged a radical tradition of trying to educate themselves and one another according to their own terms.

An 1892 essay in the *Journal of Prison Discipline and Philanthropy* articulates a conception of penal education that retains currency today. The essay, published by the Pennsylvania Prison Society, advocates making "moral education" rather than "mental education" the focus of penal education. Prior to 1892, the authors note, the purpose of prison education had been to teach illiterate white males how to read and write. Yet because prisoners' literacy levels have risen, the authors ask, "Is it mind alone that must be educated? Are we not to cultivate the better purposes of the heart? . . . 'Knowledge is power' has often been quoted and repeated, but it may be a power for evil as well as for good. The very powers that might be useful may be prostituted to bad uses, and thus disgrace the very name of education." The authors therefore suggest that penal education should foster prisoners' use of knowledge for socially sanctioned "moral" ends.[90]

Education in penal contexts has often been yoked to moral aims. As I discuss further in Chapter 5, penal institutions increasingly frame prisoners' opportunities for education in religious or moral terms, as in "faith and character" prisons and prisons whose sole educational programming is sponsored by Christian organizations. However, the history of U.S. penal practices offers glimpses of alternative possibilities for conceptualizing education in prisons. Austin Mac-Cormick offers an interesting conception of penal education in his *Education of Adult Prisoners*. At times, MacCormick constructs penal education in terms of treatment and discipline. He argues that penal education should be yoked to the goal of "individual diagnosis, prescription and treatment" for every prisoner. Moreover, penal education should foster "conformity *with* understanding" and help prisoners to "fit into the social scheme understandingly and willingly." A prisoner makes "a better candidate for education than the corresponding free man," MacCormick asserts, because "it is possible to control all his activities and to direct his thoughts to a degree not possible with free students."[91]

At other times, however, MacCormick gestures toward a model of education that foregrounds prisoners' intellectual development, independence, and empowerment. Coining the term "prisoner-students," he argues that every prisoner should be viewed "primarily [as] an adult in need of education and only secondarily as a criminal in need of reform"; indeed, "discipline should be education." One can "seriously cripple" educational efforts, MacCormick contends, by treating prisoners as "men and women to be 'saved'" and by designating moral education as the sole aim of the prison. In his view, penal education should inculcate "civic ideals" and increase each prisoner's "understanding of human beings, himself included, and of human motives, impulses, habits, tendencies and development." Such education should include literature, music, drama, and art, as well as sociology, psychology, philosophy, and the history of humankind—in short, "knowledge of what the world of thought has to offer." Although such "cultural education" has no relation to earning power, MacCormick argues, it plays a crucial role in making prisoners "better citizen[s]" by introducing them to "new ways of living, new competence . . . in living itself in the complex social relationships of modern life, . . . new richness, new outlooks, new horizons." In MacCormick's view, reading that "tends to enrich life and to increase its satisfactions" plays as important a role in prisons as that which "tends to make life more orderly and law-abiding."[92]

Notwithstanding the considerable disciplinary impulses of his argument, MacCormick's construction of prisoners as "adult[s] in need of education" and his conceptualization of penal education as a portal to "knowledge of what the world of thought has to offer" resonate in important ways with the radical tradition of prisoners educating and empowering themselves through reading and writing. Political prisoners outside the United States, such as Antonio Gramsci, Nelson Mandela, Bobby Sands, and Nawal el Saadawi, have drawn attention to the ways in which prisons can serve as schools for political education. In *Robben Island and Prisoner Resistance to Apartheid*, Fran Lisa Buntman describes how prisoners in South Africa organized reading programs designed to educate their fellow prisoners for political resistance. "The determination with which prisoners forged and fought for meaning in their lives in prison was a remarkable act of resistance," Buntman writes, "a refusal to let the state destroy their minds, bodies, or spirits." Resistance, as these prisoners practiced it, entailed efforts to maintain their "dignity and self-consciousness," their "sanity," and "a sense of human community." In educating themselves and one another, prisoners at Robben Island were engaged in "a positive act of remaking and reconstruing the dominant world."[93]

U.S. political prisoners—including George Jackson, Angela Davis, Assata Shakur, Leonard Peltier, Mumia Abu-Jamal, Laura Whitehorn, Linda Evans, Susan Rosenberg, and Marilyn Buck—as well as lesser-known "social" or "ordinary" prisoners have similarly refused state control of their minds and spirits by educating themselves and others. When more than 500 Attica prisoners were transferred to New York's Greenhaven Prison, they helped to establish an on-site, four-year college program that lasted from 1973 until 1995. Men and women in prison also serve as peer mentors and teachers for one another. As one among countless examples, political prisoners Linda Evans, Susan Rosenberg, and Laura Whitehorn have struggled for women prisoners' rights to education and worked as peer educators to increase other women's knowledge of HIV and AIDS. Furthermore, prisoners organize education circles, writing groups, and study groups that sometimes focus on readings deemed subversive by penal authorities. As Viet Mike Ngo explains, he and other prisoners used to read materials that were "contrary to the United States' ideology. So it allowed us to be more critical of our space and where we live."[94]

Prisoners have also authored underground publications and publications that circulate outside prisons. *Prison Legal News*, a monthly newsletter that has been published since 1990, addresses a host of issues that concern prisoners, their families, and their advocates, from visiting and telephone privileges to the abuse of women prisoners. Anthologies such as *Prison Masculinities*; *The Celling of America: An Inside Look at the U.S. Prison Industry*; *Doing Time: Twenty-Five Years of Prison Writing*; and *The New Abolitionists: (Neo)Slave Narratives and Contemporary Prison Writings* also feature prisoners' critical reflections about imprisonment and U.S. penal policy. Works such as Michael Hames-García's *Fugitive Thought: Prison Movements, Race, and the Meaning of Justice* and Dylan Rodríguez's *Forced Passages: Imprisoned Radical Intellectuals and the U.S. Prison Regime* further illuminate prisoners' theorizations of justice and freedom, their critiques of state violence and U.S. penal practices, and their efforts to maintain "political, intellectual, and personal connections" with others in civil society. Whether they are high-profile political activists, jailhouse lawyers, or people who have become activists and intellectuals while imprisoned, prisoners perform crucial acts of survival through their writings and their efforts to educate themselves and others.[95]

However, since the spate of prisoner rebellions in the 1970s, penal authorities have increased their efforts to circumscribe prisoners' intellectual autonomy and limit the influence of imprisoned radicals and intellectuals. In *Forced Passages*, Rodríguez contends that, since the 1960s, states have tried to "absorb and institutionalize the political-intellectual work of imprisoned intellectuals and activists" through prison education, which is often linked to religious and twelve-step therapy programs. According to Rodríguez, the prison school is "an extension of the prison regime's technologies of coercion and bodily violence," since it aims to "repress, expel, or liquidate" prisoners who use knowledge "against the liberal humanist aims of prison philanthropy." Moreover, teachers involved in such education are "embodiments of the prison's extended technologies of surveillance" and agents of its "functioning, expansion, and self-preservation" because their efforts make the prison seem more humane.[96]

On one hand, Rodríguez's critique of prison education risks throwing the baby out with the bathwater. As Barbara Harlow argues in *Barred: Women, Writing, and Political Detention*, prison education often "functions to undermine the very walls and premises that contain it." Rodríguez himself acknowledges that the prison classroom "is frequently transformed, appropriated, or rearticulated by imprisoned radical and protoradical intellectuals, who may galvanize new communities of solidarity or political kinship among and between course participants (including, at times, volunteer teachers, tutors, and teaching assistants from the free world)." On the other hand, Rodríguez draws important attention to the punitive consequences that prisoners can face when they try to use prison classrooms for "antisystemic political activities." He offers a recent example of four prisoners who wrote a proposal to introduce Asian American studies and ethnic studies courses into the Paten College Program at California's Soledad Prison. In response to their proposal, which suggested that the college include prisoners in deciding which electives should be taught and by whom, the director of the education program argued that ethnic studies courses would be inappropriate due to their "political content." Furthermore, the four authors were placed in solitary confinement and were barred from classes and extracurricular programming; two were then transferred to other prisons. As this example illustrates, education for prisoners often remains tightly wedded to penal imperatives.[97]

Moreover, prisoners' opportunities for education have precipitously declined in recent decades. As I discussed briefly in the Introduction, Congress eliminated Pell Grants for prisoners in 1994, leading to devastating cuts in educational programming for prisoners. Higher education was not available in U.S. penal institutions until 1953, and by 1965, only twelve postsecondary correctional education programs existed in the United States.[98] In 1965, however, Congress passed Title IV of the Higher Education Act, which authorized prisoners to apply for tax-supported Pell Grants that could help to cover the cost of college-level studies. Although prisoners received less than 1 percent of yearly Pell Grant funds, these merit-based grants greatly increased the availability of higher education in prisons; by 1982, 350 postsecondary correctional education programs existed in the United States. In the early 1990s, however, there was a groundswell of resistance to tax-supported funding for prisoners' higher education. Whereas Tennessee congressman Bart Gordon suggested that funding higher education for prisoners is like trying to help "blind hogs" to "find an acorn," Massachusetts governor William Weld argued that prisons should be "a tour through the streets of hell" and that prisoners should only learn "the joys of busting rocks."[99] Compared to such descriptions of prisoners as "nonhuman 'nonentit[ies]'" and "public enemies," MacCormick's 1931 conception of "prisoner-students" seems radical indeed.[100]

Although support for education in prisons had already been waning, the elimination of Pell Grants vastly accelerated this decline. For instance, New York State—which previously funded college programs in forty-five of its prisons—abolished all public funds for college education in its prisons. Nationwide, all but 8 of 350 prison college programs were closed due to lack of adequate funding. Moreover, almost every literary journal that published prisoners' writing collapsed with the reduction in college-level courses.[101]

The three prisons featured in my study illustrate how penal education remains a site of contest and struggle. For instance, the prisons block women's efforts to educate themselves about prison-related issues by banning books, periodicals, and pamphlets such as *Prison Legal News*; *Journal of Prisoners on Prisons*; *The Celling of America*; *Prison Nation: The Warehousing of America's Poor*; and "Prisons and their Moral Influence on Prisoners." Left-oriented periodicals are also forbidden. As Solo says of the library where she is incarcerated, "They'll give us a few *Newsweeks* or whatever, but the *Nation*—they won't let us have that"; authorities forbid "anything that will cause [us] to get passionate and want to rise up" or "incite us to become conscious of the fact that you may be infringing on my rights." In terms of educational offerings, the three prisons offer Basic Education, GED preparation, some college-level courses, and "career tech" classes such as cosmetology, horticulture, upholstery, and building maintenance. Each prison currently requires that women without a high school diploma or GED enroll in an appropriate academic education program. However, because long waiting lists often exist for educational classes, women are actually eligible to take classes only within three years of their release date. All three prisons also limit higher educational opportunities for women with sentences of ten years or longer. Women serving a sentence of ten or more years may attend college classes if space permits, but such classes are effectively off-limits to most women because they cannot afford the cost of tuition, books, and fees. Furthermore, both the Ohio and Pennsylvania prisons limit the number of college credits that women can earn; they cannot earn enough credits to complete a college degree.

In fact, according to the chief librarian of the Ohio Department of Rehabilitation and Correction, it is no longer "politically correct" to refer to "college" courses for prisoners. "We're not allowed to call them college classes any more," she explained. "Starting about five years ago, we call them AJT: Advanced Job Training." The librarian went on to explain that prisoners in Ohio penal facilities could earn B.A. and M.A. degrees until the officers' union complained that prisoners were getting free educations through Pell Grants. In response to this complaint, the Ohio state legislature limited the number of college credits that prisoners could earn, shifted the focus of higher education to advanced job training, and called for increased emphasis on "career tech" programming. "Now that AJT emphasizes job training," the chief librarian explains, "all classes are geared toward that." Literature courses are no longer offered because society is becoming "more technological" and "literature is not practical." Such restrictions on prisoners' educational opportunities help to explain why many women with longer sentences were particularly eager to participate in my study.

Given the decline of prison libraries and increasing restrictions on penal education, the radical tradition of prisoners' self-education is useful for understanding contemporary women prisoners' reading practices. None of the women involved in my study could be classified as a political prisoner or a radical. The women's preferred reading materials are neither explicitly political nor subversive; indeed, many scholars would characterize them as conservative and even reactionary. Whereas San Quentin prisoners were circulating handwritten pages of *The Communist Manifesto* in the late 1960s, women involved in my study circulate urban fiction such as *Thugs and the Women Who Love Them* and Christian self-help books by televangelist Joyce Meyer. However, this contrast indicates more about the climate for prisoners' reading in the two time periods than about the readers themselves. Like the male prisoners who were reading Marx in the 1960s, female prisoners who read self-help books and urban-fiction may look to reading as a tool for understanding sources of oppression, as a path toward empowerment, and as a means to survive the fierce economic, racial, and gender inequalities that a capitalist system fosters. At a time when our highest court has authorized the *denial* of reading materials as an "incentiv[e] for inmate growth"—indeed, at a time when we "have all but forsaken those who are marked as criminal"—women involved in my study are using the reading materials at hand to forge and fight for meaning in their lives; to maintain their dignity, self-consciousness, and a sense of human community; and to remake and reconstrue their worlds.[102] By focusing on women's issues, and by reading popular, female-gendered genres, these prisoners are extending the radical tradition in important ways as they navigate newly repressive conditions of confinement.

IN *Total Confinement: Madness and Reason in the Maximum Security Prison,* Lorna Rhodes suggests that "if we cannot escape our history, we might at least make better use of it."[103] The history that I have traced in this chapter provides useful starting points for understanding cultures of reading in contemporary women's prisons. As subsequent chapters demonstrate, racial and gender ideologies continue to shape penal policies about reading, education, and rehabilitation. To the limited extent that penal authorities support reading, they tend to conceptualize it in therapeutic terms and to sanction reading materials that explicitly encourage self-improvement, rehabilitation, and healing.[104] Many women prisoners themselves frequently adopt a therapeutic model of reading. Their reading practices and book choices nonetheless remain circumscribed by the disciplinary aims of penal authorities. Within the context of increasing restrictions on reading and educational opportunities in prisons, readers involved in my study engage in vital forms of self- and peer education that enable them to resist penal control of their minds and spirits. Although reading has too often served as a tool of discipline and normalization in the penal context, it is crucial to recognize the possibility—embedded in this history of reading and education in U.S. prisons—that reading can play other roles in the lives of women prisoners. I begin exploring some of those roles in Chapter 2.

CHAPTER TWO

The Underground Book Railroad

MATERIAL DIMENSIONS OF READING

I *have* to have a book. I *have* to, for when I'm bored or having a hard time sleeping, and I try to stay away from all this craziness here, and just to keep my mind right.—DARLENE, Northeast Pre-Release Center

I eat at least three books per week. I devour them.—CANDY, State Correctional Institution at Muncy

DESCRIBING HER reading habits in prison, a thirty-nine-year-old African American woman named Cassandra explains, "I read every night faithfully from nine to midnight. Lights have to go off at eleven, but I'm still up in the bed reading. I have the bathroom light on." Because she often has to wait for months before a library book becomes available, Cassandra explains that she and other women cooperate among themselves to gain access to books. "All the book readers, we all hang together," she says. "If [someone] is just about to bring this book back to the library, we say, 'Let me go with you to the library so I can check it right back out.' Or if they have a book that's due the next day, I can read real fast and I'll tell them, 'I'll give it to you in the morning' or 'I'll take it over there.' I mean, we got that bond and trust." In her continuous search for good books, Cassandra regularly approaches women who own books and says, "Please can I read this book? I will not write in your book. I will not bend no pages in your book. I will not eat with your book." By now, she explains, "everyone knows how serious I am about books so they'll come up and they'll give books to me and be like, 'I have this,' or 'Have you read this?' I run around here to find books, and if I don't have anything, I'll just be like in a real cruddy mood."

An African American woman named Denise coined the phrase "the Underground Book Railroad" to describe the informal networks through which she and other prisoners share books. The Underground Book Railroad serves as a crucial reminder of the historical continuities between slavery and incarceration, as well as the ongoing ways in which racial ideologies delimit conceptions of prisoners' humanity and capacity for change. The phrase also underscores the connections that reading can foster in prison—connections that sometimes trespass the boundaries separating incarcerated women from one another, from people outside prison, and from the world of ideas. Furthermore, the Underground Book Railroad evokes the imaginative, emotional, intellectual, and spiritual ways in which reading allows some women to proceed to new destinations, even if they will spend the rest of their lives behind bars. In this chapter, I focus primarily on the Ohio and Pennsylvania prisons in addressing how the spatial organization, regulations, and material conditions of prisons and prison libraries delimit women's access to books. I then explore the daily, pragmatic ways in which prisoners engage with books as "equipment for living" in spaces of confinement.[1]

Library Settings, Procedures, and Holdings

Access to books is limited for women from the moment they pass through the prison gates. Consider, for instance, how the location, visiting hours, and physical setting of prison libraries affect access to books.[2] In both the North Carolina and Pennsylvania prisons, the library is located in a building where educational classes take place. Some women thus have occasion to pass the library during the course of their day. In the Ohio prison, by contrast, the library is located in a building that houses several administrative offices, so prisoners only see the library if they have deliberately planned to visit it. The relative accessibility of the libraries in the North Carolina and Pennsylvania prisons is offset, however, by the fact that women can only visit the libraries by appointment. Prisoners in North Carolina can go to the library only when their particular housing unit has been scheduled for a visit. The Pennsylvania prison recently instituted a similar policy whereby women must sign up one week in advance to visit the library. Women whose names are on the callout sheet arrive at the same time and must leave together thirty minutes later; those who have scheduled time for legal research can remain for one and a half hours. Because this new policy makes it more difficult to visit the library, women are now permitted to check out six books rather than four.[3]

According to a librarian in the Pennsylvania prison, the new scheduling policy "has eliminated girlfriends and socializing," and it ensures that "mostly the real readers come." The librarian's comment highlights the extent to which penal authorities have shifted away from the public library as a model for prison libraries. The 1981 edition of *Library Standards for Adult Correctional Institutions* figures the prison library as a social space. The authors argue that it should include an area for talking, playing games, listening to music, viewing or listening to materials as a group, and small group conferences, and it should be large enough to seat "a minimum 15% of the population" at one time. In sharp contrast, current penal officials routinely express fears that prison libraries serve as a social space—indeed, as "a gay bar" and "social club"—rather than as a place where "real readers" gather books.[4]

Such fears lend added significance to the restrictive physical settings of the libraries featured in my research. The North Carolina prison library is about the size of a large living room, but it offers little of the physical comfort that the term "living room" suggests. The room has bookshelves around its perimeter and down its center, leaving very little space for a circulation desk and two small tables where a total of about five women can sit. The Ohio prison library is comparable in size but feels even more cramped, yet as the librarian and several prisoners informed me, its current location is twice as big as its former one. Bookshelves line every available portion of the library's perimeter, and several two-sided shelves occupy most of the floor space. The little remaining space contains a circulation desk, a desk for library clerks, two computer stations for legal clerks, and a few tables where a total of about ten women can sit. The Pennsylvania library is approximately four times larger than the libraries in North Carolina and Ohio. Although half of the floor space is filled with bookshelves, the room is large enough to accommodate several large tables where more than fifty women can sit. However, the Pennsylvania library restricts socializing by limiting the number of women who can visit the library at one time. A total of twenty-four women can be in the general library, and a total of six women can be in the legal library, an alcove that includes computers for legal research, some shelves of legal materials, and a large table with several chairs.

Because states cannot promote particular religions, the prisons house religious books and periodicals in a separate chaplain's library. In Ohio, the chaplain's library is in the chaplain's office, and the tiny space can accommodate only four standing women. In addition to a few shelves of books, the library has a small desk with a VCR where women can watch religious videos or a tape of a family funeral that they were unable to attend. Whereas penal officials discourage socializing in the general library, the Ohio chaplain characterizes her mini-library as a "safe haven" and "meeting place" where women "can feel at peace," "get away from the racket," and "really talk and pray together." In Pennsylvania, the chaplain's library is down the hall from the chaplain's office, and it consists of a video station and three small storage areas lined with books. As in Ohio, the library can accommodate only four standing women. Prisoners can visit the library three days a week for fifteen minutes at a time.

In addition to the location, visiting hours, and physical setting of prison libraries, their funding structures and acquisition procedures shape women's access to books in significant ways. In Ohio prisons, the general libraries are funded entirely by revenue from each prison's vending machines and commissary, a store from which prisoners buy toiletries, snacks, and other small personal items. This revenue, known as Industrial and Entertainment funds, is divided among the library, the recreation department, and religious services, which means that very little is available for the library. "Sometimes the library is looked on as extraneous," explains the chief librarian for the Ohio penal system. "Most institutions are happy to have a library because it gives inmates something to do that they don't worry about as much. But that's the extent of the enthusiasm for the library. If the library had to be a line item on the budget, wardens would be unhappy." Given these funding limitations, librarians in Ohio prisons have devised creative means to acquire books. At the Northeast Pre-Release Center (NEPRC), the librarian goes to the Cleveland Public Library once a month and borrows fifty books that she puts into temporary circulation at the prison library. Librarians also rely on an Inter-Library Loan (ILL) system with state and local libraries, and they receive donations from public libraries, local colleges, used book sellers, and the public. For instance, the Cleveland Public Library donates 200 paperback books, many of which are romance novels, to the prison every month. The difficulty with the ILL system is that book requests from nonincarcerated readers take priority over requests from prisoners; one librarian told me that he deliberately waits to submit prisoners' requests so that demand for the books can dwindle. Relying on donations is also difficult because the quantity and quality of donations have sharply decreased as online sales of used books have increased.

In Pennsylvania prisons, the main libraries are similarly funded by the Inmate General Welfare Fund (IGWF), which consists of revenue from the commissary, vending machines, and the phone cards that women purchase to make outgoing calls. This IGWF funding is divided up among an astonishing array of constituents, including the general library, the chapel library, and several programs related to recreation, rehabilitation, and job training.[5] Unlike in Ohio, however, the Pennsylvania Department of Corrections pools the IGWF funding from all of the state's penal institutions and apportions money to each institution on a yearly basis. The general library at the State Correctional Institution at Muncy is relatively well funded, and its book collection is by far the largest of the libraries featured in my research.[6] Eighty percent of the library's books are purchased with IGWF funding, and 20 percent are donations. The library also relies on ILL with other state and institution libraries; in 2006, for instance, women made 500 ILL requests, 342 of which were filled.

The procedure for purchasing books for prison libraries is more formalized in Ohio than in Pennsylvania. At NEPRC, the Library Advisory Committee meets twice a year. In addition to the librarian and the school administrator, this committee includes employees from Mental Health Services, Security, the Business Office, and Recovery Services, which addresses drug and alcohol abuse. In recent years, the committee's purchase plan has consistently included—in order of priority—"reentry" materials, large-print books for visually impaired women, and African American fiction. "The big buzzword is reentry material," the librarian explained; this category includes books about starting your own business and obtaining small business grants, guidebooks for writing résumés and cover letters, and informational books about college. Such materials are the target of Solo's critique when she argues, in the opening paragraph of the Introduction, that the prison library caters to women's fantasies of "being an entrepreneur."[7]

The book acquisition policy in Pennsylvania is more idiosyncratic because the librarian makes all decisions about acquiring books; the education director and deputy warden must approve her list of desired materials, but she can otherwise stock the library according to her preferences. As we shall see, this unusual amount of control is evident in the library's holdings, which reflect the librarian's interest in crime and mystery novels and her resistance to prisoners' requests for books by black authors. Every month, the Pennsylvania librarian orders books in the categories of fiction, nonfiction, romance, biography, murder mystery, and health. She explains that she determines what to purchase by browsing in local bookstores and by looking at book lists published by *Booklist*, *Romantic Times Book Reviews*, and *USA Today*, which typically list books by categories such as mystery, romance, and inspirational.

The funding structures and acquisition procedures for chaplain's libraries shape their holdings in even more pronounced ways. Because money from the IGWF can only be used to purchase nondenominational items for all faith groups, the chaplain's libraries in both Ohio and Pennsylvania consist entirely of donated books, most of which come from Christian authors, ministries, churches, and volunteers. As the Pennsylvania chaplain explains, "We're proactive with thank-yous. We can't solicit books but we let our needs be known." As will become more evident in Chapter 5, this funding structure has led to a predominance of Christian and evangelical reading materials. For instance, many women in Ohio and Pennsylvania prisons have read *Chicken Soup for the Prisoner's Soul*, which is "supplied in bulk to prison inmates," as well as numerous books donated by tel-evangelist Joyce Meyer.[8] Furthermore, a five-volume cartoon version of the *Left Behind* series, which depicts the assumption of Christians into heaven during the Rapture, was recently available at no cost to all women in the Ohio prison.

A final factor that shapes women's access to books is each institution's policy for banning books. The prisons featured in my study forbid books that discuss the manufacture of weapons, terrorist tactics, witchcraft, magic techniques, sa-tanic rituals, rape, or homosexual sex, as well as books that include pictures of guns, nudity, or explicit sexual material.[9] As we saw in Chapter 1, these prisons also ban most books and periodicals that address contemporary U.S. punishment practices, particularly materials written by prisoners. As one example among many of the unfortunate effects of these restrictions, the Ohio prison banned Random House's recent edition of Maya Angelou's *Phenomenal Woman: Four Poems Celebrating Women* because it includes images of Paul Gaugin's paintings. "It had naked women's pictures in it!" one librarian said of this edition. "That couldn't come in."[10] Penal officials also make specific decisions to ban genres and individual books that they deem particularly controversial or countercul-tural. As I discuss further in Chapter 4, officials in Ohio and Pennsylvania have essentially banned the genre of African American urban fiction. An example of a particular book that has been banned is Richard Dawkins's *The God Delusion*, a nonfictional work that some women wanted to read for a group discussion.

In the Ohio penal system, Legal Services is now responsible for deciding which reading materials should be banned; the screening process was trans-ferred from the Chaplain's Office to Legal Services because prisoners initiated so many lawsuits about banned materials. Once a publication is added to the list of screened materials, it stays on the list for two and a half years, at which point it must be formally re-added to the list. Prisoners can send a written com-plaint to Legal Services if they would like to appeal a decision to ban a particular book. In the Pennsylvania penal system, each facility has a Publication Review Committee—formerly called the "Smut Committee"—that is responsible for screening books and informing the Department of Corrections' Central Office of any books that they would like to have included in the Publication Denial List. At the facility where I conducted research, the five-person Publication Review

Committee is supposed to meet weekly to discuss books deemed questionable by the librarian or the property sergeant who works in the mailroom. The librarian informed me, however, that the committee rarely meets, and when it does convene, members "just skim" materials because they have only forty minutes to discuss them.

Given the myriad factors that affect prison library holdings, what kinds of books are available in the Ohio and Pennsylvania prison libraries?[11] Both libraries are organized by categories such as the following: New Books, Fiction, Non-Fiction, Large Print, Biography, Spanish, and Law, and both offer a range of magazines such as *Glamour, Oprah, National Geographic, Essence,* and *Jet.*[12] The collections of fiction, which comprise about 65 percent of the total holdings in each library, share striking similarities. Crime and legal thrillers, suspense novels, and detective and mystery novels predominate in both collections. James Patterson's crime thrillers, John Grisham's legal dramas, and Stephen King's horror and suspense novels are particularly prevalent. Other highly visible crime and mystery writers include Janet Evanovich, Stuart Woods, Robert B. Parker, Dean Koontz, Patricia Cornwell, Jonathan Kellerman, John Sanford, John Saul, Tess Gerritsen, Sue Grafton, Rita Mae Brown, and Mary Higgins Clark. Vampire books by Ann Rice and Laurell K. Hamilton are also well represented. The second major category of fiction in both libraries is romance and romantic suspense. Both libraries include rows and rows of romantic suspense by Danielle Steel, Jackie Collins, Nora Roberts, Linda Howard, Barbara Taylor Bradford, Joy Fielding, Sandra Brown, Sydney Sheldon, and Andrew Greeley. The shelves are also filled with contemporary and historical romances by authors such as Jayne Ann Krentz, Fern Michaels, Maeve Binchy, and Cassie Edwards. Another striking similarity in the libraries' collections is the preponderance of V. C. Andrews's highly sensational fiction, which regularly depicts girls and teenage women embroiled in incestuous relationships and other taboo forms of sexuality.

The Ohio library includes a notable collection of contemporary novels featured on *Oprah,* such as Wally Lamb's *She's Come Undone,* Sheri Reynolds's *The Rapture of Canaan,* Kaye Gibbons's *A Virtuous Woman,* and Jane Hamilton's *The Book of Ruth.* Neither the Ohio nor the Pennsylvania library contains many works deemed "classics," although the fiction section in the Ohio library includes single works by authors such as Charles Dickens, Virginia Woolf, Fyodor Dostoyevsky, Jonathan Swift, Mark Twain, F. Scott Fitzgerald, Ernest Hemingway, and Nathaniel Hawthorne. The Pennsylvania library lists "Ten American Classics" on a laminated placard, but none of these books is available in the library.[13]

Despite the overlaps in their fiction collections, the two libraries sharply differ in their holdings of African American fiction. The Ohio library has a "Black Authors" section that includes books by canonical authors such as Toni Morrison, Ralph Ellison, James Baldwin, Ernest Gaines, Gloria Naylor, Alice Walker, Richard Wright, Paule Marshall, Octavia Butler, John Edgar Wideman, Alex Haley, and Lorraine Hansberry. The "Black Authors" section and the rotating collection from the Cleveland Public Library also include numerous books that the librarian calls "relationship books": popular novels by contemporary black authors such as Terri McMillan, E. Lynn Harris, Carl Weber, Eric Jerome Dickey, Michael Baisden, Omar Tyree, Donna Hill, Kimberla Lawson Roby, Mary B. Morrison, and Mary Monroe. The Ohio library even has a collection of black genre fiction: mysteries and detective novels by Walter Mosley, Stephen L. Carter, Trisha Thomas, and Jake Lamar; romance novels by authors such as Doreen Rainey, Linda Hudson-Smith, and Crystal Wilson-Harris; and science fiction by Nalo Hopkinson.

The Pennsylvania library, by contrast, offers a comparatively small selection of fiction by African Americans, and it does not group these books in a separate section. Its collection focuses primarily on contemporary authors such as McMillan, Weber, Dickey, Tyree, Hill, and Monroe.[14] The status of the African American collection is a point of unspoken contention between the assistant and head librarians, both of whom are white women. On multiple occasions, the assistant librarian told me that the library needs to increase its holdings of African American fiction. She emphasized prisoners' repeated requests for more black-authored books—verbal requests and pages of ILL requests—and argued that women "want to know their history." The head librarian, however, repeatedly dismissed such requests. As she said to me more than once, "Some inmates only want African American authors and won't look at the rest. But if someone's writing a book, they don't know what type of person the inmate is. I tell them it shouldn't matter if the author is black."

The nonfiction collections in the Ohio and Pennsylvania libraries include books that address a wide range of subjects, such as parenting, adoption, cults, economics, gay rights, cooking, and needlecrafts. Two aspects of the Ohio library's collection seem noteworthy. First, it contains a range of books that address women's health and wellness, including titles such as *Surviving Schizophrenia*; *Co-Dependence*; *Breaking Point: Why Women Fall Apart and How They Can Recreate Their Lives*; *A Woman's Book of Grieving*; and *In the Company of My Sisters: Black Women and Self-Esteem*. Second, the collection includes a notable number of books that focus on African American women's history and experiences, including Zora Neale Hurston's 1942 autobiography, *Dust Tracks on the Road*; Darlene Clark Hine and Kathleen Thompson's *A Shining Thread of Hope: The History of Black Women in America*; Barbara Smith's 1983 collection, *Home Girls: A Black Feminist Anthology*; and Gloria T. Hull, Patricia Bell Scott, and Barbara Smith's 1982 collection, *All the Women Are White, All the Blacks Are Men, but Some of Us Are Brave: Black Women's Studies*.

Two aspects of the Pennsylvania library's nonfiction collection seem noteworthy. First, in addition to books about dysfunctional families, incest, sexual abuse, and domestic violence, the collection includes a striking number of books that focus on medical issues, diseases, and medications. These books address subjects such as chronic pain, heart attacks, hepatitis, AIDS, diabetes, personality disorders, eating disorders, and menopause. The librarian considers medical books a priority because some prisoners recently sued a Pennsylvania prison for its inadequate medical services.[15] During their individual interviews, some prisoners also emphasized their desire to educate themselves about medications because they believe that prison health professionals overmedicate and incorrectly medicate them. A second noteworthy feature of the library's nonfiction holdings is its fairly substantial collection of crime-related materials, including true crime books by authors such as Ann Rule and Jack Olsen, several police stories, *America's Most Wanted*, and titles such as *Lawmen, Crimebusters, and Champions of Justice*. As I discuss further in Chapter 4, these holdings reflect the librarian's privileging of certain crime narratives over others.

The general library at each institution holds some books that contain information about various world religions as well as a few particularly popular religious novels, such as T. D. Jakes's *Woman, Thou Art Loosed!* and Tim Lahaye and Jerry Jenkins's *Left Behind* series. However, most denominational religious books are housed in the chaplain's libraries.[16] The chaplain's library in Ohio includes sections for "Islamic," "Jewish," and "Catholic" books, but the overall collection is quite modest. According to the chaplain, the most popular items are Christian self-help books by authors Joyce Meyer, T. D. Jakes, and Juanita Bynum. If she acquires multiple copies of books, the chaplain will sometimes give them to women to keep as their own. The chaplain's library in Pennsylvania is far more extensive, with 2,850 books and between 4,000 and 5,000 audiotapes. The books are organized into the following categories: General Books, Self-Help, Devotionals, Buddhist, Catholic, the *Left Behind* series, Faith and Bible, Spanish Books, Muslim, and Christian Novels. The collection includes numerous self-help books by popular Christian authors such as Joyce Meyer, T. D. Jakes, Gloria and Kenneth Copeland, and Max Lucado; Christian novels by authors such as

Karen Kingsbury, Janette Oke, and Frank E. Peretti; and multiple copies of the Bible, the Qur'an, and the Torah. The library also offers nondenominational magazines such as *Today's Christian Woman* and *Darshan*, as well as magazines purchased through prisoners' tithing, such as *Saudi Aramco World* and *Aljumuah Magazine*, both written for Muslims practicing in the West.[17]

Equipment for Living: Women's Uses of Books

During my initial meeting with one group of women prisoners, a fifty-two-year-old African American woman named Rhonda asked if she and each of the other participants "could just choose one book to keep" for themselves. Rhonda's request clarified for me the added significance that books can assume in prisons, given the many difficulties entailed in procuring them. As Rhonda went on to explain, the loan period in her prison library is only seven days, and she finds it difficult to finish her books in that amount of time. Other women added that it is almost impossible to regain access to a book after returning it. "A good book here, it takes forever for it to get around to you," Denise explained, "'cause, for some reason, they only have one or two copies." After readers put their names on a waiting list for a library book, they sometimes have to wait several months for the book to become available.[18]

Given women's widespread sense that "the library doesn't have enough good books," readers who can afford to do so order their own books and share them with other women. For instance, a thirty-nine-year-old African American woman named Miekal has amassed a significant collection of books written by black authors. She had "no choice" but to order her own books, Miekal explained, because the prison library contains mostly white-authored books with unrealistic plots about "werewolves" and "a blob that ate up the city." Some readers borrow from Miekal's mini-library far more than from the prison library, and she has developed the following policy for circulating books: "I take my cover off and put your name in there, then I know you got my book. I have restrictions on my books. No bending my pages. No eating in my books and I don't like my book left facedown 'cause it breaks my binder. . . . I expect for you to bring me my book back in three days."

For many women, however, acquiring books from outside sources is a prohibitively expensive and cumbersome process. In all three prisons where I conducted research, prisoners can only receive brand-new books sent directly from publishers; they cannot receive books sent by family members or friends, and they cannot receive used books. Books that are currently out of print are thus totally inaccessible to incarcerated women unless they are available through the prison library or ILL. "Getting book clubs to send books in here is real difficult," Eleanor explains. "I fill out the form, mail it to my family, they have to mail it to the company, and the bill has to go to my family, and then the books come here and the mailroom has to go through it."[19] Further clarifying the practical and financial challenges entailed in ordering books, Shelly explains that prisoners are forbidden to mail cash to a publisher, yet they can only get a money order once every three months. "And we don't have so much," she adds. "We have kids out there. Our family is struggling to take care of us. It's hard on us to take out a little money and send to get a book."[20]

As Cassandra describes in the opening pages of this chapter, readers often navigate these access issues by "rotating" books among their friends. The woman who checks out a book from the library will maintain a written or mental list of others who want to read it before she returns it. Readers also alert one another when they have returned particular books to the library. Denise, who rarely goes to the library herself, explains, "I usually like network around with people. Sometimes they'll tell me, 'Oh, I read this good book but I had to return it, but it's over there now. If you go now you can get it.'" According to Denise, accessing books can involve a lot of footwork:

> I can go to Susie and say, "Are you through with that book?" She'll be like, "Well, Such-and-such has got it next." So I've got to go find her to let her know I want it next. She may be like, "Well, somebody already got it next." Then I'll have to find that person and say, "Well, can I get that book after you? Who got it after you?" And then they'll say, "You can get it next." So then I know when my turn is. And I ask each person, "Well, how long it's gonna take you to read it?" And they'll tell me and then I'll go to that person that day and say, "Did you get that book?" 'Cause I'm tracking the book so I can get it.

At times, a woman's desire to find a good book is so powerful that she will "walk the yard"—walk all over the prison grounds—in search of a particular title or interesting book that she might borrow from another prisoner.

In the prisons featured in this study, the accessibility of television stands in sharp contrast to the inaccessibility of books. Prisoners are permitted to have their own TV sets in their cells, and the institutions are wired for local broadcasting by ABC, CBS, and NBC. As I discuss further in Chapter 4, prisoners thus have unlimited access to television shows that focus on crime. According to the chief librarian for Ohio prisons, correctional officers "wouldn't like it" if penal administrators limited prisoners' access to television because it keeps them "occupied thinking about something else, [and] they're not thinking about doing something to the officers." A selection of films is also available in the prison libraries, and the institutions sometimes broadcast a film on the televisions in the housing units. A few women involved in my study compared their experiences of reading and watching television. For these women, reading seems to allow for deeper and more deliberate reflection, possibilities for revisiting materials, and greater autonomy of thought and imagination. Maisey explains, "You see things one way on TV but you can perceive them differently when you read. Your imagination takes you further. . . . I like quiet time. I like to reflect. . . . You can read a book twice and get more out of it the second time. . . . A book has a 'why.' TV just is." Heidi laments that "the TV is never off. It drives me crazy. I try to block it out." Television presents "what you should think, and there's always a real clear good guy and bad guy," Heidi argues, whereas "books are more in depth. . . . You can draw your own conclusions when you read. Someone else doesn't wrap it up for you. You do it yourself."

Many women who now consider themselves avid readers were not readers before they came to prison. Some were struggling to make ends meet by working two or three jobs, some were deeply involved with drugs or alcohol, and some were barely literate and had never experienced the pleasures of reading. "When I was on the street, I wouldn't read," says Mildred. "I was too busy in the streets, running the streets, getting in trouble. But once I came to prison, it's like you gotta do something to stay out of trouble," especially "if you don't have the luxuries of a TV or the luxuries of a CD player." Mildred now reads "four hours a day, every day. That's what I get my knowledge from, is reading in prison," she asserts. "Here in prison, it's like after you get off work, you want to get back to where you left off at that book. I mean, you're thinking about that book all day!" Sakina explains that she was "lacking in words and knowledge of reading" when she first got to prison, so she "read day and night" and now reads very well. Many women report that they started reading in county jail while awaiting trial. They got "hooked" on reading after encountering the jails' plentiful collections of donated true crime books, urban fiction, and crime fiction by James Patterson. Other women do not discover reading until well into their prison sentences. "I was in prison probably about three years before I even picked up a book," Melissa explains, but now "it takes me about two days to read a book." Those who were avid readers before their incarceration sometimes dive even more fully into reading as a coping strategy. Donna says that she spent 30 percent of her time reading when she was at home, but now she spends 85 percent of her time reading because she wants to "stay removed" from the "crowds and drama" and "the prison mentality." In Monique's view, reading assumes added importance for some prisoners because "we don't have anything but time, so we pay attention to the books moreso than maybe if we was outside in the free world."

In negotiating their limited access to books, incarcerated women adopt a range of strategies for choosing what to read. Because they cannot access a computer database or card catalog when visiting the library, women browse the shelves, ask a librarian or clerk for suggestions, or simply choose something from the New Books shelf. Several women learn about books on *Oprah* or through the *Black Expressions* book catalog, and some consult the bestseller list in the Sunday newspaper. Women also start reading authors whose books they have encountered as films, such as James Patterson, Stephen King, and T. D. Jakes. Some readers jot down additional titles mentioned in an advertisement at the end of a novel or embedded in the novel itself. In urban fiction, for instance, characters sometimes refer to the author's earlier books or mention books by different authors. Women now frequently request Sun-Tzu's *The Art Of War*, an ancient Chinese text that imparts strategies for dealing with conflict, because it is mentioned in two different urban books: Sister Souljah's *The Coldest Winter Ever* and Teri Woods's *Dutch*. If readers have no prior knowledge of a book, they will sometimes read the first and last pages to see if they like it. Others set out to read everything in a particular section of the library, such as the Black Authors section, or they decide to read everything that a particular author has written. Books written as series tend to facilitate such a single-author approach to reading. Indeed, Janet Evanovich's numbered mystery series, which features bounty hunter Stephanie Plum, has produced what one librarian calls a "cult following."

As they discuss their reading practices, some women emphasize their desire to read materials that take them away from real-world problems, while others express a preference for books that relate to "the real world." Whereas Breeanna says that her reading material has "got to be light," such as romances and vampire novels, Valhalla argues that "the crappy, romantic dribble" is "like cotton candy." "It tastes really great, but there's no substance there. When it's gone, it's gone, and there's nothing left." Other readers explicitly distance themselves from "light" reading, suggesting that it is wasteful and frivolous. "I read with a purpose," asserts Karimah, "either to get more knowledge for myself or to help other people. I do very little recreational reading." Karimah's preference is for "true stories" and "healing books for abuse." Emphasizing that she does not read "love books," Sakina similarly asserts, "I try to read true stories, 'cause that's what's happening in the world. I try not to read fiction." Since she is "trying to find [her]self," Sakina prefers reading books about her "African heritage" and books that show her "where other people started from, other people's insights." Because women cannot write in books borrowed from the library or from other prisoners, they often take notes or copy helpful passages from books on single sheets of paper or in a binder.

To a significant extent, imprisoned women's reading preferences reflect the books that are available in the prison libraries. Because many women first become readers in county jail or in prison, their tastes are shaped by the available genres. My subsequent chapters focus on women's engagements with highly popular genres such as victimization narratives, urban fiction, and Christian self-help books, but I could write a second book about women's readings of the thrillers, mysteries, true crime books, vampire stories, and contemporary and historical romances that occupy several library shelves. Also worthy of further investigation are women's engagements with a range of autobiographies and biographies about individuals as varied as Whitney Houston, Donald Trump, Frederick Douglass, O. J. Simpson, Martha Stewart, and Betty Ford. Two autobiographies that Ohio prisoners mention with particular frequency feature former gang members: Carl Upchurch's *Convicted in the Womb: One Man's Journey from Prisoner to Peacemaker* (1997) and Stanley Tookie Williams's *Life in Prison* (1998). Some women enjoy reading books from all of the major genres represented in their library. Bobbie, for instance, characterizes herself as "well-rounded" because she reads urban fiction, romances, autobiographies, and black history. Other women have far more difficulty moving across genres and limit their reading to one. "Sometimes it's hard for me to kind of go between a John Grisham book, a spirituality book, and maybe a book written by Bill Clinton," explains Peggy. "They're all so separate, you know, and on different paths. So it's easier for me just to read all the same thing."

In exploring broader cultures of reading in women's prisons, I do not want to overlook the unique reading preferences of individual women. Rhonda, for instance, loves books by Alice Walker, while Raylene cites James Baldwin's *The Evidence of Things Not Seen* as the best book that she has read in a long time. Alice's abiding interest—in addition to magazines such as *Architectural Digest, Southwest Art*, and *Art and Antiques*—is books that foreground strong women and women's struggles, and she is currently reading as many novels as possible about Latina women and women from other countries. Kimmie's daily reading practice includes biographies of Catholic saints, Donna reads every book that she can

WINTER's vision of respect was how devoted her father was to the dope game and the power and money he show to her.

This Book has taught me things Myself as a Black Woman didn't know.
Such as Black people were the first humans to inhabit this earth.
and in knowing that, I understand better How we are Survivor ion poverty. and any of lifes Challenge

PAGE 464

We need to come together as a Community to voice our cries of the youth and ask local Businesses to please help a good Cause for the youth and donate Funds to start a program for teens to bring out their talents and offer them classes free of Charge for photography, graphics, Clothing design, Hair Dz real estate, Video directing ect. Just so these children will have a direction in which they want to go. also an outlet to the ghetto or the Pain emotional

PAGE 466

Notes that Mildred took while reading Sister Souljah's 1999 novel, The Coldest Winter Ever. In the second paragraph, Mildred cites "page 464" and writes, "This Book has taught me things myself as a Black woman didn't know. Such as Black people were the first humans to inhabit this earth. and in knowing that, I understand better How we are survivor in poverty and any of lifes Challenges."

parental Guidance is very important today
and Winter Santiago had none of that
She was not encourage to attend School or
to become independent

our youth today don't have a positive figure
in the Community to look up to or direct them
to use their time wisely. or to try speak to
them in a language they only know.

We need to speak up in ourhomes about the reality everyday of
whats going on with, drug, Pregnancies,
prison, Money, How important Education is, positive living.

PAGE 470.H TALK ABOUT This page

Young Mothers & Father today need to take back their
place from there daughters and son as the parent
and run the house like a responable Parent adult.

Children follow there parents footprints to keep a
Cycle repeating its self.

The second page of Mildred's notes about The Coldest Winter Ever. Above a circled note
that says "page 470—Talk About This Page," Mildred writes, "We need to speak up in our
homes about the everyday reality of whats going on with drugs, pregnancies, prison, money,
How important education is, positive living." Below the circled note, she writes, "Young Mothers
& Father today need to take back their place from there daughters and son as the parent and
run the house like a responsible parent."

find about the teachings of the Buddha, and Solo reads Islamic philosophy and the Qur'an. Many women also complete Bible study mini-courses sponsored by organizations such as Gospel Express and Hope Aglow Ministries. Kate enjoys books about playing the guitar, Kerrie likes reading about Verde and his operas, and Christine loves biographies of musicians such as Jim Morrison, Janice Joplin, Jerry Garcia, and John Lennon. After completing the prison's horticulture apprentice program, Eleanor feels passionate about seed catalogs and books about gardening, and she "can't wait" to "fix up [her] yard!" Some women especially enjoy reading about current penal policy. Caesar is always on the lookout for "statistical materials about prisons." Starr regularly reads *Graterfriends*, a monthly newsletter published by the Pennsylvania Prison Society, and *The Grapevine*, a bimonthly magazine published by the Pennsylvania Lifers Support Group. Liz has been reading legal cases about religious discrimination and about sentencing policies for juvenile offenders. These unique reading practices merit further analysis that this book cannot provide.

Women involved in my study offer widely divergent estimates of how much they read: six books per month, one book per day, one hour per day, five hours per day, or "every chance I can get." The daily schedule is very segmented in penal institutions, so women have difficulty finding a sustained block of time for reading. Most women spend part of the day at their job or in school.[21] Eating meals and waiting in line for meals, medications, and supplies can take up another significant portion of the day. "Count times" also happen four times each day, in the early morning, midmorning, late afternoon, and late evening. Women must be in their cells and on their beds during count times so that the institution can account for all of its inhabitants. In navigating such a daily schedule, women find opportunities to read during count times, while waiting in lines, or when possible, if there is a lull at work. The best time for reading, most prisoners contend, is late at night when they are lying in bed and the lights have been extinguished. Although it can be difficult to read by the bathroom light or foyer light, such late-night reading allows women to take advantage of the rare calm and quiet. Many women also particularly enjoy reading during the weekend, when fewer activities are scheduled, and during the winter, when it is too cold to socialize outside. As Miekal says of her weekend reading, "Don't mess with me on Saturday. Because I'm reading all day Saturday. . . . And Sundays, too."

Although having "a room of one's own" is not possible for most women featured in my study, curling up in bed with a book of one's own—even if it is borrowed from the prison library—can provide a rare sense of peace, solitude, fantasy, or escape in the midst of a life governed by constant struggle and the realism of others. The unrelenting noise level in prisons can seem almost unbearable. Most spaces are open and crowded, and sound echoes off the metal surfaces and concrete walls and floors. Officers regularly summon women by shouting their names, and they often shout instructions to an entire housing unit from their central station. Being in their two- to four-person cells hardly increases women's sense of privacy or tranquility. At least one person in each cell is usually watching television, and many penal authorities show no respect for prisoners' privacy; while I was touring one prison during my orientation, my guide barged into some women's rooms—with no greeting or apology—and told me to look around. The library can serve as a respite from such a loud environment, but women have very little time for reading during their thirty-minute library visits. Raylene highlights the challenges that imprisoned readers face when she describes herself as "a determined reader": "I get real agitated because somebody will see me reading, and I'm still in with my book, and they're still talking to me and I'm still ignoring them," she explains. "You know, I just don't like my realm messed up when I'm reading." For determined readers such as Raylene, books can serve as a shield, and reading can serve as a means to exercise a modicum of control over a chaotic environment. Rae describes reading as "a therapeutic outlet," while Karen argues that reading offers "a peace of mind" and enables her to "shut out all the bad things around [me], the noise, the chaos." As prisoner Mark Medley explains in another context, imprisoned readers can "just absorb themselves in creating a fantasy. . . . It's like a resting period for the mind, almost like sleep, but it can be used in a sense to resist being conditioned."[22]

Reading also serves as a means for women to exercise some control over time. If the temporality of imprisonment is segmented, it can also seem like an "endless sameness" that "transforms time to timelessness."[23] Readers often emphasize the pace of their reading, noting that reading allows them to speed up the passage of time, alter the nature of its passage, or pass time in a more deliberate manner. For instance, Cassandra enjoys racing through books so that reading "is just an ongoing continuous thing." Urban books, in particular, serve as her "getaway" books. "If I just want three hours or a half day to go by, give me three or four of those books, and my day is almost over," she explains. Breeanna describes reading as a form of self-imposed discipline that will help her to do her time in a productive manner. "I'm trying to get through as many [urban books] as possible," she explains. "They'll keep me occupied until my parole comes through. I'm always running my mouth when I'm not reading. I get into a lot of shit." Angel describes reading as a way to "make time pass" and to prevent herself from engaging in regret and self-recrimination: "If I'm reading, I'm not sitting there saying, why? I'll beat myself up if I'm not busy." Rose suggests that reading offers her a chance to slow down and savor the worlds that she enters through books. "I like to read like every word, and because of that, it stays up here in my head," she says. "Like after I read a chapter, I'll always stop and I'll think about what I just read. And then I'll go on and read about it again. I'll really try to picture the things that are going on that they talk about in the book."

In addition to regulating the passage of time through reading, several women mark the passage of time by keeping charts, lists, and records of the books that they have read in prison. Cassandra maintains a detailed chart that includes a summary, brief evaluation, and number rating for every book. Olivia writes a review of each book, including "how [she] felt about the book" and "the publisher's information," and she keeps her reviews in a folder. Christine, who notes that she "read one hundred books" when she got to prison, records all of the books that she reads in order to give herself "a sense of accomplishment." Kimmie keeps a notebook—organized by author's last name—in which she records descriptions of each book that she has read, a list of the steps that she took to procure each book, and information about other books available by each author. She also keeps track on a more short-term basis by recording "Last Week's Reading List" and "This Week's Reading List." Like Kimmie, Helen maintains a reading log alphabetized by author's last name. Doing so helps her to remember what she has read and pushes her to "introduce myself to new authors because I'll see I need an author that starts with a C." According to these readers, reviewing their book logs reminds them "where [their] mind was" at different points in their incarceration and helps them to recognize how they have changed. Such records seem all the more important given that states such as North Carolina forbid prisoners to keep any kind of journal pertaining to their incarceration or the institution. In this context, women's reading records thwart attempts by penal officials to halt all activity that they have not deemed useful, tolerable, or necessary.[24]

At times, women use books pragmatically, combing them for information that can be of practical use. Such is frequently the case with John Grisham's legal dramas, which numerous women describe as sources for learning about the law. Women across racial lines explain that Grisham's novels teach them about "the whole judicial process," including jury selection, "how they go and talk to witnesses," "technicalities that people get off on or get caught on," legal vocabulary, and most importantly, "what they do behind the scenes." Olivia, a twenty-seven-year-old white woman, compares the actions of her own lawyer with those of lawyers in Grisham's novels. The novels help her to see that her court-appointed

Author	Title	Description
Russell, Insta	Going Broke	Damian / Chips Bank Accts ...
Dickey, Eric Jerome	Chasing Destiny	CARMEN, KEITH DESTINY – 15 yr old daughter ... taped on DVD. Keith got girlfriend pregnant
Ramsey, Gail	Tick Tock	Craig, James, Breanna – murdered in Bermuda ...
McGlothin, Victor	Autumn Leaves	Marshal & Kennedy James + Simpson – College
Dickey, Eric Jerome	Drive Me Crazy	artist – scam author of books Mr Freeman
Hill, Donna	Rhythms	
McFadden, Bernice	The Warmest December	
Roby, Kimberla Lawson	A Taste of Reality	woman works in a racist environment ...
Roby, Kimberla Lawson	Behind Closed Doors	Regina + Larry – husband ...
Whitfield, Van	Guys in Suits	2 Guys dating same woman Eve/Lynn, So-So
Riley, Ken	Harlem – slow & boring	Geneva – light skin about to marry rich man ...
McClain Watson, Teresa	Seven Year Scratch	Alexis + Nikki are gold diggers ...
Urban Griot aka OmarTyree	College Boy	TRAY POTTER who's black going to a mostly white college he's trying to be a basketball star
Lee, Tony / Lewis, Anthony, Crystal McCrary	Gotham Diaries	
Thomas, Jacquelin	Defining Moments	
Monteith, Marissa	Chocolate Ship	
Dixon, Colleen	Simon Says	
Chiles, Nick & Millner, Denene	A Love Story	Best friends ... sleep together after 25 years
Butler, Tatiana	The Night Before 30	
Graines, Patrice	Laughing in the Dark	She went from prison to being a reporter @ the Washington Post ...
McBride, James	The Color of Water	Black man tribute to his Jewish mom ...
Lambright, Slim	The Just Us Girls	4 girls from the 60's Peaches – Allie Mae, Jan ... get murdered by a jealous lady ...
Baisden, Michael	God's Gift To Women	How men play w/ women ...
Roby, Kimberla Lawson	Too Much of a Good Thing	
Turnipseed, Erica	A Love Noire	love story about Noire / Innocent (very drawn out boring)
Butler, Tatiana	Hand Me Down Heart	

A portion of Cassandra's reading chart, which includes author, title, and a brief description of each book. Cassandra draws a circled asterisk or smiling face next to books that she considers especially good. In her description of Van Whitfield's Guys in Suits, by contrast, she has drawn a frowning face and included the words "So-So." Ken Riley's Harlem likewise merits a frowning face and the words "slow & boring."

The Coldest winter Ever - Sister Souljah.
A Pocket Star book Published by
Pocket Books a division of Simon & Schuster Inc
1230 Avenue of the Americas, ny, ny 10020.
- originally published by Atria Books 1999,
- While the main character in the novel
is growing up in the ghetto in Brooklyn.
learning the game, her father was knocked
leaving her family devastated +
separated, the novel, goes through winters
trials, through the Top + Bottoms of NY
only in the end to be knocked.

Olivia's review of Sister Souljah's 1999 novel, The Coldest Winter Ever. Note that Olivia even records the book's original publisher: "originally published by Atria Books 1999." The final line of her summary states, "The novel goes through Winters trials, through the Top & Bottoms of NY only in the end to be knocked."

Dutch ⎫ teri woods
Dutch II ⎬
Game Over
Baby Girl
Crack head
Let that be the Reason
what goes around
Drive Me Crazy ~ a. Jerome Dickey
Janis Joplin Autobiography
Jim morrison Autobiography
Jerry Garcia- what a long strange
    trip its been...
Maya {Even the stars look lonely
Angelou {Singing & Swinging & getting merry
    Like Christmas-
    Everything i need to know, i learned in
        kindergarden- Robert Fulgham
Cash Rules
Gangsta's Girl
Deadly Reins
is it a Crime?
Payback
Triangle of sin
Rectangle of Sin
True to the Game

A page from Christine's reading record. The list includes an array of genres, including urban fiction, autobiographies by famous musicians (Janice Joplin, Jim Morrison, and Jerry Garcia), and essays and an autobiographical text by Maya Angelou.

Confessions of a video vixon
Harlem Confidential
Run for your Life
Death Sentence
A million Little Pieces
Shell Game
Angels & Demons } Dan Brown
The Divinci Code
1st to die
2nd chance
the Beachhouse   } James
when the wind blows   Patterson
maximum Ride
Beach Road
malice - Danielle Steel
mary, mary } James Patterson
  Cradle & All
love & Loyalty
To Smithereens
Atlantis Found - Clive Cussler
which lie did i tell - William Goldman
Step on a crack - James Patterson
Death Before Dishonor - 50 cent &
                    Nikki Turner
Forever & a day

A second page from Christine's reading record. This portion of the record includes several more urban books, numerous crime thrillers by James Patterson, and James Frey's controversial autobiography, A Million Little Pieces.

Last Week's Reading List
The Deathly Hallows JK Rawlings
Captivated Nora Roberts
With Open Arms Nora Roberts
Born in Death J. D. Robb
The Quickie James Patterson
Free Fall Fern Michaels
The "Stonewyck" Legacy Judith Pella + Michael Phillips
New V. C. Andrews book

This week's Reading List
High Noon Nora Roberts
Crown Jewel Fern Michaels
Rope and Jared Nora Roberts
Entranced Nora Roberts
Late Bloomer Fern Michaels

Kimmie's "Last Week's Reading List" and "This Week's Reading List." When she discovers an author whom she really likes—such as Nora Roberts—Kimmie reads as many of that author's books as possible.

lawyer acted "for his benefit" instead of hers, and they enable her to advise "the next person down the line" about what to do in a similar legal situation. Mildred, a forty-two-year-old African American woman who has "always wanted to be a lawyer or a judge," would spend "every day" in the prison law library if she were "educated enough to understand," but she finds legal reading too difficult. She therefore reads Grisham's fiction as a sort of ersatz legal training. "Like if I have to write a letter to a judge," Mildred explains, "I reflect back on what I've read . . . and I use that reading knowledge that I learned in those books to prepare a letter that's more presentable." Reading Grisham's novels also helps Mildred to gain "a better understanding of the prosecutor, the judge, and the defense attorney" and to "understand the law . . . more on the opposite side of the fence." Knowing "how to talk to the judge and the prosecutor" is crucial, Mildred explains, because her son will likely get into legal trouble, and she does not "want to see [her] child in prison." Mildred notes that she also gains particular pleasure from Grisham's focus on white-collar crime because it highlights "that white and black people think alike, as far as trying to get money" or "a little extra something in life." In her experience, the judge and the prosecutor are "usually white men," so Grisham's novels enact a "turn of the card" in depicting legal authorities' encounters with "their own kind."

Even the most unlikely reading materials provide useful information for some women. A case in point is V. C. Andrews's sensational series, perhaps the most famous of which includes *Flowers in the Attic*, *Petals on the Wind*, and *If There Be Thorns*. Marlena, a twenty-four-year-old white woman who was raised by an adoptive family, uses Andrews's novels to come to terms with the fact that she was conceived in an incestuous relationship. Describing how the books portray parents who "psychologically screw up" their children and bring them into "their twisted morbid game," Marlena explains, "In some weird way, I tried to figure out why my family did what they did through [Andrews's] books. . . . I wanted to understand where my mother was thinking this was right." Reading the novels "brings me peace" and "answers my internal questions," says Marlena, such as how the incest affected her. "It helps me deal with it" and "gives me a little bit of closure. Now I can accept it and move on. . . . It's not my fault that they did that. I'm just a product of it."

In addition to using books as sources of practical information, women prisoners often use them to increase their vocabulary, improve their spelling, and keep their minds as active as possible. Many women—particularly fans of John Grisham's books—note that they "read with a dictionary." When Jill—who "was not a reader" before coming to prison—encounters an unfamiliar word, she records its meaning in a little book. Peggy recounts that she would read the newspaper "from front to back" when she was in the county jail because she had read most of the available books. "I was teaching myself about the stock market and about different things about the Middle East," she explains. "I was learning all kinds of things. Then if I got stuck on something that I didn't know, I would call my mom the next day and she would go on the computer and she'd get information and mail it to me." Olivia, who is currently ineligible for GED programming due to the length of her sentence, likewise describes reading as a form of self-education: "I read to keep my mind busy. I'm trying to get smart and trying to educate myself, and I think that's the only way I can do it right now. . . . Even if it is just a love story, well at least I'm reading something, and it's sharpening my mind up a little bit, you know, how you think, how you talk, how you speak."

In a space that offers few sanctioned opportunities for soothing human touch, intimacy, or sensory delight, the tactile and aesthetic properties of books can assume added significance. For instance, Olivia informed me during her first interview, "I don't read hardbacks. I haven't read one since I've been locked up. It's more comfortable to read paperbacks. I lay in my bed all day long with a paperback, but I can't get past the first chapter in a hard book." Olivia was "dead set on finding John Grisham books," yet she refused to read the library's collection because they are hardbacks. "I cannot force myself to pick up a hardback," she reiterated. "It's not comfortable."[25] In an environment that creates "the impression of illness, demise, and death," Olivia is also keenly attuned to the sight and smell of books.[26] She often comments on a book's appearance—"It's a pretty pink book"—and expresses a strong preference for books that "smell fresh" and do not have creases in the spine, which she views as a sign of disrespect for the book. Although the reader's body has been effaced as reading practices have developed over time, some women prisoners bring bodies back into the picture through their vital attention to the sensory and embodied dimensions of reading.[27]

Moreover, in an environment that thwarts possibilities for interpersonal connection with people inside and outside prison, books often serve as "a carrier of relationships."[28] Reading allows some women to develop relationships at the level of the imagination. They develop a sense of familiarity or intimacy with characters who reappear in several books, such as detectives Alex Cross from James Patterson's books and Kay Scarpetta from Patricia Cornwell's. "I like to get to know the person," Liz explains. "You get to know them personally." Some women develop a more complex, quasi-dialogic relationship with book protagonists, a relationship that entails less vulnerability than communicating with other prisoners. Melissa, a twenty-seven-year-old Native American woman, develops such powerful affective bonds with the white, middle-class women featured in true crime books that she has made concrete efforts to get in touch with them. As she recounted after reading Clark Howard's *Love's Blood*, which features a young woman who kills her parents and younger brother, "After I had read the book, I was like, God, can I get the address to this Chicago prison so I can write [to the protagonist]? I mean, this was on my mind for like a week. This was something I felt I had to do. I even asked my mom . . . and she even tried to get it for me." Melissa explained her sense of connection with the protagonist in terms of a deep personal understanding: "I had sympathy and empathy for her. . . . It's like she's going through so much and she had no one else left in this world. . . . If I get out and she's still in the same prison, I probably will try to make an attempt to contact her. I want to ask her, 'How have you been making it in prison all these years?'"

For some African American readers, true crime books also enable an imaginary, cross-racial encounter with the white women featured in the genre.[29] Grace, a young black woman who "did not know it was so many white people that got in trouble 'til [she] came to prison," explains the importance of such book-based encounters in these terms: "I want to see what happened to them when they went to court. After they get sentenced, I want to know how do they cope with going to prison and how they're doing. . . . Do they regret committing the crime? If they could turn back the hands of time, what would they do? . . . Is anybody supporting them out there? Are they doing anything to better theirself while they're in prison?" Although she may not interact frequently with other white prisoners, Grace underscores her particular sense of connection with white true crime protagonists who, like her, have been convicted of killing their children. In discussing Barbara Davis's *Precious Angels*, a vilifying true crime book about a privileged white woman who allegedly killed her sons, Grace explains, "I cried about that book. The only thing I saw that lady needed was help. . . . I wanted to write her and ask what was going through her mind. I wanted to know what was going on. . . . I come from a good family, too, and I went through a lot of mental abuse, too."

In addition to fostering imaginary social bonds, reading enables some women prisoners to cultivate actual relationships with people outside prison, thereby challenging the penal system's prerogative "to define inside and outside" and to bring prisoners "out of social circulation."[30] Women share with their children books that they've read, in the hope of teaching them particular lessons; several have asked their daughters to read Sister Souljah's *The Coldest Winter Ever* so that they will "see what happens from living that fast track life style." Women also send books to family members or friends as a means to explain—through another's story—the path that led them to prison. Furthermore, books serve as a focal point for dialogue between prisoners and their relatives and friends. Helen and her mother regularly share and discuss books, and once a year, they both "find a new author and introduce him or her to each other." Valhalla and her incarcerated male cousin write each other letters about their favorite urban books, and Valhalla frequently discusses books over the phone with her female relatives. As she said of Jeannette Walls's *The Glass Castle*, a book that I discuss further in Chapter 3, "As soon as I finished it, I called home to my grandma, and I was like, 'You gotta read this book! This book is amazing!'" Her grandma, cousin, and aunt all read the book, Valhalla recounted, and a few weeks later, "we got on the phone, a three-way, and we all sat and talked about it." Reading serves as a means for some women to keep in touch with the outside world in nonpersonal ways, too. Heidi regularly reads the apartment rental ads when she reads the newspaper, while Kate reads the grocery ads. "I go through the store visually as an exercise," Kate explains, "to keep in touch with the outside world."

Within prison, readers frequently talk to one another about books and sometimes read to each other as a form of nurturance, underscoring the social dimensions of an activity most often parsed as individual or even individualistic.[31] An older woman involved in my study reads books about eating disorders to her younger cellmate, who is struggling with anorexia. Another woman whom I met in the prison library told me that she reads aloud to an illiterate friend every morning; their favorite selections include books by televangelist Joyce Meyer and an inspirational book by Iyanla Vanzant called *In the Meantime: Finding Yourself and the Love You Want.*

Even when women can barely read, books sometimes serve as an important means for them to connect with others and participate in the life of the institution. As Leah Price argues, literary critics "tend to act as if reading were the only legitimate use of books. They forget that the book can take on a ritual function (even, or especially, for nonliterates)."[32] According to one prison librarian, a woman who struggled to read the easiest materials in the basic education program "took out a library book every day, and she pretended that she read the book and came to get another one the next day. That was her joy every day." This woman especially liked Janet Evanovich's numbered mystery series and was determined to check them out in the correct sequence. Every day, the reader would come to the librarian's office—where the books were stored, due to their popularity—and ask, "Ms. [X], you got the book for me?" Once she received the numbered volume that she desired, she would return it the following day and request the next one. Whether or not she actually read the books, her daily visit to the library and systematic pursuit of the books seemed to provide welcome contact with others, a sense of purpose, and a means to share in others' enthusiasm about reading.

Indeed, books serve as a special kind of cultural capital within the prison. During one of our group conversations, participants in my study were laughing about the thrill they experienced from walking around with books not yet available in the prison library. Although all incarcerated women were eligible to participate in the study, the participants joked about being members of "the elite group," "the reading club," and "a private literary meeting." They experienced immense pleasure from recommending books "to the old timers" and from being able to say, "That's alright, I already read it" when someone said, "I've got a book you have to read." In Miekal's words, "It feels good 'cause WE got the first read! We! *Then* it goes to the library!"

Having outlined the history of reading in prisons, the material dimensions of women's reading practices in contemporary prisons, and some of the daily uses that women prisoners make of books, I will now explore how women involved in my study engage with a particular category of books: narratives of victimization.

CHAPTER THREE

Between a Politics of Pain and a Politics of Pain's Disavowal

There are many ways to victimize people. One way is to
convince them that they are victims.—KAREN HWANG,
The Humanist

It started as anger about what happened to other women.
Then I learned that I was worth being angry about what
happened to me.—KARIMAH, State Correctional
Institution at Muncy

Bookseller Magazine recently adopted the term "mis lit"—short for "misery literature"—to describe the growing number of memoirs that recount their authors' experiences of abuse and trauma. A paradigmatic example of mis lit is Dave Pelzer's *A Child Called "It": One Child's Courage to Survive*, which chronicles Pelzer's struggle to come to terms with having been beaten, starved, stabbed, burned, and poisoned by his alcoholic mother. The "public exposure of psychic suffering [has become] central to the account of oneself," Eva Illouz argues, noting that even autobiographies of "successful and glamorous" women are told as "tales of past wounds" in which the author "is perpetually overcoming her emotional problems."[1] Mis lit has become immensely popular in the United States and Britain, with women accounting for 80 to 90 percent of its consumers. The genre is also highly popular in women's prisons; indeed, several women involved in my study have read *A Child Called "It"* and its two sequels.[2]

The popularity of so-called mis lit has sparked considerable cultural debate in both popular and academic contexts. Fears that readers are indulging in "voyeurism, even salaciousness" in "snapping up" such memoirs dovetail with broader cultural concerns that Americans' preoccupation with victimization has created a culture of dependency and attachment to suffering.[3] Some feminist theorists have also expressed concern that the "cult of victimization" reifies women as victims and has led to a "mass infantilization of women."[4] In fact, although "breaking the silence" and "coming to voice" were touchstones of second-wave U.S. feminism, the recent proliferation of mis lit has increased concern among some feminist theorists that speaking out about sexual victimization produces negative effects.[5] For instance, noting that survivor discourse "is accessible every day on television talk shows, on talk radio, and in popular books and magazine articles," Linda Martin Alcoff and Laura Gray-Rosendale caution that "survivor speech" has become "a media commodity that has a use value based on its sensationalism and drama." Within such a context, the victim of physical, sexual, or emotional violence gets "reified as pure object, in need of expert interpretation, psychiatric help, and audience sympathy." Moreover, "the discussion of the survivor's 'inner' self and feelings" eclipses discussion of how to transform the sociohistorical, political, economic, and institutional forces that undergird practices of gendered violence. Alcoff and Gray-Rosendale contend, therefore, that "the primary political tactic for survivors should not be a simple incitement to speak out, as this formulation leaves unanalyzed the conditions of speaking and thus makes us too vulnerable to recuperative discursive arrangements."[6]

Influential essays by such theorists as Wendy Brown, Renee Heberle, and Sharon Marcus likewise foreground the danger of reification: the risk of reifying women as victims and reifying suffering as the foundation of one's subjectivity. In "Freedom's Silences," an essay from her 2005 collection titled *Edgework: Critical Essays on Knowledge and Politics*, Brown cautions that it is "possible to make a fetish of breaking silence." This "ostensible tool of emancipation" not only "establishes regulatory norms" and "coincides with the disciplinary power of ubiquitous confessional practices," Brown argues; "confessing injury" can also "become that which attaches us to the injury, paralyzes us within it, and prevents us from seeking or even desiring a status other than that of injured." Citing Primo Levi, who argues that "a memory evoked too often, and in the form of a story, tends to become fixed in a stereotype . . . *installing itself in the place of the raw memory and growing at its expense*," Brown then contends:

> Many contemporary narratives of suffering would seem to bear precisely this character; rather than working through the "raw memory" to a place of emancipation, discourses of survivorship become stories by which one lives, or refuses to live, in the present. There is a fine but critical distinction here between, on the one hand, reentering a trauma, speaking its unspeakable elements, and even politicizing it, in order to reconfigure the trauma

and the traumatized subject, and, on the other hand, narrating the trauma in such a way as to preserve it by resisting the pain of it, thereby preserving the traumatized subject. While such a distinction is probably not always sustainable, it may be all that secures the possibility that we dwell in something other than the choice between a politics of pain and a politics of pain's disavowal.[7]

In Brown's view, a fragile distinction thus exists between narratives of suffering that enable traumatized subjects to come to terms with their experiences and those that wed traumatized subjects to their painful pasts.

The stakes of debate about narratives of victimization are particularly high in the penal context, given that a majority of women prisoners have sustained victimization. According to the most recent statistics published in the 1999 Bureau of Justice Statistics Report, "Nearly 6 in 10 women in state prisons had experienced physical or sexual abuse in the past; just over a third of imprisoned women had been abused by an intimate in the past; and just under a quarter reported prior abuse by a family member."[8] Of women involved in my study, 89.4 percent reported sustaining physical or emotional abuse, sexual abuse, rape, or domestic violence, and many witnessed significant violence in their childhood homes. Some of these women have also perpetrated acts of victimization themselves, making them both objects and subjects of violence.[9]

Resources for helping women to address such experiences nonetheless remain scarce in the prisons where I conducted research. Indeed, prisoners counter Christina Hoff Sommers and Sally Satel's glib claim that "finding solace and strength after grief without professional help has become an anachronism."[10] The prisons featured in my study offer some treatment programs conducted in group settings, and they offer individual counseling on a limited basis.[11] However, women in all three facilities report that group treatment programs usually have extensive waiting lists—some women have waited six years to get into a therapeutic program—and they accommodate only a small percentage of those who would like to participate. As Monique argues, prison is "just one big waiting list. . . . You want the help, but you have to sit here so long either you get deterred from it or you just lose interest in it." A yearlong wait for individual counseling is also quite common. Heidi, who is serving a life sentence, recounted that she ultimately abandoned her efforts to meet with a therapist after months of trying to arrange counseling. Although Heidi "kept writing and writing," it took five months for someone to acknowledge her requests, and then she heard nothing more. "I saw one person for one hour," she explained. "Now I don't want to try

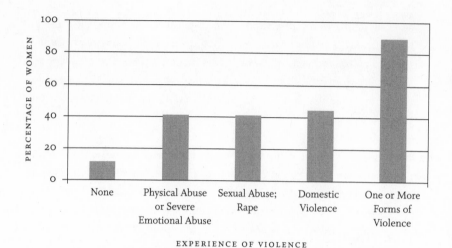

FIGURE 4 Experiences of Violence Reported by Eighty-Five Study Participants

anymore." Several women also express fears that they will be put on medication if they talk to a counselor. "A lot of people need psychological help," says Nicole, but "the only help that they're giving them is [to] put them on mental health medication, and mental health medication is only making it worse!" Furthermore, some prisoners feel reluctant to speak with prison counselors due to concerns about confidentiality. Counselors "work for the state" and will "use what you say against you when it comes to parole," some women argue, or they will "try to lock you up and send you to [segregation] because you're telling them how you really feel." The extremely high turnover rate for prison counselors exacerbates the situation. According to a former counselor in one of the prisons, counselors quickly develop burnout because they carry enormous caseloads and face considerable resistance from correctional officers, many of whom contend that prisoners need discipline, not coddling and pampering through therapy. Indeed, penal employees sometimes conflate treatment with the "amelioration of deserved suffering."[12]

Given the prevalence of victimization among women prisoners and the paucity of resources for addressing such experiences, many women involved in my study are urgently seeking "something other than the choice between a politics of pain and a politics of pain's disavowal."[13] However, the available frameworks for narrating victimization often fail to account for the complexity of women's experiences. Indeed, discourse about victimization often assumes polarized forms; at one extreme, popular culture invites sensational confessions, while at the other extreme, some feminists endorse silence as a means to counter disciplinary recuperations of survivor discourse. Moreover, feminist theorists often make normative claims about what "we" must and must not do in navigating the terrain of victimization: we must speak out, we must not speak out, we must fight back, we must foreground resistance. Such theorizing leaves little room for the varied, strategic and contingent, and even surprising ways in which women grapple with their experiences of victimization.

In an effort to open up possibilities for more nuanced dialogue about victimization, this chapter creates a conversation among women prisoners, feminist theorists, and five literary texts that foreground issues of victimization. The texts include two first-person fictional accounts, Gayl Jones's *Eva's Man* and T. D. Jakes's *Woman, Thou Art Loosed!*, and three autobiographical texts: Wally Lamb's edited collection *Couldn't Keep It to Myself: Wally Lamb and the Women of York Correctional Institution*, Iyanla Vanzant's *Yesterday, I Cried: Celebrating the Lessons of Living and Loving*, and Jeanette Walls's *The Glass Castle*. These texts greatly differ in terms of form and style. For instance, *Eva's Man* is a highly symbolic and temporally disorienting account of a woman who defies familiar categories of victim and agent, whereas *Woman, Thou Art Loosed!* is a straightforward, sympathetic portrait of a woman who can easily be classified as a victim. Furthermore, only two of the texts—Jakes's *Woman, Thou Art Loosed!* and Vanzant's *Yesterday, I Cried*—are widely read by women prisoners. I introduced Jones's *Eva's Man* for a group discussion, and a few women requested that we read Lamb's collection and Walls's memoir. I have nonetheless grouped these texts together because women involved in my study classify all of them as "adversity stories": narratives that recount women's efforts to overcome a range of difficult experiences, including abuse, poverty, and racism. Making no distinctions between fiction and autobiography, the women read all of these works as realist narratives that capture aspects of their own experiences. They look to the protagonists for lessons, both positive and negative, about making meaning from past experiences in ways that seem empowering in the present.[14]

As I weave together women prisoners' readings, theoretical essays, and literary texts, I explore five issues that emerged as focal points of prisoners' engagements with adversity stories: (1) the silences that continue to surround experiences of victimization, (2) the potential relationship between experiencing victimization and committing a crime, (3) the politics of "fighting back," (4) the importance of feeling and emotion as pathways to healing, and (5) the social and intersubjective dimensions of grappling with victimization. In discussing these issues, I highlight the particular ways in which the atomizing world of the prison shapes women's engagements with narratives of victimization. Furthermore, I explore how efforts to articulate one's own experiences both overlap with and diverge from reading about others' experiences.

As I struggled to organize this chapter, I gained deeper awareness of the fact that women's responses to their own and others' experiences of victimization cannot be reduced to neat or simple categories. Indeed, the notion that "no experience is pretheoretical" serves as a crucial reminder that women attempt to make meaning from their experiences in myriad, shifting, and sometimes contradictory ways.[15] Underscoring this sense of messiness and thereby granting women prisoners what Avery Gordon calls "the right to complex personhood" are central aims of this chapter. Complex personhood, Gordon argues, means that people are beset by contradiction; they are neither mere victims nor superhuman agents, they "recognize and misrecognize" themselves and others, and they variously "get stuck in the symptoms of their troubles" and "transform themselves." Furthermore, complex personhood means "that the stories people tell about themselves, about their troubles, about their social worlds, and about their society's problems are entangled and weave between what is immediately available as a story and what their imaginations are reaching toward."[16] In the spirit of honoring women prisoners as complex persons and complex readers, this chapter resists theoretical closure and normative claims about the proper way to address experiences of victimization and injury. I suggest, instead, that prisoners' complex engagements with narratives of victimization open important avenues for thinking and talking about victimization and agency in more nuanced, grounded, and productive terms.

Silence and the Politics of Speaking Out

Theorists Renee Heberle and Wendy Brown articulate similar concerns about the political effects of women speaking out about victimization. In her well-known essay, "Deconstructive Strategies and the Movement against Sexual Violence," Heberle questions the assumption that "more stories must be told and retold" in order to convince society of "its reality as a rape culture." In Heberle's view, a political strategy based on "exposure of women's suffering" and "continued insistence upon the reality or truth of women's pain" confers a monolithic reality onto "an otherwise phantasmatic, illegitimate, and therefore fragile edifice of masculinist dominance." As "the ever-enlarged map of women's sexual suffering is pieced together," she argues, it becomes "the social insignia of male power" and establishes the event of sexual violence as "a defining moment of women's possibilities for being in the world."[17] Clarifying that her essay "should not be taken as an argument against giving voice to suffering or bearing witness to suffering," Heberle asserts, "I am considering the political effects of speaking out about sexual violence rather than denying its therapeutic and cathartic effects." Feminists "should be conscious of the performative and interventionist quality of our representations," she argues, "rather than assuming we are telling society something it did not already know." In order to counter "totalizing" descriptions of women as victims, Heberle advocates discussing sexual violence "as the signifier of the impotence of masculinist social power," and she calls for women to speak out about their "successful" attempts to thwart sexual violence.[18]

In cautioning that representations of women's pain can inadvertently shore up male power, Heberle decontextualizes the situation of the speakout and posits a generic deliverer and recipient of testimony. Likewise, in questioning the political sagacity—rather than therapeutic value—of speaking out against violence, she relies on a generic notion of the political sphere and its actors. Yet if we view the prison as a political arena and recognize prisoners as potential members of the movement to stop violence against women, Heberle's distinction between the political and therapeutic effects of speaking out about violence no longer seems tenable. Indeed, given that many women prisoners feel intensely isolated in their victimization, lack knowledge about the dynamics of abuse, and blame themselves for their experiences, it seems crucial—on a political level—for them to learn that they are not alone and that their experiences reflect wider structural patterns. Furthermore, because many women prisoners embody the effects of being silenced in the social, legal, and penal spheres, it is politically imperative that members of their families, communities, and the penal system gain greater understanding of the astonishingly high correlation between victimization and incarceration. In suggesting that speakouts tell society nothing that "it did not already know," Heberle thus overlooks the need for deeper understanding of the potential relationship between sustaining and perpetrating violence, and for greater awareness of race and class as factors that contribute to the social recognition or disavowal of women's victimization.

Heberle's critique of speakouts about victimization also relies on a static and unidimensional conception of narrative. Her argument reinforces conceptualizations of victimization and agency as mutually exclusive and suggests that narratives of victimization produce homogeneous political effects. As this chapter demonstrates, however, narratives of victimization almost always encompass elements of agency and resistance. Moreover, readers adopt an array of perspectives in engaging with such narratives, including partial, shifting, and often contradictory forms of identification and distancing.

Whereas Heberle argues that speaking out about victimization reifies male power, Wendy Brown argues that narratives of suffering reify subjects as victims. In "Freedom's Silences," Brown thus champions a politics of silence as a means to prevent subjects from becoming wedded to their pain. A line from Adrienne Rich's "Twenty-One Love Poems" plays a key role in Brown's argument. The ninth stanza of Rich's poem begins, "Your silence today is a pond where drowned things live / I want to see raised dripping and brought into the sun." The speaker of the poem wants to surface the drowned things and help the addressee to "ma[k]e the unnameable nameable," because "whatever's lost there is needed by both of us," and "even the silt and pebbles of the bottom deserve their glint of recognition."[19] In her first interpretation of Rich's poem, Brown acknowledges that silence deployed from below rather than enforced from above can function as a mode of resistance to domination. It can serve as a method of "refusing complicity in injurious interpellations" and as a "reprieve from drowning in words that do not communicate or confer recognition." Furthermore, for those who are not yet fully "heard, seen, recognized, [or] wanted as a speaking being" in the social realm, silence can serve as "a place of potentially pleasurable reprieve in newly acquired zones of freedom and privacy."[20]

Brown's discussion of silence as a means to "refus[e] complicity in injurious interpellations" helps to explain why some women may remain silent about their experiences of victimization. This issue surfaced in women prisoners' discussions of Gayl Jones's 1976 novel, *Eva's Man*. Jones's novel offers the first-person fictional account of Eva Medina Canada, an African American woman who is incarcerated in a prison psychiatric hospital for poisoning and castrating Davis Carter, an acquaintance with whom she spent four days in a hotel. In her circular, repetitive, almost affectless narrative, Eva chronicles her continual exposure to sexual harassment from multiple figures—primarily men—including her cousin, her mother's boyfriend, a plant foreman, and a man who tried to grab her between her legs. Conveying her profound sense of imprisonment in others' misreadings and misprisions—their refusals to hear and concomitant demands that she speak—Eva maintains silence when others harass her or insist that she explain her violent acts. "I said nothing," she writes over and over, in response to Carter's insistent "I want to know you inside out," to her psychiatrist's continual demands for explanation, and to countless others' plaguing refrain, "How did it feel?"[21] *Eva's Man* suggests that those who demand that Eva speak could never really hear her even if she did answer their questions; they would merely fit her story into reductive, ready-made interpretive frameworks that cannot account for the complexity of her experiences. As Brown suggests, Eva seems to remain silent as a means to refuse complicity in injurious interpellations and to avoid drowning in words that do not confer recognition.

In their individual and group discussions of *Eva's Man*, several women noted that they could identify with Eva's failure to tell her parents about men's attempts to molest her. Although critic Melvin Dixon faults Eva for "rebelling against language" and imprisoning herself in silence, these readers related Eva's silence to a broader cultural refusal to hear accounts of molestation.[22] Melissa, who was molested by numerous male relatives, surmised that men must have greater freedom than women to voice their victimization: "When men are sitting around getting drunk . . . they might be like, 'You know, man, when I was little, what my uncle come and did to me?' . . . Then all the men can sit and relate to that." By contrast, Melissa argued, "a woman was never able to feel. If they were angry or something had happened to them . . . [or] if they were hurt, they were never able to feel that." Women "have these things happen to them, and they just bury them," she continued. "We're not allowed to talk about them. We're not allowed to deal with them. They say, 'You need to dry your eyes' and 'You just need to go on and forget about that. . . . Just don't even worry.' . . . So all that builds up and then more experiences happen and happen and happen, you know what I'm saying?"

For many readers, the accumulation of violences and silences to which Melissa refers helps to explain why Eva refused to defend her actions after murdering Davis Carter, just as she refused to defend herself at age seventeen after knifing a man who was harassing her. Janelle Wilcox claims that Eva's silence "functions as a metaphor for the unhearing audience that confronts her. . . . What can a bitch-cunt-hussy-whore say that will counter what is inscribed in the dominant male discourse?"[23] Echoing Wilcox's claim, Nicole—a twenty-two-year-old African American woman—assumed Eva's voice in saying, "Why talk? They ain't gonna believe me. They got their set of stories." This "set of stories," several prisoners insisted, systematically elides the factors motivating women's violent crimes. Eva's community assumed that "she was crazy, she's a savage, but what was going on in the house 'til it got to that point?"

Brown's helpful attention to silence as a mode of resistance to domination is counterbalanced, however, by her tendency to privilege silence in ways that preclude possibilities for addressing pain. For instance, in her second, more developed interpretation of Adrienne Rich's "pond where drowned things live," Brown suggests that experiences of suffering, subordination, and trauma "must be allowed residence in a pond of silence rather than surfaced into discourse if life is to be lived without being claimed by their weight." Experiences such as childhood abuse or living in a concentration camp "claim" subjects, she argues, "when they are incessantly remembered in speech, when survivors can only and always speak of what they almost did not survive and thus cannot break with that threat to live in a present not dominated by it." Given her fear that "speak[ing] repeatedly of a trauma" cements suffering "as identity," Brown concludes that "our capacity to be silent in certain venues might become the measure of our desire for freedom."[24]

Although Brown briefly acknowledges the possibility of "reentering a trauma, speaking its unspeakable elements, and even politicizing it, in order to recon-figure the trauma and the traumatized subject," her endorsement of a politics of silence ultimately seems to foreclose possibilities for addressing or politicizing trauma. Indeed, despite her suggestion that we "consider modalities of silence to be as varied as modalities of speech," Brown discusses speech and silence in reductive and monolithic terms. Arguing that "we" are producing "an endless stream of words about ourselves," she conflates several radically different forms of speech—including narratives of sexual abuse; tales of Holocaust survivors; chronicles by those "subjected through sexuality, race, and gender"; and "diar-rhetic speech and publication" on A.M. talk radio and Internet blogs—in critiqu-ing efforts to speak about suffering.[25] Furthermore, Brown repeatedly character-izes various forms of speech about victimization as "incessant," "compulsive," "endless," and "exhaustiv[e]," creating the impression that only two options exist for addressing a painful experience: one can either speak about it incessantly, thereby drowning one's present and future, or one can bury it once and for all in a silent pond.[26]

In critiquing the public narration of pain or victimization, Brown also dis-cusses the privileges recently gained by "queer, colored, or female" subjects, in-cluding "the pleasures of writing and other artistic practices, therapeutic work intended to fortify or emancipate rather than discipline . . . relatively uncoerced sexual lives, and some modicum of choice in reproductive and productive work." When "queer, colored, or female" subjects publicly chronicle their experiences, Brown argues, they "imperil" their recent attainment of "autonomy, creativity, privacy, and bodily integrity." Using an all-inclusive "we" yet pointing an accu-satory finger at "those subjected through sexuality, race, and gender," Brown derisively asks, "Are we compelled to reiterate the experience of the historically subordinated: to be without a room of one's own, without a zone of privacy in which lives go unreported, without a domain of creativity free from surveil-lance—this time by our own eyes? Are we so accustomed to being watched that we cannot feel real, cannot feel our experiences to be real, unless we are watching and reporting them?"[27]

Despite her adoption of the universal "we," Brown speaks from a position of race and class privilege that demonstrates little awareness of the realities of marginalized women's lives. Women in prison, for instance, have no "room of [their] own" to facilitate writing or artistic expression, no domain of creativity free from surveillance, little access to "therapeutic work intended to fortify or emancipate rather than discipline," and no zone of privacy or bodily integrity. Many of these women have never led lives that "go unreported," since poor women and women of color are subject to greater scrutiny than white and middle-class women. Furthermore, women in prison are not producing "an endless stream of words" about themselves, and they remain severely marginalized in discourses about victimization. Indeed, many women have not felt their experiences to be "real" or legitimate because those experiences have been disavowed in familial, cultural, political, and legal arenas and have not been reflected back to them in cultural discourse. Brown's claim that "our capacity to be silent" might be "the measure of our desire for freedom" seems ill-attuned to the experiences of such women. At the end of her argument, Brown acknowledges that embracing silence "requires carefully distinguishing between the pleasures and freedoms of silence on the one hand and habituation to being silenced on the other." Nonetheless, her essay offers little sense of how women who have repeatedly been silenced might reckon with or politicize their experiences of trauma. In fact, aside from calling for "speech that is neither confessional nor normative," Brown leaves little room for dialogue about experiences of victimization, and little room for the possibility that developing a sense of solidarity or collective understanding might help some women to live in a present not fully scripted by the past. In critiquing "a politics of pain," Brown thus risks promoting "a politics of pain's disavowal."[28]

In writing this book, I gained a renewed sense of how difficult and significant it is for some women to counter the many silences that surround experiences of victimization. With uncanny repetition, the maxim "What happens in the house stays in the house" emerged in prisoners' conversations. Wendy, a young black woman, described her experience of this maxim in the following terms: "I don't care if somebody got killed and they're laying in the middle of the kitchen floor bleeding to death and there's a whole uproar in the house. That phone rings, there better be dead silence, because . . . what happens in the house, stays in the house." In emphasizing their own experiences of being silenced in their families, their communities, and the justice system, women often drew attention to the overlapping ways in which self-silencing, cultural silencing, and social disenfranchisement delimit women's ability to voice their experiences of victimization.

The synergistic effect of multiple sources of silencing was of central concern to a thirty-year-old African American woman named Shelly. During her group's discussion of *Eva's Man*, Shelly insisted that Eva was being molested by her mother's boyfriend and that Eva's mother was allowing the sexual abuse to continue. Given her own mother's refusal to recognize Shelly's molestation by her stepfather, Shelly's insistent naming of Eva's molestation—which is not fully supported by the text—might be viewed as an act of resistant reading. During an individual interview, Shelly suggested that silence "in the house" can contribute to a sense of social disenfranchisement: "I guess this is another reason why a lot of black women, you know, silence [themselves]," she explained. "When [Eva] got older, she probably felt like, well why say anything? No one's gonna do anything." Shelly's own sense that "no one's gonna do anything" was corroborated when she was raped two times in her early twenties. She tried to press charges after the first rape, which was committed by a man who also burned down his mother's house, but the man was convicted for the arson and not the rape. "He was given more attention and time for this fire that he set than for what he did to me," Shelly explained. "Once that happens to so many black girls, they be like well, why should I even go downtown? They're not gonna do anything about it." Calling to mind the refrain that Eva continually hears—"If you don't want a man to speak to you, you ought to stay in the house"[29]—Shelly added that both white and "upper-class" black people assume that a poor black woman is "probably a prostitute anyway" when she tries to press charges against a rapist. Because of the silencing forces at work from "the house" to "downtown"—which dictate that "when a black girl gets raped, it's just swept to the side"—Shelly maintained complete silence the second time that she was raped.

In their discussions of T. D. Jakes's 2004 novel, *Woman, Thou Art Loosed!*, many women likewise manifested a desire to acknowledge, understand, and counter the layers of silence around victimization. Based on an eponymous film, *Woman, Thou Art Loosed!* tells the story of Michelle, a young African American woman who struggles with poverty, abuse, addiction, and imprisonment and ultimately ends up on death row for killing her abuser. When her murder conviction gets reduced to manslaughter, Michelle is released from prison on parole, and she begins a much-needed process of reconciliation with her mother, who did nothing to stop her boyfriend from molesting Michelle over the course of several years.[30]

During four different group discussions of *Woman, Thou Art Loosed!* women emphasized the ongoing cultural silence about abuse, as well as their sense that women's experiences of victimization remain inaudible in the legal system. Echoing another group's discussion of *Eva's Man*, Sissy asserted, "Men make the law. They rule the law. They control the law. . . . So what good is it to even say anything? Because they're gonna do what they want to do anyway." Several readers also argued that the maxim "What happens in the house stays in the house" governs life in prison, too, since penal employees fail to address women's histories of abuse and fail to understand how such histories can affect women's behavior. Explaining that correctional officers place her in isolation when she attempts to manage pain or anxiety by self-cutting or by cutting chunks of her hair, Wendy argued, "We need to educate them on what this disorder is and why you do what you do. But they'd rather just, you know, shut you up. Let me dope her up and get her high. . . . They don't want to get to the root of the problem and deal with it." Insisting, "I don't want to be high. . . . I just want to talk with someone," Wendy noted that although the prison is called the "Department of *Rehabilitation*" and the "Department of *Corrections*," there are "a lot of repeat offenders because people aren't getting the help they need the first time."

Women prisoners' discussions of *Woman, Thou Art Loosed!* also highlighted many women's pressing need to understand how those who have sustained victimization—themselves included—can maintain silence about others' victimization. Because the novel emphasizes that Michelle's abuser and her mother, Cassey, also sustained abuse, *Woman, Thou Art Loosed!* prompted several readers to reflect on their own involvement in cycles of abuse. As they discussed Cassey's denial of Michelle's molestation, various women offered their hard-won, first-hand knowledge about why a mother might deny her daughter's victimization after sustaining victimization herself. Tyra, a forty-six-year-old white woman, recounted that her mother "was in complete denial" when Tyra told her that she was being molested by her grandfather. Drawing parallels between herself and Michelle, Tyra explained, "I was so angry at my mother for so long because I thought, you know, she's supposed to be my protector and everything." After her mother died, however, Tyra discovered that her grandfather had molested her mother, and her grandmother—who was aware of the situation—did nothing to stop it. "After I found that out," Tyra shared, "it helped me to understand that maybe that's what was wrong with my mother. She didn't know better, you know, because of how her mother handled it. That was the best she could do."

Whereas Brown dismisses narratives of victimization as problematically "crystallized" forms of "raw memory" and as "endless speaking" about past suffering, Tyra illustrates how engaging with victimization in the fixed form of a story—in this case, another woman's story—can help some women to articulate their own experiences and "live in a present not dominated" by their painful pasts.[31]

Jakes's *Woman, Thou Art Loosed!* also helps many prisoners to counter the silences surrounding victimization by enabling them to situate their experiences within a broader context. During her group's discussion, Wendy compared her experience of reading Jakes's novel to the relief that she felt when she was diagnosed with severe depression at the start of her incarceration. She felt tremendous relief in learning "that there was something actually wrong with me that had a name to it," Wendy explained, "and that's how I felt about reading this book. I'm not alone in my mindset." Reading Jakes's portrait of Michelle's mother, Cassey, enabled Wendy to recognize that she is not alone in struggling "to make safe boundaries and say no" to people. Although she does not "agree" with the fact that Cassey maintained her relationship with Michelle's abuser, Wendy explained, "I can understand that feeling that she had, that deep, deep down fear that she has of being alone. . . . I sit back and think about all the stuff that I went through, abusive relationships just to hold onto someone. . . . Everything that that man was doing to her at one point in time, the trick had been pulled on me. . . . I'm feeling where this woman's at, and that's just what stuck out to me in this book. It's like well damn, that could have been me." Seeing herself in Cassey also reinforced for Wendy the importance of finding "someone to talk to that you can just unload on, because there's a lot of stuff that you carry around that you don't even start thinking about until someone triggers it."

As they search for alternatives to "a politics of pain" and "a politics of pain's disavowal," the women involved in my study highlight the importance of making localized and grounded statements when assessing the merits of speaking out about victimization. Although speech about victimization can reify women as victims, theorists such as Heberle and Brown insufficiently account for the particular contexts in which speech and silence are embedded. For many women who populate U.S. prisons—a majority of whom are racially and economically marginalized—engaging with narratives of victimization produces important political and therapeutic effects. Reading other women's stories opens possibilities for these women to recognize the legitimacy of their previously disavowed experiences and to give "shape and name" to their own stories; articulating their stories can serve as an essential step toward creating a future "not fully given by the trauma."[32]

Wrestling with "The Abuse Excuse"

In contemporary U.S. culture, debate continues about the extent to which it is possible to account for a person's experiences of victimization while simultaneously accounting for his or her agency and responsibility. Some feminist theorists have argued that claiming a history of victimization "offers absolution and no accountability" and precludes a necessary focus on "self-determination, action, and responsibility."[33] Theorists have found it particularly difficult to account simultaneously for women's experiences as objects and subjects of violence. Two feminist criminology collections, *International Feminist Perspectives in Criminology: Engendering a Discipline* (1995) and *Criminology at the Crossroads: Feminist Readings in Crime and Justice* (1998), begin by acknowledging that feminist criminology in the United States and Britain has remained synonymous with "feminist victimology": the creation of theories and policies about women as victims.[34] Other feminists have responded to such theorizations by constructing lawbreaking women's agency as a state of unfettered choice and self-direction.[35]

In broader cultural and legal realms, references to "the abuse excuse" often thwart meaningful discussion of the potential links between victimization and criminal acts.[36] Aside from the reductive claim that "broken homes" spawn criminals, cultural and legal discourses rarely address abuse as a systemic defect of the family norm, and they rarely account for the complex ways in which abuse affects an individual's ability to lead a safe and healthy life. For instance, in his appellate opinion supporting the death sentence of Aileen Wuornos—a woman executed by the state of Florida in 2002—Florida Supreme Court Justice Gerald Kogan acknowledges that the facts of the case "present two quite different pictures of Aileen Wuornos. One of these pictures is of a woman who has lived a horrible life of victimization, violence, and little help from anyone, who later lashed out at one of her victimizers. The other is of a cold-blooded killer who lured men to their deaths to steal their property."[37] Kogan ultimately concludes that fully acknowledging Wuornos's responsibility for her actions requires remaining "absolutely blind" to the facts of her victimization. "Some might characterize trials such as Wuornos' as social awareness cases, because Wuornos herself unquestionably has been victimized throughout her life," Kogan argues. "Nevertheless, 'social awareness' does not dispose of the strictly legal issues, beyond which this Court must be absolutely blind."[38]

Given the frequent incompatibility of constructions of victimization and constructions of agency and responsibility, women prisoners often debate the extent to which experiences of victimization can help to explain one's life path. Whether or not they account for their own victimization, these women often manifest keen awareness of the dangers involved in parsing the potential connections between victimization and crime. Jones's *Eva's Man*, Lamb's *Couldn't Keep It to Myself*, and Jakes's *Woman, Thou Art Loosed!* all feature women who sustain sexualized violence from men and then commit acts of violence against a man, resulting in their incarceration. In their discussions of these narratives, some readers emphasize the potential connections between sustaining violence and committing crimes. Accounting for their own or others' experiences of victimization helps these women to make sense of their trajectories, understand their actions, and learn how to make different choices. Other women, however, refuse to rely on what they call "the abuse excuse." Adopting a stance that resembles that of Wendy Brown, these readers highlight how particular narratives of victimization can reify their subjects as victims and flatten their multidimensional experiences. For these women, embracing a different future requires putting the past behind them, accepting full responsibility for their actions, and focusing on their efforts to chart a new path. Read together, prisoners' diverse self-positionings highlight the need for sharper understanding of the correlation between victimization and incarceration and the interconnections between victimization and agency.

In her 1976 review of Jones's novel, June Jordan characterizes *Eva's Man* as a font of "sinister misinformation" about "young black girls forced to deal with the sexual, molesting violations of their minds and bodies by their fathers, their mothers' boyfriends, their cousins and uncles."[39] For many women prisoners, "the sexual, molesting violations" of which Jordan speaks are matters of fact, not "sinister misinformation." All of the women involved in discussing Jones's novel spoke of sustaining violence at the hands of men, and all spoke of coming dangerously close to killing a violent male partner.[40] Jones's novel has nonetheless confounded critical attempts to situate Eva within existing discourses about victimization. Indeed, Eva challenges the stereotype of the violated madonna, fails to comply with the sentimentality often demanded of "proper" female victims, and occupies the position of both object and agent of sacrifice. "You ain't natural," Davis Carter says of Eva, because her brief sexual relationship with him is not bounded by a romantic or economic contract.[41] Eva "ain't natural," moreover, because she occasionally expresses sexual desire even while emphasizing Carter's attempts to exert sexual and emotional control over her. By infusing her portrait of Eva's sexual victimization with an emphasis on female sexual desire, including nonmonogamous heterosexual and lesbian forms of desire, Jones demonstrates the possibility of linking the struggle against sexual violence with the struggle to expand sexual possibilities for women.[42]

In their discussions of *Eva's Man*, women involved in my study expressed some frustration with the novel because it challenged their understandings of victimization and defied their expectations for narratives about criminal women. "If you find any more books by Gayl Jones," one reader commented, "you better just put them in the trash." Noting that *Eva's Man* refuses to provide a definitive explanation for Eva's murder of Davis Carter, Rae argued that the novel offers "no rhyme or reason" for Eva's crime or for "why she is the way she is. It leaves you guessing."[43] Rae then emphasized her preference for true crime books, which clearly depict criminal protagonists as "either crazy, greedy, stupid, or very smart." In trying to make sense of Jones's "real puzzling" juxtapositions of sexual victimization and sexual desire, some readers deemed Eva a whore. Patty, for instance, argued that Eva "could be brought to submission real easy. If I walk up to you and say, 'Oh, I see it in your eyes you want me,' and then BAM! we're in the motel, I mean, come on!" The fact that Eva "didn't want to do nothing" with Davis Carter but then started "having sexual feelings" prompted Melissa to reflect on her own extended sexual relationship with her cousin. "I really started feeling a lot of guilt," she explained, because she began to think of her cousin as her boyfriend rather than her abuser.

Although Eva resists easy categorization as both a victim and a criminal, many prisoners rendered her narrative more familiar by making sexual, physical, and/or emotional abuse their central consideration in trying to understand Eva's story. These efforts to link abuse and crime do not stem from women's desires to excuse their own or Eva's actions; rather, they stem from women's hard-won and often painful efforts to come to terms with the violence that they have committed and sustained themselves. When Eva is arrested for killing Carter, the police captain asks, "She got any marks on her?" Sue directly responded to this passage in trying to make sense of Eva's crime. Referring to her own experiences of intense emotional abuse, Sue insisted, "You don't have to have marks."

Eva's murder of Carter likewise came as no surprise to Maria, a twenty-three-year-old white and Native American woman who views Eva's experiences as painfully close to her own. "I don't think there was anything bad about her and I don't think she was crazy," said Maria. "I just think that she kept all that stuff bottled up inside of her 'til she couldn't take it no more and she just went off on that man. . . . It's like they took and took and took from her, so she took from him." Whereas other readers objected to some of the literary dimensions of Jones's novel—its nonlinearity and emphasis on ambiguity—Maria especially values *Eva's Man* because it captures how memories of past traumatic events keep resurfacing and affecting one's actions in the present. Drawing connections between her multiple experiences of sexual and emotional abuse and her crimes of first-degree murder and arson, Maria noted that she likes how Jones's novel moves back and forth between past and present. "It's not like . . . something happened years ago and it's dead and gone and boom, I just killed somebody because of it," she explained. If a man approaches Eva and says something "that just clicks a memory, she goes back to something in her childhood, or something that happened a week ago. It just shows how those things connect to each other really well."

Given her own sense of imprisonment—before she came to prison—in patterns of violence and memories of trauma, Maria believes that prison serves as a refuge for Eva. "I know when I first went to jail," she shared, "that's like the first time I did feel like peace of mind because I got away from all of my relatives and you know, the different men that was doing things. . . . So then all I had to do once I was locked up is just deal with what was in my mind and then go forth on it." Jill concurred that Eva was "really free" in prison for the first time in her life: "No man could get to her, and I think she loved that probably. She probably thought it was bliss!"

Audrey, a forty-three-year-old African American woman, articulated her deep identification with Eva's cumulative experiences of violation by addressing her directly: "Man, we went through some hell, didn't we girl?" Audrey reached her own breaking point after withstanding years of life-threatening violence from her husband. One night, when a woman she barely knew came to her house and accused her of stealing her man, Audrey beat the woman to death with a brick. Her rage, as she understands it, had little to do with that particular incident and everything to do with her accumulated fury against her husband: "I guess some of that anger that I always kept packed down, packed down, it just exploded. And I hate it was her. . . . If I had to do time, I wish I was doing it for him, 'cause he's the one that really, really did me like he did, and hurt me like he have."

Reading other women's narratives of victimization helps some women prisoners to recognize, for the first time, how their own experiences of abuse may have influenced their life paths. Tyra drew attention to this dynamic in discussing the narratives in *Couldn't Keep It to Myself*. Lamb's 2003 collection features six white women, three African American women, and one Latina woman who narrate their own experiences prior to and during incarceration. Of these ten women, nine were sexually abused as children and eight were involved in abusive relationships as adults, and almost all of these writers link their eventual incarceration to their experiences with gendered violence. Tyra said of the collection, "I liked it because I could relate to a lot of the women, the abuse that they went through as children, which created who they were. And it basically said that most of the women in prison were abused." Learning to recognize how abuse has shaped other women prisoners' lives is important for Tyra, given the abuse that she sustained as a child and an adult; as she explained, her abusive relationship with a male partner led to a suicide attempt and her incarceration for arson. "I had no compassion for people in prison before I became a prisoner," Tyra acknowledged. "My attitude was lock them up and throw away the key. But [Lamb's collection] really tells you about where their soul is, what they feel, what they lived through." Tyra's comments suggest that reading about other prisoners' experiences may have enabled her to view her own actions and experiences with greater understanding and compassion.[44]

Whereas readers such as Tyra, Maria, and Audrey relish dwelling in the company of other women's stories, some women resist such company because it might eclipse the uniqueness of their own stories or restrict their sense of future-directed agency. *Couldn't Keep It to Myself* prompted this reaction from a few readers. In his introduction to the collection, Lamb argues that the authors have been "schooled in silence" through their experiences of incest and domestic violence, and he characterizes their stories as "victories against voicelessness—miracles in print."[45] While it may have been tremendously important for each woman featured in the collection to write her own story, the similarity of the narratives risks making them seem homogeneous. Indeed, when read in succession, they can assume a serial or commodified quality that threatens to reify their subjects as undifferentiated victims.

One reader's response to such reification seemed apparent during a group discussion of *Couldn't Keep It to Myself*. Although she believes that correctional officers should read the collection "because a lot of us ladies go through a lot of things, and they don't realize this," Miekal announced that she chose not to finish reading the book "because I know what they're going through, 'cause I went through it." On one hand, the similarity between her own experience and those of the incarcerated writers seemed to authorize Miekal to tell her own story. Throughout the conversation, she offered deeply personal reflections about two rapes that she sustained, one of which resulted in the birth of her eldest son. As Miekal described her ongoing struggles to develop a maternal relationship with her son, to learn healthy ways of communicating with men, and to address the lingering effects of her rapes, other women in the group listened attentively and offered supportive comments. Suggesting that Miekal's story is as important and worthy of publication as those in Lamb's collection, Mocha pointed to *Couldn't Keep It to Myself* and asked Miekal, "So where is your story?"

On the other hand, the discussion highlighted Miekal's apparent need to articulate her own story rather than read about others' stories, and to have others recognize the singular and unique dimensions of her story. Indeed, when I commented that "some women in these stories have experiences somewhat like yours," and another reader noted that Miekal's story, like the stories in Lamb's collection, helps to explain why some women end up in prison, Miekal drew a sharp distinction between her own narrative and those in the book. "Her testimony could never be like mine," she insisted, suggesting that another woman's story could never stand in for her own or fully capture her experiences. During the remainder of the conversation, Miekal continued to foreground her own experiences and never allowed the published authors' stories to be conflated with, or to eclipse, her own. After the group discussed the importance of therapy—agreeing that "more people would not wind up in places like this if they knew at a younger age where their problems stemmed from"—Miekal and several other women expressed how much they enjoyed the discussion. Although she may one day be able to craft a different story, Miekal currently seems to find it useful to dwell in, as a means to work through, her own narrative of victimization. Her efforts to claim a unique autobiographical identity serve as a crucial reminder that every woman's experience of victimization is unique—even if it has occurred in similar outline millions of times—and every woman should have the opportunity to make her own meaning from such an experience.[46]

In another group's discussion of *Couldn't Keep It to Myself*, some readers also seemed to be resisting the collection's inadvertent reification of victimization. Two African American women—Monique and Bobby—echoed Wendy Brown in arguing that the authors featured in *Couldn't Keep It to Myself* use their victimization as "an excuse" and wallow in the past rather than focusing on the future. "I'm not putting down sexual abuse and everything," said Monique, "but every story in there led to someone in their earlier years touching them as a child, something like that. And it was just like by the time I read all these stories, I was like, that's not the only reason people grow up and start making bad decisions. I know when they talk about it, they want to express theirself and get it off their chest, but . . . [they were] using their situations as a crutch to get sympathy."

Bobbie first responded to Monique's argument by emphasizing the reality of abuse in her own and other imprisoned women's lives. "A lot of women in prison are abused, but a lot of women don't tell that they were," she insisted. "I mean, I was [abused] by four different family members . . . but it's not like I

talked about it until the last couple of years, since I been in jail." She and Monique reached a point of agreement, however, when Bobbie clarified, "What led
me coming to jail was bad decisions. . . . I don't blame being physically abused,
mentally abused, sexually abused, emotionally abused for any of that. I blame
me. There was something in me that made me want to live the fast life." Bobbie's
subsequent comment, "I don't know what it was in me that wanted to be with
the thugs and be in the fast lane," points to a possible link between her behavior
and her extensive experiences of victimization. Yet within her framework, any
acknowledgment of such a link constitutes reliance on "the abuse excuse." As
she argues, "I really can't get into anybody using their past as an excuse, 'cause
you can always change your future. It's up to you."

For Monique and Bobbie, *Couldn't Keep It to Myself* seems to represent a cli-
chéd form of mis lit. Indeed, the two women adopted a mocking tone in offering the following caricature of the authors' narratives: "Oh, I've been molested.
My father left me. Oh, my husband beat me. I'm in prison because we had to
struggle to pay bills." Emphasizing her need to overcome the past in order to
live in the present, Monique continued, "I've had my circumstance, and you've
had yours. But let's get over that hump. . . . You're forty-two years old and you're
still talking about what Johnnie did to you at nine? Come on! . . . You're grown.
You made your choices and you got here, so let's—we're not gonna forget about
Johnnie 'cause Johnnie played a role in your life—but let's talk about you at
fifty years old. . . . Where are you going? . . . Everybody has a story to tell. Let's
read the story after that story." Recalling Wendy Brown's counsel to bury painful
experiences in a pond of silence rather than wallowing in victimization, Bobbie
added, "I got to move on, because if I stay laying back here in this big old puddle
of bull, how could I raise my kids? How can you even survive? . . . If that's all
you're gonna do is waddle in your big pile of crap, then how are you gonna live?"
In Bobbie's view, adopting a "woe is me" stance would preclude her from acting
like a strong adult and capable parent.

Expressing their desire to hear a different kind of story, Monique and Bobbie
then developed an extended metaphor about the need to forgo "storm stories" in
favor of stories that show protagonists "on that sunny beach" or "trying to get to
the beach." "Right now we're all going through the storms," Monique said of herself and other imprisoned women. "I listen to storm stories every day. . . . And
you listen to these stories, and it's like okay, well what are we gonna do about
this? . . . Let's figure out how we're going to get out of the storm." At this point
in her life, Monique wants to read narratives that help her to develop her "inner
strength" and to recognize that "it's only you in this world really, no matter what

goes on. . . . At the end of the day, what's important is that you kept going." In fact, Monique criticized Lamb's collection for failing to include information about the authors' accomplishments in prison or after their release. Although the narratives actually include such information, it was eclipsed, in Monique's reading, by their emphases on the authors' struggles to overcome experiences of victimization. Bobbie suggests that reading storm stories jeopardizes the difficult work that she has performed in overcoming her victimization. "I pulled myself out of that misery hole a long time ago," she asserted, "and me reading a story about somebody else's misery ain't gonna pull me back in it. I just can't let it do that to me." Monique and Bobbie's discussion of *Couldn't Keep It to Myself* thus manifests their future-oriented desires to move beyond their painful pasts and focus, instead, on shaping their futures in active and purposeful ways. According to these women, moving beyond mis lit is essential for creating "the story after that story."

A bit later in that conversation, however, Bobbie complicated her refusal to dwell on her abuse by acknowledging that she was coerced into silence by threats of violence from family members. "I have a very volatile family," she explained, "so I knew that if I said anything, there was going to be repercussions behind what I said. So I was scared of the repercussions. . . . And then when I got older and I said something to one of my brothers, he was like, 'Don't tell me that 'cause I'll fuck you up.' And I was like, 'Okay. No, it didn't happen.' So that's how come I always kept it to myself." Bobbie's experience offers an important reminder that the ability to acknowledge one's painful past in a supportive environment is a luxury that many women do not have. As Alcoff and Gray-Rosendale argue, "Survival itself sometimes necessitates a refusal to recount or even a refusal to disclose and deal with the assault of abuse, given the emotional, financial, and physical difficulties that such disclosures can create." In keeping her experiences to herself, Bobbie strategically transformed a violently imposed silence into a sign of her agency and resilience.[47]

Bobbie's efforts to rescript her abuse as a source of strength were particularly evident during her group's discussion of Jakes's *Woman, Thou Art Loosed!* Criticizing Michelle for being weak and allowing the abuse to dictate her life, Bobbie argued, "She was an eggshell waiting to crack. You know, Humpty Dumpty sat on a wall. . . . She fell and once she fell, they couldn't put her back together any more. She just could not get it together." By contrast, Bobbie constructed herself as a survivor, a term that some members of the antiviolence movement use to underscore women's active resistance to harm: "I've never forgot what they did to me, but I'm stronger than [Michelle] was. I mean I'm not gonna crack. . . .

That got put in my mind: regardless of whatever happens, I have to survive. I'm a survivor. She wasn't."

Another group's discussion of *Woman, Thou Art Loosed!* underscored how difficult it is for many women prisoners—as it is for some theorists—to recognize the interplay of victimization and agency. Women involved in this discussion were debating how to evaluate Michelle's response to her experiences, particularly the extent to which she allowed her abuse to determine the course of her life. Nez, a forty-two-year-old African American woman, emphasized that things "wouldn't have went that far" if Michelle had been "allowed to talk" about her molestation, but Kaye, a twenty-six-year-old African American woman, criticized Michelle for failing to maintain a sense of self-determination. "She let her childhood dictate her life," Kaye argued. "She could have still been productive in life." When Nez argued that Michelle's drug addiction "took away her pain," Kaye countered, "Regardless of the situation, you have your own will. You could go left or right. She didn't have to do drugs. She could have been a rape counselor. Or gone to school." Echoing the widespread cultural assumption that people don't take responsibility for their own actions when they claim a history of abuse, Kaye added, "Just because you're abused, that don't have to be why you do things. You can do something positive out of everything." Although Nez insisted that "it's not an excuse" to acknowledge that Michelle "was raped but never got help," Kaye maintained that "there are other people who didn't do [what Michelle did] but they got sexually abused or mentally abused or felt alone."

Later in the conversation, Kaye's critique of Michelle merged with her critique of herself. Another woman whose experiences closely parallel Michelle's was arguing that Michelle "was very strong" despite her poor choices, particularly because she ultimately accepted her choices and realized that the only person she can control is herself. Countering this assessment, Kaye responded, "I can't agree with you saying she was strong. That would be saying my choices show that I have been strong and I haven't been. . . . In my situations that made me rebel, I was weak. I'm stronger now. But she was very weak." Because she has worked so hard to develop a sense of individual responsibility and self-determination in the wake of her own victimization, Kaye seems to have difficulty recognizing the interplay of strength and vulnerability, and of victimization and agency, in her own and other women's efforts to survive.

As women prisoners are keenly aware, the U.S. justice system leaves little room for accommodating complex and partial notions of agency, responsibility, and guilt. Through their responses to various narratives of victimization, women involved in my study nonetheless draw attention to our ongoing need, as a society, to expand the available frameworks for narrating victimization. Some readers illuminate the need for cultural and legal frameworks that remain attentive, rather than "absolutely blind," to systemic forms of violence that can lead women to become violent themselves. Other readers highlight the importance of honoring women's unique efforts to create meaning from their experiences and to preserve their sense of agency and accountability. Read together, these women's responses underscore our need for narrative frameworks that can better account for the complex ways in which experiences of victimization shape the parameters of women's choices and actions.

State Violence and the Politics of "Fighting Back"

Given the danger of reifying women as victims, some feminist theorists emphasize the need for fewer narratives of victimization and more narratives of women's resistance. In perhaps the most widely cited feminist call for resistance, Sharon Marcus advocates "a politics of fantasy and representation" that privileges images of women "fighting back." Sharon Lamb calls for "stories of everyday resistance," while Nicola Gavey calls for stories about women who have either fended off rape or experienced rape without feeling psychologically overwhelmed. Renee Heberle calls for "self-consciously performative narratives that represent diverse experiences of sexual violence," particularly stories that subvert "images of women as vulnerable." Although she acknowledges that calling for narratives of resistance may place greater onus on women to resist and cause survivors of completed rapes to "feel inadequate," Heberle maintains that "we may be able to hear in different women's strategies, failures, and successes increased possibilities for prevention and resistance."[48]

In their engagements with narratives of victimization, women involved in my study complicate such calls for stories of resistance by foregrounding how extralegal forms of "fighting back" all too often lead poor women and women of color to prison. Indeed, although some readers emphasize the importance of recognizing agency in the midst of victimization, women featured in this section elucidate the danger of privileging resistance without attending to the concrete, material ways in which race and class shape institutional responses to women's resistance. Given that women remain susceptible to gendered and sexualized forms of violence within prisons themselves, the incarcerated readers draw crucial attention to the need for forms of resistance that do not lead to the violent space of the prison.

The question of resistance assumed a central place in women's discussions of Jones's *Eva's Man*. In assessing Eva's agency and capacity for resistance, some women asked the question most often raised in discussions of domestic violence: Why didn't she leave? As Shelly commented, Davis Carter was not "keeping [Eva] hostage." Other women responded to this question by highlighting the grave danger of separation assault, as well as some of the reasons why women's sense of agency may be restricted. Maria referred to her own experiences in suggesting that Eva was suffering from "a guilt trip" with Carter because she was unaccustomed to men "being nice" to her. She was "in her own prison, within herself," Maria argued, regardless of whether she "physically could get away." Calling to mind how her boyfriend's violence left her psychologically shackled to his demands, Tanya asserted that Eva is like a dog who refrains from urinating in the house for days, despite great need, because he knows that "you're gonna beat him up" if he ruins the floor.

In discussing *Eva's Man*, two African American women illuminated the limitations of existing narratives about black women's resistance to sexual violence. Whereas Audrey closely identified with Eva as a model of violent resistance—which she came to see as the only way out of her own abusive situation—Shelly disdained Eva for allowing herself to be victimized in the first place. As Audrey tried to explain why Eva stayed in the hotel room with Davis Carter, she emphasized her own contradictory desires to protect herself from, and to sustain her relationship with, her extremely abusive husband. On one hand, Audrey graphically depicted how utterly dismissed she felt when seeking legal protection from her husband: "One of your eyeballs is springing out, and they're not even gonna talk to this man who done knocked it out!" On the other hand, she expressed a deep sense of shame about her own lack of resolve to put an end to the relationship, even after her husband severely beat her when she was five months pregnant: "My brother was wearing his ass out and I'm sitting there hollering like a fool, 'Leave him alone!' . . . I was sick."

Audrey's admiration for Eva, who reached a point of violent resistance earlier than Audrey did, seems evident as she imagines what Carter's wife must have been thinking when she saw Eva after the murder: "If I had had the nerve to do what you did, then I wouldn't have went through all of this." During an individual interview, Audrey expressed considerable pride in describing her own resistance to her husband's violence: "One night . . . I didn't even try to wake him up. I said, 'I'm gonna kill you, you black son of a bitch,' and I had the meat cleaver and it come down. He was grabbing for it, and these fingers fell off in my bed, all three of them, and he went out that damn window, took the window stash and everything. 'Cause I had took enough, took enough, took enough." Deeply identifying with Eva, who likewise "took so much, took so much, took so much," Audrey explained that she, too, was deemed "crazy" by her community when she turned to violent resistance "because they don't think women supposed to have the nerve to strike back at the men." Furthermore, Audrey seconded Eva's admiration for the Queen Bee, the novel's quasi-mythical castrating woman who allegedly causes the death of all men who love her. Emphasizing the Queen Bee's ability to remain "in control" and "do her own thing," Audrey shouted her admiration: "Queen Bee! Oooooo, oooooo, I wouldn't mind being her!! Ohhhhh! I don't think I'd have wanted the men to die, but if she did kill them, I mean that's too bad!" Audrey's reading of *Eva's Man* thus points to her powerful identification with women who have resisted male domination; at the same time, her reading highlights the need for interventions that adequately protect black women without contributing to the massive incarceration of black men and women.

Audrey's hearty admiration for Eva's resistance sharply contrasts with Shelly's disdain for Eva's passivity. Eva defies Shelly's conviction that black women, unlike white women, will not tolerate abuse. Reflecting the almost unanimous, cross-racial sentiment that emerged during her group's discussion of *Eva's Man*, Shelly asserted that a white woman "will take that abuse and take that abuse 'til she really can't take it no more" because "that's the way she's raised, to stay there and try to work it out." She argued that black women, by contrast, are "very seldomly" victims of abuse because they say, "I watched my mom get beat all her life, I'm not fixing to get beat," or they say, "You're not gonna beat me 'cause my daddy been beating me. I took too many beatings. I'm gonna fight you back or bust you down." When I asked whether black women always fight back, Shelly responded, "The majority. Now you have some that stays there and constantly get beat over and over and over again, but it's not many." While she empathizes with the victimization that Eva endured as a child, Shelly disdains her for mimicking white female passivity as an adult, when "she knew better than to let this man take advantage of her." Eva, who "took so much," defies Shelly's conviction that black women "won't take it" and prompts her to state, "I couldn't, I mean really, I couldn't put a name on Eva."[49]

At the same time, however, Shelly seems to be struggling to "put a name" on herself within the polarized terms of the victim/agent script, which offers her few possibilities for acknowledging—without shame—that she, too, remained in a physically abusive relationship with her son's father. When she states, "The first time you hit a black woman, she's gonna hurt you badly and leave 'cause she's not gonna let it happen again," Shelly seems to be speaking not from past experience but from an intense desire for a different history and a different future. Embracing this narrative—which does not reflect her own experience—may function for Shelly as a rhetorical willing-into-existence of that which does not yet fully exist: consistent communal valuing of black womanhood, and women's ability to extricate themselves immediately from abusive situations.

On another level, Shelly's embrace of the culturally dominant narrative of heroic black female resistance leads to a form of self-silencing; she disavows in herself the vulnerability and ambivalence that she disdains in women, like Eva, who remain in situations of violence. When Shelly argues that a black woman stays in an abusive relationship "because that's what she want[s]," she seems to be seeking possibilities for naming her own experience with as little stigma as possible; she attributes greater agency to black women, who want to stay, than to white women, who "know no better." Yet even this formulation disavows the pain that African American women like Shelly endure in abusive relationships, occludes the multifaceted reasons why women remain in situations of abuse, and renders invisible the less obvious and more partial acts of resilience and resistance that women perform in trying to make abusive relationships work. Shelly thus participates in a pattern whereby the desire to maintain a sense of empowerment leads women of color to disavow the extent and seriousness of their violent treatment. Indeed, black women are far less likely than white women to report rapes and to seek support services and counseling. This reluctance, in turn, reinforces the social erasure of sexual victimization among women of color.[50]

Although Shelly disdains Eva's passive victimization, she simultaneously critiques black women such as Eva who "kill [a man] the first time . . . when she could have walked away." Because she is "not looking to come back to prison," Shelly has abandoned her previous vow to kill any man who touches her without permission. "Depending on how bad he hurt me," she now argues, "I would probably walk away. I would go and get the police and, knowing all the things that I know now—'cause I'm more educated than . . . when I came in here—something would be done. Where one authority won't, the next one will." Shelly's newfound determination to find justice within the system and her faith that "something would be done" stand in sharp contrast to her earlier sense that black women remain silent about sexual victimization because "no one's gonna do anything." A sense of individual empowerment and renewed faith in the system will not suffice, however, to eradicate the large-scale communal problem of sexual violence. Such a task requires shifting away from prisons—which exacerbate violence by siphoning off resources that could reduce economic, educational, racial, and gender inequalities—and focusing, instead, on policies that address such systemic inequalities.

Moreover, such a task requires elucidating the systemic nature of sexual violence in prisons themselves. Indeed, despite some women's descriptions of prison as a peaceful refuge from unwanted sexual advances by men, Human Rights Watch reported in a 1996 study that the custodial environment in women's prisons "is often highly sexualized and excessively hostile." In a 1998 report, the United Nations Special Rapporteur for Violence Against Women corroborated that "sexual misconduct by prison staff is widespread in American women's prisons."[51] Correctional employees have "vaginally, anally, and orally raped female prisoners and sexually assaulted and abused them," and they have awarded and withheld goods and privileges in order to compel prisoners to have sex. Furthermore, mandatory pat-frisks, routine strip searches, body cavity searches, room searches, and medical examinations serve as occasions for male prison employees to grope women and view them in a state of undress. Given widespread evidence of women prisoners' susceptibility to violence, Angela Davis argues that "prison is a space in which the threat of sexualized violence that looms in the larger society is effectively sanctioned as a routine aspect of the landscape of punishment."[52]

As women prisoners search for forms of resistance that will not lead to the violent space of the prison, they provide an important counternarrative to unnuanced feminist calls for "fighting back." For instance, in advocating "a politics of fantasy and representation" that privileges images of women "fighting back," Sharon Marcus quickly slides into a call for physical forms of "fighting back." Critiquing antirape manuals that advise against resistance, and urging women to exercise their "will, agency, and capacity for violence," Marcus argues, "Simply by fighting back, we cease to be grammatically correct feminine subjects and thus become much less legible as rape targets." Although she clarifies that "we should not be required to resist to prove our innocence at some later judicial date," Marcus concludes that "we should do so to serve our own immediate interests. . . . Clearly it is preferable to have stopped a rape attempt ourselves than to have our raped selves vindicated in court."[53]

When juxtaposed with women prisoners' reflections about "fighting back," Marcus's normative use of "we," "our immediate interests," and "clearly" seems troubling. Her argument insufficiently accounts for ways in which women's agency may be limited, given the multiple forms of victimization they may be negotiating. As women involved in my study repeatedly emphasize, the issue of fighting back is complicated by the fact that, in the words of Tanya, "the ones closest to you is the main ones . . . that mistreat you." For some women, preserving their chances for housing, financial support, or employment takes precedence over "fighting back." Other women who have endured years of rape by family members emphasize that fighting back is not something they can simply will themselves to do. As Maria explains, "Even now, still, I get in that little shell where it's like I just can't do anything."

Furthermore, Marcus relies on a notion of white, middle-class femininity when she claims that the "grammatically correct mirror of gender" reflects back to women "images which conflate female victimization and female value," and when she calls readers to imagine the female body as "a potential object of fear and agent of violence."[54] Women prisoners' reflections rarely appear in the "grammatically correct mirror of gender," and their racial, class, and sexual identities are all too often read as indicators of violent tendencies. The pervasive cultural myth that black women will always "fight you back or bust you down" stands in tension with many prisoners' firsthand knowledge that women of color, lower-class women, and lesbians face disproportionate punishments for aggressive behavior.

As women involved in my study repeatedly emphasized, the costs of "fighting back" in states such as North Carolina are particularly high, given the state's restrictive definition of self-defense. Sakina, an African American woman convicted of killing her rapist, captures some of these tensions when she states, "I promised myself that a man would never do what my father done to me. But once we start trying to defend ourself, it's like we're back in slavery. This place right here's a slavery place."[55] A young black woman named Tamia likewise emphasizes the inextricable links between interpersonal and state violence. Referencing the myriad women prisoners who have murdered their husbands or boyfriends, Tamia states, "I think about all those broken bones that these women done had, all the black eyes, I mean, all the bruises and stuff, and how many times we done went to the police for help, help, help, and nobody does anything. But as soon as we get to the point where it's a life or death situation, either he dies or I die, and I end up killing him first, I get sentenced to life in prison. OK, where's the justice in that?" Arlene fears that fighting back will lead to an entire generation of African American women spending their lives in prison. "The generation that's coming up after me, I see them fighting back more," she explains. "They're not taking it. . . . It's good in one way, but then in the end, it seems like the woman gets the worst. Seven times out of ten, she winds up in a place like this because she had tried to defend herself." Although Arlene says that she is "not one to take licks," her urgent message for younger women is, "Don't come here. Don't come here."

Poor, working-class, and racially marginalized women face what Angela Davis calls "surplus punishment," given the "pandemic of private punishment" and the soaring numbers of women being sent to prison, where sexual abuse "has become an institutionalized component of punishment behind prison walls."[56] With their firsthand knowledge of surplus punishment, the women featured in this chapter offer a powerful reminder that calls for a politics of fantasy about women's violent resistance must be contextualized in relation to the historical and material contexts in which variously situated women do and do not fight back. Only by fully acknowledging these contexts can such a politics help to push the boundaries of women's current social positioning.

Bodily Acts: The Labor of Feeling and Healing

In her highly popular autobiography, *Yesterday, I Cried* (1998), Iyanla Vanzant argues that expressing one's feelings is an essential component of efforts to heal from painful experiences. In narrating her personal history, Vanzant emphasizes her myriad experiences of abuse, including emotional and physical abuse from her grandmother (her primary caretaker), a near-fatal beating by her father, sexual abuse by another caretaker's husband, and severe physical and emotional abuse from two husbands. She recounts that after bearing three children and surviving two suicide attempts, she eventually entered a healthy marriage and became a lawyer, Yoruba priestess, and award-winning author.[57]

Because she believes that remaining silent about victimization "can destroy your identity and your spirit," Vanzant insists that expressing one's feelings is necessary for healing, and she foregrounds tears as a privileged medium for such expression. Distinguishing among angry tears, sad tears, frightened tears, shame-filled tears, combination tears, and joyful tears, Vanzant argues that "unshed tears" cloud our thoughts, and she contends that we will repeat our mistakes if we "try to move forward without allowing the tears to flow freely." Each tear "contains a seed of healing," she asserts, so we can cry "with an agenda" and "float on our tears to a new and better understanding of ourselves and the things we have experienced in life." Linking the acts of crying and telling one's story, Vanzant promises that her book will help readers to "find the courage to cry and the understanding of why [they]'re crying" and thereby "wash away the fear and shame" that have prevented them from telling their stories. She also invites readers to inhabit her story vicariously, reassuring those "who have not yet been able to tell their story" that *Yesterday, I Cried* "is not just my story, it is *our* story" and "my healing is our healing."[58]

In touting tears as necessary for healing from victimization, Vanzant makes precisely the kind of argument that theorists such as Wendy Brown and Renee Heberle want to resist. Vanzant's call for women's tears not only risks fetishizing suffering; it also flouts evidence that people who experience trauma or significant loss are not always "helped by talking about it."[59] Nonetheless, because so many women prisoners have felt forbidden—in their families and in the broader culture—to grieve or even to acknowledge interpersonal and structural sources of harm, Vanzant performs important work in legitimizing women's emotions and experiences. If social "uptake" is essential for the successful expression of emotions, reading *Yesterday, I Cried* gives many women a sense that their own feelings are being heard and understood. Moreover, as Eva Illouz argues, books "offer scenarios through which [subjects] can cognitively rehearse their emotional experience and reflect on others' emotional transactions and expressions." Vanzant's narrative enables some women to recognize, reflect on, and express their own feelings, thereby increasing what Illouz calls their "emotional literacy"—their understandings of possible ways to "transform emotional experience into words."[60]

Sentimentality serves as a helpful framework for comprehending the central role that emotion plays in some women's engagements with narratives such as *Yesterday, I Cried*. As June Howard explains, sentimentality entails emotion and sympathy. Emotion is "embodied thought that animates cognition with the recognition of the self's engagement," while sympathy is "based in the observer's body" but "imaginatively link[s] it to another's [body]." Sentimentality thus "locates us in our embodied and particular selves, and takes us out of them." Karen Sánchez-Eppler suggests that reading sentimental literature is "a bodily act" that "radically contracts the distance between narrated acts and the moment of their reading, as the feelings in the story are made tangibly present in the flesh of the reader. . . . Tears designate a border realm between the story and its reading, since the tears shed by characters initiate an answering moistness in the reader's eye."[61] Howard's and Sánchez-Eppler's conceptions of sentimentality elucidate how a sentimental text such as *Yesterday, I Cried* enables some women prisoners to feel intimately involved in Vanzant's story, to "become in some measure the same person with [her]" and feel some of what she is feeling. This "empathetic identification" allows women to counter their sense of isolation and to experience potentially frightening emotions in the company of someone who shares and understands those feelings.[62] As Nena said of the books that she read for this study, "I can relate to every thought and behavior, and they really help me out. Reading these books has helped me identify things in a safe environment and feel feelings without chemicals. It's really helping me out to be an adult." Furthermore, as embodied thought that animates cognition, emotion can catalyze new thoughts and serve as a conduit for readers to learn from the stories that they temporarily inhabit.

As they discussed *Yesterday, I Cried* and Jakes's *Woman, Thou Art Loosed!*— both of which may be classified as sentimental texts—women prisoners drew attention to the ways in which sentimentality serves as a protocol for reading narratives of victimization. Women frequently mentioned that they were crying while reading and made statements such as "When she was sad, I was sad. I felt her pain." Jacqueline is a forty-one-year-old African American woman who best illustrates the kinds of emotional labor that some women perform in their engagements with such texts. Emphasizing the extent to which she inhabited Vanzant's story, Jacqueline described her reading of *Yesterday, I Cried* in these terms: "Sometimes I got really emotional, and I had to stop because I was crying and I didn't want anyone to see me crying, and [a friend] said, 'You leave here when you're reading that book,' and it wasn't like I was in this prison, I mean, I was having flashbacks." Vanzant's narrative pushed Jacqueline to engage in the difficult work of reckoning with her past. As she explained, "Reading about the abuse [Vanzant] experienced emotionally, mentally, physically, sexually, I mean I can relate to all of that. . . . [But] I don't want to believe that that stuff happened to me. So when I was reading this, it was so emotional for me." In discussing *Woman, Thou Art Loosed!* Jacqueline similarly recounted, "I've never read anything so emotional. . . . And I never cried so much since I've been locked up because I was having flashbacks. . . . This book was very, very hard." Highlighting how difficult emotional labor can lead to self-understanding, Jacqueline then described the insight that she gained from comparing how Michelle's mother and her own mother had to choose whether their priority was to protect their daughters from abuse or to maintain their relationship with their daughters' abuser. "My mother didn't choose me and my sister," Jacqueline explained. "Reading this woman's story, [I realized] that's why I was drinking. That's why I started using drugs. That's why I got high and it escalated to crack cocaine, you know, trying to work from the pain, and eventually I ended up in here."

In contrast to Wendy Brown's suggestion that focusing on pain almost inevitably "chain[s] us to our injurious histories" and precludes possibilities for "identifying as something other than [our suffering]," Vanzant acknowledges the difficulty and struggle, as well as the risk and agency involved in efforts to move beyond experiences of pain. Pain sometimes becomes "familiar," Vanzant cautions, and "patterns of pain become etched in your mind." You "become so caught up in surviving, you forget that there is another way of living. You forget about the joy and the gentleness and the softness. You forget about the communication and intimacy."[63] Vanzant's emphasis on the potential difficulty of relinquishing pain resonates with many women. As Jacqueline said in discussing *Yesterday, I Cried*, "It's time to let go of the past. Not forget it, but let it go so I can move forward. I've been so accustomed to so much pain in my life that when something good happened, I would sabotage it. . . . Joy was foreign to me. . . . But I don't want to be like that anymore. I know now that I deserve better."

What seems most important to many women about Vanzant's narrative is her recognition—which is lacking in Brown's work—that attachment to pain can result from not taking the time to heal. Vanzant suggests that eradicating an attachment to injury requires dwelling, for a time, in the wound; as she explains, "You must take your time remembering, cleaning up, and gaining strength." Referencing her former self in the third person, Vanzant recounts that she had to learn "that the only way to heal her wounds was to acknowledge them. She needed to remember how she had been wounded. She needed to look into her heart and make peace with those who had inflicted the wounds."[64] Responding to Vanzant's call for readers to clean up the "crap" from their pasts, Jacqueline offered the following reflection: "She talked about how you have to get rid of all that crap, you know, and you have to let it come to the surface. And it's a hard thing to deal with painful things, but you have to do that in order to grow, in order to continue. I'm not saying being stuck in the past. I'm saying just you have to deal with what happened and realize it wasn't your fault. . . . You have to forgive yourself and love yourself."

Many women value the advice that Vanzant offers for learning to love and forgive oneself and to fulfill one's emotional needs. Jacqueline describes *Yesterday, I Cried* as "therapeutic" because it teaches her "to let people know how I feel instead of shutting down. . . . This book made me know that I matter."[65] Sissy, a forty-six-year-old African American woman who sustained extensive abuse from her childhood until her incarceration, particularly appreciates Vanzant's acknowledgment of how frightening it can be to ask for help when one is accustomed to having one's needs denied. Noting that "asking for help" is her "greatest fear," Sissy explained, "The times when I needed help, nobody would help me. So I don't want to ask nobody for help. . . . One of the proverbs that was said was 'A folded arm never receives.' And that meant a lot to me. Sometimes I fold my arms, and I don't mean to, but I had them opened so many times and never received the things that should have helped me or made life better for me and made me feel, you know, a better person. And I always got them like cut off at the elbow. So I closed my arms." *Yesterday, I Cried* offers Sissy the encouragement to let go of the "defenses that are [her] known strength" and acknowledge her needs.[66] Several women also appreciate Vanzant's suggestion that "healing, growing, and learning never stop" and that healing is a layered process: "Each time you peel back one layer, you discover a new level of healing that needs to be done." The prospect that the healing process will continue—in Starr's words—"to the grave" can seem comforting rather than daunting because it suggests that the difficult emotional labor of reckoning with the past need not be completely overwhelming or accomplished all at once.[67]

Reading Vanzant's *Yesterday, I Cried* offers some women a form not only for recognizing but also for expressing their own feelings. Indeed, readers often suggest that Vanzant's narrative puts their own emotions and experiences into words. During the group discussions, several women reported that they copied passages of the book onto pieces of paper or into their personal notebooks because it seemed to speak directly to their own lives. Mildred—the avid John Grisham fan whom I introduced in Chapter 2—conveyed a sense of amazement in describing the overlap between her own and Vanzant's stories:

> She was a very, very brave child. And her story told my story. . . . I couldn't, I couldn't word my life that way if I wanted to word my life that way. I couldn't word it that way 'cause I didn't know how to put the words together. I would have stumbled on the words trying to put my life on paper or explain it to somebody. But I had to copy some of these pages down because this was my life she was talking about! I mean, . . . my abuse wasn't as graphic as hers was. . . . But this was my life story. As she got older, as she had the baby, she was telling my life! I had to copy some of it down!

Unlike Miekal, who insisted when discussing *Couldn't Keep It to Myself* that the author's "testimony could never be like mine," Mildred seems to find it fulfilling that Vanzant's story can stand in for her own.

In fact, Mildred used Vanzant's words to articulate some of her own insights about her growth. "I wrote a letter to someone!" she enthusiastically explained. "Some of the passages in the book, I used in my letter. Like the passage of 'Who I am is not who I used to be. But who I am is all of who I used to be.' I love that! . . . It spoke to me so much those words!" A bit later in the conversation, Mildred further elaborated on the ways in which Vanzant's narrative articulates her own story:

> In a period in her life she was trying to kill herself, I mean, taking all the pills, and then when she went to the psychiatric hospital. That part right there, you know, I've experienced all of it. Several times. . . . I knew where she was coming from. I mean, she didn't feel she was wanted. She didn't feel loved. . . . She didn't know about herself. And she was hurting. And her pain and her hurt was my story *all day long*! I just keep saying it because it was. But all the books we have read, it's words, the words taught me, it shows how to put your pain and your hurt on paper when I never knew how to do that.

For Mildred and some other readers, *Yesterday, I Cried* not only validates their painful feelings; it also illustrates the possibility of owning, narrating, and transforming those feelings by putting them down "on paper."

Although *Yesterday, I Cried* generally conforms to women's expectations for sentimental narratives of victimization, Vanzant occasionally offers suggestions that challenge such expectations. At the end of her narrative, for instance, she argues that the man who sexually abused her when she was a child "was innocent" because she was "a loveless child, crying out for love and attention." He "tried to love me the only way he knew how, sexually," she explains. "He was not trying to hurt me, he was trying to love me. . . . We both did the best we could do based on what we believed to be true at the time."[68] Reinterpreting an experience of victimization can do nothing to alter the fact of physical violation, but it can enable women to create a "countermemory"; as Vanzant demonstrates, women can "remake their understanding of the 'truth' of the past and reframe the present by bringing it into a new alignment of meaning with the past."[69]

Some women found it liberating to adopt such an interpretation of their own childhood abuse. Explaining, "This book really told my story," Mildred emphasized that Vanzant's perspective makes it possible not only to forgive her abuser because "he didn't know no better," but also to forgive herself because they were both doing the best that they could. Jacqueline, who began to cry in discussing Vanzant's countermemory, explained that she had always interpreted her abuse as a negative consequence for being "bad" and having "sex on the brain." Vanzant's narrative reminded her that she used to confide in her abuser that she wanted to kill herself, and he would console her by saying that the feeling would go away if she would pray. Viewed through Vanzant's interpretive lens, this memory of her abuser enables Jacqueline to "sort of forgive him" and re-frame her conception of herself in line with this understanding of her past.

Vanzant's countermemory did not sit well, however, with some women in another discussion group. In fact, these women described her reinterpretation as "disappointing," as evidence that "she's still struggling with herself," and as a sign of "going backwards." According to Karimah, Vanzant "forgave herself but she's still blaming herself for what happened" in arguing that she gave her abuser messages that he misinterpreted. Heidi asserted, "To forgive [her abuser] is one thing, but it's wrong to say he did nothing wrong." Starr acknowledged that "if you make peace with someone, it doesn't mean that you want that person in your life," yet she vehemently disagreed with Vanzant's reinterpretation of her abuse, dismissing it in these terms: "My mind fixed it like it was a misspelled word. I think you should apply the idea of a deadly disease to molesters. You should execute them all." Women prisoners' divergent responses to this issue underscore, once again, the danger of prescribing how women should respond to victimization: no single approach can accommodate the wide range of women's feelings and needs.

In contrast to Vanzant's *Yesterday, I Cried*, Jeanette Walls's *The Glass Castle*—a best-selling, award-winning memoir published in 2005—offers women a decidedly unsentimental medium through which they can "cognitively rehearse their emotional experience and reflect on others' emotional transactions and expressions."[70] In spare and often humorous prose, Walls—a middle-aged, white reporter and contributor to MSNBC—describes her hardscrabble, nomadic existence as the child of a highly intelligent yet alcoholic father and a highly creative yet emotionally unstable mother. While highlighting the hunger, homelessness, danger, and sometimes serious injury that she and her siblings experienced, Walls also conveys the powerful blend of love, admiration, loyalty, betrayal, anger, codependency, and guilt that characterized her relationship with her parents.

Despite all of the trials and tribulations that Walls endures, *The Glass Castle* includes none of the intimate, revelatory conversation expected in narratives of victimization, and it defies classification as mis lit or a storm story.[71] Indeed, in identifying what she liked about the book, Olivia read aloud a review from the *Chicago Tribune* that emphasizes Walls's refusal to "whine" about her experiences: "On the eighth day, when God was handing out whining privileges, He came upon Jeanette Walls and said, 'For you, an unlimited lifetime supply.' Apparently, Walls declined his kind offer." Walls's refusal to whine was also appealing to Candy, who enjoyed *The Glass Castle* because "it's a tragedy, but there's not a lot of tragedy in the book. They're not always talking about hard things and crying. Or victimization. They're not victims even though they went through a lot. . . . There was no 'poor me' for them." Kerrie interpreted Walls's relatively affectless stance as evidence that she had successfully gained mastery of her emotions. "It must have been therapeutic to write it," Kerrie argued. "She seems indifferent to everything. She scripted it without feelings. It must have been healing for her. She could cope with all that out of writing the book."

Olivia, who often writes her own reviews of books, states in her review of *The Glass Castle* that Walls "spin[s] an autobiography that'll make you laugh and cry" and "tells her story with rigorous honesty and emotion." Yet for Olivia and other readers, *The Glass Castle* represents a refreshing twist on what it means to tell one's story with "emotion." Walls's narrative enables women to increase their emotional literacy and expand their emotional repertoire by presenting a larger spectrum of emotions on which they can draw for expressing and responding to pain. For instance, *The Glass Castle*'s ability to make some readers laugh was central to its appeal, particularly for women who "don't laugh real easy." Walls's narrative seemed surprising—and deeply enjoyable—to these readers because they had not previously encountered narratives that address suffering through humor. As Monique realized from reading *The Glass Castle*, "When you look at the pain and hurt, you need to laugh about it in the end. . . . A lot of things that we went through we can laugh about it and be like dang! I can't believe I did that."

However, some women found it disorienting and even disquieting to encounter the unconventional emotional landscape of Walls's unsentimental tale. They wanted a more introspective and familiar account of what it must have felt like to be part of such a complex and potentially damaging family. Yet unlike Vanzant's or Jakes's narratives, *The Glass Castle* offers neither a therapeutic nor a didactic perspective, and Walls resists the sort of emotional revelations that characterize so many books and talk shows geared to female audiences.[72] Because she does not, like Vanzant, invite readers into her inner world or claim that "my story is your story," Walls prompts some women to characterize her narrative as too remote, inadequately revelatory, and insufficiently focused on her own and her family members' feelings.

One such reader is Liz, a twenty-five-year-old white woman who began serving a life sentence at age sixteen. "I was expecting more of a sense of her emotions and her mental state," Liz said of *The Glass Castle*. "But it was more matter-of-fact. There wasn't enough about herself. . . . I had my own feelings from what I read. But I didn't know if we should just assume what she was feeling? . . .

The Glass Castle - written by Jeanette walls.
Copyright 2005 by Jeanette walls.
Scibner 1230 Avenue of the americas
New York NY, 10020.

  Jeanette walls, does spin an autobiography
that'll make you laugh and cry make
you think, and know life is not perfect
and truly that others may have been
dealt a bad hand, that you go through
things + know that it could still be
worse; Since the time she could
remember Jeanette was poverty-stricken
and truly a overcomer. all through
out her novel she tells her story
with rigorous honesty and
emotion. I felt like a sibling
of hers, through her trials.
I really admire her courage,
innocence + honesty, as her familys
Mom + Dad included.

Olivia's review of Jeanette Walls's 2005 memoir, The Glass Castle. Her review includes the copyright date and address of the publisher, followed by this assessment of the novel: "Jeanette Walls does spin an autobiography that'll make you laugh and cry[,] make you think, and know life is not perfect and truly that others may have been dealt a bad hand, that you go through things & know that it could still be worse. Since the time she could remember Jeanette was poverty-stricken and truly a overcomer. All through out her novel she tells her story with rigorous honesty and emotion. I felt like a sibling of hers through her trials. I really admire her courage, innocence & honesty, as her familys[,] Mom and Dad included."

You have to look between the lines." Liz's desire for a deeper understanding of Walls's emotions seems significant given her emphasis, during her individual interview, on the profound extent to which she was out of touch with her own emotions before coming to prison. As she now describes it, Liz's childhood was characterized by an intense sense of pain, loneliness, and abandonment, which she attempted to mask by engaging in a range of extreme behaviors. Since her incarceration, Liz explains, she has increased her awareness of her own and others' feelings and has been learning to recognize how her actions affect others. As evident in her reading of *The Glass Castle*, Liz seems particularly attuned to the emotional landscapes of books and to characters' efforts to manage their feelings. She therefore seems to find it more satisfying to read sentimental narratives—which are marked by conventionalized invitations to emotional response and deep concern with human connectedness—than to read emotionally abstruse texts such as *The Glass Castle*.[73]

As with Eva in Gayl Jones's *Eva's Man*, Walls's relative lack of affect prompted some readers to express concern about Walls and to fill in what they believe is missing from her own account of her experiences. Readers whose own pain has been ignored found it particularly alarming to hear Walls's parents insist that "suffering when you're young is good for you" because it "immunize[s] your body and your soul"; these readers interpreted Walls's silence about her feelings as a reflection of her parents' refusal to acknowledge her pain.[74] Referencing the parents' failure to respond when they discovered that their son was being molested by his grandmother, Rose argued that it's okay to let your child know "you're gonna be okay because of this, you know, don't let this destroy you. But it's not okay if you just brush it off like it's nothing, 'cause when your children get older, like what if they have kids and their kids go through something? You're gonna raise generations and generations and generations of just crazy people. . . . You still have to let them know that this is not right." Some women also read between the lines of Walls's silence and insisted that she was being abused by her father. "She doesn't talk about abuse but it's in the periphery," Donna argued. "There was more than she says." Furthermore, even as they acknowledged that the Walls children developed incredible strength and resilience as a result of their experiences, some women argued that such strength came at too high a price. In the words of Genevieve, who particularly appreciates Vanzant's emphasis on the value of tears, "I'm beginning to think that maybe all this no crying thing is going to catch up with [Walls] and really kind of depress her. Sometimes you really have to cry. I mean, I just don't understand how someone cannot cry after so many things."[75]

Whether they are engaging with a sentimental narrative such as *Yesterday, I Cried* or an unsentimental text such as *The Glass Castle*, women involved in this study perform both emotional and cognitive labor in discussing their own and others' painful experiences. For some women, it feels deeply comforting— even liberating—to discover that another woman's narrative articulates aspects of their own experiences and emotions. Reading such narratives enables these women to give shape to their own feelings, sometimes in vicarious form. Other women increase their emotional literacy by engaging with narratives that open up alterative possibilities for responding to and expressing pain. As they "rehearse their emotional experience and reflect on others' emotional transactions and expressions," women prisoners suggest that learning how to feel constitutes another important form of resistance to victimization.[76]

"You Don't Know How Many People You Touch": Intersubjectivity

In critiquing speakouts about victimization, some feminist theorists caution that public discourse about violence against women has too often "replayed confessional modes that recuperate dominant patriarchal discourses without subversive effect." According to Linda Martin Alcoff and Laura Gray-Rosendale, confession is always implicated in "an unequal, nonreciprocal relation of power" that involves "an imperative to speak" issued by a dominant figure to a subordinate one, and its goal is always the "normalization of the speaking subject." The confessional framework also sets up a binary between "raw" experience and feelings, on one hand, and theory, on the other. Wendy Brown, who generally categorizes speech about victimization as confession, adds to these concerns in arguing that confessional practices "reinstate a unified discourse in which the story of greatest suffering becomes the true story of woman." Brown does not explore alternative possibilities for public expression of pain or victimization, but Alcoff and Gray-Rosendale seek to cultivate discursive environments that might enhance "the autonomy and empowerment of the survivor who is speaking as well as of survivors elsewhere."[77]

As they discuss narratives of victimization, women prisoners sometimes create "new discursive forms and spaces" in which they "gain autonomy" in the process of "bringing sexual violence into discourse." Rather than replicating the power dynamics of the confessional mode, prisoners' engagements with narratives of victimization sometimes entail social and intersubjective dimensions that foster women's sense of empowerment in a context of mutuality. As we saw with Miekal during her group's discussion of *Couldn't Keep It to Myself*, interacting with others enables some women to occupy the role of "a survivor/expert" who is "still working through and theorizing her own experience."[78] Furthermore, women frequently mentor, teach, and support one another in discussing their own and others' stories. Engaging in dialogue opens up possibilities for women to bestow and receive recognition—a form of affirmation that is "premised on the existence of an empathic other who validates and recognizes the speaker's self-narrative."[79] At times, women seem to call for such recognition by publicly articulating how they have inflicted harm on others. Rather than enacting a disciplinary form of confession, these women seem to be asking others to reflect back to them a sense of their humanity and capacity for change. Through their engagements with narratives of victimization, women prisoners attempt to reclaim their places as healthy citizens, and they spark dialogue about the ongoing need to address systemic sources of injury and violence; in so doing, they illuminate the ways in which "individual empowerment" is "itself a political action with social consequences."[80]

A particularly interesting dimension of prisoners' intersubjective engagements with narratives of victimization is their use of such narratives to tell others, by proxy, about their own experiences. Tanya is a thirty-one-year-old African American woman whose own story closely parallels that of the protagonist in *Eva's Man*. In talking with me about Jones's novel, Tanya noted that she feels a sense of connection with Eva due to her own experiences of sexual assault and her decision to remain silent in the midst of escalating problems and violence. She also noted, however, that although she fully understands Eva's refusal to speak, she now feels wary of succumbing to silence. "They done Eva dirty so long the woman won't even talk," Tanya said. "I know what it's like not to talk to people, I really do. And I still find myself doing it. But there's no sense shutting yourself from the world." In an effort to articulate her own experiences, Tanya decided to tell her parents about *Eva's Man*. Because they "still don't really know the full extent of what all happened," she told them Eva's story, explaining that it "might sound twisted, but it makes all the sense in the world, you know, because everything's not A, B, and C. There's a motive behind whatever. It might not mean anything to you, but it means a world to the other person." In articulating her own experiences through Eva's story, Tanya offers a reminder that no easy formula can capture the accumulation of lived experiences that lead so many women to prison: "Everything's not A, B, and C." Her reading calls us to abandon "know-it-all criticism"[81] and attend more carefully to the kinds of stories that make "all the sense in the world" to women who end up in prison.

For women who are grappling with their own victimization *and* with the fact that they have harmed others, engaging in dialogue about narratives of victimization can open up possibilities for complex and multifaceted forms of recognition. Publicly articulating their harmful actions can feel urgently important to some women, not because they desire the absolution that confession affords, but because they seek recognition of their humanity, an affirmation—however fleeting—that who they are and who they might become is not encompassed by the self who performed reprehensible deeds. A young Latina woman named Nena often seemed to be seeking such recognition through the group discussions. During a discussion that focused on Jakes's *Woman, Thou Art Loosed!* some women were denigrating Michelle's mother, Cassey, for denying Michelle's abuse, particularly since Cassey had been abused herself. Comparing herself to Cassey, Nena acknowledged, "I think about what I did with my son. I let him be abused even though my sister abused me. I have to stop the cycle now." When another reader said of Cassey, "It's I hurt, so you hurt. Isn't that crazy?" Nena responded, "That's like me. I was in denial for twenty-one years until I realized that I can't be OK unless I count on others to help me. I have to . . . get help for future generations." A bit later in the conversation, Nena again identified herself as both victimizer and victim when she shared,

> This book makes me bawl. It brought out a lot of guilt and shame for me.
> I was the youngest of four girls. My sisters locked me in the trunk, put me
> in the dryer, did all kind of things to me. I was the black sheep. I was even
> shipped off to my grandmother's. But then I chose a man over my own
> daughter and I lost my parental rights. I felt really messed up reading this
> because my daughter was molested due to my drug use. I bawled in this
> book. I had feelings of hurt, rage, anger, loneliness, bitterness. It reopened
> scars I try to keep hidden.

At other points in the discussion, Nena emphasized the difficult decisions that she has recently made in trying to change the course of her life. For instance, she reported her sister to Child Protective Services for abusing Nena's son, and she has cut off ties with her family because "none of them were good for me. . . . It was all chaos, hatred, jealousy, and grudges." Referring to a statement that Michelle makes when she is first released from prison, Nena said, "On page 32, I could relate to where she says, 'That ain't my home. That's just a place where a piece of me is buried. I won't be staying in that house.'" Adding another layer of complexity to the idea that "what happens in the house stays in the house," Nena explained that she has decided not to return home upon her release from prison because "all [her] abuse issues are buried there." Although she would rather not live in a halfway house, Nena plans to do so because she now believes that she needs "rules, guidance, authority, consequences."

A pastor's statement in *Woman, Thou Art Loosed!* that Michelle needs to lead her own life also powerfully resonated with Nena. Acknowledging, "It took a drastic change for me to look at me and not blame others for me being a victim," she asserted, "I have to grow up and be responsible. I have to care for myself." Nena then harshly characterized herself as "immature," "stubborn," "belligerent," and "obnoxious," concluding, "I used to be a clown. I was a complete jerk. I've learned that my life from birth to twenty-nine years old was a play. Now it's time to put the masks away, pull down the curtain, and pack up fantasy island. . . . I want to do something better. . . . I got to do some work." At various points, Nena emphasized how difficult she finds this process of reckoning, noting that she feels "emotionally, physically, and spiritually drained." Nena is fighting bulimia, struggling to forgive herself "for how [she] hurt others," and working hard to like herself although "the bad outweighs the good." She periodically reminded herself, however, that "positive thoughts lead to positive actions," and she noted that Michelle's story gives her "strength and hope."[82]

As Nena offered these reflections, other women involved in the discussion responded with expressions of understanding, support, and encouragement, occasionally offering comments that might help Nena to interpret and theorize her experiences. A forty-six-year-old African American woman named Boo, who has been incarcerated since age seventeen and serves as a mentor for many women, reassured Nena, "You're really maturing. I believe you're gonna be alright. You'll do what you have to do. It's not easy. Nothing's easy. But if you believe in a higher power, you'll make the right choices for you and others." At other points, Boo offered nurturing comments such as "See, you're smart" and "You don't know how many people you touch. It gives me something to think about when I listen to you. Some people need to hear you and get where you're at. Your story can save a life. You could help another child not to be hurt."

Whereas Wendy Brown cautions that "confessing injury" often "attaches us to the injury, paralyzes us within it, and prevents us from seeking or even desiring a status other than that of injured," Nena's efforts to articulate her experiences of sustaining and inflicting injury suggest that a different outcome may be possible. According to Eva Illouz, publicly narrating one's injuries allows for "symbolic reparation" in the form of recognition, while at the same time compelling one to assume responsibility for improving one's condition. In a slightly related vein, bell hooks argues that "story-telling becomes a process of historicization. It does not remove women from history but enables us to see ourselves as part of history." As she narrates her experiences as victimizer and victim—weaving between her own story and the stories of women featured in books—Nena seems to be engaged in a process of historicizing her life. Situating herself both as part of a larger history and as an individual whose own history is unfolding, she seems to be seeking confirmation of her ability to redeem herself, to rescript her life story—in its past and future forms—in more bearable and even hopeful terms.[83]

As they discuss narratives of victimization, women prisoners also highlight their efforts to interrupt cycles of violence by educating themselves, their violent partners, and/or their children about alternatives to perpetrating and sustaining violence. Explaining her resolve to leave her husband after nine years of abuse, Arlene recalled how she and her siblings would be "crying, beating on the door" in their attempts to save their mother from their father's violence. "I wasn't going through it," she finally decided, "and I wasn't having my son go through it." During her subsequent twenty-year relationship with another man, Arlene engaged in a long-term process of teaching him an alternative to "that fight thing." He eventually "got the message," she explained. "Keep your hands to yourself so I don't wind up coming to prison for killing you!" Arlene has also tried to teach her sons to keep their hands to themselves, reminding them, "This woman is somebody's child, somebody's daughter, and think about if you have kids, if you want somebody abusing your children."

For Audrey, violence has been the controlling feature of her life narrative, from witnessing her father stab her mother in the head nine times, to enduring several years of abuse from her extremely violent husband. Defiantly declaring, "The cycle stops with me," Audrey proudly recounted her daughter's rewriting of a life script potentially filled with violence: "Let me tell you what my daughter did. . . . She brought that boy['s] clothes home to that boy's mama, sure did, took that boy's stuff and told her, 'Miss [X], I don't want your son no more.' Said, 'Here go his stuff. You can go get him, 'cause I tried to tell him to come off me but he [wouldn't, and he] ain't living with me no more.'" As Audrey and other prisoners reckon with their own and other women's stories, they illuminate the underrecognized social, intersubjective, and political dimensions of women's engagements with narratives of victimization.

IN EXPLORING women prisoners' readings of this diverse array of "adversity stories," I have learned some valuable lessons about the creative, varied, and strategic ways women engage with narratives of victimization. Whereas theorists such as Brown and Heberle assume that codification and fixity will result from putting experiences of victimization into public discourse, the incarcerated readers illustrate that one cannot preordain the effects that literary narratives of victimization will have on their tellers or hearers. In deeply identifying with protagonists' experiences of victimization and adversity, some readers recognize the legitimacy of their experiences and discover the healing potential of putting their own stories and emotions into words. Through the difficult cognitive and emotional labor of temporarily inhabiting others' stories, these women gain insight and inspiration for creating a future not fully determined by the past. Other women sharply disdain narratives of victimization, arguing that the protagonists should "shake off" their painful pasts rather than invoking them as "an excuse." In such cases, women refuse to make abuse "the central meaning-making incident" in their lives, and they find it more empowering to read about women who are "on [their] way to the beach" than about women struggling to survive "the storm."[84] Prisoners have taught me that their responses to narratives of victimization are never a onetime, all-or-nothing, static affair. They are always context-specific, contingent, and deeply inflected by women's race and class positionings. Furthermore, women sometimes manifest conflicting needs in engaging with narratives of victimization, as when they desire the company of others' stories while at the same time wanting assurance that their own story is unique. Regardless of whether they embrace or resist others' stories, however, women use those narratives to facilitate self-reflection, reckon with their roles as objects and agents of violence, authorize their own stories, and narrate the person they have been and the person they might become. Such narratives also serve as vehicles for women to publicly recognize one another's humanity and capacity for change.

Although some feminist theorists rightly warn of the potential pitfalls of "giving voice" to victimization, I have learned that recognizing the possibility of speaking out and realizing that one's experiences form part of a larger pattern constitute important discoveries for some women. The silence around victimization is not old news; it remains a pressing issue for many women prisoners. At the same time, I have learned that silence plays a strategic and protective role in some women's lives, and that women sometimes turn coerced silence into a sign of strength. As they grapple with representations of victimization and adversity, the women featured in this book contribute to and underscore the need for theorizations of resistant agency that accommodate the complexity of women's lives: the tangled interplay of sexual desires and desires for protection from violence, the manifold reasons why women of all races sometimes remain in situations of violence, and the difficulty of finding adequate means to resist violence without contributing to its vicious cycle. Moreover, the readers illuminate the many forms that resistance to victimization can take, including efforts to feel and express the full range of their emotions, to reframe their stories in more sustainable terms, to assist others as they struggle to reckon with their experiences, and to promote alternatives to violence. Through their diverse responses, women prisoners help to "mak[e] room for a respectful plurality" of voices about victimization.[85]

Because the law revolves around ritualized battles over competing narratives and cultural stories, women's engagements with narratives of victimization can also serve as a resource for challenging the law's prevailing stories about victimization and agency. As Toni Morrison argues, "Oppressive language does more than represent violence; it is violence; does more than represent the limits of knowledge; it limits knowledge."[86] Through their discussions of literary narratives of victimization, women prisoners generate insights for developing more complex, multilayered, accurate, and compassionate narratives about women whose lives have been touched by violence. Feminist theorists, myself included, face the ongoing challenge of translating those insights into stories that—rather than being dismissed as mis lit—might help to counter the immiserating forces that undergird our culture of incarceration.

Interlude 1

Denise: A Portrait

It's my time to come out of the wilderness
now, and I saw all that in this book.
—DENISE, Northeast Pre-Release Center

DENISE IS PASSIONATE about reading. Her favorite reading materials include books about the Holocaust, historical romances, Toni Morrison novels, and newspapers. "You don't know what you'll find in the newspaper from day to day," Denise explains, "so I read every inch of it. The NASDAQ—I have no clue what all that is about, but I read it anyway because what I don't know, I create my own story for what it is." Her ability to inhabit whatever she is reading makes the act of reading particularly intense for Denise. "It's like I visualize that book sitting there and me just melting into the pages," she explains. "When I read, I take myself so deep I can smell smells. You know, if I go to the rainforest, I can see bugs crawling on the leaves. I can see water dripping off the leaf. I can hear the snake on the limb crawling."

Although she acknowledges that she "may take books a little too serious," Denise does not mince words in criticizing books that disappoint her. For instance, she considers many Christian self-help books "just mediocre jargons." Referencing Jack Canfield, Mark Hansen, and Tom Lagana's edited collection, *Chicken Soup for the Prisoner's Soul*, Denise asserts, "It didn't have, like, a soul! . . . A person that can take a *Chicken Soup* and think it's the all-in-all is shallow." She says of herself, by contrast, "I want a book to stay with me. . . . I want it to make me think. I want it to change something about the way I view tomorrow. I want it to . . . change the way I see the next person, the way I treat that next person."

At the heart of Denise's current reading practice is her attempt to differentiate between "fantasy" and "reality," since fantasy has played a central role in her long-term practice of shoplifting. Denise, who was born forty-six years ago in a poor, black community in the South, notes that her earliest reading experiences involved fantasy: "I would take the pictures from the Sears catalog and I'd make my own stories to them. I'd go out in the cornfields and fantasize. . . . I think that's where my love of fashion and clothes come from."[1] Now, however, Denise expresses a strong preference for books in which "everything could happen in everyday life. None of it is really fantasy. It's real." She likes reading about "everyday common people" who "work hard at a menial job" and "just make it, not with this big grandiose house and all of this," and about people who start off "hard-pressed, like from the farm and abused or mistreated" and learn "to cope" with their backgrounds. In Denise's view, "it's not healthy" to read books about "people living lavishly" when "they came from humble beginnings" because such books can lead a reader to think "this is gonna happen for you" and "you end up in the malls, like me."

Denise developed an addiction to shopping malls during her fifteen-year relationship with an abusive man who forced her to shoplift as a means of financial support. During this long-term relationship, her partner would come over in the morning and demand that Denise make a certain amount of money by a given time. If she failed to generate the desired amount, her partner would say, "You can't do shit right. And you wonder why I knock you upside your head." She would then go to another mall, since "it might be easier on [her]" when she got home if she could acquire the money. In recalling this time in her life, Denise emphasizes her sense of entrapment in a seemingly endless stream of physical and emotional violence from her partner. He prevented her from having any friends and would "just do stuff to humiliate [her]," such as pushing her in the bathwater when she was bathing her kids. "I learned not to even cry," Denise recounts. "One night I was in the bed with my kids, and he came in, and he just punched me maybe twenty times in my head, and my little girl was laying there just squeezing my hand. I could feel her little hand just squeezing my hand every time he hit me, and I had to not cry for her."

In the midst of this violence, the shopping mall became "a safe haven" where Denise and her daughter would stay "from the moment it opened 'til the moment it closed. . . . It almost became like my home," she explains. Furthermore, the mall came to represent a space of magical possibility for Denise. Her neighborhood and the mall were "two different worlds. The malls was things I saw in magazines, like a dream world, where home was reality. Home was dark. Home was pain. . . . I could be anything I wanted to be in that mall. But at home I couldn't." Denise's almost rapturous description of the shopping mall underscores her fantasy-based attachment to the world it represents:

I can't even imagine my day without a mall. It's almost like it's a part of my arm or something. . . . I love the smell of them. I love the lighting. I love the floors, like going from the cushion to the cement. I love that feeling. And I love the domes of the light, the way the dome lights are shaped, and the way they shed the light on certain items. . . . I like the music that plays softly over the air. I like the whole atmosphere, and stealing the clothes is just like icing on the cake. . . . It's just a beautiful place to me.

The mall also became the basis of Denise's identity. As she describes it, "The malls was—is—everything to me. . . . I feel like that's the only place I'm gonna reach what I'm trying to be or what I want to be. . . . This is where I should have been in my life. I should have been successful like that where I would have been able to bring my children to the store and shop." At the mall, Denise can maintain the illusion that she has actually attained such success, even though she acknowledges, "I have to fake it. I have to pretend." It therefore seems "worse than going to jail" when stores require Denise to sign a document that bars her entry. "I don't even know how to explain the feeling in the inside when you get caught," she says, because "they're telling me I'm a failure, that I don't belong. That I'm less than."

Currently incarcerated for her sixth shoplifting offense, Denise feels determined to change her life, yet she frankly acknowledges, "I'm in a messed-up place. Shoplifting led me into a hole, a hole that I don't know how to come out of." Although she has participated in Narcotics Anonymous and Alcoholics Anonymous in prison, Denise finds these programs inadequate for curbing her shoplifting addiction. "They tell you to apply those same steps to your life, which could possibly work, but it doesn't work for me," she explains. "The shoplifting is stronger than the drugs."[2] Describing the isolation that she feels in grappling with her problem, Denise offers a highly insightful conclusion about the fantasy that undergirds her addiction:

When I talk to other boosters, you know they talk about, "Yeah man, we cleaned up at this store. We cleaned up at that store." It ain't like that with me. It's not about cleaning up. It's not about outrunning the police. I don't want the police after me at all. I want to walk out of there like Elizabeth Taylor or somebody. You know, I want to be able to be back tomorrow, and this lady greet me with respect because she thinks I'm a shopper. . . . I'm not the enemy. . . . I'm a part of the scene, you know. . . . But see, that's my illusion.

Because Denise now looks to reading as a means to counter this illusion—her belief that she belongs to the world of prosperity and prestige embodied by Elizabeth Taylor and wealthy shoppers—she expresses sharp disdain for African American urban fiction. As I discuss in Chapter 4, urban fiction typically depicts male and female protagonists who live a glamorous lifestyle through participation in crime; although the protagonists sometimes face arrest or decide to stop participating in crime, they typically retain their financial prowess. In Denise's view, some women can only see "the big cars with the big rims" when reading urban books; they fail to recognize that "only about one out of a hundred people" manages to achieve such a lavish lifestyle.

Denise's determination to engage in a reality-based reading practice nonetheless allowed her to experience a powerful shock of self-recognition when she read Sister Souljah's 1999 urban book *The Coldest Winter Ever*. This best-selling novel features Winter Santiaga, the selfish daughter of a wealthy drug kingpin whose own ruthless criminal acts land her in prison. Although Denise objected to the novel's thinly portrayed characters, she felt a strong sense of identification with several characters after reading the supplementary character analyses that Sister Souljah includes in an appendix. "That's where I saw the way I raised my children in each one of those characters," Denise said during our group discussion. "I saw Winter in me. I saw Winter in my daughter. . . . I saw Winter's father in me, with me trying to make my children flash for all their schoolmates. I realized that I'm creating a Winter." Referencing her twenty-one-year-old daughter, she then added, "After I read that ending, I understood why my daughter thinks it's the best book she ever read: 'Cause she saw me. She saw herself. She saw my lifestyle." Noting that her eight-year-old daughter wants to be a "hoochie" like her status-obsessed sister, Denise acknowledged that she felt "ashamed" and "sick at [her] stomach" from reading the book. "Little pieces [of the novel] would jump out at me and would like stab me," she said. "Like oh God, this is what I done did to my child."

Denise's reading practice often involves this kind of intense identification with one or more characters. According to Elizabeth Long, such identification entails "a complex, messy commingling of subjects." Because identification "pulls a reader into a dynamic relationship with a character who must be reckoned with almost like another person, it can lead to deep personal insights and to critical reflection about literature and the social order."[3] This dynamic is evident in Denise's deep identification with the protagonist of Iyanla Vanzant's *Yesterday, I Cried*. Grappling with Vanzant's conclusion that she abused her own children even though "everything she did was so they could have a better life," Denise reflects: "I thought I was giving my kids the best of everything, but I really was abusing them by making them think that everything was easy, just ask for it, and somebody's supposed to give it to you. You don't have to work for it. . . . That's abuse when you don't teach your kids how to live in the world. That's abuse to cut them off like that from reality."

Denise's intense identification with protagonists likewise leads her to reflect on the ways in which she has been complicit in her victimization. For instance, she focuses on her own abusive relationship in discussing various elements from Vanzant's list of "things I have done that are not in my own best interest," such as "staying in a situation when I know it is causing me pain." Denise says that she has learned from Vanzant's book "to stop thinking that it's love" when someone else is "controlling everything or telling [you] how to do things" as if "they know what's better for you than you do." As part of her effort to ground herself in reality, she has also adopted the questions that Vanzant regularly poses to herself to assess her development, such as Who are you? What is your greatest strength? weakness? fear? mistake? accomplishment? What is the experience that brings you the greatest amount of joy? If you were to die today, what is the one thing that everyone who knows you would say about you?[4] Denise plans to send these questions to her older daughters every year on their birthdays, and she wants them to send their replies to her so that she can "see where they're going."

Through her identification with book characters, Denise also deepens her understanding of how larger structural and historical forces, such as poverty and racism, have shaped her actions. She has found Dorothy Allison's 1993 novel, *Bastard out of Carolina*, especially useful for contextualizing her experiences in relation to broader social patterns. Allison's novel features a poor white family from South Carolina and is narrated by Bone, a young girl who sustains physical and sexual abuse at the hands of her stepfather. Although Denise is African American and Bone is white, Denise considers Bone's story a stand-in for her own. "I *lived* that book," she says. "You read this book, I ain't got to tell you my story. . . . All I got to tell you is this is me."

Denise's profound sense of identification with Bone relates, in part, to their shared experience of sexual abuse. Denise left her childhood home at age fifteen when a young man whom her mother had agreed to raise began sexually abusing her. During our group discussion, Denise said of Bone's experience, "It felt like it hurt me physically when he raped her that day in that house. I feel so sad for her that I have to tell myself she's a character. But to me, she's a little girl still running around in North Carolina somewhere." Allison's novel may prevent other children from being molested, Denise argues, since "here I am standing here in front of you telling you it happened to me." She believes that "every woman should read" the book, and it should be in men's prisons, too, since "it might make men be better fathers."

Denise also deeply identifies with Bone's experiences of growing up in an extremely poor, fiercely protective, and insular community. *Bastard out of Carolina* seems "really profound," she explains, because Bone's family is "the exact same as my family, the way we keep secrets and keep everything in the family." Denise, the youngest of twelve children, was raised in a predominantly African American town. Her father was an alcoholic gambler and the owner of a "juke joint," and her mother worked as a maid for a white judge. Her family had no running water, heat, or indoor toilet, and she and her siblings rarely had shoes. Through commingling her own and Bone's stories, Denise has deepened her understanding of the fierce sense of pride that she and her family developed from banding together in their destitution. "We could protect [ourselves] as long as we stayed together," she reflects, but "when you put us somewhere where don't nobody know us, they're gonna shame us. They're gonna damn us. They're gonna see that we're less than. And they're gonna treat us as such." This understanding has, in turn, helped Denise to articulate the potential links between men's social marginalization and their abuse of power within their families. As she said in discussing *Bastard out of Carolina*, "I believe that's where the liquor and the alcoholism and the abuse stems from: the frustration of not being nothing in society. . . . But you're king when you come home. . . . You are the protector and the ruler of everybody with your last name. . . . And you can dominate and tell everybody what to do." Such insight seems particularly important given Denise's ongoing efforts to understand why her own abusive partner treated her as he did.

Her identification with book protagonists likewise enables Denise to understand how racial inequality has shaped her involvement in shoplifting. For instance, in discussing her hope that Bone will escape from her childhood home, Denise simultaneously reflects on her own conflicted relationship to the town in which she grew up. On one hand, she occasionally returns to the town for her "salvation," since her siblings take good care of her and town residents "don't care about Liz Claiborne." On the other hand, Denise had to leave the town in order to realize that white people are "just people, just like me." If she returns to her hometown, which she associates with racialized poverty and stagnation, Denise fears that her past self will obliterate the more empowered person that she has struggled to become—she will "resort back to that cotton picking, tobacco picking person that [she] was," who is "submissive" and believes that "white people won't let you" succeed.

Our group discussion of Patrice Gaines's 1994 autobiographical narrative, *Laughing in the Dark: From Colored Girl to Woman of Color—A Journey from Prison to Power*, triggered a particularly painful memory of racialized shame that has increased Denise's understanding of her shoplifting. Gaines's narrative details how the author became a successful journalist at the *Washington Post* after battling with racism, sexual and physical abuse, drug use, shoplifting, and a prison sentence. In her reflections about *Laughing in the Dark*, Denise acknowledged her tendency to "pass into characters' heads" and not "let the story evolve" because she wants it to convey her own rather than the author's experiences. As she said of Gaines's narrative, "I was in the story like it's *my* story! She ain't handling that right!" Noting numerous parallels between her own and Gaines's experiences, including their shared anger about their parents' willingness to work for whites, Denise then meditated on a powerful memory that surfaced while she was reading *Laughing in the Dark*:

> I was at school one day and this little girl said, "That was my dress." I had on one of the dresses my mama had got from her mama. And when I got out of school, my friends was saying, "You got on a white girl's dress! You got on a white girl's dress!" And I wonder if somewhere that's what led me into boosting. I had this thing where my kids would never wear nobody else's clothes. And when I read this book, it jarred little things, like *that's why you act like this*. And it all go back to the racial prejudice that you experience as a child, how it affects you. . . . Even today, I hate when anybody treat anybody like they're less than. That's like the worst thing in the world to me.

In her ongoing efforts to reckon with feelings of shame about her childhood poverty, Denise also looks to book characters as sources of inspiration and guidance. Because she now considers continuing her former lifestyle futile, she conveys an urgent need for such guidance. "All the stealing I have done for twenty-five years has profited me nothing," Denise concedes. "My kids are struggling. So all the years I done missed out on their lives [while] in prison, what was it all for? . . . I have nothing and nobody in my life." At times, book characters serve as negative examples from which Denise distances herself. In discussing *The Coldest Winter Ever*, for instance, she emphasized that Winter had "no God in her" and "no relative to instill in her a different life," whereas Denise herself has a strong spiritual foundation and supportive relatives who have instilled some good values in her children. At other times, characters serve as positive sources of inspiration for Denise. As she said of *Laughing in the Dark*, "This book, it touched every part of my life, but it also showed me that I could come through it. . . . Every opportunity is available now for myself, and that's what this book help[ed] me see, that I can't keep living like this as an excuse for things that happened in my past. . . . I, me, can step out of this situation any time I want to."

In addition to learning from the examples of various characters, Denise remains keenly attuned to metaphors that might help her to narrate dimensions of her own story. She particularly values Joyce Meyer's Christian self-help book *Battlefield of the Mind: Winning the Battle in Your Mind*, because it fulfills her long-term desire to read a book that explains "the mental state of a person that's caught up in shoplifting." From reading Meyer's book, which claims that God and the devil wage a continual battle for control of our minds, Denise believes that the devil "knows your weaknesses" and uses them "to bind your mind. He knew that wealthy things was what I craved for because I was so poor as a child," she explains, and he "deceived me into feeling like I was doing something good, like a Robin Hood." Before reading *Battlefield of the Mind*, Denise never believed that it was wrong to steal expensive merchandise for the homeless, a prom dress for a needy teen, or clothes for family and friends. Now, however, she interprets her compulsion to shoplift as an ongoing battle between God's angels and "those demons that was trying to convince me mentally that I was a thief," and she cherishes the thought that God will help her to vanquish the urge to steal: "Even when I be asleep at night, and demons come at me, God fights them in my unconscious. . . . I know to call on Jesus, and they'll leave me alone."[5]

From reading Vanzant's *Yesterday, I Cried*, Denise has gleaned another helpful metaphor for understanding how destructive and empowering impulses battle for dominance in her psyche. Referencing Vanzant's description of her two competing selves—Rhonda, who refuses to move beyond her painful history, and Iyanla, who is "creating her own [history]"[6]—Denise said during a group discussion, "This book showed me that I'm not the only person that has two people living in them. I've had this person I called Mattie, and she's the person that I blame for the hard times and did all the wild stuff, but Denise didn't do those things." She then experimented with this framework as a means to articulate her conflicted sense of self. Although she described Mattie as always trying "to knock [her] down" when she does something right, she also described her as the strong, adaptive self who helped her to survive her abusive relationship and life in the city. Denise's sometimes contradictory descriptions of these two selves and her occasional confusion about which self she should leave behind indicate her ongoing uncertainty about how to cultivate a strong, adaptive, yet law-abiding persona. As she works to integrate her "weaker" and "stronger" selves, Denise is trying to emulate Vanzant's self-forgiveness and her recognition of the important roles that her past self has played in "preparing her for her life."

Furthermore, Denise is experimenting with Vanzant's maxim—"Always be grateful"[7]—as a framework for reenvisioning in more positive terms the deprivations that she experienced as a child. During our discussion of *Yesterday, I Cried*, Denise rescripted her poverty as a source of strength in asserting, "I can survive under any conditions. I can work hard 'cause I worked in those tobacco fields sun up 'til sun down. . . . It's in me to be a survivor. It's in me to be strong." She then enumerated several aspects of her childhood for which she now feels grateful, from seeing a chicken lay an egg to sleeping in the same bed with her four sisters. Recalling how she always wished that "somebody else" could be her parent when she "would look at books and see these little girls on TV" with cinderblock houses, carpeting, "cushy" chairs, and their own rooms, Denise added, "But today, when I think about all of us sitting around in that living room spreading newspaper on the floor to eat our meals, that was love. That was love 'cause all of us was there. . . . And I recognized that in [Vanzant's] book, how some of the things that you thought was so harsh in your childhood you could turn out to be grateful for." Moreover, Denise explained that she is learning to value her experiences by having them reflected back to her through reading and discussion: "I have learned so much about myself that I didn't realize, about my upbringing, about my past. How valuable those hard times are. . . . When I read about them in those books, I treasure every day of my youth, I do, because it's a time that will never come back."

Although she risks romanticizing the dire poverty that engulfed her family, Denise contextualized these statements as part of her efforts to acknowledge—without shame—the economic circumstances that contributed to her shoplifting addiction:

> When I think about how ashamed I was of those times, talking about them now helps me get over the shame. A little bit of me is still ashamed. Like I remember last week when I spoke out about having to use newspaper in the toilet, that bothered me all day. . . . And just now when I said it, a shame thing still came over me. And it's the shame thing that made me grow up to be in abusive relationships and made me grow up to be a shoplifter. 'Cause

to go in Dillard's and walk in the stores with rich people meant that I wasn't poor no more.

Denise is also learning to reclaim the knowledge that she has gained from her experiences and to share this knowledge in intellectual discussions. Conveying her excitement about this development, she offered the following reflection during her final group discussion:

> Finally, I got a chance to say how I feel about a book to somebody that was willing to listen, somebody that understood, somebody else that saw some of the things I did. I got excited about every book I read because it was like a me inside of me getting a chance to come out, and it would just live! It was like getting a chance to see home and to see my childhood and to talk about it when somebody else was talking about it too; even though this person was in a book, they were talking about it, too. It's like it stirred up something in me and it would just come out like, "I gotta say this . . . I know this!"

As Denise's reading practice illustrates, "A momentary loss of barriers between self and fictional 'other'" can "reintegrate aspects of the reader's self in almost therapeutic fashion."[8]

As she "remak[es]" herself "in dialogue with others and with literary texts," Denise is particularly attuned to metaphors that suggest some sort of plan, as well as meaningful progress, in the life path that she has followed.[9] Her readings frequently focus on images of thresholds, plans coming to fruition, and future days of fulfillment. Vanzant's narrative reassures Denise that what awaits her, in terms of self-development, exceeds what she is currently able to perceive. She summarizes the book's message in the following terms: "Just 'cause you're crushed right now, don't stop because it look like this. It won't look like this in the end. There's a greatness in you that you couldn't even see when you was little. You know, there's a greatness in you that you couldn't see when that man was beating you. . . . But if you keep on and keep on, God will be in your path and will keep on elevating you. And finally you'll get in that spirit realm where you can see everything." Denise likewise feels inspired by Patrice Gaines's ability "to look back over her life and see that it was all a plan set out," even if "she made twists and turns in it"; by "pulling it all together" in her book, Gaines can help others and "be free." Denise finds especially useful the metaphor of coming out of the wilderness, which frequently appears in Meyer's *Battlefield of the Mind*. "I've been in the wilderness long enough, and it's my time to come out now," she asserts. Describing some of the changes that she already perceives in herself—including her decision to purchase clothing from the Goodwill store upon her release—Denise reflects, "I don't know what life's gonna be like not shoplifting again. But I'm ready. [The Israelites] didn't know what it was gonna be like coming out of the wilderness. But God . . . promised when he brought them out of the wilderness he was giving them a land of milk and honey. So I know it's good things in store for me when I come up out of there."

The powerful role that books play in Denise's life is perhaps best captured by her description of *Battlefield of the Mind* as "not just a book to read. . . . It's life, breathing. It's alive. It lives. . . . This book is a living book because I can go back to it, and it strengthens you so you'll be able to fight the things that come into your mind" and "progress instead of being defeated." Underscoring how important the book has become to her, Denise announced during our final discussion, "Matter of fact, I'm keeping this book! The library can't have this one back! . . . Every day I go back in here to read something, and I find something to share with people I see going through things. And I tell them, 'Read this book. It'll help you.'"

Using books as life-breath, Denise is learning to acknowledge her illusions, deepen her self-awareness, create new meanings from her experiences, and experiment with new subject positions. In reckoning with the many forms of loss that mark her life story, she draws attention to the systemic forms of inequality and violence that have shaped her story from the beginning. At the same time, reading narratives about other women inspires Denise to carve out a different future. As she describes it, her life as a reader is intimately connected to her ongoing project of imagining new ways of being in the world: "I don't think it's too many people know me like this. They don't know I read books. . . . They wouldn't believe this me could sit in a room and talk like this." Denise now realizes, however, that this reading self is her "power," and she feels eager to share her knowledge with her children and nieces. "My life with them has been, 'Oh you want a new outfit?'" she explains, "so now I got to get them to know me another way."

Reading her own story—from the transcripts of her interviews—underscored for Denise how far she has come in understanding herself. "You know, I related to all these books," she said, "but when I read about me, I was thinking that person is crazy! She's living a fantasy life." In encountering her earlier self on paper, Denise recognized that shoplifting has served as her "defense mechanism for dodging pain," and she reaffirmed her resolve to inhabit the remaining pages of her life story in a healthier fashion. "This started as just a book club," she said, "but it was kind of life-changing for me."

CHAPTER FOUR

Fear of Books

READING URBAN FICTION

I try to say there is more to life than urban books or true crime.—PRISON LIBRARIAN

This book, it gives me goosebumps how real it is! . . . I was Amen-ing at all this stuff going on because . . . there's a lot of things in this book that I know.—WENDY, Northeast Pre-Release Center

AFRICAN AMERICAN urban fiction—also known as gangsta lit, street lit, ghetto fiction, and hip-hop fiction—has taken the U.S. publishing world by storm. Bearing titles such as *Thugs and the Women Who Love Them*, *Forever a Hustler's Wife*, and *Thug-a-Licious*, urban books feature African Americans who are involved in urban street crime, including drug dealing, hustling, prostitution, and murder. The genre has gained immense popularity, particularly among young black women, since the 1999 publication of Sister Souljah's best-selling novel *The Coldest Winter Ever*. Its roots extend further back, however, to African American novels about ghetto life such as Iceberg Slim's *Trick Baby* (1967) and *Pimp: The Story of My Life* (1969) and Donald Goines's *Dopefiend* (1971) and *Whoreson: The Story of a Ghetto Pimp* (1972).[1] Although urban fiction writers struggled to find publishers for their work in the late 1990s—they often self-published their books and sold them on street corners, in clubs, and in barbershops and salons— some authors now sign six-figure contracts with major publishing houses, and urban books dominate the African American collections in large chain bookstores.[2] Triple Crown Publications, an urban book publisher that was founded in 2001 by former prisoner Vickie Stringer, is now the largest independent publishing house in the country, and both Borders and Waldenbooks have established specific sections of Triple Crown books. Many urban fiction writers are first-time authors, and a substantial number of those writers are prisoners; for instance, seven of the twenty-six authors sponsored by Triple Crown Publications are incarcerated.[3]

In the prisons where I conducted research, urban fiction is particularly popular among young, lower-class black women, but it has also gained popularity among some white women and middle-class black women. According to women involved in my study, urban books typically feature "a pimp or killer or drug dealer" or "just a everyday life situation: prison, baby mama drama, having a guy being a player." The books often emphasize how characters "used to see their mother get beat up, or how they went to different groups and foster homes and prison," and they sometimes involve courtroom scenes and characters' efforts to "flee the police." The genre has opened up a world of reading for many women who were not readers before coming to prison. Ronnie "didn't read hardly at all," but she "was hooked" after discovering urban fiction. Now, she explains, "I keep reaching out and reaching out until I find more and more. They all just been good books. They talk about real life." Urban books are a frequent topic of conversation among prisoners as they sit in the cafeteria or spend time outside, and when I began my study, a few of the participants were involved in an informal reading club that focuses on Triple Crown books.

From immersing myself in the genre, I have learned that urban books frequently foreground racial disparities in the administration of justice and underscore the difficulty of trying to achieve economic security in a racialized capitalist system. Many of the books pay particular attention to the toll that urban living takes on black men; the protagonists' fathers are often dead or imprisoned, and most male characters have been involved in the criminal justice system. Urban books also underscore the struggles that black women face in trying to achieve economic security and establish healthy, long-term relationships with black men. Some novels emphasize the sexual needs and desires of their female protagonists, and they question the physical, emotional, and sexual abuse that female characters endure in order to secure men's financial patronage.[4] In focusing on the hardships that men and women of color face in the United States, many urban books implicitly justify characters' criminal actions as legitimate resistance to white oppression. At the same time, the books typically feature protagonists who survive the system. They often portray a black male character who is extremely powerful, wealthy, wise enough to survive the game, and gentle enough to meet all the needs of the female protagonist and her existing or soon-to-be-born children. Several urban books also offer portraits of strong

TRIBLE CROWN
A Hustlers Wife
Triangle of Sin
Rectangle of Sin
Grimy
Crackhead
Bitch
Bitch Reload
Stacy
Whore
Conviction Candy
Its like Candy
Hustlers Wife II

A list of the Triple Crown books that Gypsy Rose has read. Although not all of the books on this list are published by Triple Crown Publications, the publishing firm has played such a central role in shaping urban fiction that some women identify all urban books as Triple Crown books.

black women who "get knocked down" but remain "the last one standing." At the conclusion of many novels, these women finally lay down their burdens and allow the hero of the story to "be the man [they] need."[5]

Some critics argue that urban fiction glorifies crime, reinforces stereotypical images of African Americans, and crowds out far better literature by African American writers. Indeed, some of my colleagues have skeptically asked me whether urban fiction can even be classified as literature. In "Their Eyes Were Reading Smut," a frequently cited Op-Ed published in the *New York Times* in 2006, Nick Chiles describes the proliferation of urban fiction as "these nasty books . . . pairing off back in the stockrooms like little paperback rabbits and churning out even more graphic offspring that make Ralph Ellison books cringe into a dusty corner." From Chiles's perspective, "serious" African American writers such as Toni Morrison, Edward P. Jones, and himself are being "surrounded and swallowed whole on the shelves" by "pornography for black women" and "books that glamorize black criminals." Chiles feels "thoroughly embarrassed" by the current state of black book publishing and deeply troubled by "the future of [his] community." In her 2007 essay "Writers Like Me," Martha Southgate likewise criticizes urban fiction in lamenting the proliferation of "commercial genre fiction by African-Americans" and the relative invisibility of "ambitious, thoughtful" writing by black authors. Corroborating Southgate's viewpoint, one African American author informed me that several publishers have rejected her novel, which focuses on imprisoned men and women, because it offers neither "real" portrayals nor the sensationalism common to urban fiction; in fact, one publisher requested that the author make her fictional account nonfiction.[6]

Critics' anxieties about urban fiction are matched by penal officials' anxieties about the genre. Despite women's daily requests for urban fiction, prison librarians in both Ohio and Pennsylvania exclude the genre due to its emphases on drug dealing, hustling, prostitution, and violence. One Ohio librarian acknowledges that urban books "will hit home to a lot of women" because they "basically depict a woman hustler, and a lot of the women in here are either former drug addicts or were on the streets selling themselves." However, this librarian has set aside her preference for "noncensorship" because she believes that the books should not be permitted from a "corrections" perspective. The librarian in the Pennsylvania prison likewise characterizes herself as "not big on censorship," but she, too, refuses to allow urban books in the library. Although she has not read any urban fiction, she justifies the genre's exclusion on the grounds that the Department of Corrections has banned several titles, and the books "disappear too fast" due to theft.[7]

I realized the extent of prison officials' anxieties about urban fiction while I was conducting group discussions with women incarcerated in Ohio. Although we had received permission to discuss a few urban books, a prison official burst in to stop one of our discussions after learning that the books were published by Triple Crown Publications. The official told me to collect the books and immediately remove them from prison grounds, as if, one prisoner noted, they were "a bomb that no one can touch." Since we were not permitted to read any additional urban books, I asked if we might have a group discussion about two particularly popular books that most of the participants had already read. A penal official insisted, however, that "there can be no discussion of the work."

Although some prisoners echo the concerns of various scholars, librarians, and penal officials in voicing disdain for urban fiction, other prisoners draw attention to the inconsistency of penal officials' attempts to guard the literary gates. Several women foreground the racialized dimensions of the ban on urban fiction, noting that white author James Patterson's violent crime thrillers are the most abundant books in their prison library. In fact, the Pennsylvania librarian orders six copies of each of Patterson's novels and has established a separate section for his books.[8] Miekal, who claims that the Ohio prison library has "about seventy" of Patterson's crime thrillers, asserts, "I think it's racism, and I think it's prejudice, and I don't think it's right, because you got James Patterson and all these killer books," with men who "kidnap women . . . and put snakes in their rectum and kill them, and they're rapists. . . . [But] in urban books, it's not horrifying. It's just something that's going on in everyday life. It's happening whether they want to face it or not." As for the specific ban on books published by Triple Crown Publications, Miekal argues, "Let's just keep it 100 percent real. They ban them because half of the authors is from prison, and it's based upon some form of what they done went through in their life. And they don't want us to read it 'cause they want to keep us in here." A young white woman named Valhalla reasons that "the one who decides what we can and cannot get tends to be a white man," not "a bunch of urban project women with a bunch of kids. I'm sure it's highly educated men that went to a good college and [had] a good life, and they don't understand. Those books are ridiculous to them."

Imprisoned readers also note the discrepancy between their restricted access to urban books and their freedom to watch countless movies and reality television shows that focus on crime. Lakesha, a twenty-seven-year-old African American woman, suggests that the prohibition of urban fiction contests incarcerated women's status as readers. In an imaginary dialogue with penal officials, Lakesha said, "I just want to read this book. . . . Why don't you want me to read it? . . . Why are you trying to take another black author off the shelf? But then you allow me to watch 'Prison Break'? I can watch 'Prison Break' and I'm sitting in prison! So what's really your story?"[9] Lakesha's deep concerns about penal control over prisoners' reading became apparent during her initial interview. As she was discussing some of her favorite books, including older urban fiction by Donald Goines and works by revolutionary black women such as Assata Shakur, Elaine Brown, and Waset, Lakesha seemed increasingly anxious about mentioning books that she suspects are not sanctioned by the prison, even though she found one book in the prison library and received the others through the mail.[10] "I don't want to go to [segregation] over no book," she said, wondering aloud if it would be better to discuss Euripides' Medea or books by Socrates "so I won't get my books taken." By the end of the interview, Lakesha decided to drop out of my study because she feared that it would lead to further restrictions on women prisoners' reading. "I don't know if I should be talking about this stuff," she concluded, "'cause I love my books. I want my books, and I want other inmates to get the opportunity to read stuff, too." Just before leaving the room, Lakesha added, "Maybe you should write another book called 'Fear of Books.'"[11]

Lakesha's comments have stayed with me over the course of my study, serving as a crucial reminder of what is at stake in my exploration of prisoners' reading practices. I must acknowledge that I have felt reservations about the ideological underpinnings of many urban books. For instance, although urban books often reference the racial oppression that African Americans face, intraracial class conflicts take center stage in many of the books, and black characters destroy one another in their often ruthless efforts to gain class ascendancy and maintain their economic power. The books frequently define success in terms of vast material wealth and often romanticize the role of drug dealer. Furthermore, they tend to portray female characters as viciously vying for the financial patronage of male drug dealers; many books suggest that supportive relationships among women are well-nigh impossible, and that women can only achieve well-being by establishing a heterosexual, reproductive family unit with a wealthy man. Indeed, the genre may perpetuate the fantasy that African American women can game and romance their way to the top of a system that routinely excludes them from equal opportunity and economic success. Finally, urban books often espouse a notion of justice based on individual enactments of revenge, thereby leaving little room for imagining mutuality, cooperation, or shared struggle for collective benefit.

Notwithstanding these ideological criticisms of urban fiction, my interactions with women prisoners pushed me to abdicate the role of literary prison guard and try, instead, to understand how readers use available narrative forms to negotiate their place in the world. As we have seen, women prisoners have been stripped of their agency as readers throughout U.S. penal history, due to cultural anxieties about women's corruption through reading, racialized assumptions about prisoners' lack of capacity for reflection, and fears that criminals will increase their criminality by reading inappropriate books.[12] Given the important roles that urban fiction plays in the lives of many women prisoners, carefully analyzing how they engage with the genre is essential for honoring their agency as readers. In an essay titled "Can the Penitentiary Teach the Academy How to Read?" H. Bruce Franklin argues that Donald Goines's ghetto novels push teachers and students of literature to think about questions such as the following: "Are aesthetic standards expressions of class, gender, and ethnic values? Are complexity and ambiguity the hallmarks of literary excellence, or are simplicity and accessibility literary virtues?" Because books that are popular among prisoners tend to foster such reflection, Franklin concludes that "the penitentiary can help the academy learn to read." In the following pages, I underscore the complex and varied ways in which women prisoners engage with books that many members of "the academy" consider unworthy of reading. Although it remains crucial to address how publishing and market demands restrict the range of representations of African Americans, I believe that it is equally crucial— lest we participate in creating a "prison-house of language"—to understand how women prisoners use the narratives at hand as tools for shaping their own experiences.[13]

Toward such ends, this chapter explores individual and group discussions of urban fiction. My analysis focuses on the five urban books that we were permitted to read: Sister Souljah's *The Coldest Winter Ever*; Tu-Shonda Whitaker's *Flip Side of the Game* and its sequel, *Game Over*; Shannon Holmes's *Bad Girlz*; and Danielle Santiago's *Grindin'*. I also draw on prisoners' and my own readings of urban books by popular authors such as Noire, Nikki Turner, Vickie Stringer, Teri Woods, T. N. Baker, Lisa Lennox, and Chunichi.[14] As the chapter illustrates, women perform a range of readerly negotiations as they engage with urban fiction. At times, women "keep it real" with the books' depictions of familiar characters, scenes, fashion trends, and speech patterns, which enable them to maintain a sense of connection to a community beyond the prison walls. Drawing on urban books' realistic and fantastic elements, readers grapple with the ways in which racial, class, and gender inequalities shape their access to the American Dream and their social position as women. Because urban books rarely offer developed portraits of their protagonists, some women add layers of complexity to the novels by writing themselves into the narratives, and they use the books as templates for reflecting on their own experiences. Readers also establish standards of aesthetic judgment and literary value in assessing the genre, and as we shall see, some women gain inspiration to write their own urban books.

Keepin' It Real with Urban Fiction

Because urban books are not available through their prison libraries, women sometimes ask family members and friends to order books for them through online catalogs such as BlackExpressions.com. When a book arrives in the mailroom, a prison official decides whether it is acceptable, and if it is not, the prisoner must destroy it or return it to the sender. The acceptance rate of urban fiction fluctuates depending on the whims—and sometimes the race—of the official involved. On a few different occasions, women involved in my study tried to teach me how to order urban books that might be deemed acceptable. Cassandra informed me that "as long as the cover don't look too racy and crazy" and "as long as it doesn't say Vickie Stringer or Zane, they would let it come in." Monique explained, "Sometimes the titles won't let them get in more than the contents. . . . It's probably like their impression of the book, like what they see at that moment. If they see oh no, no, no, you got naked people on the cover, oh no, you can't have this in there. You got 'bitch' on the cover, or something like that. No, you can't have that in there." Given the mercurial nature of the screening process, a substantial number of urban books have made it into the Ohio and Pennsylvania prisons, and correctional officers cannot penalize women for having those books in their possession. In fact, many correctional officers read urban fiction themselves, and they sometimes assist women in procuring books; during one woman's monthlong stay in the segregation unit, sympathetic officers brought her more than forty urban books. Women who receive books through the mail often share them with others via the "Underground Book Railroad." "You'll have about 300 people in this compound waiting to read a book," explains a young black woman named Darlene, "so it's like a list that the [book owner] keeps on who got the book and how much time they got to read it and get it to the next person. . . . These books, they really keep us going."

Like literary critics and penal officials, prisoners sometimes debate the merits of reading urban fiction.[15] The category of "the real" plays a wide range of shifting roles in such debate; women both critique and laud the genre on the basis of its realism. Perhaps in response to the power that penal authorities confer on urban fiction through their efforts to ban it, women sometimes characterize the books as powerful agents that can either enable positive transformation or contribute to one's downfall. Whereas Ronnie argues, "I probably won't come back to prison if I keep reading them books" because they "help me keep my mind straight" and "not get involved," Marisa claims, "Most of the ones who read urban books come back. . . . They don't want to change mentally."

Prisoners who criticize urban fiction express particular concern that the genre leads women between the ages of eighteen and thirty down the wrong path. Denise acknowledges that some fans of urban fiction were not readers before they came to prison, so they find it "just amazing that somebody has put their lives, or the lives that they want to be, in a book." She considers urban books "garbage," however, because they depict "what these girls have lived all their lives. It's what brought them to the penitentiary, and it gives them a hype that this is what they should [a]spire to be." Denise goes on to explain, "I listen to them when they're playing volleyball, calling out these characters' names and saying little lines of these characters. In one of these books, there's a guy named Vegas. He was a real big drug dealer. . . . And I watch girls walk around like, 'Yeah, I've gotta call Vegas to send me a money order.' . . . Or, 'Just call me Ms. Vegas.'" In Denise's view, urban books are "tragedies" in which "a lot of people die," yet many readers can only see characters' "flashy" and glamorous lives. Whereas books by Toni Morrison and Alice Walker "show true black life, like the struggle, the strength, the honor, the history, the respect," urban books "do black life injustice." Some other black women likewise lament urban books' representations of African American life. Sixty-six-year-old Caesar argues, "I can't stand black books. They're all about drugs and gangsters. My people used to have morals [but] now they don't." Twenty-six-year-old Lefty asserts that urban books "are a reminder of home, but they're too ghetto for me. They're popular because they're big print and small books, and a lot of girls have small minds."

According to women who criticize urban fiction, its realism makes it unhealthy to read. "What you take in, comes out," Omega argues, "and that part of the world caused me nothing but trouble." Some women—including fans of the genre—argue that urban books discuss drug use in ways that can reactivate readers' addictions. Miekal, who owns an extensive collection of urban books, asked the prison librarian to ban two books—Lisa Lennox's *Crack Head* (2005) and Y. Blak Moore's *Slipping* (2005)—because she believes that their descriptions of crack use will make addicts "slip when they could have wanted to be clean." Starr argues that women prisoners should be reading "imaginative books, science fiction, and fantasy" rather than books "based on real life," since "people might run out and shoot somebody from seeing what's on television or reading." She expresses particular concern, as a black woman, that urban books keep younger black women "linked" to the world of crime. "They're like an old song that filters through your brain and gives you a memory of why that song was good," Starr contends, and they keep women "plotting to make that stuff come true. Those books glorify their addictions to drugs and money."

Women who enjoy reading urban fiction also evoke its realism in expressing their appreciation for the genre. Making few distinctions between characters and actual people, these women argue that urban books "keep it real" by depicting characters and dilemmas that relate to their own experiences. According to Darlene, the books are "so real you can actually feel what they're going through or been through. I can find bits and pieces of me or somebody that's close to me in the urban books." Distinguishing urban fiction from "love story tales," "science fiction," and "alien comic books," Monique explains, "I like reading books that pertain to life. Real life. . . . You know, reading about somebody that came from nothing and has everything, or reading about somebody who was born into it and lost it all." Angel notes how ironic it is that her prison library includes true crime books about local murderers yet does not include "books about the lives we've lived." Nena and Boo argue that their warden restricts urban fiction because she is out of touch with the realities that the genre depicts. "We're not all rich people," Nena insists. "We came from the streets. We've been raped doing tricks and left for dead in alleys with dead animals on us." Boo echoes this sentiment in saying of the warden, "She needs to get out of herself and her fantasy world. Life is not a bowl of cherries. Put your feet in someone else's shoes."[16]

By depicting familiar characters, scenes, fashion trends, and speech patterns, urban books enable some women to maintain a sense of connection to their communities, and they conjure a realistic world that exists outside the control of penal officials. For Darlene, the best part about reading urban books is "the realness that can take me out of here and away somewhere else other than in my room on my bunk. . . . I mean, it's very interesting to the point where you put a face on the characters . . . or when they're out at the club dancing and stuff, you can imagine all that, just put it all together in your head." During an early phase of her incarceration, Darlene felt particularly comforted by Vickie Stringer's urban books because they mention the names of streets and buildings with which she is familiar. "In one of her books she's even talking about Tower City and the hotel next to Tower City," Darlene explained, "and I was so glad to read that book and be familiar [with] what she is talking about 'cause I was so homesick." Miekal similarly describes urban books as a means "to keep it together" by staying connected to life happening outside the prison. "Urban books is basically just keeping you in touch with what's going on in the streets," she explained. "The latest words they're saying out there, the latest things they're wearing, the latest things they're doing. I like to hear what the lady's got on, you know, she's wearing her miniskirts, and she got on stilettos, and she's looking good, her skin glistening like mocha chocolates. It gets me going all deep." Miekal also likes to read books in which men "take care of their women" by buying them designer jewelry, clothing, and perfume, but she remains fully aware of the consequences that such a lifestyle invites. "It's not like no fantasy or nothing of mine to sell drugs," she clarified. "'Cause that's drug money, and if you read the book, it tells you eventually he goes down, you know. He's looking at ten to fifteen years or he gets killed." From Miekal's perspective, it makes no sense that women are permitted to read about serial killers but not about what she finds most captivating in urban books: "black men sporting Timberland boots and women wearing Prada."

The fact that urban books employ the vocabulary and speech patterns of African American urban culture is particularly attractive to some readers. An African American woman named Soso specifies that she likes how characters in urban books "use slang, like 'da' instead of 'the,' and 'what fo?' I like how they say 'dat' and not 'that' . . . and things like, 'yo,' 'hey ho,' and 'wassup.' That's how it is in the streets. People use those terms. . . . That excites me." Wendy argues that Sister Souljah's use of "the common everyday slang" allows *The Coldest Winter Ever* to "speak volumes to people because it's on a level where they can understand everything that's going on. They don't have to feel stupid" or keep stopping to "get the dictionary" in order to comprehend. Readers find it especially inspiring that urban fiction writers have withstood pressures to use standardized English. As Darlene says of the author Zane, "They wanted to change her words around. They say our language is Ebonics or whatever. But she didn't change nothing what she wrote. She stuck with it and now she's like a *major* writer." The mass-produced feel of the genre also adds to readers' sense of its authenticity and accessibility. Nena appreciates Shannon Holmes's *Bad Girlz*, for instance, because "it's not elegantly produced. It doesn't have no extra cover, no picture of the Taj Mahal or magnificent trimming. . . . It's simple. And he explains his whole story in three sentences."

The verisimilitude of urban books in terms of their details and settings enables some readers to participate vicariously in the stories while remaining aware of their fictionality. As a young African American woman, Kaye relishes the fact that urban books feature people and situations that seem familiar. "A lot have to do with growing up in the projects, selling, and using. I did all that," she explains. Invoking the titles of two popular books—*Sheisty* and *A Project Chick*—she adds, "They're about people like you know. I know people who did sheisty things. I've known that project chick." Kaye nonetheless emphasizes that urban books are not "real." "If it was real," she says, "it would give me more sadness of how their lives turn out." She recognizes that urban books "have to keep the momentum" and "the momentum comes from fights, action, and drama. If [the characters] have a job, kids, and a nice life, it levels out. It would be like going from the New York City streets to the country roads of Alabama." In fact, noting that her taste in books is like her taste in movies—she prefers murders, comedies, and suspense—Kaye suggests that characters in urban books serve as surrogates, allowing her to experience things that she does not want to experience in her actual life: "In everything I read, I like stuff that I don't like in my life." Bobbie similarly describes urban books as a means to get her "thuggish feeling out of the way. I put myself where the characters are," she explains, "so it's like okay, you're dealing drugs, I'm dealing drugs. You're killing people, I'm killing people. But I wouldn't really be doing it, you know what I'm saying? I'm just standing back there watching what you're doing."

The genre also offers opportunities for vicarious pleasure through its frequent depiction of African American characters who resist or undermine the legal, political, and economic power of whites. Only a few women openly acknowledged experiencing such pleasure, but I suspect that my presence as a white authority figure deterred others from sharing similar responses. Monique, who always spoke with great candor, readily asserted that she enjoys "rooting for the bad guy . . . the underdog, or the guy that they think is a threat." In her view, the underdog in urban books is typically the male drug dealer or his family; it can be anyone who experiences great loss but "keeps pushing" and emerges "still breathing." Rooting for these underdogs seems important to Monique because she believes that members of dominant white culture "are pleased as long as they see that you're not living up to your potential, but as soon as they feel like you're starting to gain an edge . . . that's when all the problems start." Discussing Teri Woods's 2003 novel, *Dutch*, Darlene likewise conveyed a sense of delight in recounting the protagonist's ability to escape punishment. "Dutch is just this drug lord right now, and many people praises him," she explained. "But also many people hate him because of the murders he has committed. And then he ends up where he's in the courtroom and the judge is sentencing him, and he got these three girls that's on his team that's gonna come and rescue him from this courtroom before the judge sentences him to life or even to death." When I asked whether Dutch manages to escape, Darlene replied, "Yes! That's what's so awesome about the book! I can't wait to read part 2. I mean, it's make-believe, but you know, everybody loves Dutch."

For women with middle-class backgrounds, urban fiction can provide a vicarious experience of—or association with—a world that seems more "real," gritty, or authentic than the world represented by the suburbs. Bobbie, who grew up in a black, middle-class, suburban household, acknowledges that urban books depict "a life that I've never personally lived," yet she values them because they portray a "real" side of life that gets overlooked in cultural representations such as *Pretty Woman* and "fairy tales like the Huxtable family" from *The Cosby Show*.[17] Referencing *Pretty Woman*, Bobbie insists that "nobody lives this life," but she says of urban fiction, "I don't feel like I'm in a fantasy world reading that. I don't feel like I'm a six-year-old. . . . I'm into things that faces reality because even though I would love to live in a rose-colored glass world, I am a realist so I know that this happens." For Cassandra, who was raised in what she calls a "stuffy, sheltered" environment, urban books seem to buttress her sense of racial authenticity or affiliation with street culture. In discussing her passion for urban fiction, she draws a sharp distinction between her own fluency in the language and culture of the street, and the cultural illiteracy of her "clueless" parents and "straight-laced" white women—like me, she notes—who need explanations of urban vocabulary. Signaling her eagerness to affiliate herself with urban culture, Cassandra signed up for my study in order to increase her interactions with women who read and own urban books.

Other readers emphasize their distance from the lifestyle depicted in urban fiction and suggest that the books foster their understanding of, and identification with, women whose experiences seem to be reflected in the texts. Wendy says of her fellow prisoners, "There's no way on God's green earth I would have ever been around any of these people outside of prison." Because urban books—like the people around her—have a "hustler, ghetto-type feel," Wendy uses them to understand why her fellow prisoners behave as they do. "In some way," she claims, "I'm doing research." Valhalla, a white woman who grew up in upper middle-class suburbs, likewise explains that she reads urban books to gain "empathy" and "understanding" for people whose lives are "so far from anything I've ever known." When she cannot understand the books' vernacular speech, Valhalla asks her roommate to "translate" it for her. "I don't know nothing about pimps and the crack dealers on the corner and placing all your happiness on how nice your boobs and fur coat is," she acknowledges, "but it's interesting."

Rescripting the American Dream

During one of our group discussions, Kaye characterized urban fiction in these terms: "Hustling is always gonna be on your mind. It's the American dream to live comfortably and to take care of your own. These books are about another way of getting the American dream than the honest way." Kaye's insightful comment highlights the capitalist ideology that undergirds urban fiction. The books insistently focus on the moneymaking prowess of characters and their right to a bigger slice of the economic pie. The desire for class ascendancy is racialized, with African Americans trying to wrest from whites the wealth and privilege that whites have unfairly hoarded. Yet this desire is also the primary motivation for the intraracial conflicts in the novels, and it serves as a point of cross-racial identification for many white readers. For instance, a young white woman named Angel observes, "Some [people] say white people can get a job, get all the breaks, and go to rehab, but if you're mixed, or black, or Spanish, you don't get that. But [those people] don't understand that people of all races have different lifestyles. . . . I'm not from a rich family. The street is what I know." In plotting stories of lower-class African Americans rising to prosperity, urban fiction may tap into what Claudia Tate calls the "political desire" of readers; it may reflect readers' "racial and gender aspirations to live in a world where such stories [are] possible."[18]

Indeed, women prisoners who have struggled for economic survival often appreciate the genre's over-the-top portrayals of characters' moneymaking abilities and lavish lifestyles. Participating vicariously in the exciting and luxurious lives of the characters is some women's favorite aspect of reading urban fiction. Says Charmaine, a twenty-seven-year-old African American woman, "Fast lives, fast money. Shopping, new cars every week. That's what makes them attractive." As some prisoners fear, urban books can fuel the fantasy that one might actually achieve the kind of easy wealth that protagonists enjoy. For instance, Touché— an African American woman who has written three urban books—recounted in an individual interview that she was attracted to the genre because of the "flashy" look of the men and women depicted on the covers. "They represented money to me," she explained. "Some type of hustle was transpiring and some money was being made."[19] Touché also acknowledged that writing urban books sometimes reactivates her desire to make fast money: "Talking about my crimes gets me hyped, and the hype happened as I was writing my book." Furthermore, she recognizes that her books' emphases on designer clothing and the protagonists' moneymaking prowess make readers "want material stuff. A few [incarcerated] women have said they wish they were with me at the time I was out there," Touché explained. "They wanted clothes and jewelry and weren't seeing that in their own hustle, so they want to be a part of mine."

Soso is a reader who particularly enjoys "the money part" of urban books. On a few occasions, she has tried to discern whether a particular story is "a myth" and whether the author "hyped it up a little" to make it "more exciting in the book than in real life." Most often, however, Soso expresses her desire to replicate the characters' ability to make fast money. "It excites me to read them," she says of urban books. "I like how they're hustlers, how they con someone. I look at all this money they're making. It gives me a feeling of oh man, is it that easy? I could have tried that!" During our discussion of Shannon Holmes's *Bad Girlz*—which she read in its entirety four times in a row—Soso acknowledged, "When I'm reading, I can't wait to see the dollar signs. They made money just like that! I wish I had options like that for fast money, with no strings attached." *Bad Girlz* features Tender and Goldie, two young women who save themselves from homelessness by becoming wealthy strippers and prostitutes. When other women in the discussion group tried to imagine how Tender and Goldie might have survived without hustling, Soso conceded, "I can't see an alternative. They would just move from house to house being used up." During a group discussion of Danielle Santiago's *Grindin'*—which begins with the exciting adventures of two female hustlers who seduce, drug, and rob extremely wealthy white men— Soso similarly commented, "I wish I could do that, make this much money. . . . I'm older now and I can't get all dressed up like they did and get men. But they really were getting paid! They got $100,000 from that man! . . . You take one weekend trip and you're set. I'm thinking if I was their age, I'd get money like they were getting and sit back and relax. You give men drinks and get them high and get their money! I wouldn't have to worry about hustling." For Soso, the excitement of dwelling in "the money part" of urban books may reflect her desire "to posit an alternative reality which cannot be fully contained in the novels' construction of the real."[20]

Other women communicate a tension between their lingering hope that they might replicate the wealth and power that characters achieve and their sense that the books may present an unrealistic picture of such power. A Latina named Marisa experiences a vicarious rush from sharing in the adventures of female hustlers, particularly since she suffers from debilitating rheumatoid arthritis. "I put myself in their shoes," she explains. "With all the details about sex, I get those feelings. If they have money in their hands, if they're taking drugs, I feel it. I get that thing in my stomach to want to go [double] the money or do heroin. . . . I want money and drugs to relieve my pain and so I can do whatever I want physically." At the same time, however, Marisa tries to inject some realism into the portrayals of the protagonists, tempering her envy of their hustling prowess by wondering how they might fare if they put themselves in *her* shoes as a forty-six-year-old, struggling mother. "There are never urban books about women my age who struggle," she observes. "They're always young and beautiful. . . . One character has six abortions. What if she kept one or two [babies]? . . . I wish they had babies in the beginning [of the book], because as a mother, it would slow them down some."

While inhabiting the alluring worlds that urban fiction conjures, some women draw a clear distinction between the books' fantastic and realistic elements. "You have to know where to draw the line from fantasy to reality," Cassandra asserts. Urban books serve as "get-away books" that evoke "a nice, kinda lightweight fantasy-type world," she explains, but she would never want to experience the real dangers that attend such a lifestyle. Cassandra acknowledges that urban fiction writers "stretch" the truth in depicting drug dealers who always sell huge quantities of drugs and make enormous profits, and they "bring out a little extra umph just so they can keep you glued to the pages." Dismissing the concern that reading such books will make women "want to go out and commit crimes," Cassandra defends urban fiction as "just fun entertainment. Reading it's just like a fantasy type thing. . . . It's not like watching 'Thelma and Louise' and then you go out robbing."[21] Sahara, a forty-six-year-old white woman, emphasizes that urban books offer an unrealistic portrait of drug dealing. "The books focus so much on money and the lifestyle that they might have people thinking they can live like that," she explains. "But the dealers I know are just making it. They don't have a Benz and millionaire houses and wads of cash. That's fantasy! You hardly ever see a drug dealer living like that. They're in cartels, not in inner-city Philly!"

Over the course of the group discussions, I began to recognize that a few urban books present more opportunities than others for contextualizing characters' actions in relation to broader social and political issues. For instance, Sister Souljah's *The Coldest Winter Ever* and Danielle Santiago's *Grindin'* generate divergent interpretive possibilities through their depictions of the drug trade. Although *The Coldest Winter Ever* is often deemed the progenitor of contemporary urban fiction, it differs from most of its literary offspring in explicitly critiquing the drug trade for spawning destruction and ruthless competition within the African American community. *Grindin'* seems more typical of the urban fiction genre in its legitimization of the drug trade as a means of "stackin' for the future" and its endorsement of endless revenge—the ethos of "Fuck with mines and I will annihilate yours."[22] In comparing *The Coldest Winter Ever* and *Grindin'*, I do not mean to champion Sister Souljah's novel as the ideal to which urban fiction should aspire. In fact, I find problematic the novel's homophobic vision of the monogamous, heterosexual, male-governed family as the salvation of the African American community. The comparison nonetheless seems instructive because it draws attention to the kinds of interpretive possibilities that urban books do and do not open up for readers.[23]

The Coldest Winter Ever features Winter Santiaga, a selfish young woman whose father is an extremely wealthy drug kingpin. When Winter's father gets arrested, her mother becomes addicted to crack, her younger sisters end up in foster care, and Winter herself engages in ruthless criminal activity that lands her in prison. Winter nonetheless valorizes her father's criminal activity in these terms: "He got at least *twenty years of good high living* out of the business" while a "regular nigga worked all week for change to get to work plus a beer to forget about how hard he worked." Winter also contends that drug dealers help America "to be rich" and employ "half the men in the ghetto," who otherwise cannot get jobs. Sister Souljah—who appears as a character in the novel—counters this logic, however, by arguing that "drugs is a government game. A way to rob us of our best black men, our army. Everyone who plays the game loses. Then they get you right back where we started, in slavery! Then they get to say 'This time you did it to yourself.'" *The Coldest Winter Ever* reinforces this perspective in an appendix—which has no parallel among other urban books—that includes detailed analyses of the novel's main characters, as well as Sister Souljah's responses to ten interview questions.[24]

As women debated the merits of Winter's logic during our group discussions, some argued that "the good living, the cars, the clothes, the jewels, all that stuff—I don't think it was worth it," while others maintained that it would be worth spending time in prison if you made a million dollars, "as opposed to struggling until you're seventy-five and you never get a million dollars." All of the women felt persuaded, however, by Sister Souljah's argument that the drug trade is a form of modern-day slavery. Her argument prompted Monique to reflect on her own role in enslaving others through selling drugs: "You're putting boundaries and holds on a whole 'nother being because when you do sell the drugs . . . you limit other people's ability to do certain things, whether it's provide for their family, take care of theirself, or get an education because they're just gonna continue to chase that high, you know. Instead of just having them straight put shackles on us and take us to another country and put us to work, we're shackling ourself." Valhalla reflected that drug dealers themselves become slaves because "they don't prepare for anything else" and then "they can't get out of it; they're trapped." *The Coldest Winter Ever* thus opened up possibilities for women to reflect critically on commonsense justifications of the drug trade.

By contrast, Danielle Santiago's *Grindin'* implicitly justifies participation in the drug trade as necessary for achieving economic success. Although Chaz, the protagonist's boyfriend, has suffered because of his mother's drug addiction, *Grindin'* does not critique his role as a drug seller. In fact, when Chaz asks if the protagonist, Kennedy, can live with the fact that he's going to stay in the game, Kennedy says, "I guess I don't have a choice if I want to be with you."[25] For some readers, the novel's endorsement of a ruthless capitalist ideology accords with their sense of what is required for success in a fiercely competitive world. During a group discussion, Kaye argued that Chaz "won't make someone else's mother stop using if he stops selling. The dealers are not the ones making the problem." Drawing on media representations of the high cost of being a star, several women also asserted that despite Chaz's huge success as a rap star, he must continue selling drugs in order to have enough money. "After they pay for the videos and all that, stars don't have any money," Nez argued. "That lifestyle's expensive. So Chaz had to hustle." Readers in the group agreed, moreover, that Kennedy had no choice but to allow Chaz to continue selling drugs because she "gets a lot of money from him" and understands that "once you see how much money you can make, it's hard to let go." For women who look to urban fiction as a reflection of the real world, *Grindin'* thus generates few possibilities for imagining employment options that do not revolve around "the game." In fact, Nez—who wants to "go legit" upon her release from prison—has learned from *Grindin'* that strip clubs have become popular, so she plans to open a business that can supply strip clubs with sex toys and exotic costumes.

The constructions of the drug trade in *The Coldest Winter Ever* and *Grindin'* are yoked to their constructions of education. *The Coldest Winter Ever* depicts Sister Souljah, the character, as an avid reader who is always surrounded by books, and it emphasizes that a former drug dealer named Midnight is able to leave the game because he has educated himself. The narrator specifies that Midnight has read books that ostensibly deepen his awareness of his position as a black man in a racist society: Frantz Fanon's *The Wretched of the Earth*, which critiques colonial power; Sun-Tzu's *The Art of War*, which highlights strategies for dealing with competition and conflict; and Karl Evanzz's *The Judas Factor: The Plot to Kill Malcolm X*, which chronicles the history of the Black Power movement and CIA involvement in the assassination of Malcolm X. In their readings of *The Coldest Winter Ever*, women in my study tend to follow the novel's lead in emphasizing that Midnight's education enables his escape from a criminal lifestyle, while Winter's lack of education keeps her wedded to the game. Such a perspective resonates with women who prioritize education in their own efforts to leave crime behind.

At the other end of the spectrum, Santiago's *Grindin'* suggests that higher education leads to a false sense of superiority and a distance from the realities that most black people face. Kennedy refers to her aunt who has a master's degree as a "snooty rich know-it-all . . . whom no one got along with," and she tells her aunt to take her "snooty, I-got-my-master's-degree shit back to Queens and shove it up [her] tight ass!" Later in the novel, Kennedy has a meeting with Brooke, a "black yuppie" marketing executive who graduated from Yale University and believes "that she [i]s better than most black women." Kennedy says to Brooke, "Your skin may be black, but you don't know shit about being *black*."[26] During the group discussion of *Grindin'*, women indicated that Kennedy's comments resonate with their own suspicion that education can distance people from their communities and from the realities of everyday life. My status as a middle-class university professor and the fact that most of the women had dropped out of high school seemed to inflect this conversation in significant ways. Nez and Soso discussed the characters' education levels in ways that enabled them to feel empowered. "Kennedy could survive in Brooke's world but Brooke couldn't survive in Kennedy's world," Nez argued, suggesting that "street smarts" are more versatile than formal education. She and Soso then characterized well-educated people as emotionally fragile. "They have breakdowns. They're the ones who turn to drugs," Nez said, and Soso added, "They always have complicated problems in their lives." Soso went on to suggest that educated people are prone to dissimulation and likely to conceal who they really are—they "wear masks"— while "people from the projects just do what they know how to do."[27]

Kaye responded to Kennedy's comments by announcing, "I still want education" and by emphasizing her own ability to be "a chameleon" and function in "two different worlds." "I can talk business but I can also swear with the best sailor," she asserted. Kaye nonetheless drew attention to the gulf between Brooke's experiences and her own. "I'm from the projects," she emphasized, adding that Brooke "probably never had to endure life or steal something to survive. Students from Yale think they're the best and they get the top jobs." This sense that those who "never had to endure life . . . get the top jobs" undergirds the suggestion, in many urban books, that people from the projects must participate in crime in order to succeed. On one level, then, *Grindin'* speaks to the disparity that exists between the opportunities that are available to some readers and to more privileged and well-educated people. On another level, however, the novel provides few possibilities for readers to gain new information about alternative worlds and subject positions that they might inhabit. As they invoke the American dream, urban books thus prompt some readers to grapple with issues of power and privilege, yet they often reinforce ideologies that help to maintain current structures of inequality.[28]

Gender and Power

Although the gender balance of contemporary urban fiction has begun to shift, with more male writers and readers arriving on the scene, the genre has been dominated by female writers and readers since it started to gain prominence in the late 1990s. The female gendering of urban books seems evident in their frequent focus on the violence that female characters sustain at the hands of their boyfriends and husbands. Most often, the books depict women who endure physical, emotional, and sexual abuse from their male partners because they fear losing the financial security that the men provide. Although most books implicitly and sometimes explicitly critique violence against women, some books threaten to naturalize and sensationalize such violence with their extreme and graphic portrayals of men's brutal treatment of women.[29]

In discussing urban fiction, several women note that they cry a lot or feel "very emotional" or "extremely sad" when reading about female characters' experiences of gendered violence. As with the narratives of victimization that I examined in Chapter 3, readers often draw direct correlations between their own and the protagonists' experiences of being raped or abused, and some women insist that the authors must be depicting experiences that they themselves have sustained. Books that offer particularly graphic depictions of violence against women prompt some readers to assert their own capacity for resisting violence. Arguing for the importance of such depictions, Bobbie said during a group discussion, "Number one, it's life. And number two, when I read stuff like that, it teaches me what not to do. I'm not gonna go get involved with a man that wants to whup my ass like that all the time, or hold a gun to my head, or put a gun in my mouth. No. I'm not gonna be bothered with you. You only got one chance to do that to me and I'm outta here, for real." Noting that "some women allow that kind of treatment," Bobbie insisted, "I don't care how much money you have. You are not going to mistreat me! . . . I won't allow that to happen to me anymore. And if I see it happening to me, I know how to get out of it. I know how to walk away."

As I indicated in my overview of the genre, urban books frequently conclude with the female protagonist falling in love with a man—typically a former or current drug dealer—who is highly wealthy and powerful, yet gentle, sensitive, and committed to fulfilling all of her economic, emotional, and sexual needs. Aside from comments by a few women that they either liked a book's happy ending or found it "kind of corny," women prisoners paid strikingly little attention to the books' emphases on "patriarchal responsibility" and long-term heterosexual unions.[30] Their apparent lack of interest in such outcomes may stem from the fact that these women have very different goals in mind when it comes to relationships with men. While urban books often emphasize female characters' ultimate financial and emotional dependence on men, many women in prison are actively working to achieve a sense of emotional independence from men, and many are well aware of the liabilities of financial reliance on male partners. Readers involved in my study were thus more inclined to critique female characters' dependence on men than to celebrate urban books' romantic conclusions. As Kaye commented, "Women sell themselves short. Women do everything for money. Being wifey is all that matters.[31] Just bring me diamonds and cars and I don't care how much you run around. . . . It's messed up that men treat us that way, but they only do what we allow them to do."

Moreover, readers often showed greater interest in the relationships among female characters than in their romantic, heterosexual relationships. In sharp contrast to many urban books, which typically depict women as locked in bitter competition with one another, *The Coldest Winter Ever* explicitly addresses issues of female power, cooperation, and solidarity. The character Sister Souljah holds meetings with young women during which she encourages them to educate themselves, cultivate their inner rather than outer beauty, gain control over their own lives, and work together rather than constantly competing. Sister Souljah asks each woman to state what she believes and then asks questions such as "What is so important to you that you would risk your life for it. Fight for it, die for it?"[32] During our group discussions of *The Coldest Winter Ever*, several women commented that these meetings made them think about how they are raising their daughters and inspired them to tell their daughters, "You're beautiful, you're smart, and not just the outer beauty." In Jacqueline's view, Sister Souljah teaches women "to realize who they are, and the strength that they really do have. And stop being an object for men."

Readers were less persuaded, however, by Sister Souljah's call for women to cooperate with one another. Although they found the idea appealing, they described such cooperation as an impossible ideal, emphasizing the extreme difficulty of learning to trust one another and work together in prison. In Miekal's words, "So many people jack you around. I mean, one after another after another after another. . . . When I came in here, I was not like this. I was *made* to be like this. I was too giving, you know, and I got screwed." Monique reflected on Sister Souljah's vision in these terms: "For me, her perspective is way out of line because it's not reality. . . . I think she's a hopeful type of person like Malcolm X, like Martin Luther King. Everybody wanted peace, and everybody wanted everybody to mesh together, and let's all just be one world. But reality is not gonna strike it like that because people tend to play up other people's downfalls." Both Miekal and Monique went on to describe how women who seemed like family have abandoned them since they came to prison. Underscoring the sense of isolation and atomization that imprisonment breeds, Monique concluded, "Yeah, I was hopeful like [Sister Souljah] was. . . . But as soon as real shit sets in, reality hits, and then you see people's true colors. . . . Everything that we build is built for self now, you know what I mean?"

Grindin', which pits female characters against each other in vicious competition for men's financial patronage, resonates more with some readers' sense that "women are against each other," that "women are jealous, devious, and envious," and that "women are always fighting about sleeping with another man." This sense of women's fierce rivalries serves as an important context for understanding how some readers navigate the book's contradictory messages about violence against women. Early in *Grindin'*, a protagonist named Nina is beaten to death by her abusive boyfriend, and later in the novel, Kennedy is brutally beaten by Chaz's rivals, causing her to miscarry and sustain an emotional trauma that requires a year of recovery. Women responded very emotionally to these scenes. Nez, for instance, shared that she "couldn't stop crying" in reading Nina's story and insisted, "Nina said she provoked him, but he still had no right to put his hands on her." At the same time, however, *Grindin'* implicitly supports the view that Chaz should be violent toward Ria, the mother of his child. As Chaz's sister puts it, Ria "is one them hos a man have to beat. I told him a long time ago to punch that bitch in her face. That's the problem now. She knows he won't fuck her up. That's why she keeps on disrespecting him."[33]

Women in the group unanimously agreed with the novel's attitude toward Ria. Although Nez insisted that Nina's boyfriend had no right to hurt her even if she provoked him, she argued that Ria "is asking for it" and that Chaz "should have stopped her the first time." Nez's statements seem contradictory at first, yet they illustrate how she and other readers construct an ethics of interpersonal relations in their interpretations of *Grindin'*. According to Nez, Nina's unjust subjection to male violence and Chaz's right to be violent toward Ria represent "two different situations." In her view, Ria has "handled the situation wrong" and behaved highly unethically toward her rival, Kennedy, even though Kennedy helped to care for Ria's children on a few occasions. Kaye argued that some women will take advantage of men and "do anything" because they know that these men "will never put their hands" on them. Chaz should "put his foot down," Kaye insisted, because Ria "spanked his butt." Soso agreed that Chaz "should have dealt with" Ria because "Kennedy didn't deserve" Ria's poor treatment. I felt uncomfortable with these sentiments during the discussion because I am personally averse to endorsing violence as retaliation. In reflecting on the conversation, however, I have come to recognize the readers' responses as part of their efforts to navigate a complex moral universe. Rather than simply presuming women's status as victims of male power, these readers evaluate female characters' adherence to broader standards of mutuality and ethical treatment. Within such a framework, interpreting fierce rivalries among female characters entails scrutinizing how particular characters handle issues of reciprocity, jealousy, boundary setting, loyalty, responsibility, and friendship.

Writerly Reading Practices

As we have seen, urban books reflect settings and social contexts with which many readers are familiar. Their social realism is not matched, however, by psychological realism; in other words, many of the books are plot-driven rather than character-driven, and their thin character portrayals offer few insights into the psychology, motivations, or internal struggles of the protagonists. On a few occasions, women involved in my study expressed disappointment with the portrayal of characters in particular books. During one group's discussion of *The Coldest Winter Ever*, for instance, most of the participants were staunchly defending the novel's realism. "I don't think anything is written that's more real than what Sister Souljah wrote," Jacqueline asserted. She went on to insist, "For people who have *lived* this, okay, they can look at this book and be like, 'Wow, this is me!' And for people who don't have any knowledge of what goes on in this world, this is what this book is telling you. This is how it goes down! This is life! This is it! So I think she did a wonderful job enlightening the public as far as drugs!" Sissy, however, voiced her strong dislike of *The Coldest Winter Ever*, noting a discrepancy between the novel's monochromatic character portrayals and Sister Souljah's more nuanced and thorough analyses of the characters in the appendix. Referencing the novel's depiction of Winter's mother, Sissy argued, "I'm quite sure she had thoughts of what could have been and should have been, but [Sister Souljah] didn't bring those to life. [The novel] wasn't put together because she talks about all that at the end of the book when she could have incorporated some of that into her book to bring out the character of the people . . . and bring us to a better understanding."

Whereas Sissy expressed a desire for a deeper understanding of the characters, many women—including Jacqueline—respond to urban books as if they offered deeper character portraits than they do. These readers seem to assume such a close proximity between their own and the characters' experiences that they use urban books as a template, a paint-by-numbers canvas that allows them to fill in characters' portraits with their own psychological interiority. These women assume authorial agency by essentially writing themselves into the narratives, adding layers of complexity and sometimes putting the stories to alternative uses. In this sense, the women engage in what José Esteban Muñoz calls a practice of "disidentification," which entails "tactically and simultaneously work[ing] on, with, and against a cultural form" in order to "invest it with new life."[34]

For some women, performing writerly readings of urban books entails intuiting connections between their own and the characters' behaviors and attributes. Several women engaged in such critical self-reflection as they analyzed Winter. As we saw in Interlude 1, Denise acknowledged, "I saw the way I raised my children in each one of those characters. . . . I realized that I'm creating a Winter." Olivia explained that Winter "irritated" her, but she feels "a bond with her" because Winter refused to listen to others' advice, much like Olivia did when she was younger. Mildred admonished herself for the fact that like Winter, who started "taking the role of the parent" when her father was in prison, her own son had to "take the role as a parent" because Mildred was not around to raise him. Barbara emphasized how much it bothered her to read about Winter selling crack to her own mother: "I sold drugs to my old man's mom! I'm no better than this woman in this book! It makes me sick to think that I did that!" Barbara then added, "I'm getting ready to leave in thirteen days, and I'm scared shitless because I don't want to be a Winter. I have to start all over and I'm scared, because all I know was to sell drugs, trick, rob, steal, be a mule. I'm not gonna know how to act to have a real life. This book was so real for me because somewhere in this book that was me."

Despite their thinly drawn characters, Tu-Shonda Whitaker's *Flip Side of the Game* (2004) and its sequel, *Game Over* (2004), also prompted in some readers a deep sense of connection with the characters that led them to reflect on their own actions and relationships. Whitaker's novels focus on Vera Wright-Turner, a young woman who is struggling to develop a healthy relationship with her mother and with a man who wants to marry her. Vera's mother, Rowanda, tried to abandon her when she was born by placing her in a trash can; Rowanda was fifteen years old and addicted to crack, and she did not believe that she could provide a good home for her daughter. Vera was rescued and raised by her aunt, and during the present time of the novels, she is learning to forgive her mother— who is recovering from her addiction—and to accept responsibility for her own choices and actions. Vera is also learning how to value herself enough to receive love from Taj Bennett, a former drug dealer who has become an upstanding doctor. Whitaker's books are the ones that I had to remove immediately from the Ohio prison grounds, a fact that seems especially ironic given that women view the novels as different—and less exciting—than other urban books because Vera is "college educated, she has her own business, and she doesn't live a sleazy lifestyle."

Vera's struggles with her mother led many women to reflect on the long-term effects of their own relationships with their mothers and on their own roles as mothers. Nena, who engages intensely with every urban book that she reads, identified so strongly with Vera's feelings of neglect from her mother *and* with Rowanda's neglect of her daughter that she said of Whitaker's novels, "On a scale of one to ten, I'd rate these books a twenty!" Although she deeply sympathizes with Vera, Nena said during a group discussion, "The number one thing is how [the books] make you think about choice. I have choices to make in my future. One bad choice will bring me back here. It's up to us. We can't blame others for our consequences." Referring to Vera's tendency to blame Rowanda for her problems, Nena added, "I could have just kicked her ass sometimes. I wouldn't have such a strong opinion if I hadn't experienced it. But when I've experienced 98 percent of the book—all the consequences, wanting to kill myself, all her thoughts and feelings—I could really relate to her. It helps me keep my own head on straight." Just as Vera had to learn that "she's not eight years old," Nena acknowledged that she is learning to view herself as "a twenty-nine-year-old woman and not a three-year-old. I'm learning to get comfortable in my own skin." Later in the conversation, Nena also drew parallels between the guilt and shame that Vera feels for being Rowanda's daughter and the feelings that her own son may have toward her, particularly since he was born addicted to heroin. Furthermore, referencing Vera's decision to monitor her mother through a hidden camera while she is babysitting Vera's child, Nena shared, "I was thinking about how I would feel as an addict, like they're never gonna trust me. I would be upset and hurt. But then I flipped the script and realized I was only clean eight out of twenty-nine years of my life. I've been in mental hospitals, rehab, and every time I said, 'I'm gonna be mature, etc., etc.,' and every time I got high." Reaffirming her resolve to follow a new path, Nena concluded, "My family abandoned me, but I can't change anyone but me."

Urban fiction writers often present their books as cautionary tales, and in so doing, they implicitly and sometimes explicitly invite readers to write themselves into the narrative. According to Noire, author of well-known urban books such as *G-Spot: An Urban Erotic Tale* (2005) and *Candy Licker: An Urban Erotic Tale* (2005), "I show people exactly what happens when they choose that fast, get-money, grimy life, and that's what real street fiction is all about. I have a lot of teenage girls who email me and say they've learned a lot just from reading my books, and that way they don't have to go out there and experience all of that pain and drama for themselves." In *Let That Be the Reason* (2002), author Vickie Stringer includes an afterword in which she suggests that her fictional tale directly reflects her actual experiences. "I've exposed myself with the prayer that my life can be used as an example to warn others of the awful dangers of the drug Game," she writes. "Do not allow my mistakes to become yours. Please become cognizant. Your awareness may save someone else." Stringer also asks for forgiveness from her family, community, and the addicts to whom she sold drugs, claiming, "I knew not the extent to what I did."[35]

In discussing *Let That Be the Reason*, a young African American woman named Natasha emphasizes what she has learned from comparing her own life and Stringer's. She particularly values Stringer's eventual realization that she should "not put everything into a guy" and that "it's more important to be a mother." Stringer's book offers "a lot of encouragement to a lot of women," Natasha explains, "'cause it's a true book that somebody had done been there, done that, wrote it." When reading urban books as cautionary tales, other readers note that "the glamorous life" does not last, and that characters who commit crimes or do wrong to others "reap what they sow" and "get back three times what [they] gave." Whereas "rich people books" by authors such as Jackie Collins regularly portray characters who "break law after law after law, but they never get caught," urban books always remind readers that "you have to deal with the police and prison." Angel explains that urban books teach her about "how people can come up out of the ghetto and make something of themselves," but if they "step on" others along the way, their "past catches up with them eventually." Although she acknowledges that some readers might conclude from reading urban books that "if you're into the fast life, there's no escape," Angel conforms the books to her own purposes by insisting that "the message of the books is change. You just can't run from your past. You have to make your past right, try to apologize and ask for forgiveness. There *is* hope. You *can* change."

Other women likewise perform acts of disidentification as they read urban fiction, working on, with, and against the books in order to suit their own needs. During one group's discussion of Whitaker's *Flip Side of the Game* and *Game Over*, Tyra drew attention to the books' quasi-obsessive emphases on brand-name clothing, cars, and furniture. Vera is "too materialistic," she argued, and the novels focus excessively on the fact that she is "wearing Prada" or sitting "on a Coach red leather sofa." In responding to Tyra's critique, some other readers insisted that the novels offer a realistic representation of life in the ghetto. According to Mocha, "A lot of people are materialistic that's from the ghetto. . . . That's what everybody looks up to, the Donna Karan, the JLo, the Sean John." Monique, who was deeply invested in urban fiction at the time of the conversation, performed a particularly striking disidentificatory reading by insisting that Whitaker's inclusion of brand names merely represents effective description. Drawing comparisons with writers outside the urban fiction genre, Monique argued, "The writer was just very detailed in all of her descriptions . . . so you could just visualize for yourself and take a walk with [Vera]. . . . It's not necessarily being materialistic, but they just describe it to a 'T' so you can get a feel for what they want you to feel. . . . I've read books where I never attached to the book because they didn't put me in that walk with them."

Although Monique subsequently stopped reading urban books, her efforts to deflect Tyra's critique, and thereby defend urban fiction as a whole, reflect her appreciation for the genre. Urban books have been important to Monique because they contribute to her focus on "getting [her]self together." She finds Whitaker's novels inspiring, for instance, because they "tell you the real deal while also showing you . . . that you can make a better life for yourself." Monique likes that Vera "came from a trash bag, and her mother was strung out, but she also owned her own business and got herself together and wasn't using that as a crutch. She used that as a building tool. Through all her struggles and her strifes and her history and her past, she overcame that, and she built a firm foundation with her husband, who's educated." Even when Vera was trading sexual favors for men's financial support, "she didn't just go and buy cars and go to clubs," Monique noted. "She went to college. . . . She had a business. . . . So I respect her hand and how she played it." Because she is struggling to develop a good relationship with her own mother, Monique also deeply admires Vera's efforts to repair her relationship with her mother. Monique's disidentificatory reading of Whitaker's novels thus enabled her to protect a genre that has played a crucial role in her efforts to make positive changes in her life.

Women whose racial and class positions are not represented by the characters in urban books sometimes perform disidentificatory readings in an effort to make the texts more meaningful. During one group's discussion of *The Coldest Winter Ever*, Marlena—a twenty-four-year-old white woman who was raised in an upper middle-class family—acknowledged that the novel "frustrated the hell out of [her]" because she wanted it to reflect her own experiences of selling and using prescription drugs. Insisting, "I am no better than a heroin addict," Marlena explained that "the whole situation in this book made me mad because they're just portraying it that it happens in the ghetto like that. No, it happens in the suburbs like that, and it happens to rich families and poor families. . . . It was so centered on the slang and stuff like that that I just didn't understand it, and I wanted to, because it could happen to your all white, Republican family from some uppity snooty town, too." Marlena subsequently added that *The Coldest Winter Ever* "really hit a nerve" because her brother had just been charged with a serious drug offense in a "snooty" town. Her frustrations with *The Coldest Winter Ever* suggest that Marlena may desire a cross-racial, cross-class identification with other women who have been involved with drugs, a desire that Sister Souljah's novel ultimately did not satisfy.

As writerly readers of urban fiction, women prisoners also formulate their own standards of literary excellence and make discernments about the quality of particular texts. Readers sometimes argue that a book is particularly "exciting," "deep," "overrated," "all-out," "corny," or "too much." Some women who read a variety of genres note their preference for the direct writing style that urban books employ. Drawing a distinction between the spare writing style evident in most urban books and the more descriptive literary style of Eric Jerome Dickey's novels—such as *Milk in My Coffee, The Other Woman,* and *Thieves' Paradise*—Miekal says of Dickey, "He's too drawn out for me. He got to tell you the painting on the wall was this and the coffee table had the candles and the placemats, and the floor had the burgundy carpet. . . . By the time you finish, you're like, what was the point?" Cassandra draws a humorous distinction between the writing styles of "white folks" and authors of urban fiction. She argues that white authors such as Jackie Collins or Danielle Steel will write, "He laid her down and he stroked her face and looked in her eyes. And the candles were slowly burning and then they made love," while urban fiction authors will simply write, "He was in the shower with her, and he was hittin' her from the back."

In assessing urban books, a few women critique them for their poor editing. A young white woman named Christine notes that urban books are "so poorly edited" that it drives her "crazy." Rose argues that books published by Triple Crown Publications manifest particularly poor editing. As she said of Nikki Turner's first novel, *A Hustler's Wife,* "It's like half the words are misspelled, and I'm like, who wrote this book? . . . I'm real good with language and stuff like that. Like every time I take a test, I score high. I know how paragraphs are supposed to be, where punctuation marks and stuff like that goes. And it was just kind of like everything was all ran together. . . . It was weird. I didn't care for it too much." Although Rose's own comments include nonstandard grammar, she draws on her knowledge of grammar in evaluating the merit of urban books.[36]

Urban fiction inspires such enthusiasm in some readers that they transition from the role of writerly reader to the role of literal author. The genre enables readers to consider their experiences and speech patterns as worthy of representation in a book, and it suggests that readers can become authors simply by writing about what they know. Indeed, many writers of urban books promote a democratization of authorship, inviting their readers to correspond with them and to engage in dialogue about reading and writing. "Some of the authors even ask you do you have a story to tell, or how could you relate to this book," Darlene explains, and "they even say you could write me a letter here and I will respond." Touché, who published her first urban book in 2007 and has two others under contract, began writing after seeking advice from authors Vickie Stringer and Teri Woods.[37] She handwrote her manuscript in pencil, asked another prisoner to type it, and asked her sister to send the manuscript to several publishers whose addresses were listed in the back of urban books.

Darlene, who is currently writing her first book, conveyed great excitement in describing what the process has been like for her. Referencing her recent stint in a segregation cell, she recounted, "I just sat in the hole and wrote a whole 'nother chapter on it in like two and a half days, just nonstop! And I'm using [request forms] and everything 'cause I ran out of paper!" Darlene uses other urban books as a guide for her writing. "You have to get fictional with it a little," she explains, "so I think I've learned a lot from them. . . . But I don't mimic them. I want to put my own little something in it that could stand out different than theirs and stuff. . . . [I'll] say well, damn, this thing in her book was just the bomb! How can I make mine better? So I'll go back and read it like three or four times, but I want mine to be ten times better than hers, the high point of the book. So people can remember and so they can talk about it." Another significant source of inspiration for Darlene is the stories of other women prisoners. "It's some crazy ass stories here to tell, you know what I'm saying?" she says. "And my thing is, they got these movies about 'Prison Break,' even the 'oz' movie thing, but they ain't really did nothing about a woman's point of view of prison yet. . . . The Martha Stewart thing wasn't nothing. Shoot. . . . And [rapper] Lil' Kim . . . she only did ten months, so what would she know for real?" When I asked Darlene how her urban book will end, she replied with a grin, "with Part 2."

"I've Been Down That Road": Moving beyond Urban Fiction

Although women often acknowledge that urban books seem repetitive—"they're mostly the same books with different names" and they depict "the same thing, same thing, over and over and over"—they provide enough entertainment or sustenance for some women to keep reading and rereading them. Other women, however, distance themselves from urban fiction over time. John Frow argues that genres construct "genre-specific worlds" as "a preexisting state of affairs," and they position readers to respond to these worlds in pragmatic and affective ways. Moreover, in bringing various discursive worlds into being, genres "create effects of reality and truth that are central to the ways the world is understood."

In their efforts to pursue a different life path, some prisoners develop a critical stance toward the discursive worlds that urban books conjure, at times moving beyond the genre altogether.[38]

In order to manage their anxieties about the potential negative effects of reading urban books, women sometimes displace or project those anxieties onto other readers. Reading urban books is "good for me" but bad for others, these readers suggest, and they occasionally advocate restricting other women's reading. For instance, although Marisa acknowledges the excitement that she feels when she reads about characters hustling and taking drugs, she expresses concern about her roommate's habit of reading one urban book per day. "It's not good for her to read them," Marisa contends. "She gets excited. It triggers her." Wendy contends that reading urban books is "good" for her—because "it makes you think, 'OK, I'm not gonna do that'"—but the books can be "bad" for others because they glorify the "easy money, fast lifestyle." In projecting their anxieties onto others, readers may also be engaging in what Irving Goffman calls "face-work": efforts to ward off criticism for reading culturally devalued materials. Facework strategies include criticizing devalued materials to others, citing the intellectual value of the materials, and distancing oneself from "typical" readers.[39] Barbara, a white woman who loves urban books yet worries that Christians should not read them, seems to engage in facework as she justifies her practice of reading the books. Although she acknowledges that reading urban fiction helps her "just to release energy and relax," Barbara also argues that such reading serves as important preparation for doing prison ministry with other women. Urban books help her "to really, really feel where these girls come from," she argues, while at the same time reminding her "not to go back out there." Underscoring her lingering fears about the genre, Barbara nonetheless responded, "Definitely not!" when I asked whether she planned to use urban books as part of her ministry. After reading such books, she explained, other women "would go back to that lifestyle!"

Readers who are actively seeking to forgo a criminal lifestyle sometimes develop perspectives that enable them to question the worldviews that urban books construct. In Shannon Holmes's *Bad Girlz*, an older stripper advises the young protagonist, "Use da game as a stepping-stone. Or it'll use you. . . . Make it out da game fo' it's too late."[40] During one group's discussion of the novel, some women argued that this philosophy seems sound, since you can get a car and nice things for your children "in days," rather than struggling for years, and then get out of the game and start your own business. However, a young black woman named Lefty sharply criticized the older stripper, vehemently arguing,

"It shows you how people feel like there's no other way to start a life. But there are so many other routes to get started in a beauty parlor. She shouldn't say use the game as a stepping stone! She should say you should do something else to get started with your life. . . . Work at McDonald's! Get financial aid!" Lefty's comments seem particularly significant because she is incarcerated for several robbery charges and has only recently begun to reassess her own efforts to achieve wealth. Earlier in the conversation, Lefty acknowledged that hustling was "a fun life," but she now realizes, "In a lot of black families, money rules. People are materialistic. They feel that's happiness. But when you meet the Man, none of it matters. . . . A lot of people don't realize that the best things in life cost nothing." This discussion of *Bad Girlz* concluded with the following poignant and good-humored exchange, in which Lefty challenged the novel's framework by offering an alternative vision of what matters:

LEFTY: When you're in jail—I've got robbery cases and bank cases—you think about all the money you got, but it don't be shit now that you're in jail. My Pop-pop said you appreciate all you've got when you work hard for it. He worked and had benefits. It sounds corny but when you experience it, you wish you would have listened. It took years to get what they get in a day, but you probably had something to show for it. And all these people who have SUVs with movie screens and everything else, who wants to watch TV when you're going down the street?
CANDI: She did have big speakers. [laughter]
NENA: When people have a fifteen-inch TV screen in their car, *that's* corny.
BOO: Yeah, you should save that for the house.
LEFTY: You could invest in college, not a TV or a pair of Jordans. I didn't appreciate that before.

Some women ultimately conclude that they must leave urban books behind if they want to embrace a new way of being in the world. Natasha, who first started reading in prison and has focused almost exclusively on urban books, now acknowledges, "The books that I read, they might not be good for me, 'cause they're like violence and sex books . . . and I'm trying to get away from all that." When she was first incarcerated, Natasha found urban books "exciting because what I was reading is what I was, and I wasn't ready to change that environment that I was in." Explaining her current desire to read other kinds of books, she asserts: "I owe myself that. I want to have a better life and a better relation with my family and my kids. I don't want to keep looking over my shoulder worried about going back to prison." Christine, who has read about thirty urban books during her incarceration, similarly explains that she wants to read other kinds of books because she is "getting out of the street mentality" and feels "like a different person." In fact, Christine now believes that urban fiction is not good for incarcerated women because it suggests that "no matter how hard you try to escape" a criminal lifestyle, you will never be able to do so. As Natasha and Christine illustrate, women usually decide to leave urban books behind not because they tire of the narratives but because they want to go somewhere else on their personal journeys; they are looking for other ways to script their own realities and other stories to tell about their lives. In the words of Rose, "If I'm reading to take my mind to another place, obviously I don't want to read the Triple Crown books because I don't want to go to that place. . . . I've been down that road."

"MAYBE YOU should write another book called 'Fear of Books.'" As I reflect on women prisoners' engagements with urban fiction, Lakesha's comment pushes me to reckon with the lingering discomfort that the genre inspires in me. This discomfort does not stem from women prisoners reading these bestselling books. As this chapter illustrates, women read urban fiction in complex and varied ways. Although some urban books script a self-referential universe that provides few avenues for readers to "take [their] mind to another place," women demonstrate resourcefulness and creativity in using the books as tools for lending meaning to their experiences. As they enter the protagonists' stories, women sometimes reflect on their own experiences as children and parents, drug users and drug sellers, victims and perpetrators, and enemies and friends. Some women gain greater self-awareness, learn from the characters' mistakes, increase their sense of agency, and even develop empathy for others. In their group discussions of urban books, readers sometimes push one another to think about important issues such as the ethics of the game, gendered violence, and possibilities for carving out new ways of living. While some women find pleasure and comfort in maintaining a singular focus on urban fiction, others determine that they must leave urban books behind as they seek to rescript their lives. Regardless of the particular outcomes of women's engagements with the genre, I firmly believe that neither penal officials nor literary critics should police these engagements.

Notwithstanding my desire to recognize imprisoned readers' agency, I continue to feel uncomfortable about urban fiction because it reinforces dominant ideologies that fuel conditions of inequality and thereby help to create a pipeline to prisons. Like so many other cultural forms—from true crime books to countless law-and-order television shows such as *Crime Scene Investigation*—urban fiction offers no "trace of an imagination of a society without crime as we know it" and no sense of "a collective fate" or "shared destiny" necessary for imagining a society without crime. Narratives about murder, Sara Knox argues, say "so much about *what a culture knows* and *what it will not let itself know*."[41] By focusing on drug dealing and involvement in "the game" as necessary for gaining a foothold in our racist, capitalist economy, urban books divert attention from our need, as a society, to change the structure of the game and make the playing field more fair. Moreover, in celebrating protagonists' mastery of the game, urban fiction often reinforces an ethic of violence, ruthless competition, materialism, and revenge, thereby occluding possibilities for mutuality and collective efforts to achieve social justice. It bears repeating, however, that this ethic is not unique to urban fiction; the genre is but one manifestation of the sacrificial logic that pervades our culture and governs U.S. penal policy. Our current failure to approach communal safety and well-being from the perspective of social equality and social justice—rather than from the perspective of "Fuck with mines and I will annihilate yours"—represents an impoverishment of our social imagination.[42] This limited social imagination, far more than any book that could make it into prisoners' hands, is what truly warrants fear.

CHAPTER FIVE

To Set the Captives Free

SELF-HELP READING PRACTICES

"A book must be the axe for the frozen sea within us,"
Kafka wrote. Self-help is how we skate.— WENDY KAMINER,
I'm Dysfunctional, You're Dysfunctional

It don't matter if it's foreign to me. If I feel it's going to help
me, I'm going to read it, and I haven't found a book yet that
didn't help me.—ELLEN, Northeast Pre-Release Center

IN WOMEN'S PRISONS, narratives of self-improvement and religious transformation have largely replaced narratives of political transformation, reflecting a broader cultural shift from the politicized climate of collective activism
and social critique during the early 1970s to the self-help climate of the 1980s
and beyond.[1] As Eva Illouz argues in *Saving the Modern Soul: Therapy, Emotions,
and the Culture of Self-Help* (2008), therapeutic discourse has gained primacy
across the spectrum of U.S. social life, from families to prisons to corporations.
Such discourse has become a central means to "express, shape, and guide selfhood" in the United States, Illouz contends, and "self-change is perhaps the
chief source of contemporary moral worth."[2]

Self-help discourse has a Christian inflection in the women's prisons where
I conducted research; indeed, the majority of available self-help books are written by Christian authors and geared toward a Christian audience. As I explained
in Chapter 2, the chaplain's libraries in both the Northeast Pre-Release Center and the State Correctional Institution at Muncy consist entirely of donated
books, most of which come from Christian authors, ministries, churches, and
volunteers. In prisons throughout the country, the decrease in state and federal
funding for rehabilitative programming has been matched by an increase in the

presence of Christian volunteers, reading materials, and educational programs. As a 2007 federal appeals court decision underscored, this influx has meant that some opportunities, privileges, and reading materials are available only to prisoners who are willing to embrace a Christian perspective.[3]

In the Ohio and Pennsylvania prisons, Christian self-help authors who have gained some popularity include T. D. Jakes, Kenneth and Gloria Copeland, Max Lucado, Merlin R. Carrothers, and Joel Osteen. Some women have also developed a fondness for the *Chicken Soup for the Prisoner's Soul* series edited by Jack Canfield, Mark Hansen, and Tom Lagana, which is distributed free to prisoners across the United States.[4] These authors and materials are overshadowed, however, by the tremendous popularity of Joyce Meyer, a world-renowned televangelist, prolific author of 104 books, and keynote speaker at the 2002 Christian Coalition convention.[5] Meyer's popularity among women prisoners stems, in large part, from the widespread availability of her books. Joyce Meyer Ministries has adopted the slogan "By faith and God's grace, we will reach *every nation, every city, every day* through the spoken and written Word." The ministry might well add "every prison"; indeed, its prison outreach group has distributed more than 1.6 million "hygiene gift bags"—each containing soap and/or shampoo and one of Meyer's books—to prisoners in all fifty U.S. states and in twenty-five other countries. "Basic hygiene products, like soap and shampoo, are something most prisoners can't afford," the ministry's website explains, "and they are often the very things that open their hearts to reading the enclosed book." The prison ministry often holds religious services as part of its book distribution, in an effort to bring "eternal freedom" to prisoners.[6] Women incarcerated in Pennsylvania received gift bags from Joyce Meyer in 2006, and many continue to trade the books that they received. Prisoners regularly borrow the books that Meyer has donated to the chaplains' libraries, and some women write to Meyer for free books; they can receive a total of eight free books during their incarceration, chosen from a limited range of Meyer's works. Once they start reading Meyer's books, women often begin buying them through the *Crossroads* Christian book club, and many also subscribe to Meyer's monthly magazine, *Enjoying Everyday Life*.[7]

The popularity of self-help books in prisons generates considerable anxiety among a range of academics. As a colleague asked when I was discussing prisoners' engagements with such books, "Is *this* what's good for them?!" Many critics argue that self-help discourse effects "an individualization of social conflict" by focusing on individual transformation rather than addressing broad-scale political, economic, and social problems. In particular, Christian self-help books suggest "that religion itself is the cure for socioeconomic problems." Other critics argue that "therapism" promotes "emotional self-absorption" and offers "no basis for community" or "model for ethical action in the world."[8] Eva Illouz contends that self-help discourse risks deepening "the predicaments of modern identity" by inviting subjects to view themselves as "a 'sick' self in need of correction and transformation," thereby generating "a narrative structure in which suffering and victimhood actually define the self." Because of the risk of promoting an individualizing and pathologizing framework for understanding crime, some leftist scholars likewise eschew narratives that emphasize prisoners' "individual enlightenment and personal transcendence," calling instead for more politicized narratives like those written by imprisoned radicals such as George Jackson and Angela Davis.[9]

Although such concerns merit consideration, I want to underscore that women prisoners are doing the best that they can with available materials when they engage with self-help discourse. Given that penal systems marginalize radical prisoners and deny women access to reading materials that emphasize structural models of change, books that foreground individual models of change are some of the only available resources.[10] Moreover, because therapy and counseling opportunities are rare in prisons, these women perform therapy on themselves—self-help—with materials that are accessible, often free, and easy to read. Because books by authors such as Joyce Meyer constitute the primary materials available to women for attending to questions of the self, women's preference for self-help books must be understood as a highly conditioned choice, often made in the face of urgent need.[11]

Indeed, the search for self-understanding, growth, and empowerment can feel especially pressing for some prisoners due to their disempowered position in prison, their experiences of disenfranchisement and victimization, and their desire to carve out a different future. With many women in prison, the social and structural conditions that have shaped them as subjects can "be seen through the outlines of impacts suffered"; they register "in a kind of hauntedness, a being weighed down."[12] Yet regardless of the structural causes or political patterns of women's imprisonment, individual women prisoners have to negotiate the daily business of living; they must figure out how to live with themselves and how to live as members of various collectives, including their families and prison communities. Many women feel an urgent need to understand the psychological, emotional, and interpersonal issues that played a role in their crimes, and they often feel a pressing desire for what critics of self-help discourse dismiss as "enlightenment," "correction," and "transformation."

In coming to understand women's practices of self-help reading, I have learned to ask questions such as the following: What makes therapeutic discourse "such a seemingly useful *cultural resource*"? "What are the contexts in which certain ideas about self and self-responsibility become useful? What work is done . . . by regarding [one]self in such full . . . possession of individuality and autonomy?"[13] Narratives of individual responsibility and agency can serve as strategic resources for women as they struggle to overcome addictions, change unproductive thinking patterns or behaviors, or face new emotional, intellectual, or social challenges. Moreover, such narratives can serve as important modes of oppositional consciousness, particularly for those who have experienced marginalization, disenfranchisement, abandonment, and erasure in their families, their communities, and now in the penal system. When others have failed to take responsibility for you—when you have access to few resources and scant emotional and social support—claiming your individual agency can be the first step toward greater empowerment.

In parsing women prisoners' engagements with self-help discourse, I have also become aware that contradictory and confusing notions of the self are often at play in both criticisms and practices of self-help. For instance, Christina Hoff Sommers and Sally Satel claim that therapeutic discourse promotes a conception of Americans as "weak, dependent, . . . never altogether responsible for what they do," and in need of "a vast array of therapists . . . healers, and traumatologists to lead [them] through the trials of everyday life." By contrast, Eva Illouz argues that such discourse actually merges two contradictory constructions of self: "the self as a (potential or actual) victim of social circumstances and the self as the sole author and actor of one's life." Self-help discourse fosters a "split model of responsibility," Illouz explains, because it "promotes a self that is passive—in that it is defined by wounds inflicted by others—but is commanded to become highly active, in that it is summoned to change. It is highly responsible for self-transformation." In Christian self-help discourse, this split model of responsibility is further complicated by the notion that readers should place their trust in God and allow for the unfolding of God's plan in their lives.[14]

I have become aware, moreover, that many women prisoners comb through reading materials of all kinds for whatever clues they can find about becoming a more agentic individual. Yet far from being a solipsistic or atomistic endeavor, women's practices of helping themselves through reading often involve numerous other agents and factors external to the self. In fact, these self-help reading practices revolve around a fundamentally social and intersubjective notion of the self. One prisoner's reflections about Iyanla Vanzant's *Yesterday, I Cried* will help to elucidate what I mean by a "practice of self-help reading."

As we saw in Chapter 3, *Yesterday, I Cried* is well-loved by many women prisoners. The book recounts Vanzant's experiences with abuse, abandonment, and self-doubt, and it foregrounds the lessons that she has learned about using hardships as occasions for growth and healing. Solo shared the following extended reflection as her group was discussing Vanzant's book:

I first experienced this book when I was in County [jail], at the beginning of this case. And I was in a very dark place at that time. I didn't want to come back to prison. I felt like such a loser. . . . I wouldn't eat. I didn't shower. I just stayed in my room under this heavy, wool, grey blanket. And it got to the point that the girls would knock on the door and just say, "Do you want your [food] tray?" No one cared enough to say, "Solo, come out." You know, it was like, "Do you want your tray?" And I was in there, "Get away from me!" you know, and I was in there with these demons. And one girl came by with a book, and it was this book . . . and she said, "You may as well read it. You may as well read it." And she left. Well, I got up, and I did read. And as I was reading it, I was doing just what it says on [page] 222 at the bottom:

"There always comes a time of elimination. The earth sheds each year. The trees and flowers let go of their identity. As the old identity dies, a new identity is born. The body sheds constantly. Some of it happens invisibly, so naturally and silently that we do not realize it is happening. The heart and the spirit also shed. They shed the emotions and experiences that we no longer need. They shed the things that stunt our growth. This, too, is an invisible process. Yet because of the energy involved, we often feel the emotional and spiritual shedding. It feels as if we are dying. We are. Just like the flowers and the trees, we are dying to an old identity. This shedding, or death, is not the end of us. It is the beginning."

And that's the Solo that you see today. From that girl, having that much compassion for me, I got up, I came out, I showered. I let somebody braid my hair, and that in itself is a nurturing thing, to have someone braid your hair, and the women sort of gathered around me, and I fed from their energy. I played cards that day, I ate that day, and I smiled that day. And I had hope, and it wasn't long after that my bond was reduced, and I got out. Long story short, I got a better deal. But I think had I stayed in that dark place, fighting that shedding, trying to hold onto everything that I thought was still mine . . . Had I not read this book, I don't know what would have happened to me because I was so close to that brink, there's no telling.

And if you stay in that darkness too long, you become it, and then you fall over into the abyss. All it took was one kind gesture, and that was this book.

Vanzant's narrative assumes tremendous agency in Solo's account of her experience. Serving as a vehicle of resurrection, the book enabled Solo to step back from "the abyss" and begin a painful yet hopeful process of rebirth. The book also served as a source of spiritual food that gave her sustenance at a time when she would not eat the food on her prison tray. Furthermore, *Yesterday, I Cried* provided a means for Solo to participate vicariously in Vanzant's healing. "As I was reading it," she explained, "I was doing just what it says." The narrative enabled Solo to reflect on her own life and to reemerge into the present rather than remaining in the "dark place" of the past. In constructing the book itself as a "kind gesture," Solo actually conflates the book and the unnamed woman who performed a kind gesture by giving her the book. In Solo's account, the book stands in for the woman's gesture of care; after all, the book can slide under Solo's door in a way that the woman cannot. It is crucial to recognize, however, that the book was the medium through which the woman participated in Solo's work of healing. Through her kind gesture of sharing Vanzant's book, the woman enabled Solo to enter a community of women, feel nurtured and energized by them, and summon the courage to face her future.

Solo's account of reading Vanzant's narrative illustrates important aspects of what I call a practice of self-help reading. By reading *Yesterday, I Cried*, Solo helped herself: she pulled herself into the present and opened herself up to a different future. Yet even as her account emphasizes the individualist outcome of getting "a better deal," it draws attention to factors external to the self that contribute to Solo's process of helping herself, including prisoners' gestures of care for one another and Vanzant's invitation for her readers to participate vicariously in her work of healing. Although both reading and self-help are most often parsed as individual or even individualistic, Solo's story suggests that a practice of self-help reading is fundamentally a social and intersubjective process; the self is not left to its own devices to help itself.[15] In fact, self-help reading often depends on a structure of surrogacy in which a book serves as a surrogate or stand-in for a reader's relationship with an author, a parent, a higher power, a lover, or herself. The "self" in a self-help practice of reading is thus a self-in-relation. It is also a narrative self, one that is participating in a progressive unfolding or writing of itself. Frequently, the self's journey assumes spiritual—

typically Christian—overtones of redemption or resurrection, as with the resurrection imagery in Vanzant's narrative and the ways in which "the word" serves as spiritual sustenance.[16]

My conception of a self-help reading practice is also informed by Michel Foucault's later writings about care of the self. In his earlier work *Discipline and Punish: The Birth of the Prison* (1975), Foucault constructs the self as an effect of disciplinary power in arguing that "knowable man (soul, individuality, consciousness, conduct)" is the "object-effect" of the carceral network. He argues that, like criminology—which establishes a fixed notion of who "the criminal" is, "will be," and "may be" by seeking the causes of his crime "in the story of his life, from the triple point of view of psychology, social position and upbringing"—emphases on "the biographical" establish a fixed notion of the self and serve as an "alibi" for normalization and discipline. Because self-help discourse can encourage individuals to scrutinize their psychology, social position, and upbringing, and because it can promote efforts to achieve socially defined standards of health, happiness, and success, the early Foucault might view it as a means by which individuals subject themselves to the disciplinary and normalizing demands of institutional power.[17]

In his later writings, however, Foucault manifests an increasing fascination with "technologies of the self," which he defines as practices that "permit individuals to effect by their own means or with the help of others a certain number of operations on their own bodies and souls, thoughts, conduct, and way of being, so as to transform themselves in order to attain a certain state of happiness, purity, wisdom, perfection, or immortality." During the Hellenistic and Roman periods, Foucault explains, the "care of oneself" entailed continual self-analysis, taking notes on oneself, and becoming "the doctor of oneself."[18] Taking proper care of yourself entailed knowing "ontologically what you are," "what you are capable of," what it means "to be a citizen of a city" and a member of a household, "what things you should and should not fear," "what you can reasonably hope for," and "what things should not matter to you." Foucault argues that in the modern era, care of the self has likewise entailed a willingness and an obligation to engage in an "elaboration of the self," an ongoing effort to make one's "very existence" a "work of art."[19] The "exercise of the self on the self in order to develop and transform oneself" is not a once-and-for-all liberation from constraints but, rather, an "aesthetic experience" and an active, ongoing "practice of freedom" that draws on models of selfhood suggested and imposed upon us by culture.[20] According to Foucault, care of the self requires a "historical investigation into the events that have led us to constitute ourselves and to recognize ourselves as subjects," and a commitment to explore "the possibility of no longer being, doing, or thinking what we are, do, or think." In other words, Foucault calls us to perform a "critical ontology of ourselves": to adopt "an attitude" or "ethos" in which "the critique of what we are is at one and the same time the historical analysis of the limits imposed on us and an experiment with the possibility of going beyond them."[21]

Although he briefly touches on the fact that a "limited margin of freedom" may exist for exercising care of the self within "states of domination," Foucault never fully engages with the question of prisoners' margin of freedom for undertaking the aesthetic work of self-creation, and his discussions of self-transformation never attend to subjects' particular race, class, and gender positionings. The women involved in my study help to bridge Foucault's earlier emphasis on the totalizing power of the prison and his subsequent emphasis on the aesthetic work of self-creation because they demonstrate some of the forms that care of the self can take in the heart of the carceral continuum. Through their self-help reading practices—which foster self-invention, self-education, and self-repair—women prisoners examine their "thoughts, conduct, and way of being, so as to transform themselves." Performing a critical ontology of themselves, they continually examine the limits imposed on them—external limits such as poverty, racism, gender inequality, abuse, and imprisonment, as well as internal limits such as addiction, mental illness, self-doubt, and self-defeating behaviors—and they experiment with the possibility of going beyond them, "shed[ding] the things that stunt [their] growth." Women cultivate a relationship "of differentiation, of creation, of innovation" with themselves, and with the artistry of a composer, they work to integrate new ways of being, doing, and thinking into "the score of their existence."[22]

Through their practices of self-help reading, women involved in my study also illustrate the intersubjective dimensions of care of the self. By "their own means [and] with the help of others," these women learn how "to occupy [their] rightful position in the city, the community, or interpersonal relationships." They illuminate the importance of having "a guide, a counselor, a friend, someone who will be truthful with [them]" as they work on themselves and negotiate their relationships as members of communities on both sides of the prison fence.[23] In dialogic relation with others, and sometimes in a figurative relation of co-authorship, women prisoners engage in an ongoing practice of freedom that entails claiming authorship of their lives. Refusing the narrative closure of previous scripts and of others' definitions of "what [they] are, do, or think," the readers struggle to realize "the instinct for freedom" even while their existence is overdetermined by prison life.[24]

As previous chapters illustrate, women prisoners engage in processes of self-reflection and self-empowerment while reading a wide range of texts, including narratives of victimization and urban fiction. To summarize the preceding pages, I argue that a practice of self-help reading is distinct in the following four ways: First, such a practice not only describes women's engagements with self-help books; it also describes an approach to reading that is geared toward a broader process of care of the self. Far from implying that women prisoners can simply "def[y] physical incarceration by finding (intellectual/spiritual) freedom in the creative act," self-help reading involves the difficult, ongoing labor of practicing freedom in conditions of confinement. For many women, practicing freedom entails learning to feel worthy of self-care when they are wracked with guilt, grief, and self-recrimination; learning to maintain control of their own minds in an environment in which they can control little else; and learning to find purpose and beauty in lives that may otherwise look like "an abandoned battlefield."[25] The second distinguishing feature of a self-help reading practice is its status as a processual, long-term regimen. Whereas women will often read urban fiction or crime fiction with great speed, they tend to engage in "intensive reading" or "reverent rereading" in their self-help reading practices, approaching a small number of texts slowly, deliberately, and when possible, "over and over and over again."[26] Third, a practice of self-help reading involves a structure of surrogacy in which books serve as vicarious means to experiment with other ways of being and to engage in intersubjective dialogue and relationships. Fourth, self-help reading tends to involve a narrative conception of the self: the idea that the self is always in process and that one constitutes oneself through narratives and lends meaning to one's experiences by putting them in narrative form. Even when a woman's life story seems to have been scripted by forces outside her control, a narrative understanding of the self enables her to exercise some control over her life story in terms of how it is written, by whom it is written, and how it will unfold.

In the remainder of this chapter, I analyze how women prisoners adopt practices of self-help reading when engaging with two extremely popular self-help books and one work of fiction: Iyanla Vanzant's *Yesterday, I Cried* (1998), Joyce Meyer's *Battlefield of the Mind: Winning the Battle in Your Mind* (1995), and Pearl Cleage's *What Looks Like Crazy on an Ordinary Day* (1997). I also draw on Meyer's *The Confident Woman* (2006) and on Rhonda Byrne's bestseller, *The Secret* (2006), in exploring women's practices of self-help reading.

"A Good Book for Growing Up": Tools for the
Intersubjective Practice of Self-Care

As we have seen in previous chapters, many women prisoners are seeking models of change as they read. They feel inspired by protagonists' efforts to overcome their difficult childhoods, reckon with experiences of abuse, and renounce
their criminal lifestyles. In their practices of self-help reading, women often look
to the authors, characters, and books themselves not only as sources of inspiration but also as friends, guides, mentors, counselors, and even parental figures
who model practical techniques for undertaking the care of the self. In these
instances, the book mediates intersubjectivity; it serves as a surrogate for, or
conduit to, other agents who can assist the self with helping itself. As Charmaine
says of the *Chicken Soup* series, "*Chicken Soup* books are the best books! I've
read every one written. . . . There's hope in them. You get to see someone else's
struggle and see how it helped others and they overcame. They're so inspirational!" Valhalla explicitly describes books in terms of friendship. "Some of the
books I've read are like my friends," she explains. "There's characters I've met
who I keep with me inside me." Denise similarly characterizes books as friends
who can help to extricate their readers from harmful habits and relationships:
"Sometimes you need a book to come at you like your best friend. You need a
book that comes at you strong like you care, a book really to snatch you out of
it." The slippage between "a book" and "you care"—rather than "a book that
comes at you strong like *it* cares"—suggests the extent to which Denise personi-
fies books as nurturing companions.

Prisoners from a variety of religious, racial, and class backgrounds specify
that they have received guidance from Joyce Meyer's books and from Meyer herself. Olivia captures the sense of connection that many women feel in reading
Meyer's books when she explains, "Max Lucado—he's a male writer—he's not
really talking about his life. . . . He's just saying it from somebody's point of view.
Now Joyce Meyer, she speaks it from her biography, you know what I mean? She
speaks from her experiences." Indeed, Meyer discusses almost every aspect of
her life, from her long-term sexual abuse by her father, to her resultant tendencies to be aggressive, controlling, competitive, anxious, and critical, to how she
handles frustration about a wrinkled pair of pants. She also assures her readers and viewers, "I know you can change because I did." For Meyer's audience,
which is primarily female, her persona becomes an important part of the help
that her books offer.[27]

Meyer actually positions herself and her books as means through which readers can access God's help. Arguing that she "graduated from the school of life" and that her qualifications "come from personal experience," she communicates ambivalence about formal therapy or counseling but positions herself as a surrogate counselor.[28] For instance, in her popular 1994 book, *Beauty for Ashes: Receiving Emotional Healing*, Meyer instructs readers to ask God "whether it is His will that you go to another human being for counsel or whether He desires to counsel you Himself." Meyer herself went to a counselor only once and did not find it helpful. "It was better for me to receive the truth I needed directly from [God]," she explains, but others may need "someone to assist them in setting goals for themselves and to keep striving toward those goals." Constructing herself as such a guide, Meyer promotes her own books and audiotapes as gateways to God's cure. After all, she quips on her television show, her products cost less than the fees that counselors charge. "Read some good books about God's love," she says to those who struggle to receive God's love. "I recommend that you start with the ones I have written called *Tell Them I Love Them*, and *Reduce Me to Love*." Meyer encourages those who have a difficult time "hearing from God" to "read my book titled *How to Hear from God*," and she advises those who need inner strength that God's word "is medicine for your soul. . . . I encourage you to read my daily devotional, *Starting Your Day Right*."[29]

Many women prisoners cherish the mentoring role that Meyer and her books play in their lives. They look to Meyer as a "strong," "smart," "funny," "down to earth," "blunt," and "inspiring" role model who "tells it like it is" and who gained tremendous success without even going to school for ministry. Women identify with Meyer's resilience and toughness in the face of suffering, and they feel confident that "she's not lying to you" because she speaks from her experience. Underscoring the intersubjectivity at the heart of a self-help reading practice, some prisoners have developed a quasi-counseling relationship with Meyer. Nena says of her intense sense of personal connection with Meyer, "I saw her address in a book and told her where I was, and I told her about myself, and what I was struggling with at the time. And she sent me *Beauty for Ashes*. . . . It's about how she was abused by her dad and neglected, and how she went from the lowest pit to being very successful." Nena now regularly writes to Meyer about her efforts to follow a new path:

> I write to her two or three times a month. I explain my rapes, my abuse, my abandonment by my family—how they turned my collect calls off and stopped returning my letters. I talk about my depression, my health problems, and how I'm trying to gain stability. I get back typed letters

signed by her and her husband. In her letters, she quotes Bible verses. Sometimes she'll send a book on related issues that I'll be able to read. I've read about twenty books by her. I read all these books like within the last six months. . . . I like Joyce Meyer because she doesn't play the victim role. She deals with it. . . . She teaches me about not giving up.[30]

According to Wendy Kaminer, "Merely buying a self-help book is an act of dependence, a refusal to confront the complexities of a solitary creative act and to endure the loneliness and failures that are the price of its surprises."[31] Offering a powerful challenge to this dismissive construction of self-help reading, women prisoners suggest that the project of self-elaboration is an intersubjective rather than solitary endeavor. At the same time, however, they often emphasize the difficulty and the emotional risks involved in performing a critical ontology of themselves through their self-help reading. Many women adopt a practice of intensive reading, poring over texts carefully, slowly, and repeatedly in order to grapple with their implications. As Barbara explains, "It takes forever to get through books by Joyce Meyer 'cause you want to . . . let it soak in and understand it more." Readers often take notes on a separate sheet of paper or underline passages in the book if it is their own copy, as if they are decoding their own lives as they decode Meyer's messages.

Olivia illustrates both the intersubjective and lonely dimensions of a self-help reading practice as she discusses her encounters with Meyer's *Beauty for Ashes*. In *Beauty for Ashes*, Meyer discusses in detail her efforts to reckon with the fact that her father sexually abused her over a fifteen-year period while her mother did nothing to stop it. Olivia found the book too painful to read the first time that she checked it out. When she returned the book to the library after reading only a small portion of it, the librarian asked her if she liked it. As Olivia recounts,

I said, "No, 'cause I got frustrated with it. And I don't like the way she writes." . . . And then all three ladies that were sitting there, the old-timers, they all put down their books and they were all looking like, "You don't like Joyce Meyer?" I'm like, "No, I don't like her." They was like, "What? Did something hit home with you?" And I was like, "I'll see you later." I walked out and then it crossed my mind: . . . This must be a sign, 'cause if three old folks are sitting here telling me why they like Joyce Meyer, then I better take a look at the book again. So I walked right back in and picked the book back up and checked it back out. I went back, you know, started to read the book, and then I really enjoyed it.

Demonstrating that self-help entails figuring out how to be helped by others, Olivia looked to experienced prisoners as her teachers and took the risk of trying to read Meyer's book again. She now realizes, "I guess I didn't like it 'cause it's kind of like looking in the mirror, you know, when I was young what I went through. I kind of related with her sexual abuse. It's like it touched home with me, exactly like [the old-timers] said. It was the reality that I was trying to deny, you know, trying to hide behind. . . . Right away, I had feelings drawn out of me that I didn't want to address, so I didn't want to read that book or anything written by her." Although she still has not finished reading *Beauty for Ashes*, Olivia could handle it better the second time because she "paced" herself and "took [her] time with the book." Now that she knows Meyer's "life story and what she's been through and how she overcame," Olivia explains that she will "read her stuff because I look up to her." Far from using Meyer's books to skate on "the frozen sea" within her, Olivia—in company with Meyer—reads them to undertake the courageous work of cracking the ice and encountering what has been frozen.[32]

Like Nellie, who argues that "reading is like my mother . . . because it's teaching me more than the prison is teaching me itself," Olivia describes Meyer's books in quasi-parental terms. During a group discussion, she said of Meyer's *The Confident Woman*, "I think the *Confident Woman* is like preparing us for our future, and you know, kind of growing up into a woman again." Suggesting that the book offers what she needs for assuming her place as an adult woman, Olivia explained, "After I started getting high and drinking and getting into abusive relationships, I stopped caring about my woman [i.e., the female part of herself]. So I think this kind of reiterates what we need in order to be a woman. You've got to have confidence to be a strong woman, you know. So I think it's kind of like a good book for growing up."[33]

Iyanla Vanzant and her works also serve as guides for many prisoners as they engage in the creative project of self-elaboration. During a group discussion of *Yesterday, I Cried*, Solo emphasized an episode in which Vanzant finally gained a "sense of self" that allowed her to stand up to her abusive husband and refuse "to react to his actions." Describing her own long-term journey to develop such a sense of self, Solo acknowledged, "I've yet to see if my journey's gonna lead me to that. I believe I'm here but I gotta do a test. . . . I'm excited to see if this discipline that I've been fusing within my personality for the last five years is really set. 'Cause I don't want to step out the door and be like a little robot and, you know, fall over." Also invoking Terry McMillan's 1992 novel, *Waiting to Exhale*, Solo emphasized that she wants her sense of self "to be like [Vanzant's]. I want it to be where I can reflect and say okay and I can inhale, waiting to exhale."

Arguing that Vanzant models how to "take a stand for yourself" and "establish your boundaries," Solo then assumed the role of mentor in the discussion and encouraged other women to establish their boundaries. They should develop an "invisible fence" or "invisible screen" that people "won't see" but "will sense," she argued. Drawing attention to the social and intersubjective nature of the self, Solo continued, "Every week you're gonna encounter new faces, and each week you have to reinvent you for the new person. 'I have boundaries, this new person. Do not exceed them.'" To illustrate how to establish boundaries, Solo recounted how she stood up to a prison staff member who merely "grunts and makes motions with his head" when he wants prisoners to do something:

> Everybody goes along with it, but I said, no. Let him know that this will not work. So I said, "Are you communicating with me sir?" [Unintelligible sound]. I said, "I don't know what that means. If you're communicating with me, can you articulate that?" So the [other] women were like, "[Solo], you're gonna get yourself in trouble." But I wouldn't move. And finally I said, "If you will explain to me what you want me to do, then I can do it." He said, "I want you to move." I said, "Okay, I can do that."

Bridging the emphases in Foucault's early and later work—and conveying the "palpable pleasures" of "coming to rest outside [of power's] whirlpool even for a minute"—Solo demonstrated how to practice freedom and care of the self even under the watchful eye of disciplinary power. "Don't let people just treat you any kind of way," she encouraged other women in the group. "Don't accept grunts and groans when he can open his mouth and talk."[34]

In discussing *Yesterday, I Cried*, some women explained that the book has inspired concrete changes in their lives and become part of their practice of freedom. Jacqueline shared, "It gave me hope, and it made me want to get closer to my God. It made me want to be patient. It made me want to be still and listen. It made me want to not take not one day of my life for granted, no matter how bad it is. It made me appreciate life." Quoting the scripture "This is the day that the Lord hath made. Let us rejoice and be glad in it," Jacqueline added, "I say that to myself every morning since I read this book." She also regularly invokes an epigraph from Vanzant's book "that says when you meet someone, remember that that person is holy so you have to be holy." Noting that people "get on [her] nerves," Jacqueline said that the epigraph reminds her that "this is a human being; this is a beautiful creature that God has created." In practicing care of the self, Jacqueline thus learns to care better for those whom she encounters.

In looking to self-help authors and books as mentors and guides, women prisoners strategically choose which messages and techniques they want to adopt; they are not—as Wendy Kaminer suggests—following "rules on how to be an individual." Women's selective reading strategies are particularly evident in their discussions of Joyce Meyer's views about gender roles. Meyer consistently maintains that "God's revealed plan for families" entails wives submitting to their husbands "as head of the home." In *Battlefield of the Mind*, she features a couple— Mary and John—who are having problems because Mary "doesn't know how to let John be the head of their home" and resists becoming "a sweet, submissive, adoring wife," while John allows her "to run the household. The finances, the children and him." In explaining that Mary should be submissive to John, Meyer writes, "I don't mean that [John] should come on like 'Mr. Macho,' ranting and raving about his authority," yet he "should be firm with his wife—loving but firm."[35]

When readers do not agree with Meyer's claims about women's submissiveness, they sometimes dismiss those claims as unpersuasive rhetoric: as "just an opinion" or "just her interpretation." For instance, although Monique often emphasizes that Meyer offers "the hardcore facts" and "has a Bible verse to back up every point," she says of Meyer's arguments about gender roles,

> That didn't stand out in my mind because that was just an opinion, you know. And I don't look into that as deep as I did the rest of the book because it was just like, okay, we've heard that already, that the man is this, the man is that. But everybody knows what's really going on [laughter], you know what I mean? . . . Women are more educated than their men nowadays, and they have better-paying jobs than the men. . . . Like there's a lot of equal rights going on. So that was a minor, minor part I read, and I was like okay, flip the page.

Other women who have been in long-term abusive relationships with men read Meyer's depiction of husband/wife relationships as an appealing ideal to emulate. For these women, being submissive in the way that Meyer describes means feeling safe enough to allow a man to assume some appropriate power and responsibility in their relationship. For Deven, a thirty-six-year-old white woman, such a model is attractive because it suggests that "it's not me always giving and [him] taking. It's 50/50." Deven pictures a partner who is "the breadwinner, the grass-cutter, the window-cleaner, the fix-it man, good with the kids, good with me, complimenting of myself, the house, the kids, good lines of communication." She nonetheless qualifies her embrace of the book's gender norms by arguing, "If the man is head of the house and you're letting him do that, then you should be submissive. But if he's beating your butt, no." Reflecting on her actual experiences of abuse by men, Deven adds, "Now all the men I find? Hell no! [laughter] Hell no! I've been way too submissive! [laughter] . . . I would like to have that relationship, very much so, but I have yet to have it."

In one group's discussion of *Battlefield of the Mind*, women debated about whether it is possible to find someone who fits Meyer's male gender ideal. Some readers suggested that such an ideal is a fantasy, while others held fast to the model that Meyer promotes, arguing, "That tells me that's the type of man I am to expect. . . . I know that's far-fetched, but that's what I look for." Women also debated the meaning of Meyer's claim that women should be "submissive" to their husbands, drawing on their own experiences to assess the value of the claim. Sissy, who was in a severely abusive relationship for several years, insisted that a man "is supposed to respect my wishes as well as I do his," and she characterized Meyer's claim as "just her interpretation," arguing that everybody "has their own way of looking at how God said it's supposed to be." Meyer's argument would be acceptable to her, Sissy added, if she replaced the word "submissive" with the word "humble," which would help to "make peace in the household" and encourage both members of a couple to "let go" of strife.

From Olivia's perspective, Meyer's *The Confident Woman* illustrates the important lesson that even a wise mentor like Meyer can grow and change her way of thinking. During a group discussion, Olivia argued that Meyer's position "on that husband and wife submissive thing" in *Battlefield of the Mind* "is totally switched up since *The Confident Woman*." In *The Confident Woman*, Meyer continues to assert that a woman should "be submissive to her husband," but she acknowledges, "I know that a lot of women don't like that particular 's' word. But think of it this way: You can't have two people driving a car at the same time. . . . By necessity, one person has to occupy the driver's seat." Furthermore, Meyer argues that "it was never God's intention that women be dominated and made to feel as if their opinions were of no value," and she insists that men's treatment of women should never include "abuse, control, manipulation, or mistreatment of any kind."[36] Positioning Meyer as a self-in-process and a model for change, Olivia noted a parallel between her own and Meyer's changing perspectives: "My thoughts and opinions have changed. . . . Six months ago, I wouldn't read a hardback book but I've read several of them since then. Maybe between [*Battlefield*] and [*The Confident Woman*] [Meyer] might have grew some, 'cause she really goes into it in [*The Confident Woman*]. So I guess that makes it okay for me 'cause then I feel like we can all grow."

From Loveless to Beloved: Reckoning with
Guilt, Grief, and Abandonment

Performing care of the self poses particular difficulties for women in prison because they often feel utterly unforgivable, forsaken, despised, and unlovable, even by themselves. As Audrey says of the heavy weight of guilt that she bears for her crime: "When you take somebody else's life, that's a heavy load to carry. It liked to fuck me up real bad. For about the first three to four years, everybody thought I was really loony and I was on a lot of mental health medicine . . . 'cause I mean, that's all I thought about. Like when the breeze blow outside, I think, that woman can't feel that breeze on her face. Or when I get up in the morning time . . . I would think, that woman can't get up out that grave."

The haunting presence of the past assumes even greater significance given women prisoners' limited opportunities for addressing their crimes in therapeutic settings. Tamia, who has been on a waiting list for a counseling group for more than two years, tells a story of determination and isolation in describing her efforts to reckon with the past: "I've dealt with my crime by myself for so long. The incest—the molestation and stuff—I've dealt with that. . . . About the deaths of my mom and my grandmom, I've dealt with it, I've lived through it, and I've moved on from it. With the abusive boyfriend, I've dealt with it and I've moved on from it. So all the issues that I have or had, I really feel there's no help for me, because I've helped myself." Because Tamia wanted help from others but it was not available to her, she claims her individual agency and autonomy—which were necessary for survival—as signs of her strength. Yet even as she says that she has single-handedly "dealt with" her issues and "moved on," Tamia acknowledges that she remains locked in guilt and grief about her crime: "I thought it was gonna really kill me because I just held it in for so long. And to this day, I haven't forgiven myself."

Heidi, a white woman who is serving a life sentence, describes the weight of the past in these terms: "I have to live with the fact that someone's dead because of me, and I can't live with that. . . . Time doesn't heal all wounds. The pain gets worse with time. . . . It affects me every day." Adopting what John Berger calls a "stance of undefeated despair"—despair "without resignation, without a sense of defeat"—Heidi holds on to the hope that God's agency combined with her own may enable something positive to emerge from her crime: "God may make something good out of [my crime]. I don't know what that might be. . . . If I make the best life that I can, I'll have a chance to redeem myself. . . . But if it wasn't for prayer, praying for [the victim's] family and his soul, I don't know where I would be. The guilt would crush me."[37]

Many women also struggle with feelings of profound abandonment related to their experiences prior to and during incarceration. Some women have never felt loved or supported to begin with, while others have been disowned or cut off by their families since they came to prison. Even those who feel well-supported by family members and friends can feel deeply isolated due to the expense and difficulty of both phone communication and in-person visits.[38] Furthermore, many women experience multiple deaths in their families while incarcerated— Deedee, for instance, has had eight deaths in her family, including one suicide and one murder—and few have opportunities to mark those deaths in significant ways. As I mentioned in Chapter 2, prisoners are permitted to watch a video of a family funeral in the chaplain's library, but few women have such videos at their disposal. Moreover, if women are in solitary confinement when they learn of a family member's death, they cannot even make contact with their families. Solo learned that her brother was murdered while she was in punitive segregation, and she was not permitted to call her family until two months later when she had finished her term of solitary confinement.

For women struggling to manage feelings of guilt, grief, and abandonment, a self-help reading practice offers opportunities for strengthening or developing their belief in some sort of god, spirit, or higher power that loves them unconditionally and allows them to bestow their love in return.[39] As Vanzant writes in *Yesterday, I Cried*, "I was in the prison of needing to be loved for most of my life. Now I know I am loved and that God loves me." Avery Gordon notes that "love enters the prison and the prisoner's life" in numerous books and films, "ameliorating the dehumanization, hatred, and loneliness to which he or she is usually subject. Sometimes this love is romantic, sometimes it is Christian, sometimes it is familial, and sometimes it is called friendship." Through their efforts to cultivate spiritual forms of love, women prisoners once again underscore the social and intersubjective dimensions of self-help. As Heidi explains, turning her attention to building a relationship with God helps her to survive the "incredibly hostile environment" of the prison.[40]

Joyce Meyer's books emphasize God's unconditional love as the source of his forgiveness, a forgiveness that operates outside the dictates of state-administered justice. "God doesn't delight in punishing us," Meyer writes. "He is merciful, and if we are able to receive His mercy, He frequently gives us blessings when we legally deserve punishment." Asking, "Are you a son or a slave?" Meyer insists that readers inherit God's grace and do not have to labor for it. "How much time do you waste living under guilt and condemnation?" she asks. "Don't think about how terrible you were before you came to Christ" or "how God must be so disappointed with [you] because of all [your] weaknesses and failures." God loves unconditionally, she argues, and readers must learn to receive God's complete forgiveness no matter what they have done.[41]

Some Christians criticize Meyer for preaching a "self-love, self-image, self-esteem" gospel, but for women who feel overwhelmed with guilt and shame, Meyer's emphasis on God's forgiveness helps them to move beyond a paralyzing sense of self-recrimination.[42] Genevieve, a middle-aged black woman, describes the solace that she gains from her intensive and deliberate practice of reading Meyer's books: "When I think about the past, some thoughts come, and it's like one part of me saying oh, you're so bad, you can't be forgiven. You know, all those regrets come back. But reading what [Meyer] wrote, God forgives us and he really forgets. So sometimes when all those thoughts from the past have been coming and I feel so overwhelmed, I dwell on what I've read." A young white woman named Drea likewise experiences tremendous relief from reading Meyer's work. "It's like she really understands what I was going through in my mind!" Drea exclaims. "I lived in the past for so long. It's a waste. You can't do anything about the past. It's a nowhere land." Meyer's books have taught Drea to understand that "if you make a mistake, you correct it. The only bad thing is if you don't do anything."

Some women have great difficulty internalizing Meyer's message of self-forgiveness even though they understand that "the past is past. You have to remain positive. . . . Otherwise, you'll torture yourself." For a young white woman named Candi, Meyer's message of forgiveness creates anxiety because she fears that she will never be able to forgive herself, and "if you don't forgive yourself, God will never forgive you." However, Candi greatly appreciates Meyer's emphasis on forgiving others. "I like that she didn't hold on to her abuse that her dad did to her," she explains. "When her dad got older, he needed her. She didn't push him away. She still accepted him and took care of him. Most people wouldn't want to help him, but she teaches about letting go." Breeanna, a young white woman who sustained abuse from her own father, acknowledges that she started reading Meyer's *Beauty for Ashes* but had to put it down because she is "struggling with forgiveness. If I forgive my dad, it feels like I'm saying it's okay," she says. "The Bible says forgive and pray about it, but I'm stuck there. And it's hard to move on without facing it and dealing with it, but I'm not ready to fully face it. I hope I will be, but maybe it won't be until my dad passes." Breeanna's admission that she currently feels "stuck" and unable "to move on" signals her absorption of both therapeutic and Christian concepts of the self, which highlight the self's involvement in a journey toward healing or redemption.

Just as they use Christian self-help books to experience a sense of being loved, women prisoners sometimes make similar uses of other kinds of books in their practices of self-help reading. Sissy offers a particularly moving account of how she taught herself about love by reading Sidney Sheldon's novels. Currently age forty-six, Sissy entered prison as a very young woman, and she sustained years of abuse and violence prior to her incarceration. Discussing the role that reading has played for her in prison, Sissy explained, "I've read so many spiritual books it isn't even funny, and that taught me about life in general as to how I want to be talked to and how I want to be treated." She then described how Sidney Sheldon's "sex books" taught her about physical tenderness, pleasure, and intimacy and thereby taught her to take care of herself, in literal and philosophical terms. From Sheldon's books, Sissy learned "about another side of sex" and discovered that "sex can be enjoyable." Explaining that she only knew how to "shut my mouth and let him do whatever he wanted to do" during sex, Sissy continued,

> I never had a man rub my body or give me massages or anything like that, or just rub my arm. None of those nice things that you do. I've never had anybody do anything like that to me. And to read about those things? I felt sad, you know. But then, I was like that's alright, that's alright because now I know. Now I know that you can be intimate with a person without having the penetration. You can have a man kiss your cheek, or just run their hand through your hair, or just tell you that you're pretty or beautiful and not have to feel that you have to give them something in return for it.
> I know that now.

Sheldon's books also "taught me how to take care of myself if I want to look nice," Sissy explained. "I know how to do it for me; not for them or my child, for me. . . . Even the spiritual books I read, I learned to love me. And not worry about what someone thinks about how I smell . . . or how I speak." Drawing on books as surrogate parents, teachers, and gentle lovers, Sissy has learned about other ways of being. Although she used to be "a wallflower" who "was there but wasn't there," her self-help reading practice has enabled her to claim her space in the world as one who deserves to be treated—and to treat herself—with the tenderness reserved for the beloved.

"We Are Engaged in a War": The Battlefield of the Mind

In the prison environment, where prisoners are totally dependent on others for their basic physical needs, and where the constant threat of physical and emotional violence replicates experiences of domestic violence, many women struggle to maintain some sense of control over their lives.[43] For some women involved in my study, self-scarring, anorexia, and bulimia serve as means to exercise domain over their own bodies. For these and other women, maintaining a sense of control over their own thoughts can also assume paramount importance. As Olivia says of being in prison, "In here, everybody is stripped of everything but our minds. Everything physical, we're stripped of." Feeling in control of her thoughts is crucial, Olivia adds, because "anything physical couldn't really hurt me 'cause I've been through a lot physically, so it's usually with my mind that somebody can hurt me."

For many women, trying to maintain some control over their thoughts is a central aspect of their practices of self-help reading. A middle-aged white woman named Maisey describes Robin Casarjian's *Houses of Healing: A Prisoner's Guide to Inner Power and Healing* as helpful for "reprogramming your thinking." The book helps you to "reevaluate your losses and your traumas and then go on," Maisey explains. "It teaches you about how not to stay stuck." Donna, a middle-aged white woman who is currently serving her second prison sentence, considers Buddhist reading materials an invaluable resource for getting in touch with, and altering, her thinking patterns. Donna did not "work on [her]self" during her first imprisonment, but after returning to prison, she felt determined not to waste her time and "started getting into books." Her decision to try a Siddha-Yoga Correspondence Course led to her abiding interest in Buddhism, which she pursues by requesting books through interlibrary loan. As Donna describes the effects of her reading practice, it has taught her "to maneuver through life with a more expanded perspective," to love herself and heal from "guilt and shame," and to "recognize everyone's divinity." Furthermore, she explains, "It helps me to watch my thinking, pay attention to things, and change my thoughts. You do have power over which thoughts you run with."

In addressing how readers can learn to control "which thoughts [they] run with," both Iyanla Vanzant and Joyce Meyer employ metaphors of captivity and freedom. The authors' use of these metaphors seems deliberate; like Meyer, whose ministry sponsors an enormous prison outreach program, Vanzant coordinates a correspondence-based prison ministry with more than 3,500 people incarcerated in U.S. penal institutions. In *Yesterday, I Cried*, Vanzant invokes metaphors of imprisonment in urging her readers to maintain sovereignty over their minds and spirits: "There are many types of jails. Some people are in the jails of their limited minds. Many people are in the jail of drinking alcohol, taking drugs, working on a job they hate, or living in bad relationships. We are all doing some kind of time. The only difference is that some of us have keys to our cells and others do not. Nobody but you can imprison your mind. Nobody can imprison your spirit." Meyer likewise adopts metaphors of imprisonment and freedom in urging readers not to be held captive by their emotions and thoughts. The verse "Jesus came to open the prison doors and set the captives free" appears in several of her books. In *Beauty for Ashes*, Meyer writes, "I know what it is to be an emotional prisoner. . . . When I put up walls to keep others out, I also wall myself into a solitary place of confinement," and she cautions that "prisoners, whether physical or emotional, become so accustomed to being in bondage that they settle in with their condition and learn to live with it." Meyer calls her readers to "refuse to live the rest of your life in a prison of suspicion and fear!" and to allow God to "open your prison door" and "liberate you in every area of your life."[44]

Meyer's *Battlefield of the Mind* combines metaphors of captivity, an ongoing war between God and Satan, and computer programming in discussing how readers can maintain control over their minds. "We are engaged in a war," Meyer asserts. "Our enemy is Satan. The mind is the battlefield," but "the good news is that God is fighting on your side." Drawing on the work of Alon Nahi and Haim Omer, Eva Illouz argues that the therapeutic narrative is inherently a "demonic narrative" because it "situates the source of suffering in an evil principle that is outside the subject, whether Satan or a traumatic event," and it suggests that "the identity of the person is taken over and transformed by the evil principle, which has insidiously entered his or her soul or body."[45] In Meyer's work, Satan seems to be located both inside and outside the subject. At times, Meyer invokes the devil as a surrogate for structural inequalities or the effects of such inequalities. In *The Confident Woman*, for instance, she acknowledges that women have not been respected throughout history, but she uses the figure of the devil as a placeholder for the structural inequalities and contingent social arrangements that have created women's devalued position. Constructing Satan as an external agent, Meyer argues that the "attack on women is from Satan himself," and she asserts that "the war between women and Satan got its start in the Garden of Eden and has not stopped. Satan hates women because it was a woman who gave birth to Jesus and it is Jesus who has defeated Satan." Rather than acknowledging historically shifting constructions of male power and privilege, Meyer presents gendered conflict in eternal terms, making it difficult to imagine individual or collective efforts to alter currently existing gender inequalities.[46]

More frequently, Meyer constructs Satan as an evil principle that enters subjects through their minds and holds them in bondage through "certain types of wrong thinking," or "wilderness mentalities," that make them wander in the desert like the biblical Israelites. Among other things, these wilderness mentalities include believing that one's future is determined by one's past and present, self-pity, and failure to assume responsibility. According to Meyer, winning the war against Satan requires joining forces with God to change such unproductive patterns of thinking. Reframing the captive subject as the captor, Meyer argues that readers must "brin[g] every thought into captivity, into obedience to Jesus Christ"; they must capture their own thoughts and "submit" them to God's thoughts in order to combat Satan's control of their minds. Meyer reinforces this idea through the language of computer programming. "Your mind is like a computer that has had a lifetime of garbage programmed into it," she contends, so readers must "reprogra[m] a very carnal, fleshly, worldly mind to think as God thinks." Assigning primary agency to God, Meyer assures her readers that God is "the best 'computer programmer' around," and he will "reprogra[m] your mind" if "you have invited Him to have control of your thoughts." By relying on God to resist Satan's efforts to hack into their minds, readers can experience "freedom from every bondage" and find "the Promised Land."[47]

The layered metaphors that Meyer adopts in *Battlefield of The Mind* resonate with women prisoners in numerous ways. The language of the battlefield speaks to some women's sense that life is a constant battle that leaves them feeling besieged, scarred, sometimes shell-shocked, and compelled to fight for survival. Whether they interpret the titular battle as a controversy between God and Satan, good and evil, Satan and "my own mind," or "yourself versus whatever is coming your way at that time," women frequently emphasize that *Battlefield of The Mind* helps them to live with a sense of strategy, control, and the ability to make choices in facing life's battles, rather than feeling helpless, reactive, or immersed in chaos.

Indeed, several women describe *Battlefield of The Mind* as an invaluable "guide" that they continue to consult over time as part of their self-help practice. Underscoring how Meyer and the book become intertwined in the role of mentor, Lefty explains, "I love *Battlefield of the Mind* and I'm not even Christian. I love the title because your mind is always in a battle and it teaches you how to control your thoughts. . . . I read it a long time ago and I've been using it in my life ever since. She teaches you to be a stronger person and to focus on what you're good at." Olivia says of *Battlefield of the Mind*, "If I'm going through a struggle, I know that's the book to go find. I've read that book probably five times in the past year. Every time I start to get frustrated about something, I'll go to one of those verses, and I'll read in-depth into it. . . . I know the material in there will pull me through." For many women, simply knowing that such a resource exists to help them in their time of need is itself a resource that they may have never had. Monique suggests that *Battlefield of the Mind* serves as a reference book; although she is planning to donate her other books to the prison library upon her release, she will take *Battlefield of the Mind* home with her because "you can always refer back to this book as like a guide." Calling to mind how Vanzant's book served as mental sustenance for Solo when she could not eat the food on her prison tray, Monique describes *Battlefield of the Mind* as something that both feeds her and helps her to assess her personal growth: "I like to read it and then try to take notes and see where I've come from the first time that I've read it to the point later on down the road, and see if I'm really paying attention to it. This is mental food, which makes you think and grow."

Although Meyer never discusses the game of chess, the front cover of *Battlefield of the Mind* includes a life-size photograph of a hand moving a chess piece— the queen, which is the most powerful piece on the board. Highlighting how images can also play a role in a self-help reading practice, several women note that this photograph occupies a central place in their understanding of the text. Olivia says of the book's cover, "The way they did this picture on the front, I always think about it. . . . Controlling your mind and what you're thinking about and what you speak out of your mouth and what you let come into your being will affect the things that are going to happen to you." Monique also loves the cover of *Battlefield of the Mind* because "dealing with everyday struggles" is "basically brought down to a game of chess. Like you cannot win your struggles just by physical strength alone. You have to use your mental, and I like how [Meyer] deals on the mental, as far as building your mind up, getting your mind together, getting it in shape." As I will discuss further in Interlude 2, Monique wants to live her life "like a game of chess," which entails strategizing, making deliberate moves, staying focused on the big picture, and making thoughtful choices.

Women involved in my study also find Meyer's conception of the devil helpful for maintaining control of their minds. Some women invoke the concept of Satan or the devil to name feelings or situations that they cannot fully articulate or explain. Drea, who "didn't know where fear comes from" and often feels paralyzed by it, finds especially helpful Meyer's claim that fear "is the devil's tool to keep people from enjoying their lives and making progress." Drea is now trying to adopt Meyer's stance that "the only acceptable attitude we can have toward fear" is "I will not fear." Denise finds Meyer's conception of the devil useful for explaining the tremendous anxiety that she feels in being separated from her children. Many women in prison—including those who have lost their parental rights—convey a sense of continuous anxiety about the health and safety of their children, an anxiety that is greatly exacerbated by institutional impediments to maintaining family ties. Denise makes meaning from her anxiety, and manages to contain it, by interpreting it as "mental attack" from the devil.[48] Highlighting how Meyer's book serves as a vehicle for God's work in her life, Denise explains:

> Something that gave me peace in this book and that I really needed—and I believe this book was the way of God helping me deal with that—when I don't hear from my children, I instantly think they're dead. And I get so scared, and my mind goes all the way to, oh, nobody gonna come see me because they don't want to tell me my kids are dead or that my little daughter burned up in a house fire. These are thoughts that go through my mind. And I'm like, Oh God, [my daughter]'s gonna burn up! She done burned up! And I run around to the phone trying to call. I go through all that. But . . . ever since I read this book, every time one of them thoughts come to my head, I say those are from the devil, 'cause the book told me that. . . . I say no, I rebuke these thoughts 'cause I know they're not from God. . . . That's that battlefield of the mind again. But that's one war I fought and that's one war I won.

As we saw with Denise in Interlude 1, Meyer's conception of the devil is also useful to many women as they contend with thinking patterns related to addiction. "This book changed me," Jacqueline said of *Battlefield of the Mind*. Recounting how a friend said, "I changed my way of thinking" when she asked him how he stopped using crack, Jacqueline explained, "I really didn't understand what he was saying until I read this book." She now believes that holy words can vanquish unholy thoughts inspired by Satan. Meyer "is teaching you [to] meditate on the word of God," Jacqueline argued, "because when them thoughts come, you can just shoot that scripture at them. And I like that a lot." For Jacqueline and other women, *Battlefield of the Mind* thus extends beyond a single instance of reading; it serves as a resource for women's broader processes of making meaning from their experiences.

"You Can't Make a Pact with God to Get What You Want": Negotiating Agency

In their practices of self-help reading, women prisoners often wrestle with the age-old question of free will versus determinism. As I noted toward the beginning of this chapter, self-help discourse fosters what Eva Illouz calls a "split model of responsibility" because it merges two contradictory constructions of self that are at work in contemporary culture: "the self as a (potential or actual) victim of social circumstances and the self as the sole author and actor of one's life." Christian self-help discourse further complicates the matter of agency by suggesting that subjects should allow God to direct the course of their lives. At times, a practice of self-help reading requires sorting out competing models of agency: a structural model, which entails changing social and political systems; a Christian model, which entails asking God for healing; and a self-help model, which entails changing one's thinking patterns and claiming "a voluntarist responsibility for the future." Sorting out the parameters of individual agency can assume particular urgency and importance for women prisoners, some of whom will never again have sovereignty over their time or living conditions, and all of whom must regularly confront the concrete limits of the prison walls and the infantilizing and dehumanizing forces of institutionalization. For women who have faced numerous social and structural obstacles, including poverty, racism, abuse, and/or violence, and for women who live with daily and sometimes violent reminders of their captivity and dependence, understanding the extent to which they can reclaim their lives and shape their futures often becomes a matter of pressing need.[49]

I gained a much deeper understanding of this need—and began to recognize how a practice of self-help reading addresses such a need—during a group discussion that took place toward the beginning of my research. The discussion focused on Pearl Cleage's bestseller *What Looks Like Crazy on an Ordinary Day*. Cleage's novel tells a three-part tale of redemption. Ava Johnson, who has been diagnosed as HIV positive, returns to her hometown to visit her sister. Although she faces discrimination from community members and struggles with bitterness and self-blame, Ava undergoes a process of transformation through which she learns to embrace the present and her home. The primary inspiration for Ava's transformation is Wild Eddie Jefferson, a Vietnam veteran and former cocaine addict who spent ten years in prison for a double murder. While in prison, Eddie decided to turn his life around, and in the present time of the novel, he fills his days by meditating, doing carpentry, and cooking vegetarian food. The third tale of redemption in Cleage's novel features Imani, a crack-addicted baby whose mother abandoned her in the hospital when she was born. Imani eventually thrives under Ava and Eddie's care and emerges as the real heroine of the tale. Ava, Eddie, and Imani embody the novel's credo that "people have a right to change, to grow, *to get better.*"[50]

Cleage's threefold tale of redemption is predicated, however, on another story about an unredeemable class of "crack-heads" who must be expelled from the community—and the narrative—in order to ensure the health and safety of the main characters. The text depicts its representative male drug users, two teens named Frank and Tyrone, in terms that reinforce dominant constructions of black male "superpredators"; Ava insists that the teens are "destroyed" and that nothing will "transform [them] from predator to productive citizen." Cleage also depicts poor, drug-addicted women of color as so expendable that she never even assigns a name to one woman who sustains sexualized violence from Frank in two scenes. Rather than exploring the social factors that contribute to the crack epidemic, *What Looks Like Crazy on an Ordinary Day* suggests that death or incarceration are the only means to contain the threat that crack-heads pose to the community. Indeed, by conflating the threat posed by black male drug addicts with the threat posed by "the Klan and other renegade white folks," Cleage's novel characterizes those involved in the drug culture as menacing communal safety from the outside, as pathogens that must be excised in order to restore communal health.[51]

To my surprise, women involved in the group discussion—many of whom have struggled with an addiction to crack—embraced Cleage's novel as an accurate and warranted depiction of crack-heads. As I now understand, the women were performing a self-help reading practice, and their primary interest was in the lessons that the novel and its characters offer about individual agency, responsibility, and transformation. In discussing various characters, readers focused on the extent to which each was attempting to change. Patty characterized Frank, Tyrone, and the unnamed female crack-head as "examples of where your life could head if you choose for it to do that." Eddie, Ava, and Joyce, by contrast, are "people making a difference" and "making a change," even though they have "obstacles" in their lives. Rae likewise distinguished between Frank, who is "not even making the effort," and Eddie, whom she considers her "hero" because he "wanted to be reached" and "came out on top" after "everything that he had gone through." Some women also argued that the unnamed woman was complicit in sustaining violence from Frank. As Patty insisted, "You simply have to at some point and time accept responsibility for what you have chosen to put yourself in." The group concluded that Frank will never change, since prison will only "make him harder," and they proceeded to discuss fellow prisoners who remain "unreachable no matter how hard you try." Claiming her place within a community of women who are actively trying to help themselves and one another to change, Arlene said of Cleage's novel, "To me, that book gives a lot of ladies in here as well as myself a lot of support. Because a lot of us are trying to change."

Women prisoners' discussion of *What Looks Like Crazy on an Ordinary Day* served as an important reminder for me that concepts of individual agency and personal responsibility can be used both for and against prisoners' best interests. On one hand, jurisprudential practices and cultural narratives about prisoners often rely on notions of individual choice and responsibility that fail to account for the social and structural factors that shape lawbreakers' agency and sense of alternatives. Within the prevailing framework of "punitive individualism," lawbreakers are constructed simply as willful actors who chose to do wrong, and attempts to contextualize their actions are frequently construed as efforts to excuse their behaviors. Such a framework presumes that the lawbreaker is "the only appropriate target of intervention," thereby precluding a necessary focus on communal responsibility and the ways in which society itself needs to be transformed. On the other hand, I have come to recognize that notions of autonomy and individual responsibility can be strategic and crucially important resources for women prisoners as they practice freedom and perform care of the self.[52]

At times, however, women involved in my study argued that particular self-help books carry the idea of individual agency too far. Rhonda Byrne's bestseller, *The Secret*, prompted such a response from many readers.[53] According to *The Secret*, "Imperfect thoughts are the cause of all humanity's ills, including disease, poverty, and unhappiness." Byrne contends that you can "completely change every circumstance and event in your entire life, by changing the way you think," so those who remain in negative circumstances deserve full blame for their suffering. In our group discussion, several women argued that *The Secret* exaggerates the control that individuals can exert simply by willing "the universe" to provide desired results. The book claims, for instance, that author Jack Canfield expressed his desire for money by hanging a fake $100,000 bill on his ceiling, and within a year he had made $92,327. Then when he tried it again with a million-dollar bill, he received a million-dollar check from his publisher. Mocha responded to this example by arguing, "I believe you have to work for it. But they just make it seem like that it came just like that!"[54] Several women also argued that *The Secret* does not illustrate a proper balance between individual striving and faith. Byrne's book "makes it seem like you got to keep thinking 'I'm gonna get it, I'm gonna get it,'" Mocha explained. "But then I think everything happens in God's will. If it's meant for us to get it, then you'll get it. I think that *The Secret* will build you up too much and let you down." Tyra, who took extensive notes on Byrne's book because she "wanted to know the secret," criticized the book's exaggerated emphasis on individual agency in these terms: "I don't believe I can pray to God and say, 'Give me my freedom.' You know, I'm going to do this, this, and this, so give me my freedom. You can't make a pact with God to get what you want. . . . They take it a little far."

Joyce Meyer strikes an uneasy balance between emphasizing individual agency and the power of positive thinking, and emphasizing the role that God should play in shaping one's path. Like Byrne, Meyer sometimes erases social and structural concerns—promoting a "blaming the victim" stance—in suggesting that individuals determine their material circumstances through the character of their thinking.[55] The prosperity gospel message in her work, which suggests that proper belief will yield material rewards, dovetails with the self-help tenet that positive thinking will yield material rewards. A prime example of this logic is Meyer's claim that people bring poverty upon themselves by having what she calls "a poverty image." "If we are in a certain class, it is because we have relegated ourselves to it or allowed someone else to do so," Meyer asserts. "God has not assigned His children to an upper class, a middle class, and a lower class. . . . Whoever will believe in God and serve Him wholeheartedly can be blessed in any way that anyone else can be blessed."[56] She similarly argues that Satan deceives people into thinking that "they are unhappy due to what is going on around them (their circumstances), but the misery is actually due to what is going on *inside* them (their thoughts)." In discussing prayer, Meyer sometimes asserts that her readers will receive what they request if they believe that they will. At other times, however, she cautions that "we can't control [God] with our thoughts and words" and will be unhappy if we are "trying to make something happen instead of waiting patiently for God to bring things to pass in His own time and His own way."[57] In discussing agency and responsibility, Meyer sometimes insists, "*We do not need self-confidence; we need God-confidence!*" and she argues that "our confidence must be in Christ alone, not in ourselves, not in other people, not in the world or its systems. . . . I know that without Him, I am nothing." At other times, Meyer suggests more of a partnership between humans and God, arguing that God "has a part and we have a part," and that responsibility is "our response to God's ability."[58]

As they sort through these sometimes conflicting constructions of agency, women involved in my study find most useful Meyer's notion that humans can work in partnership with God. A key point that Sissy takes from Meyer's work is "the responsibility that God gives us in everyday life." Underscoring the extent to which many women assume responsibility for rehabilitating themselves, Sissy asserts, "Even though we're in prison, we're still responsible for a lot of things. We're responsible for how we do as far as we rehabilitate ourselves, as far as how we change our mind; change our thinking; change the way we do, say, and act towards things. . . . We have to move on to something more positive in life." According to Mocha, "Most of what [Meyer] says is preparing you for some more struggles in the future." Meyer's emphasis on positive thinking seems "very powerful," Mocha explains, "because I don't know how I'm gonna get out there and be on my own and take care of my kids. You know, it just seems impossible. But if you say, 'I can do it,' then you'll start goal setting and write your goals down and take a step." From *The Confident Woman*, Mocha has learned that "courage is when you stand up to your fear," a message that inspires her to face the upcoming challenge of trying to get a job as an ex-felon. "As far as what people say to drown your courage," she says, "I think that when I get out there, by reading these books—*The Battlefield Of the Mind* and *The Confident Woman*—I think that it's gonna make me want to even try harder." For Mocha, Meyer's books serve as helpful tools for "break[ing] away from other peoples' expectations" and for countering the discouragement that she receives from the world. She balances her sense of self-determination, however, with Meyer's comforting promise that "if you do what you can do, then God will do what you cannot do."[59]

At times, the competing models of agency at work in self-help discourse created tensions in our group discussions. During one group's discussion of Mary and John, the couple experiencing difficulties because Mary won't "let John be the head of their home," it became clear that different models of agency point to different remedies for addressing problems.[60] As I previously noted, we discussed male/female gender roles in talking about Mary and John, in part because I was interested in the issue and raised the topic. Jacqueline expressed a keen awareness of gender inequalities in suggesting that Meyer's male gender ideal is an unachievable and dangerous fantasy. "When it comes down to it," she insisted, "the woman is the one that is keeping track of the money and paying the bills and taking care of the kids and taking care of the house," and she cautioned that men's promises before marriage never accord with their subsequent actions. Nonetheless, Jacqueline became frustrated with the discussion because she believed that our focus on gender inequalities was obscuring what she views as Meyer's central argument: that the devil causes interpersonal conflict and that one must "go to God" to resolve such conflict and receive "spiritual healing."

With mounting anger, Jacqueline said, "To me, the whole point is being missed because she's trying to tell us . . . these people are Christians, and they're having strife in their home. She's saying what are they gonna do spiritually to fix what's going on in their home?" Denise agreed with Jacqueline's reading, adding that the devil is "trying to break up their home" by "using things that they suffered as a child and bring[ing] it all the way up into their adult life." Mary, she explained, "had in her mind that men are always trying to run things," and John was too passive because he "always tried to please his mother." According to Denise, the "real message" is that "the devil can use your past only if you let him. But if you know how to go to Jesus about it, he'll fix it." Because she sensed Jacqueline's frustration with the conversation, Denise cautioned her not to "let the devil have his way," because "whenever something spiritual is going on . . . he's coming." Jacqueline nonetheless responded by angrily leaving the room, thereby strengthening Denise's conviction that the devil was at work. "It's a spiritual warfare that's going on that you can't see, and it just happened right here in front of our face," Denise concluded. "The devil used her mind to make her feel victimized or attacked in some kind of way to where she left the room. . . . So he won that little war right there."

Jacqueline's insistence that *Battlefield of the Mind* "is a spiritual book, and we done got off the subject!" ultimately deepened my understanding of how she and other women approach Christian self-help discourse. Whereas a structural model of agency foregrounds systemic change as necessary for ameliorating gender relations, Meyer's Christian model of agency suggests that God is the solution for healing Mary and John's devil-induced interpersonal strife. On one hand, it is important to recognize how *Battlefield of the Mind* thwarts structural understandings of gendered conflict. Meyer argues that Mary's and John's "problems are internal—in their thoughts and attitudes," and she constructs their personal histories in ways that obscure larger patterns of gender inequality. For instance, she counterbalances her portrait of Mary's "domineering" father with a portrait of John's "domineering" mother, and she argues that Mary has been "brain-washed for years by Satan who had told her lies" about men, such as men "think they are something," can "do anything [they] want," and "can order people around." As Janice Peck cautions about therapeutic discourse in general, Meyer's repeated counsel to resolve gendered conflict through "spiritual weapons" might "be personally beneficial," but it "may be so by helping [readers] adapt to a social order that requires analysis itself." On the other hand, it is crucial to recognize that Jacqueline remains keenly aware of gender inequality, as do other women prisoners who suggest that they would not trust any man whom they actually know to occupy the dominant role that Meyer advocates. This fact suggests that women's embrace of the model of agency evident in *Battlefield of the Mind*—the notion that Mary and John can resolve their gendered strife by "go[ing] to God"—should not be dismissed as an unfortunate adaptation to a dysfunctional social order. For women such as Jacqueline and Denise, whose lives have been shaped by gendered violence and inequality, reading "spiritual books" provides tremendously helpful reassurance that God can assist with mending gendered conflicts, even when they stem from individuals' damaging personal histories and from broad patterns of deeply ingrained cultural beliefs.[61]

"All Us Women Have a Story within Us": (Co)Authoring the Self

According to Wendy Kaminer, self-help ideology is "more conducive to totalitarianism than democracy" because it "tells us all problems can be solved in a few simple steps" and offers "rules on how to be an individual." Two of Joyce Meyer's recent titles, *In Pursuit of Peace: Twenty-One Ways to Conquer Anxiety, Fear, and Discontentment* (2004) and *Look Great, Feel Great: Twelve Keys to Enjoying a Healthy Life Now* (2006), might seem to support Kaminer's claim that self-help books offer simple plans for achieving desired outcomes. Women prisoners clearly demonstrate, however, that a practice of self-help reading does not involve quick fixes or thoughtless adherence to lists of rules. Rather, it involves an ongoing journey or narrative unfolding, a long-term process of claiming authorship of one's life and "restorying" or rescripting one's past and future experiences. Because women's self-help reading practices entail intersubjective engagements with authors, characters, other readers, and even God, this self-authorship might be more aptly characterized as collective- or co-authorship.[62]

The central role that self-authorship plays in women's practices of self-help reading seems particularly evident in their discussions of Vanzant's *Yesterday, I Cried*. In our group discussions, several women emphasized how much they love the questions that Vanzant regularly poses to herself to monitor her journey of self-discovery. For instance, What is your greatest strength? mistake? fear? accomplishment? "If your life ended today, what is the one thing everyone who knows you would say about you? . . . Why wouldn't or couldn't they say what you would want them to say?"[63] Kate, a fifty-one-year-old white woman, explained that she first read *Yesterday, I Cried* several years ago at the beginning of her sentence, and the questions were instrumental in her efforts to script a new role for herself in prison: "I could really relate to the questions. . . . Prior to coming here, you have a definition of yourself. But here, you're perceived as a number. You're no longer that wife or mother. I was always someone to somebody else: my mom's child, a wife, a mother. Here, that wasn't who I was. I had to re-explore and redefine myself. I had to ask, who am I really? It was a process of self-discovery."

Deven offers a particularly clear illustration of the central role that self-authorship plays in women's practices of self-help reading. Echoing the general enthusiasm about Vanzant's questions, Deven said, "Those questions were just so amazing! And I like the answers that she put. . . . Each time she asked herself those questions, the answers changed. She was growing, and I just loved that." Like many women, Deven wrote all fourteen questions on a piece of paper, and she plans to refer to them on a regular basis. "I answered them now, and then I figured in another month, I'll revisit them, and we'll go from there," she explained. "Even if the answers are the same, that doesn't mean I didn't grow. It might just be something that I'm beginning to acknowledge within myself." Refuting the idea that self-help offers a quick fix, Deven thus characterizes her self-help reading practice as an interactive regimen. The question that currently "strikes a chord" with her is "What was your greatest mistake?" She greatly admires Vanzant's answer, "Mistaking sexual attraction for love," because Deven has "made plenty of mistakes" in her own relationships, and she now realizes that being able to acknowledge such mistakes shows "how much you have grown within yourself to see that those relationships . . . were a mistake, and now that you know that they are what they are, learn from them and move on." For Deven, Vanzant's questions foster the process of beginning "to recognize yourself," which—in Foucault's lexicon—constitutes a first step toward "no longer being, doing, or thinking what we are, do, or think."[64]

In her group's discussion of Vanzant's *Yesterday, I Cried*, Deven suggested that the book enabled her to perform a critical ontology of herself: "I got so much out of this book from taking a deeper look at things that I've acquired in my life or things that have happened in my life, and finding peace with them. . . . It was an opportunity for me to review my life, and . . . it forced me to search my soul, revisit old wounds, assess who I am and make some decisions about where I want to go." The key, Deven emphasized, is to keep asking questions of herself. "If you're in touch with your inner self, you're going to do that on a daily basis," she argued, "and those answers are going to eventually change." As she performs care of the self, Deven remains keenly aware that her life narrative is not fully scripted; there is still room to improvise, revise, and choose new ways of living her story. As she observed partway through the study,

We've just read five different books of women telling us about themselves in like seven hundred different ways. And each of them . . . has been a wonderful learning journey for me of getting more in touch with my inner self and my inner power source, and having some different ways to look at some situations instead of starting with that tunnel vision that I've known for so long. . . . All these women had stories inside of them. All us women have a story within us, and it's just, which way do we choose to write it, you know?

For many women involved in this study, performing care of the self involves a similar process of learning to "ow[n] the stories that shape [them] as subjects." It is this sense of ownership that enables craft and artistry, the creation of a meaningful—even beautiful—narrative from the often painful fragments of a life.[65]

The idea of a narrative self—a self constructed *through* narratives and *as a* narrative that can unfold in multiple ways—accounts for the excitement that Deven feels in engaging with self-help books. "I can't put them down!" she says. "I just need to know what's gonna happen next. It's like watching a good movie and they want to break for a commercial and you're about to flip out, you know. No!!" Suggesting that her excitement stems from finding out "what's gonna happen next" in her own self-development, Deven explains that self-help books give her a language for articulating her experiences. "I'm really getting in touch with my inner self, my inner thoughts," she says, "and reading the books helps me to put my thoughts and my feelings together to explain it more to others." In Illouz's terms, self-help books develop Deven's "emotional literacy," enabling her to extract herself "from the flow and unreflexive character of experience and transform emotional experience into words." The books also provide practical strategies that Deven feels eager to implement in her daily life. "I look forward to the next chapter only to see what else that I can get out of it, and maybe experiment with, see how well it works for me," she explains. "Is it gonna be something that I need to do for thirty days? Maybe it will become a habit. . . . Maybe it's something that I need to do periodically."[66]

Deven considers Joyce Meyer's *Battlefield of the Mind* particularly "awesome" because "it gives you another way to look at things, look at people, look at society." Emphasizing the sense of contingency that the book opens up—the multiplicity of narrative possibilities and potential realities that it makes available to her—Deven explains, "Just because through all these ages, everybody said the leaves [of a tree] are green and the trunk is brown, and that's the way it should remain, with reading these books, they kind of open your mind to see that it doesn't have to be just green and brown. It could be yellow, pink, purple, anything that you want it to be." In Kathleen Stewart's lexicon, Meyer's book makes Deven feel "animated by possibilities"; it enables a "quivering in the stability of a category or a trajectory" and "gives the ordinary the charge of an unfolding."[67] The possibility of viewing things differently helps Deven to recognize that social labels and others' expectations cannot fully determine her future experiences. Although incarceration carries a stigma—"you're treated as a second-class citizen or a lower life form"—Meyer's book reminds her that others "don't need to judge me or treat me like that." At the same time, the book helps her to "be a little more accepting of others and the situations they're going through." Furthermore, *Battlefield of the Mind* increases Deven's awareness of the myriad ways in which her life story might unfold: "You know how they create DVDs now and you get three alternate endings? Life can go like that. As you look at the big picture and realize, well, before you make these choices, this could happen or that could happen, and if you weigh out all those other options, then you make better choices in the end. That's where I'm at in life. I'm trying to make better choices."

Some women take particular comfort in conceptualizing their life stories as coauthored by God and as part of God's larger plan. The redemption narrative at the heart of self-help discourse helps "to establish coherence and continuity for the self." It allows women to interpret all of their life experiences, including their incarceration, as purposeful and meaningful and as part of God's "glorious plan" for their lives.[68] In *Yesterday, I Cried*, Vanzant frequently emphasizes that readers may not be aware of God's plan, but every one of their experiences is part of that plan, and all of their troubles are preparation for something better. "Even when it seems that your life is falling apart," Vanzant reassures her readers, "there is divine restoration going on." Joyce Meyer similarly promises, "Even if your fragmented life looks like an abandoned battlefield, Jesus can reshape all the pieces of your past into something beautiful. . . . Your pain will not be wasted."[69] By suggesting that God is an artist or author who can guide the work of self-elaboration, these formulations enable women to imagine their lives as governed by God, rather than the state, and to trust that God, rather than the untrustworthy world, will offer them guidance and take responsibility for their well-being. Discussing *Battlefield of the Mind*, for instance, Genevieve acknowledged that being in prison is "overwhelming" and she finds herself "getting depressed," but Meyer's book reminds her, "All I have to do is really wait upon God, and he will direct my path. I may not really know what the future holds for me, but if I just trust in him, he has the future all laid out for me, and I don't have to even be worried or anxious about it because everything will fall in place."

During a discussion of Vanzant's *Yesterday, I Cried*, women shared their ideas about how to submit to God's plan for their lives if it involves considerable pain and suffering. Noting the subtitle of Vanzant's book—*Celebrating the Lessons of Living and Loving*—Mildred initiated the conversation by asking, "How do you celebrate these experiences she had?" Solo offered the following counsel: "If you truly, truly submit to God or the creator or whatever you want to call it . . . you will find gratitude in everything because out of everything, good can come." When you're "getting ready to go through a storm," she explained, if you "assist, instead of resisting," then "you can see all the good that's for you instead of the negative. . . . Then you don't have to end up with battle scars, missing limbs, your heart snatched out over here, people that you hate over there." Reflecting on the sense of peace that she now feels, Solo shared that she has been able to overcome feelings of bitterness about her imprisonment by accepting that it is part of the narrative that God has scripted for her: "I was supposed to go through that, experience that and the good that came at the end."

In discussing their efforts to coauthor their lives, some women also draw attention to the ways in which genre expectations shape their conceptions of their unfolding life stories. For Monique, *Battlefield of the Mind* offers a crucial reminder to "think highly of yourself because everything that you're going through right now is just the basis for you to get on that journey that you're supposed to." Quoting a Bible verse that appears throughout Meyer's work, "I am convinced and sure of this very thing that he who began a good work in you" will bring it "to full completion in you," Monique shared her understanding that embracing God's plan does not guarantee a magically happy ending: "It's not always a fairytale that God is gonna get you out of prison, because sometimes you're gonna be here and you're gonna die here. But the whole point is it's all about your growth, your personal growth. . . . You could be in solitary confinement, and still there's no telling what His plan is for you. . . . No matter what your circumstances, there's always room to grow, whether it's in your mind, whether it's in your spirit, whether it's physically." Embracing a narrative model of redemption, rebirth, and resurrection, Monique explained that she was "dead spiritually" when she was selling drugs, but she has taken time to "think about stuff that I didn't want to think about when I was younger" and now believes "that everybody's put in their circumstances to find that person that was once dead." If, as Rodríguez argues, "the fundamental logic of punitive incarceration is the institutionalized killing of the subject" and the production of a condition of "living death," Monique and other prisoners emphasize the possibility of imbuing their lives with new meaning and, sometimes, a sense of divine purpose.[70]

Indeed, reading self-help books enables some women to enter "a spiritual place of rest." Meyer describes such a place of rest in these terms: "It is the privilege of every believer to refuse to worry or have anxiety. As believers, you and I can enter the rest of God." For women involved in my study, finding a spiritual place of rest means knowing that they have not been forsaken, that they will have help and guidance in transforming the wreckage of their lives into something beautiful. For those who may feel like they have spent much of their lives running—from pain or poverty or violence, from fear of the past or fear of the future, from others or from themselves—a practice of self-help reading offers the hope of finding a refuge, sanctuary, or place of peace amidst the ongoing struggle for freedom.[71]

DURING AN individual interview, Solo showed me a poem that she had written to tell herself, "Just remember girl, you have evolved and evolution is continuous."[72] Because her poem offers an eloquent and elegant description of her practice of freedom, I quote it in full:

FREEDOM

The essence of the word freedom is a state free of restraints, liberated, independence, exempt from unpleasant or onerous conditions, free will, unrestricted access and the ability to pursue unalienable rights.

I, Solo, exemplify freedom in its totality of this description. From the covering of my splendidly natural hair, to my brown eyes which no longer endure the pain of blue and blackened eyes swollen from abuse, to my mouth unclosed and expressive, to my ears now open to receive instruction, advice, and acknowledgement, to my neck, elegant, loosed from shackles of ignorance, to my shoulders erect and bold, not bent from shame, to my heart filled with optimism and expectancy, to my stomach less flat yet more satisfying, to my broader hips, which still retain the rhythm of the drum beats, clear down to the very soles of my Black feet, calloused from all the years of walking towards freedom.

I am Free!

For me, freedom has been an *evolution* not a *revolution*. See, my freedom was gained through years of self inflicted struggle, through increments of embraced ignorance, which was demonstrated in collective acts of pure foolishness. Freedom for me was elusive. I could not purchase it; consequently, I saw no way to ever own it. I could not believe in this reality because I had no faith. Freedom for me was always close like my baby sister and like my child. I had birthed it but I would not name it, consequently, I could not claim it. Remember, freedom for me was an evolution and not a revolution. For me, freedom crept in slowly on cat's paws, quietly and unassuming.

It happened like this. One day I opened my mouth and said exactly what I meant to say and I liked it. Then, I stood up refusing to dine on entrees of morbid lies and delicacies of hypocrisy and petite deception, and I liked it. I walked away from plentiful dependence to limited independence, and I liked it too! Freedom for me was an evolution and not a revolution.

There were no star-spangled banners, no rockets red glare. Instead, it was dark and I was naked, just standing there. Standing for my faith, standing for my unalienable right to exist, standing for my children's children to have a voice and standing for my choices, which today define who I am.

Freedom for me was an evolution and not a revolution. Yes, I have run the longest race, but I have not reached the finish line. Indeed, I have developed, but only God can create. Surprisingly, I have harbored, but few have I actually helped to freedom and for this, I apologize.

Each day, I evolve the woman you perceive me to be, yet tomorrow, I will rise a new creature conceived in love and renewed hope. Freedom for me was an evolution and not a revolution. America, America, God shed his grace on thee, and crowned thy good with brotherhood from sea to shining sea! Not so, sista! Freedom for me meant shaking off the dust from the Mississippi slave cabins hot and stifling like the heavy air hanging over unpicked cotton fields to a cold and barren empty grave with the letter X as its marker.

Freedom for me crept in around my edges and around my corners, in places so unprotected that I became helpless to stop its advancement, hallelujah! Freedom landed on my shore, set up camp, declared victory, and pledged allegiance to my soul!

For me, freedom came and slept with me, it held me close during the midnight of my existence, and baptized me with my own tears until I was thoroughly thoroughly cleansed of inferiority, low esteem, and self loathing.

Then I awoke in the beautiful morning of my middle-age, early before the sun came up, then I *stood* up a woman who knew her name, knew her purpose, knew her past was that and nothing more than that, knew her life was meaningful, worthy of saving from both prison and abuse, and knew that her spirit was a merciful and most precious gift from God Almighty.

Freedom for me was an evolution, not a revolution.

As she describes it, Solo's path toward freedom has been a long, gradual, often painful process of becoming. Like Vanzant, who narrates her own process of "emotional and spiritual shedding," Solo depicts a process of cleansing herself of "inferiority, low esteem, and self loathing"; shedding the "shackles of ignorance" and "self-inflicted struggle"; and refusing lies, hypocrisy, and deception. Her practice of freedom has also entailed reckoning with historical legacies of unfreedom as she performs a critical ontology of herself: finding her place as a "sista" in the "brotherhood" of America, and "shaking off the dust from the Mississippi slave cabins." Describing concrete ways in which race, class, and gender limit her freedom, Solo asserted in discussing her poem, "I'm an American, and I love that. . . . But I don't have the same freedom in America. 'Cause there's not no brotherhood from sea to shining sea." She also underscored the concrete limits to her freedom in prison, suggesting that it is difficult to practice freedom when you're "trying to live in a grave" and "nobody hears you when you call out, 'Hey, I'm alive!'" Keenly aware of the limits imposed on her, Solo nonetheless insists that freedom has crept into her life, "quietly and unassuming," as she has opened her mouth and "said exactly what [she] meant to say"; as she has opened her ears "to receive instruction, advice, and acknowledgement"; and as she has stood up for her choices, for her "unalienable right to exist," and for her "children's children to have a voice." In creative partnership with God, Solo has become a woman who knows her name and her purpose, feels at peace with her past, and has refused to allow prison or abuse to dictate the meaning or parameters of her life story. She recognizes, however, that she has not "reached the finish line." Freedom may have "landed on [her] shore" and "declared victory," but Solo's practice of freedom is daily and ongoing. Glossing the line from her poem, "Each day, I evolve the woman you perceive me to be, yet tomorrow, I will rise a new creature conceived in love and renewed hope," she explains that "they're very quick to tell me who I am here . . . but really I'm different every day." Drawing on her own poem as her "mantra" and as part of her self-help reading practice, Solo remains deeply engaged in the ongoing work of authoring herself.[73]

The process that Solo illustrates in her poem highlights the kind of work that women prisoners perform through their practices of self-help reading. Women who have been schooled for misery and abuse use self-help books as a means of self-education, self-discovery, and self-transformation. For many women, reading such books fosters a process of reckoning: both a coming to terms with grief and guilt and an anticipation of something yet to be born. Through their self-help reading practices, some women develop or maintain their belief in God or a spiritual power who functions as a higher authority than the state. Belief in this higher power enables them to feel beloved and forgiven rather than despised, to feel in control of their own minds, to recognize purpose and beauty in lives that may otherwise look like "an abandoned battlefield," and to arrive at a "spiritual place of rest" or at least a "stance of undefeated despair." As they engage in "patient labor giving form to [their] impatience for liberty," some women prisoners use reading as a means to develop their sense of agency and responsibility, change their way of thinking, reoccupy the present, and craft their life stories as more open-ended tales of becoming, opening themselves to future possibilities even when those possibilities remain circumscribed by prison bars.[74]

Monique: A Portrait

It's all about the reading. It's like everything
that I come across now is just mental preparation
for what I'm gonna eventually be able to do.
—MONIQUE, Northeast Pre-Release Center

"MY GRANDMOTHER raised me at a young age to read the newspaper," says Monique, a twenty-nine-year-old African American woman, in describing how she has rekindled her love of reading while in prison. "On the street, I really didn't have time to read. . . . But here, it's like let me get that book! I'm all over it. . . . I read to keep my knowledge vast, so I don't just limit myself to this spot right here. . . . I don't want to be caught up in the whole prison life. This is temporary for me. I'm not accepting this, so I'll read." Monique considers reading especially important "at night if you can't sleep, or count time, or you're off of work and you don't want to be all tied with everything that's going on; you don't want to be in the day room and you don't want to watch TV." When she finds a good book, Monique will stay in her cell "and just read, cover to cover," and she often reads a 300-page book in two days.

When she was a child, Monique relied on her grandmother, great aunt, and uncle as her "backbone" because her mother "was in and out" and traveled a great deal for her job. "She always redirected me, my energies," Monique says of her grandmother, recounting that she "was real strict on education" and helped Monique to deal with the experience of seeing her father beat her mother. Monique did well in school, particularly in English courses, and she was deeply involved in sports, including volleyball, basketball, softball, and soccer. In fact, she would have attended college on a basketball scholarship if her career had not been cut short, when she was seventeen, by two broken ankles.

Things began to shift in Monique's life after her ankle injuries. "I started drinking and smoking marijuana," she explains, "and sometimes I would drink excessively and then my anger would just show. Like it would just bring the fury out. . . . Uncontrollable anger gets me into a lot of situations that I shouldn't be in such as prison, and losing people that might really care about me but I didn't give them a chance to show their true feelings." As Monique understands it, her anger comes from "people that try to get over on me . . . or I had a feeling that they were trying to get over me. And being surrounded by people that don't have the best interest of the group at heart but only focus on themselves and what they can get out of the situation." She also harbors some anger against her only sibling, a brother who is nine years older and had a "problem with his hands": a tendency to physically abuse Monique. "My brother was my biggest problem as a child," she says, "and it's to a point now where I pray for him, but I don't really speak with him."

Around the time of her incarceration, Monique had earned her real estate license, was running two small businesses, and had plans to earn a college degree with a major in journalism and a minor in business. However, "instead of going on in the positive direction that I wanted to," she explains, "I was surrounded by people who still was trying to pull me back to the negative side. And there's a lot of things that went on that strayed me from my path." Describing how she became involved in selling drugs and got caught up in making money "by any means necessary," Monique recounts: "I went all out as far as throwing caution to the wind. . . . It was just like if I got to get it, I got to get it, you know. And up all night for four days and sleep on the fifth day, and then get right back up and you're at it again. . . . My thing was just to get to the top where I didn't have to do this anymore." Monique was eventually arrested not for selling drugs but for violently resisting some men who attempted to rob her.

Since she has been in prison, Monique has grown "closer to God" and is working to "build a better foundation." This process entails "focusing a lot more on me and what makes me tick," she says. "How I react to certain situations. How I take certain things, you know, like authority or even just the other inmates' feedback." Monique believes that she landed in prison because she "never included God in any of [her] plans," so she is currently trying to "rethink" her plan and discover "what plans God has" for her. "My choices got me in here," she contends, "but God's blessings are gonna get me out of here. . . . If I focus now on what I need to do, then once I do return to society, I can be even smarter about what I was doing as opposed to just having it wash away, and then having to start the building over."

As part of her efforts to build a better foundation, Monique regularly attends church and Alcoholics Anonymous meetings, and she has attempted to enroll in a host of programs and classes, including anger management, victim awareness, and college courses offered through the local university. "They're gonna get sick of me," she says, recounting how she wrote "about 200 kites" during her first month of incarceration. She has devised a "whole plan" of everything that she wants to do, but much of that plan is "on pause" because "there's always a waiting list."[1]

Reading also plays a central role in Monique's efforts to build a better foundation. Distinguishing between "love story tales" and "realistic" books "that pertain to life," she expresses a distinct preference for books that "focus on getting myself together," "challenge my mind," and "make me rethink some things." When I first met Monique, she had recently discovered urban fiction and conveyed considerable interest in the genre. Describing books such as *Married to the Game*, *G-Spot*, and *Still Sheisty*, she explained that she was reading "two or three books at a time." Urban fiction appealed to Monique because it addresses issues that seemed important to her when she was involved in "the game": "It's basically giving you the rules of the game. . . . Just how to always be aware of your surroundings. Always stay on point. Never lose focus. Always pay attention to details." As she said of the character Winter from Sister Souljah's *The Coldest Winter Ever*, "I didn't necessarily agree with everything and the way that she did it, but I respected her for the fact that she was a hustler."

When I returned to the prison six months after completing my research, however, Monique's reading practices had shifted from urban fiction to books that she categorizes as self-help texts. Even while she was avidly reading urban books, Monique suggested that she was not learning from them. "I read urban books, but I also like books that make me think," she explained, "that open up other ideas as to what direction I might need to go." She described her ultimate decision to move beyond urban fiction in these terms: "I've been there, done that. So right now, I don't feel like reading about it any more. . . . That's not the direction that I'm going in right now." Arguing that "six out of ten" urban books seem boring and repetitive, Monique added, "They're limited knowledge of things" and "they all end up the same way."

In describing her efforts to expand her reading horizons—to find "something that I'll use my mind on that will get me thinking, instead of just reading and reading and reading"—Monique recounted how an "older friend" handed her a list of books one day as they were talking. The list included "everything from mystery novels to *Beloved*," black history books, and autobiographies. Monique interpreted her friend's act as an important form of mentoring. "I believe in blessings," she explained. "I wasn't familiar with a lot of the books but I like her as a person, and I like what her mindset is and her way of thinking. So I said well, if this is the level that she's on, that means let's go on and figure it out and start getting books like that." Monique sent the list of books home to her family and is now open to reading "whatever comes to [her]."

Overall, however, her current reading practice is geared toward books that "build your mind" and "elevate your mentality." As Monique explains, "Right now, my big thing that I'm looking for is mental strength. Whatever I do, it's my plan to live to the fullest of my ability with the best knowledge that I have. . . . So now I'm reading books about self-help, spiritual books. I'm reading more on which direction I need to maintain a vision, what I have to do to never return to this place and . . . to weed out the people that aren't beneficial for me in my life right now." Monique is especially interested in "self-motivation books. Something that just gets you up and gets you thinking on a more positive level as opposed to waking up angry." Reading is "keeping me sharper," she says, "and God is showing me different things that I probably didn't pay attention to that he was showing me before." Underscoring the extent to which she uses books as equipment for living, Monique explains that she now takes notes on almost every book that she reads: "I have a business notebook, so I jot down the title of the book and my notes. . . . It's for my own personal use" and "just to reassure me if I don't have access to the book. I don't want to ever lose that book and then have to wait for it." Because gaining access to books is so difficult in prison, Monique's philosophy is to "use everything to the fullest right now because I might not ever have that chance again."

Autobiographies play an important role in Monique's self-help reading practice. "Everything I read that's reality based, I compare myself a lot," she says. "If somebody's talking about their patience issues, I'll read that and be like *this* is what I got to work on." During our final interview, Monique was awaiting Rhonda Turpin's 2005 book, *Resilience: Living in Prison with Martha Stewart*. She wanted to read about Stewart's "outlook on being incarcerated," not only because Stewart is "so upper echelon," but also because she continues to help women in the prison where she was incarcerated and has managed to "gain more than what she lost."[2]

As "a big promoter of overcoming adversities," Monique felt particularly inspired by reading Jeannette Walls's best-selling memoir, *The Glass Castle*, which underscores Walls's indomitable spirit, resourcefulness, and determination. During a group discussion, Monique highlighted the sense of cross-racial solidarity that Walls's narrative fosters. "I like when [Walls] was in the pool with all black people," she explained, "because even the white people were shunning her, like 'You're dirty. You're gonna contaminate the water.' . . . That's some of the stuff they used to say to the coloreds. And I was like damn, she really knows the struggle! It's not about being black or white. It's just a struggle." Monique asserted that she will remember *The Glass Castle* "probably forever" because it gives her courage to implement her goals. "When [Walls's] opportunity came, she took it," she explained. "When I closed the book, I started thinking about a lot of different things. . . . Everything that I've been going over in my head on the next move that I'm gonna do either in here or out there, I just said fuck thinking about it! I'm just gonna just go for it, implement it, you know what I'm saying? The worst thing that somebody can do is say no, so you just go to another door and you knock on it."

Given her experience in business and real estate and her "vision" for her future, Monique also enjoys reading books about "moguls" and "trailblazers." Because she wanted "to see what drives Donald Trump," she asked her family to send her Trump's autobiography, *Trump: The Art of the Deal*. As she was reading *Trump*, Monique was comparing her own and Trump's "assertiveness" and "determination." "He's been through bankruptcy, and he still bounced back," she says. "Maybe there's something that I might be able to take from his circumstances and apply it to me." A second "mogul" book that has sparked Monique's interest is Russell Simmons's 2007 bestseller, *Do You! Twelve Laws to Access the Power in You to Achieve Happiness and Success*. Monique asked her family to order Simmons's book for her after she read about it in *Vibe Magazine*. Simmons has struggled with drugs and alcohol but is now the wealthy owner of DefJam Records and Phat Farm clothing. "He tells you where he is now, and what he had to go through to accomplish what he did," Monique explains. *Do You!* incorporates motivational advice from figures such as Donald Trump, Oprah, and professional athletes, as well as insights from Buddhism and the Bible. According to Monique, Simmons's book is about "how to get positive outcomes," and it highlights "steps you can take to rethink your focus so you can start achieving calmness and peace within yourself. . . . His main concern is your vision. Telling you [that] you have to start somewhere. Have a dream and stay with it. If one door closes, you can't stop there." Monique has read *Do You!* twice, and she frequently reviews her notes about the book. "That's a book that I'm definitely going to keep with me," she asserts. "I don't lend it out to too many people. That's a book that I go back to."

Monique also "go[es] back to" Robert Greene's 1998 bestseller, *The 48 Laws of Power*, which has gained tremendous popularity among rappers and in business schools. Drawing on a range of historical figures who have "studied and mastered the game of power"—including Machiavelli, Nietzsche, Napoleon, Mao

Zedong, Henry Kissinger, Casanova, and various "con artists"—*The 48 Laws of Power* discusses forty-eight precepts that illustrate a single premise: "Certain actions almost always increase one's power . . . while others decrease it and even ruin us." Among the forty-eight "laws" that Greene discusses are maxims such as the following: "Never outshine the master"; "Never put too much trust in friends, learn to use your enemies"; "Conceal your intentions"; "Court attention at all cost"; "Get others to do the work for you, but take all the credit"; "Use selective honesty and generosity to disarm your victim"; "Pose as a friend, work as a spy"; "Crush your enemy totally"; and "Do not commit to anyone."[3] According to the chief librarian of the Ohio penal system, *The 48 Laws of Power* is banned from Ohio prisons because "everything can always be misused." Reading Greene's book would be OK "if you were sitting in college and the teacher was discussing how you increase sales by telling the sales staff xyz," the librarian argued, "but if you're trying to get a gang to see that, it's a potential misuse. . . . [Prisoners] have 24/7 to think of stuff to do. You have to think in terms of could this be used in a bad way." Another Ohio librarian contends that *The 48 Laws Of Power* is banned "because it can mind-alter you."

Monique received *The 48 Laws of Power* from an older friend about five years ago, and she likes to read it before going to sleep, along with her Bible, because it helps her to "get [her] mental together" and surround herself with "positive energies." Noting that *The 48 Laws of Power* was on prison grounds only "for a minute" before it was banned, Monique argues that "anything that goes to self-empowerment, anything that goes to show that there is a brighter way to make it out of here, it's like they try to put bans on it. Anything about self-help, they try to put bans on it." Whereas penal officials fear that "you might overtake the government" from reading Greene's book, Monique argues that "it's about gaining knowledge and wisdom about yourself. . . . I don't agree with everything because it's basically about how to use people to your advantage, like self-preservation. But . . . it really sharpens your mind and sharpens your energy and keeps you on your toes."

In Monique's view, *The 48 Laws of Power* overlaps extensively with Joyce Meyer's *Battlefield of the Mind*—one of her favorite books—because "it's basically teaching you how to live your life in a game of chess moves. For every option you have like four or five other options, so you just don't box yourself in." Monique further explains,

> Chess is a thinking person's game. You don't just jump over something.
> You have to really apply your brain power, really think about your next

moves. And that's kind of like *The 48 Laws of Power* because every move you make is your life on the line. So it's basically like you're that chess piece. But you're every single chess piece. And you have to play every single row, from the bishops to the knights to the rook, the queen, king, etc. . . . You yourself is actually the game, and society is the opponent. . . . So you have to have patience, and you have to really have understanding of how can I check their queen?

The 48 Laws of Power teaches Monique that "everything that you do is a reflection of you. Nobody else can take responsibility for it." Indeed, the book "makes sure that you take care of you. . . . It gets you refocused on the things that you need to do within your life. It's basically telling you how to get ahead. How to be on top and to stay on top" without "displaying any weaknesses." In Monique's view, *The 48 Laws of Power* is "a powerful book because you can use it in anything. You can use it in the business world, you can use it in the street world, you can use it in everyday life, and you can use it in here."

In enumerating how Greene's book has been useful to her in prison, Monique explains that "never outshine the master" is a helpful stance to adopt with penal employees. "There are some staff and authority figures that you know more than them, or you know how to act more proper than they do, but if you show that, then they feel intimidated by it so they want to downplay or disrespect you," she says. "So sometimes it's good to just let the people in authority, you never want them to feel on edge, like you're coming for them or you're coming for their job. So I like that rule because it kind of tells you to stay in place for right now because there's something that you might learn and then you can move on." Monique also values the laws that counsel "never say too much" and "trust yourself." "You don't want to divulge so much information about yourself that nothing is hiding, nothing is saved," she argues. "Sometimes it's just better to be quiet and listen than it is to keep talking." Monique adds that *The 48 Laws of Power* helps her to "deal with a lot of situations that go on here that can be avoided, such as arguments and petty things that I really don't need to concern myself with." Furthermore, the book enables her to imagine a different future by helping her "to think outside of the box. Don't just go back to selling drugs or don't just go back to the streets. There's other ways that you can focus on your inner self, and it's positive. It's more of a positive energy for me."

As we have seen with readers throughout this book, Monique nonetheless reads *The 48 Laws of Power* strategically, embracing particular aspects while rejecting others. Although she "love[s] the book because it sharpens you," she acknowledges that "some of the techniques" that Greene endorses for achieving success "aren't good." For instance, "It says to get people to be a scapegoat, and to me, that's kind of a cop out. Because if you do something, you should man up to it, you know, you should own into your own actions. And I think that's a lot of problems with people—especially dealing with the penitentiary system—there's a lot of people that point fingers and blame others, or they did something and they tell on others or do what we call snitching, and I don't think that's right, you know, you should be loyal to thy own self." Monique also disagrees with the book's suggestion that you should "use people to your advantage. It's like basically you're dealing with somebody just to gain something from them," she argues, "and I'm just not that type of person to just take advantage of somebody's situation." Furthermore, Monique takes issue with the book's suggestion that you should "invest your time in someone and act like they're a protégé to you, or that you truly genuinely care about them, but in actuality you're building them up for failure. So it's like you have these people put their trust in you but in actuality you're using them as a pawn to get where you need to, and you really don't care about the outcome that you have on that person." Emphasizing the disjuncture between such a philosophy and her spiritual beliefs, Monique asserts that "the overall feel[ing] is like use people to your advantage and it doesn't matter about the repercussions because as long as you got your goal, then that's OK. But especially by me being spiritual, you're supposed to treat somebody how you want to be treated, so I don't think I'd want to set somebody up . . . and then just drop them once I was done with them."[4]

Monique's resistance to the ethic of ruthless self-interest evident in *The 48 Laws of Power*—an ethic that occludes possibilities for working with others for mutual benefit or gain—seems particularly significant given her acknowledgment that she had embraced such an ethic while selling drugs: "When I was selling drugs, I was dead spiritually because I didn't care. . . . I provided for my people, but if you weren't my people, it was basically like fuck you." Like many other women involved in my study, Monique is assiduously searching for a means to achieve personal and financial success without jeopardizing others' well-being. At the same time, however, the cultural predominance of competition over cooperation—particularly in a penal environment—seems evident in Monique's reluctance to share *The 48 Laws of Power* with other prisoners. "I'm selfish with that book," she explains. "When I got my copy I didn't give it out because I didn't want somebody else to try to think along the same lines as me or have an advantage over me because they could learn something else." Although she may allow her "close associates" to read it, Monique is wary of sharing Greene's book with others because they might replicate or challenge the power and advantages that she has gained from reading the book.

Rhonda Byrne's *The Secret*, which I discuss in Chapter 5, has also played a particularly significant role in Monique's self-help reading practice. Her grandmother learned about *The Secret* on *Oprah* and sent it to Monique as a gift. According to Monique, the central premise of *The Secret* is "If you think negative, negative things will come. It's all about your thought patterns. And if you project positivity, that's what's gonna surround you. . . . The energy that you give off is the energy that you'll get back in." Underlying the book's emphasis on the power of positive thinking is the philosophical conundrum of how to retain notions of individual responsibility and agency while accounting for social and historical forces that delimit individuals' control over their circumstances. As we have seen, Byrne responds to this conundrum by suggesting that one can exert almost complete control over one's circumstances through positive thinking. From Byrne's perspective, even victims of large-scale injustices or tragedies—such as slavery, the Holocaust, or natural disasters—attracted such negative experiences to themselves by virtue of their thinking; "thoughts of fear, separation, and powerlessness . . . attract[ed] them to being in the wrong place at the wrong time."[5] Monique finds this philosophy appealing because it "isn't anything that you can cry over and say, 'Oh, I was abused or I was neglected.' This is like dust yourself off, keep it moving, stay focused, stay positive, and then this is where you can go. Read this and get a plan." Because she privileges the concepts of individual agency and responsibility, Monique agrees with the book's contention that individuals bear some responsibility for suffering from large-scale tragedies or injustices. Slaves "didn't ask to be slaves," she acknowledges, but those who suffer are "paying for mistakes that their ancestors had made."

As I discuss in Chapter 5, we read *The Secret* for one of our group discussions, and it provoked angry responses from many women who believe that it exaggerates the power of positive thinking. Monique, who suggested that we read the book, repeatedly and sometimes defensively tried to explain how and why she finds *The Secret* useful. "The only thing that I liked about the book is just so much positivity about it," she asserted. "I like it because it's like you can start with nothing, but if you put your mind to it and you stay focused, you can end up with everything." At various points in the discussion, Monique emphasized that her reading practice entails picking and choosing what she finds useful. "Any book that I read, I take from it what I need and put the rest of it back on the shelf," she explained.

Like if somebody says, "Yeah the sky is purple and it's raining dogs out there," you're not just gonna take that and say, you know, what? The sky is purple, and it is raining dogs out there. You look into it. And like with this book, a lot of the stuff that they were talking about, I looked deeper than what they just said on the pages. I go past what somebody says in my face and I dig deeper into it. . . . Some people are far fetched. . . . But I didn't take it and critique it like that because I'm just gonna do me.

When some readers complained that *The Secret* is "a scam" because "they're using 'universe' instead of the word 'God' and instead of reading the Bible," Monique highlighted how she disidentifies with the text, filling in what is missing and reappropriating it for her own purposes. "I just put 'God' in certain places where they put 'universe,'" she explained. "Or if I didn't agree with it or it didn't go with my religion, I just disregarded that. . . . A lot of these different things that they were throwing out, I just put my own beliefs in it . . . and left the rest on the shelf for somebody else." At another point, as we were discussing a passage in which Byrne seeks to disprove the notion that "being wealthy is not spiritual," some readers vehemently objected to *The Secret*'s assertion that Jesus was a "millionaire" with a "more affluent lifestyl[e] than many present-day millionaires could conceive of."[6] "Jesus was a poor carpenter," Tyra insisted, "and he lived in poverty!" Monique countered that Byrne didn't necessarily mean wealthy "materialistically"; rather, she was referencing Jesus's mental riches. When Tyra responded, "But affluent? I mean, that man struggled! Someone always wanted to kill him!" Monique suggested that "affluent" means "your riches in your mind," and she emphasized Jesus's ability to cure the "mentally broke." When Tyra insisted that Byrne characterizes Jesus as "affluent like we see Donald Trump as someone very affluent," Monique offered her central interpretation of Byrne's work: "If a million people in this world wanted to kill me, they still can't take away my mental [strength]. So for me, it was moreso a mental thing." Tyra's continued insistence that Byrne uses the word "lifestyle" rather than "mental" led Monique, once again, to highlight her strategic reading practice: "When somebody says one thing, I don't necessarily agree with it. I take it to my level and my context."

As with *The 48 Laws of Power*, Monique also drew favorable comparisons between *The Secret* and Meyer's *Battlefield of the Mind*, suggesting that both books fuel her determination to succeed. Commenting on a verse that stood out to her from Meyer's book—"It shall be done for you as you have believed"—Monique explained,

The Secret isn't as godly based [as Battlefield of the Mind] but it's about positivity, and if you believe it, it will happen. Now I'm not saying that you're going to look at something and say, "Hey, you know what? I'm going to get that, whatever material item it is, or I'm going to get this job." . . . But it's just saying like as long as you believe and you have faith in it, anything is possible. It's like with Proverbs 23:7, "For as he thinks in his heart, so he is." If you really believe that in your heart and that's what you want to do, you can do it.

In clarifying that one cannot gain something simply by desiring it, Monique actually diverges significantly from The Secret, which suggests that positive thinking guarantees rapid material results with little to no effort required.[7] Revisiting this theme a bit later in the conversation, Monique elaborated, "It's gonna take more for you [than] to just look up to the universe or to your God and say, 'I want to be rich' and you get rich. . . . I think it's the in-between level that people forget about." She justified The Secret's failure to mention the in-between steps by arguing, "It was just their way of summing up: 'I did believe and I received it,' you know, as opposed to saying, 'I did it, and it took me eighty-five years or twenty years to get this.'" For Monique, the key concept is that positive thinking can catalyze the necessary action for achieving goals. "If you say, 'I am gonna be a millionaire,' and you keep saying, 'I am, I am, I am,' then you're gonna get in the process and . . . you're gonna go all out and get rich. . . . The Secret is saying I'm gonna throw [my desire] up out there, and I'm gonna do everything under the sun to find what I'm looking for and get where I need to be."

Whereas Monique interprets The Secret in a way that accords with her views, she simply "won't listen" to some self-help books because they offer promises that she finds unrealistic. "I think that you actually have to look within yourself to find that peace or happiness or success that you are looking for," Monique contends. "But there are a lot of books that say if you go out and buy this, then that'll help you get this, or if you wear this particular color for all day long, then you're gonna get these results. And I don't believe that." Monique increasingly prefers books "that are coming from a higher power's perspective"—such as Do You!, Battlefield of the Mind, and Woman, Thou Art Loosed!—because "they don't just say I did it on my own. They put God into it, and I like that because you can't do it by yourself, no matter what belief you have. . . . I think that our higher power really dictates and controls our life. And once we get into the swing of his beat, then the better off we'll be." Identifying two primary perspectives among the self-help books that she reads—"You get man and then you get

God"—Monique suggests that her self-help reading practice entails creating her own synthesis of secular and sacred approaches: "I figure you can keep on the right track if you find common ground in between them and you can go off on your own."

Discussing books with other women is also a central component of Monique's reading practice, and she does so "on a daily basis." "I actually like to sit down with people and kind of pick their brains a little bit," she says, "because maybe I can gain something that might build my character or something. If I see it from one angle, then maybe they can throw something out there that I'll be like no, I didn't catch that." According to Monique, she was talking about the group discussions so much that several women started asking her about how they might participate. Because I did not plan to conduct another round of research, Monique started "trading books" with some of these women, and they now discuss books "on the yard, in our unit, or at lunch, whenever we get a chance, if we're just walking around. . . . We come together and just collaborate on our ideas."

As Monique describes it, her intense practice of self-help reading is geared toward preparing her mentally for the challenges that lie ahead. One of her major goals, upon release from prison, is to carve out a living that does not involve selling drugs. She plans to earn a degree in journalism and eventually open a nightclub that would have "a business side" and "a relaxing side," enabling patrons to "make corporate deals" outside of a corporate setting. "I want to bring people together to be able to network," Monique explains. "That way you can talk business with an agent over here, or you can talk to this contractor over here. . . . I want everybody to be able to come together and make money or do everything on a better level than what they were doing it on." In preparation for opening such a club, Monique also spends some time reading legal materials that pertain to zoning codes, food and liquor licenses, and business loans.[8]

Because she "never want[s] to forget where [she] came from," Monique explains, her post-incarceration plans also include helping imprisoned women to understand that "just because we're in here doesn't mean that you have to stop. We can also use this as a beginning. You know, my favorite phrase is that it's important for time to serve you and you not to serve the time. So use everything that they have to offer, which is not a lot, but it's something. Go to school, get into a pet program, get into maintenance—whatever they have to offer."[9] In an effort to share what she has learned and to present herself as an example for "the younger generation," Monique is also considering writing a book. "I'm twenty-nine, so by my age, you're kind of set in your ways," she argues. "But maybe I can get fifteen-, sixteen-year olds, fourteen, thirteen and try to let them know that it's not about what you do, it's how you do it. . . . Life is a struggle period, but it's all about the choices that you make. It can be a hard struggle or it could be an easy struggle. I'm not saying that I want to save the world, but if at least I put a thought into their mind, it might redirect whatever direction they was going." Emphasizing that she has reached the point of "being honest" with herself and "being real" about her experiences, Monique expresses hope that sharing her story may help others: "I don't mind telling my story because I really got nothing to hide. I made some mistakes and I'm trying to correct them and just keep going. . . . If I could share my story with somebody else and they listen to it and they can get something from it, knowledge shared is knowledge gained."

CHAPTER SIX

Encounters

THE MEETING GROUND OF BOOKS

> If they really want to rehabilitate and change people's minds
> and thoughts and the way us women think and what our
> place is in the world, they would have more book clubs.
> —OLIVIA, Northeast Pre-Release Center

IN HIS 2004 WORK, *Oblivion*, anthropologist Marc Augé reflects,

> The fact of recording other people's tales, or "participating" in their "fic-
> tions," does not happen without having an effect on the life of the observer
> and on his own "fiction." The narrative of either cannot coexist without
> influencing each other or, more precisely, without reshaping each other's
> tales. This is true of ethnological investigation, from which neither those
> who were its object nor he or she who prompted it ever come out unscathed.
> Afterwards they will not quite have the same life as before; to be more pre-
> cise, everything they will have to live and to say will in one way or another
> integrate the plurality of the narratives produced on that occasion.

Augé's reflection illuminates the reciprocal nature of looking and listening,
the ways in which an encounter with the Other can change you and render
you strange unto yourself. In *Ordinary Affects*, anthropologist Kathleen Stewart
describes "encounters and interconnection across difference" as "bodies literally affecting one another and generating intensities," and as "a connection of
some kind that has an impact." Sociologist Elizabeth Long, author of *Book Clubs:
Women and the Uses of Reading in Everyday Life*, argues that participants in book
clubs create "new connections, new meanings, and new relationships—to the
characters in the books or their authors, to themselves, to the other members of
the group, to the society and culture in which they live." Each of these formula-

tions speaks to the ways in which women prisoners and I began to reshape one another's tales and create new cultures of reading through our shared engagements with books.[1]

This chapter analyzes the encounters that resulted from these shared experiences of reading. Focusing on our discussions of six books that fell outside women prisoners' usual reading practices, the first section explores the divergent needs and desires that we brought to the act of reading and the unexpected and often generative outcomes of our conversations. The second and third sections of the chapter feature reflections—first from women prisoners and then from me—about our involvement in this study. Through their encounters with various characters, with one another, with me, and with continually emerging aspects of their own subjectivity, women sometimes inhabited alternative subject positions and experimented with new ways of imagining themselves and their relations to others. I, too, do "not quite have the same life as before" after participating in 245 individual interviews and 51 group conversations with incarcerated women. My thoughts about reading, about women prisoners, and about my role as a scholar have been deeply affected by my interactions with the women featured in this book.

Going "Someplace [We] Didn't Exactly Intend to Go": Group Discussions

Kathleen Stewart's *Ordinary Affects* describes the continuous and often unexpected ways in which individual subjects are shaped through their encounters with others. "Like a live wire," Stewart writes, "the subject channels what's going on around it in the process of its own self-composition. . . . It's a thing composed of encounters and the spaces and events it traverses or inhabits. Things happen. The self moves to react, often pulling itself someplace it didn't exactly intend to go." Stewart's description resonates with my sense of the many ways our group discussions brought women prisoners and me into contact with one another, often pulling us "someplace [we] didn't exactly intend to go." Through our discussions of unfamiliar books and genres, some women connected in deeply personal and relevant ways with seemingly distant material, reexamined their assumptions through a cross-cultural lens, and delighted themselves by achieving deeper understanding than they anticipated. Together, we took texts in surprising directions and co-constructed meanings that would not have been possible had we been reading alone.[2]

When women requested that I choose something new or unusual for the discussions, I found it daunting to select the books. On one level, the task was challenging because the readers represented a wide range of interests and abilities, and some women voiced preferences about what they wanted to read. In one group, for instance, one reader requested that I avoid "black books," while another requested that I avoid books that feature violence against women. At one point, I felt at such a loss about what to choose that I polled family members and friends for suggestions and spent two weeks reading recent fiction. I also felt pressure to choose well because I planned to donate all of our books to the prison libraries and would therefore be shaping the libraries for years to come. On another level, however, I found the selection process so difficult because of my deep desire to provide opportunities for satisfying and meaningful reading experiences. I was thinking of books as a way to nurture women, to give them something, to enable them to experience the sense of transport and intense pleasure that I have experienced as particular books led me to insights seemingly unavailable anywhere else.

Ultimately, we selected the books collaboratively. I elicited suggestions from the women, gathered a range of possibilities, and presented an array of books from which each group could choose. When readers had conflicting preferences, I asked each woman to vote for her top choice, and we read the book that received the most votes. Many of the books that we selected in this manner did not satisfy the expectations or desires of the participants. As the study progressed, however, I began to realize that the actual books didn't matter that much. Many women valued our conversations—as I did—regardless of the books' content. The books served as a kind of connective tissue; they enabled interaction and dialogue, and they fostered women's engagements with characters, with other readers, with the outside world, and with developing versions of themselves.[3]

When I distributed *Anne Frank: The Diary of a Young Girl*, I was hopeful that women would love it and gain sustenance from the story. A few women had read the book long ago, but some had never heard of Anne Frank. When we reconvened to discuss the book, several women characterized it as a "struggle to read," "depressing," and full of "monotony," and one woman said that she "needed a dictionary beside [her] to read it." Yet as the conversation continued, members of the group expressed amazement about Anne's remarkable "stamina and courage," optimism, dedication to educating herself, consciousness of women's inequality, and belief that all people are basically good. Some women also drew correlations between being in hiding and being in prison. Arguing that Anne Frank and her family "were living worse than we are" and through "no fault of their own," Amy emphasized that Anne "was dealing with her internal self.

She never lost her spirit. That's the secret we have to get to. You have to hold onto that center." Referencing one of her favorite books, concentration camp survivor Viktor Frankl's *Man's Search for Meaning*, Amy added, "They can't take your mind." Kate drew a connection between Anne's use of a diary "to keep her sanity" and the strategies that she and other women with life sentences adopt to keep from going "out of [their] mind[s]." Journaling is "how we get our feelings out if we're not free to speak to someone," Kate explained. She and others noted, however, that they feel "paranoid" about journaling in prison. Given their sense that prison personnel "have a key for every lock," the women either tear up what they have written or—after checking to make sure that it "won't offend" anyone—send it home. Just as Anne Frank and her family listened to the radio to keep in touch with the outside world, women in the group talked about books as "a lifeline" and shared how they read the newspaper, including grocery ads and apartment rental ads, as a means to stay connected with the world beyond the prison gates. Some women also expressed a fear of dying in oblivion like those sent to concentration camps. Caesar argued that Jews received assistance, while prisoners—particularly women with life sentences—are essentially forgotten: "I've been here for twenty years. They put us in a hole and now they're putting the lid on it. We have to lift our voices to the outside. . . . The Jews stuck together. That's how they survived. They had people that helped them. But now it's all for self. . . . People outside are not interested in us." Although some women in the group did not enjoy reading *The Diary of a Young Girl*, readers brought the book to life for one another through the discussion.

Three groups voted to read Ernest J. Gaines's *A Lesson before Dying*; although few women enjoyed reading the book, it also sparked important insights and interchanges. Gaines's novel is set in a small Cajun community in the late 1940s, and it depicts the wrongful conviction and execution of a poor, young black man named Jefferson. The novel centers around the relationship that develops between Jefferson and Grant, a university-educated man who has very reluctantly accepted the task of teaching Jefferson how to die with dignity and reclaim the humanity that was stripped from him during his trial. In the final analysis, Grant is as much the object of the "lesson" as Jefferson. Many women found the novel "depressing" and "very dry," and they "hated" the ending; one woman asked twice for reassurance that the book was "just fiction" because she found it so sad. Furthermore, several women said that they did not understand the lesson and felt "disappointed" and "disgusted" with Grant. In struggling to engage with the novel, readers sometimes found points of connection with Grant's girlfriend, whom they considered very strong, and with Jefferson, who felt "so alone and secluded" before Grant gave him a radio as a link to the outside world. The group that had read about Anne Frank drew parallels between the books' emphases on the "resilience of the human spirit." One group also discussed the white prison guard who develops a positive relationship with Jefferson, thereby challenging the community's preconceptions about whites. "The white people who dehumanized this man dehumanized themselves in the process," Amy argued. "Nietzsche said when you're chasing a monster, don't become a monster." This comment led women to reflect on the fact that "the more human [prison] guards act, the more difficult time they have doing their job." By the conclusion of this discussion, Heidi noted, "When I first came tonight, I thought I didn't like this book but now I feel like I really like it." Kate maintained that she "didn't really like the book," but it affected her on a deeply personal level by inspiring her to write stories for her grandchildren. "Since the man was on death row writing his thoughts to people, it made me want to leave something for my grandchildren as a gift," she explained. "We all have things we don't know about our [relatives] until after they're gone. . . . The book moved me to say these things."

A few participants in the study requested that we read Khaled Hosseini's *A Thousand Splendid Suns*, a novel that chronicles the lives of Mariam and Laila, two Afghani women who are married to the same violent man. Some readers characterized the book as "horrible," "too violent," and "too traumatic to recommend," noting that they "took the book personally" and "had trouble sleeping" because it "dredged up stuff." Others said that they "couldn't put it down" and described the book as "tremendous," a "horrible story but beautifully written," and a moving portrait of "intergenerational friendship" and "unconditional love." In each discussion group, readers talked about the friendship and dedication between the two women, Laila's tremendous love and sacrifices for her children, the abuse that both women sustain, and Mariam's selfless death. The novel's hopeful ending, which portrays Laila and the love of her life reunited and poised to help with the rebuilding of Afghanistan, prompted women to debate whether such an ending seems too much "like a fairytale" or presents an inspiring assurance that "things can always get better." When Helen argued, "No matter what you endure, no matter how bad it is, how dark, there's a snippet of love or a wellspring of hope. You can see that in everything," Liz responded, "But what's peaches and cream about their situation?" Undaunted, Helen retorted, "Yeah, but what's the soul if the soul cannot climb above all that? That was Mariam's message."

Women's discussions of *A Thousand Splendid Suns* also generated particularly interesting debates about the treatment of women from a cross-cultural perspective. Some women made comments such as "I'm glad I live in the U.S. and don't go through all that they go through over there" and "This book brought home how much other countries need the U.S. I understood better why our troops are there." Other women insisted that although the United States "doesn't condone" violence against women, "the system enables" the violent treatment of women in individual households. Kate argued, for instance, "It didn't make me glad to be born in the U.S. I drew parallels between here and there. . . . The same thing happened to me. . . . Women are united around the world because we suffer the same things. . . . It seems like the stories are all the same." Kate later commented that she found it very upsetting to read *A Thousand Splendid Suns*, but "it taught me about myself. I'm a stronger person than I thought. I don't have to relive the past since I've gone through a healing process. It just caused short-term discomfort." She wants to read the novel again "several years from now" to see "if it will seem different" to her then. As we have seen in previous chapters, reading thus serves as a means for some women to gauge their personal growth.[4]

A more advanced group of readers voted to read Toni Morrison's *Beloved*, the story of a former slave woman who kills her daughter to keep her out of slavery. Women found the novel very difficult, so I took an active role in leading the discussion. Sky later said of the experience, "I didn't understand a word of *Beloved* but I tried. I wouldn't have read it on my own. It was totally frustrating. But the discussion was like a light bulb went off!" Helen said that she "saw threads towards the middle. And in the discussion, I got more understanding. I could see that I was on the right road, and it felt good." Despite their frustration with *Beloved*, the participants surprised themselves by their own abilities and insights, and they all kept the book to try reading it again. As our discussion was coming to a close, Angelique commented, "It's the intellectual conversation that we miss so much. Intellectual and emotional conversation refreshes the brain."

One group that wanted to read something historical chose Harriet Jacobs's *Incidents in the Life of a Slave Girl* (1861), an autobiographical account of Jacobs's desperate attempt to escape her master's sexual predation by hiding in a crawl space for seven years. The narrative seemed too distant to some women, and only about half of the participants finished it. It catalyzed a very lively and important discussion, however, beginning with Sissy's reflections about her great-grandmother, a former slave. "It's like rehearing her story about the struggle for finding your place when you've gone through abuse," Sissy explained, "because she went through that also." Sissy's great-grandmother repeatedly recounted how her master's son would greet her late at night and "stick that funny looking yellow thing up in me," and until the time she died, she continued to say, "I wish

I was never pretty." Discussing the effects of her great-grandmother's experiences on subsequent generations, including her mother and herself, Sissy said of Jacobs's narrative, "That's why it was like oh my God, this is really, really sad."[5]

Incidents in the Life of a Slave Girl also prompted women to compare the situation of African Americans in the contemporary United States and in the time period depicted in Jacobs's narrative. Explaining that she could "feel their pain" as she was reading *Incidents*, Jacqueline said, "This book made me proud to be a black woman. And it also let me know that there's nothing in life that I can't tackle because of the people that I come from. These people were so strong that it made me sad because black people back then, they helped each other. It didn't matter if you were a family member or not. They had a connection. We've lost that, you know. I want my children to read this. I want my grandbabies to know about this." Women in the group, all of whom are African American, then lamented that children do not learn black history in public schools, and they expressed concern that black children "don't want to hear about" black history and "won't accept it" because "they feel like it disrespects them." Moreover, contemporary black youth believe that "the only way they're going to get out of the ghetto is by either playing ball or rapping." Rhonda argued that the entertainment business "is another form of slavery" because dominant white culture only accepts African Americans in rap and sports, and "our children think this is what they got to do to survive." Wendy argued that "they're not teaching education. What you see on TV is you got to have the money, the big jewelry, the fancy clothes," and kids do not realize that "you got to work for things" and that "walking around with some twenty carat diamond on you isn't really all that important anyways."

Women in the group then debated whether the current position of African Americans reflects a lack of initiative and failure to work together or, rather, serves as evidence of the ongoing efforts of whites to exert "power and control" over blacks. Jacqueline and Wendy argued that African Americans no longer have "the hunger and the thirst" for education and equal treatment that they had during slavery and the civil rights movement. "There are no individuals, no free thinkers anymore, and that's why things are going down," Wendy asserted. "There are no people out there studying to be Dr. Kings. Studying to be Malcolm X. Studying to be Nat Turners and Nicky Giovannis, you know what I'm saying? Since the civil rights movement, we have been going backwards instead of forwards." Rhonda insisted, by contrast, that "the government planned it that way. That's why they kill whole neighborhoods of black folks. . . . The white man's still dominant. He wants to stay dominant. And he's gonna do whatever he can to try to keep us oppressed and controlled." Expressing disagreement with "the whole conspiracy thing," Wendy said to Rhonda, "If that's the way you're feeling about the situation, you're either part of the problem or you're part of the solution. What are *you* doing as an African American woman to change the way society is seeing?" Wendy and Jacqueline then discussed the importance of "joining together," as people did when Martin Luther King Jr. was alive. Jacqueline shared her plans, upon her release, to "do something with the kids because somebody has to reach them" before they end up in prison. Wendy spoke passionately about the possibilities of "the information age," arguing,

> I can be talking to somebody in Moscow or China that has the same
> ideas as me who wants to change the world, because I'm not just about
> the black struggle. I'm about the struggle in general, the endangered spe-
> cies, the rain forest. You know, there are so many things, so many atrocities
> in this world right now. The AIDS epidemic in Africa. The homeless people
> here in America. And there's so much going on that needs to be viewed
> and changed, and it's just insanity that people don't see this. And if they
> do see it, they step over it. And if I'm one of the ones that see it without
> my glasses, and I'm legally blind, I can find somebody that sees it that way,
> and then he can find somebody else that sees it that way—there's power
> in numbers.

Such enthusiasm did not move Rhonda, however, who insisted, "They're not gonna let you get to that level where they feel intimidated by you. They're gonna keep you under control. . . . The society we live in is about power and control. It's been like that from the beginning. America, with the slavery thing, power and control. That's all I got to say." This debate remained unresolved, but the overall discussion illustrates how women prisoners found ways to make a text published in 1861 relevant to their lives.

Another group's discussion of Zora Neale Hurston's *Their Eyes Were Watching God* illuminates how women learned from one another and co-constructed meaning in discussing texts. Deven first responded to the novel by saying, "I just could not get that dialect. And so it was frustrating me, and it was pissing me off." Denise responded, "I enjoyed the dialect because it takes me back home. I used to talk just like this"; she went on to argue that the characters in the novel "are very intelligent, but their intelligence come from God. It didn't come from a book. The things they know, they know from inside." Highlighting her personal knowledge of "a lot of things they were speaking about," Denise discussed some of her favorite "cute sayings" from the text, including, "Beating women is just like stepping on baby chickens." The characters "may not know how to say it in the right words," she argued, "but they said it the way they saw it in their head, and I like that." After listening to Denise, Solo commented, "This story right here, you could have written it! Because of the way you told the story, and the way you related to it, and you've done that with pretty much every book." Deven concurred, recounting that while she was struggling to read the novel, she thought about finding Denise and saying to her, "You need to read the book to me, 'cause I just can't do it." Deven then said, in the midst of laughter that morphed into happy tears by the end of her statement,

> Denise, I gotta tell you. When I came today, I was ready to tell [Ms. Sweeney] okay, this book sucked bananas, and I don't understand any portion of it. But when you sat down and blah, blah, blah, and I'm thinking oh my God, I remember that part! I remember that part, that part, that part. Just from you giving your own description about it, it helped me realize that I did understand the story. I really did. I got a lot more out of it than I really thought I did. And you know, I was trying to be very close-minded just because the dialect was not the dialect that I would choose. And I have to say even when we got the Sister Souljah book, I was like—oh, let me tell you— I was like what kind of hooey phooey bull crap shit is that? I was closed-minded. And I don't want to be that way, and I talked to [Ms. Sweeney] at length about having that tunnel vision and being close-minded, and I have to say just throughout all of this, I feel like I have evolved, and that I know more about so much, and it makes me feel good because I just didn't think I could learn that.

For the remainder of the discussion, the participants closely analyzed various events in the novel, including Janie's sexual awakening, various marriages, and arrest for shooting Teacake after his infection with rabies. They also engaged in an extended conversation about funerals and diverse ways of grieving, drawing on their own experiences of feeling pressured to grieve in socially acceptable ways. Commenting on the fact that Janie wore overalls to Teacake's funeral, Denise recounted her intensely painful experience of going straight to her mother's funeral from prison, wearing "a purple jogging suit from K-Mart," and receiving explicit and implicit criticism from others in attendance. "It's a certain kind of grief where you don't care about how your hair look," Denise explained. "I understand that kind of grief where none of this don't matter. . . . And I loved that part in that book that somebody else know that kind of grief and had the nerve to write about it." Women in the group also asked questions about the contemporaneous reception of Hurston's work, which led to a discussion of the ways in which "it's still a man's world."

As these discussions illustrate, participating in learning communities enabled women prisoners—many of whom had little experience with diverse narrative styles—to generate layers of unexpected meaning from texts and to read and understand beyond their self-perceived abilities. Encountering different characters and other readers also inspired women in various ways and enabled them to gain critical distance from, or to become more in touch with, their own experiences. In going someplace they didn't exactly intend to go, the readers gained greater awareness of where they already are.

Reading Communities, Communities of Readers

As previous chapters of this book illustrate, encounters with book characters and protagonists enabled women to inhabit alternative subject positions and experiment with new ways of imagining themselves and others. Nena described her participation in the study as a series of inspirational encounters with people and characters featured in books: "I could relate everything directly with my experience and see people who gave up or refused to give up and kept keeping on and kept it moving." Solo described her encounters with books in terms of both inhabiting and incorporating others' experiences: "The religious books, the philosophies, books about successful women—I can take stuff from that and add to like my closet. I can wear some of Oprah's dresses sometime, you know, because I know that it wasn't always easy for her. . . . I can kind of step in her shoes sometimes by her book. . . . I can take stuff from those pages, and I can put them inside of me. And then when I'm in a situation, I can use them." As Wayne Booth argues, reading often involves "*taking in* the new selves offered in stories" and "trying out"—in a low-risk "trial run"—the lives depicted in books.[6]

What seemed most striking from the book discussions, however, was how reading enabled women to encounter one another. Despite the forces arrayed against women developing relationships in conditions of confinement, the book discussions not only created reading communities; they also helped to create communities of readers. As with all communities, the burgeoning of these groups often involved discoveries of otherness and the interchange of unfamiliar ideas, recognition of commonalities across lines of difference, efforts to police one another, and efforts to support, encourage, and learn from each other. When I first began my research, I was unsure how women would respond to the format of the group discussions, given the compulsory nature of group discussions during the era of bibliotherapy and the prevalence of the group format in existing therapeutic programs. However, many women considered the group discussions one of the most attractive aspects of participating in the study. Over and over, they emphasized how much they enjoyed "hearing what others think"; discussing books with "other people that have different ideas, different opinions, and different beliefs"; and being able to "talk about these books and get real life experiences from people who lived different than you." Prisoners' uses of books as vehicles for engaging in dialogue with each other and with the world beyond the prison walls illustrate the intersubjective dimensions of their reading practices.[7]

According to women involved in the study, the book discussions provided a rare opportunity to gather for conversation. "With us being in different units, this is a chance for us to get together," Monique explained, "'cause you're not supposed to get with someone from a different unit. So now this is like a chance that you can go and talk to other people." Maisey specified that the discussions gave older women with life sentences an additional opportunity for interaction, since there is only one program geared toward their needs. Denise and Sissy, who participated in the first round of research in Ohio, found the group experience so attractive that they wanted to participate in the second round as well, even if we read the same books.

Deven, who is white, was part of a discussion group in which African American women were the most steady participants. During that group's final conversation, Solo offered the following compliment to Deven: "You, my light-skinned sister, what I like about you, you're just so genuine wherever you are. . . . And you stuck with it. Keepin' it real, I'm sure some of the books might have been uncomfortable, you know, because you're reading about a different culture than yours, but you're not letting that influence you, and you're not saying, 'Oh they only talk about black and white issues in there. I don't want to do that.'" Gesturing toward me, Deven replied with laughter, "Well see, the very first one, that Coldest Winter Ever, I thought man, is this chick nuts? Is she fricking nuts or what? We're gonna have a riot up in here! . . . I was the only white person in the bunch! And I'm thinking to myself oh, this is gonna be all bad." Solo responded, "You continually evolved as genuine, and you came in and spoke. Forget the color. You just spoke from the literature of it." Deven then went on to say, "I would have never taken the opportunity to read these books, so I'm very blessed with having the knowledge of Toni Morrison, Ms. Hurston, Sister Souljah, Patrice Gaines. For me it was just a wonderful learning experience." A bit later in the conversation, she added, "Truthfully, it made me feel good because I have to say that I was a little scared about the sessions. You know, I was thinking well, my thoughts aren't her thoughts, and a lot of people are so judgmental and critical, and I thought, I've never really spoken in an open forum. [But] we all let each other speak and we all listened to what each other said and either disagreed or agreed."

Racial tensions did not, however, magically disappear as a result of the group discussions. After her group's final conversation, Kate confided in me—presuming our racial solidarity—that Ernest Gaines's *A Lesson before Dying* "concerned" her. "I was holding my breath about the subject matter," she said. "There's reverse racism here. People have a 'woe is me attitude' if they have the wrong color skin, instead of looking at it like it's an unfortunate thing but you can still make changes. I mean, the Irish were treated worse than your people. The only jobs for stupid Mics were jobs that blacks wouldn't do. Women say they want to be treated like everyone else but they also want special treatment." Aligning herself with the white women in her group, including one who decided not to attend the session because she was wary of discussing race, Kate explained, "I was mentally prepared for nonsense to start. I was planning to steer the conversation if it starts that way. I knew Amy and Heidi would help. I didn't want something embarrassing to happen. Some women don't know how to behave with guests. I wanted to protect the integrity of the group." Although the actual group discussion probably did not alter Kate's racial views, the fact that it "pleasantly surprised" her seems significant; at the very least, the discussion demonstrated to Kate that it is possible to have a productive cross-racial discussion of race and racism. Furthermore, Heidi's perspective on the group's racial dynamics—which she voiced in front of Kate—may have challenged Kate's implicit division of the group along lines of race. "I didn't feel any racial tension," said Heidi. "I was curious to hear black women's perspectives. . . . I like hearing the diversity of thoughts and opinions. . . . I think it's great that we can have black and white women discussing a book about racism. And we can read *A Thousand Splendid Suns* with Muslims and not get into an argument about it. It's a nice dynamic to have so many women with different backgrounds."[8]

Several women suggested that the discussions helped them to understand how particular experiences shape one's perspective. Helen, who believes that "everybody is your teacher," said, "Everybody has their own life experiences, and they brought that in, too. You realize she processed the book that way because of her experiences." Sissy said of the group discussions, "It's about learning other people's ideas and opinions and seeing other people's perception and interpretation of what we read, and then it's something for us to think on. I get something every time I come here out of something somebody said because I didn't see it that way. . . . I don't have to agree, but I can understand where she's coming from because that's *her* opinion." Deven explained her new understanding of perspective in these terms:

> The thing that it showed me is that there's a book in all of us. We can write it from so many different views, so many different angles. I mean, even though we're sitting here at this same spot right now, you could go write a book, I could go write a book, and it's gonna be totally different because even though we're in the same situation, we have totally different views. . . . There might be some similarities here and there, but they're going to be descripted in a different way. You know, her dialect is not gonna be my dialect. What focal point she has from that whole situation that has taken place, it's not going to be the focal point that I have seen it from. . . . Every one of these books have taught me that there is a story within each one of us, and even though I might want you to see it from my point of view, I have to take the time out to see it from your point of view, too, or I'm not gonna get the whole well-rounded picture.

Discussing books with others also served as a kind of "consciousness-raising process" that enabled women to validate their own views as legitimate or understandable.[9] Comparing her thoughts with those of others enabled Jacqueline to discern whether her own thoughts "are crazy or reasonable." Denise found comfort in hearing others affirm her views: "It's a good feeling when you come together and all of you see the same thing. And it lets you know that it's somebody else in the world that thinks like me. I'm not wrong about the way I feel or the way I'm thinking. Somebody else done experienced this, too." Hearing other women's views also allowed readers to recognize commonalities across lines of difference. As Heidi said, "I was surprised to hear we were all having such similar thoughts, even women I don't know and thought I didn't have anything in common with." Furthermore, some women gained satisfaction from asserting their own views and developing a distinct sense of themselves in relation to others. Nena enjoyed having "a chance to speak with no specific boundaries." Gypsy Rose said, "It was a good feeling to put my words on a book," while Gracie said, "It was a positive experience to read something I didn't like but still have that right to my own opinion." Kate highlighted how a group encounter can lead to greater introspection when she said, "I related more of myself to the books through the group discussions."

Readers brought a wealth of experiences to the discussions, and many women emphasized that they "learned a lot from other people" and received "a lot of encouragement" from members of the group. Certain women emerged as mentors, and other group members sometimes commented on how helpful they found the mentors' contributions. Boo, who has been incarcerated for twenty-nine years, was a frequent recipient of such praise. During one discussion, for instance, Maisey said, "I love to listen to you talk, Boo. . . . You should be a mentor." Drea likewise said, "For a long time, I was close-minded. But here we all got something in common. Some people have valuable information. I'm amazed at how you can apply it to your life. Boo gives me hope and strength." The group discussions also gave women a chance to see one another in a new light and to discover other women who want to do their time in similar ways. As Olivia explained, "For all the women that was in the group, I got to see a different side of some of the women that I see out there on the yard, you know, or in groups." Referencing Monique as an example, Olivia said, "I seen her in the yard and stuff, but I never really knew she's really a smart girl. I didn't know her like that. She really surprised me." She likewise said to Genevieve, "I didn't know about your [education] and all that. You know, that's really inspiring to me." Olivia concluded that the book group "helps us unite a little bit" and helps her to "come out of my little shell a little bit to see what other people's perspectives are, and where you're coming from."

Several women emphasized, moreover, that they gained a sense of belonging and common purpose and even developed lasting friendships from participating in the study. Angelique and Helen, who discovered that they are similar "types" because they both like to "sit and reflect," explained that discussing books "gives you a common link, and you can build off that" and "build friendships." Valhalla recounted during one discussion, "Me and Monique were talking a couple of weeks ago how much we enjoyed it, and people were like, 'Oh I want to get in. I want to get in.' I'm like, 'No, no this is our elite reading club' [laughter]." Acknowledging that she had some hesitations about participating in the study, Monique added, "Once I stuck with it, I'm like yeah, I'm glad as hell that I got to go to group. I'll be walking in front of them and women will be like, 'Where you going?' 'I'm going to group!' Monday night, I'm like where's my pass? I got to go to group!" When I returned to the Ohio prison six months after completing the study, several women reported that they are "still friends" and "talk all the time" with other women from their discussion group. Tyra noted that she misses the reading group because she has a more "intimate" relationship with those women than with other prisoners. For Deven and Denise, developing a friendship during their group's discussions was a source of joy:

DEVEN: It helped me to get to know you, Denise. Oh my god, I know you so much! I love Denise! Denise and I, we've left here a couple of times, and we're

DENISE: still talking!

DEVEN: Yeah, we are just so overjoyed about this, you know! We always are talking about, "God, I'm so glad you said this. It's like you got it." Or you know, she says that to me.

DENISE: It's like I feed off of her.

DEVEN: Yes, we feed off each other.

One of my favorite memories from the study is of Genevieve saying to Monique as they were leaving their group's final discussion, "You know, I'm interested in chess 'cause I used to play chess in high school." My audio recording stops at that point, but the women continued their conversation; as they walked out the door, they were trying to figure out how they might play chess together. Genevieve discovered Monique's passion for chess through a discussion of Joyce Meyer's *Battlefield of the Mind*, and that discovery was the seed for a potential friendship.

Women's sense of belonging also extended beyond the confines of their discussion groups; indeed, books served as a bridge to the larger community, enabling women to feel like they are part of a conversation that usually goes on without them. In Angelique's words, "The group has made me realize that we can still be on the same page as someone out there. We can have the same thoughts and the same emotions." And as Helen said during one of our discussions, "When we're here, I don't feel incarcerated. I feel a part of society as a whole."

Because they found the social dimension of the book discussions so rewarding, many women were interested in arranging additional shared experiences of reading. Since their prison library has two copies of some books, some women planned to pair up with a friend and read the same books, and they were encouraging others to do the same. Nez said, "I'm gonna ask my friends to make a book group and each person will pick a book. We'll meet each week or every two weeks. I got the idea from this group. We would read lots of Triple Crown books and *The Confident Woman*." When I returned to the Ohio prison, some women had been encouraging others to read specific books or to read in general. Genevieve reported that two or three of her friends "always read what I do after I read them." Given the high level of interest in the book discussions, several women in both prisons were also investigating organizational and financial possibilities for continuing book discussions on their own. In Ohio, women pleaded with me to talk to the requisite supervisor because "it's not easy to get a group started here if it's just inmates. They don't like us coming together as a group. They fear an uprising or something." In Pennsylvania, some women had already started speaking with various counselors, staff members, and the new programming director to see if they might sponsor a book club. Explaining the enthusiasm about continuing the discussions, Kate said, "This book club awakened a lot of us in a way we haven't been for a long time. We're all trying to keep it going. . . . We've had a lull here. How may computer classes can you take? How many times can you take anger management because it's under a good facilitator?" Because news of the book discussions had "spread like wildfire," Heidi, who is part of an inmate organization, was investigating how the organization might sponsor book discussions. Funding might come from the Inmate General Welfare Fund, she explained, or from a fundraiser of selling sodas, digital photos, or ice cream. Heidi asked me how to lead a book discussion, so I showed her the notes that I prepared for our discussions and offered suggestions about how to involve other participants in facilitating the conversations.[10]

Over the course of their participation in the study, many women reported alterations in their reading practices. Confirming Jenny Hartley's claim that knowing that you will be discussing a book pushes you to take stock of what you really thought, readers noticed that they had begun to "look more into things," "stop and think more about the characters and the subject," "dissect the characters," and "analyze situations more."[11] Heidi explained, "It made me think more about the books knowing that I was going to talk about what a book did for me—if I liked it or didn't like it, and what's important to me. I hope that will stick with me." Echoing Kate's claim that the book club "awakened" women, Heidi added, "I'm still a little numb coming out of the shell of my other life and my addiction. It's time to wake up, so it came at a good time for me." Some women began to read with greater frequency; when I returned six months after completing the study, Olivia reported, "All I ever do is read." Others became more deliberate about reading. Genevieve, for instance, started keeping a folder with notes about every book that she reads, excluding romances.

Breeanna's comment—"I'm not afraid of new kinds of books now"—highlights how participating in the study also led many women to expand what they are willing to read. Women often described such changes in their reading practices in terms of an "opening up." Olivia commented, "It really opened me up" in describing her new willingness to read hardback books and books that "take me somewhere else from what I'm used to reading." Angelique said, "For me, a door opened up from doing this. I'm the Dean Koontz, James Patterson, Patricia Cornwell person, but now I want to read something new. . . . I would have never picked up *A Thousand Splendid Suns*. It wasn't appealing to me, and I'm not familiar with the author. . . . But I couldn't put it down. . . . I'm learning to have a more open mind about books." Some women have gained the confidence to choose "random" books because they have discovered that it is possible to make meaning from every book; as one woman put it, "We all took something from each book we read." Kaye has concluded that "sometimes it's good to just go out of the box and pick a book that has good ratings. I wouldn't have done that before, but now I'm more open to learning." Kate has decided that at least two times a year, she will "pull a book from the shelf with no thought, without even flipping through it." By asking herself, "What am I going to get out of this?" she is confident that she will "open up new doors" and "expand [her] thinking."

In the midst of the study, Deven decided to read Toni Morrison's *The Bluest Eye* on her own because "everybody kept saying Toni Morrison, and I was like oh shit! Who's Toni Morrison, and why do I need to read this?" Acknowledging that she "didn't get it" when she read it, Deven plans to reread *The Bluest Eye* "because after doing this book group study, I feel like when I read a book now, not only am I absorbing the story, but I'm really absorbing the characters and I'm really taking a look at where does this woman go? What happens? You know, it gives me a new way to read the book." Denise described the changes in her reading preferences as a matter of growth: "After all the books we've read, it's like they went stronger and stronger and stronger. It's like an elevation. They just went up and up and up mentally and spiritually for me, to where *The Coldest Winter Ever* is the last man on the totem pole now, when I thought that was just *the* book in the beginning." Arguing that *The Coldest Winter Ever* "works with somebody [age] nineteen or eighteen," Denise said of the other books that we read, "It's like *The Coldest Winter Ever* grew up." Concurring, Deven added, "And I think that we grew with them, too."

Through their participation in this study, many women prisoners also encountered newly emerging or long-forgotten aspects of their own subjectivity. "I really enjoyed this group because you don't get a chance to go in the depth of *you* often and really see what's there," Denise explained. As they encountered themselves on paper—in reading the transcripts of their individual interviews and group discussions—some women merely corrected hesitations or places where they didn't like the sound of their grammar. Other women made small changes that reflected particular desires about how they wanted to present themselves. For instance, one woman added a more glamorous pseudonym and changed her age from thirty to twenty-five, while another removed a statement that she had to attend a mental health appointment. As we saw with Denise in Interlude 1, it was a powerful experience for some women to read their transcripts. When Miekal returned with her redacted transcripts, her face was flushed and she said, "I liked this. This was good." I asked, "What did you like about it?" and she said, "Me!" Acknowledging, "I didn't think you got all that," Miekal went on to explain, "We read all these books about other people" but it was new "seeing me on paper. I liked what I read. This was me. It was my life. It was my story. This was a thrill for me. . . . It blew me away. This gave me inspiration to tell my story." Miekal then flipped through her transcript and showed me pages that were especially important to her, including her discussion of the rapes that she sustained, passages about her former partner, and her description of telling her mother that she is a lesbian. She also noted that reading about Vibe Night—a poetry club that she has started in prison—"gave [her] chills" because it concretized the possibility that she could open such a club after she is released from prison. "That's all I think about. It's my dream," she shared. "Now I know it's gonna happen."

Another woman told me at the start of her individual interview that she had never had "more than twenty minutes" to recount her life story, and she then spoke very emotionally for almost two hours. Yet in reviewing her interview transcript, she carefully redacted all references to pain, including her extensive experiences of sexual and physical abuse. She seemed to find it overwhelming to encounter her painful history on paper. This reader nonetheless loved books about women whose lives mirror her own. "Texts introduce a distance between the immediacy of experience and the self and, in that distance, codify experience," Illouz argues. Reading others' stories seemed to provide the necessary distance for this woman to encounter herself.[12]

In my introduction, I reflected on Trinh T. Minh-ha's question, "What do I want wanting to know you or me?"[13] Women's reflections about their participation in my study also prompt me to consider Minh-ha's question from their perspective: What might women prisoners have wanted in wanting to know me and in wanting to be part of my study? Which of those wants was I unable to fulfill? For a few women who have been cruelly misrepresented by journalists and the media, my book represented an opportunity for them to set the record straight and tell their side of the story. Referencing the other authors who have told her story, one woman said to me, "It seemed like you'll be one not like the rest." On a more general level, some women may have wanted to present a positive image of imprisoned women, an image that I could reflect back to them and

A heavily redacted page from one woman's interview transcript. In review-ing her transcript, this interviewee systematically crossed out all references to painful aspects of her past.

offer to the reading public. I have done my best to represent women's words and experiences with accuracy and compassion. I am aware, however, that my book falls far short of sharing the stories of all the participants.

Many women also seemed to want intellectual stimulation and validation of their thoughts and ideas. Being treated as an intelligent thinker by a white, middle-class college professor held special significance for some readers. As Solo explained to me one day, "Some people, they have tours here. Like we're a zoo. And they come in and they act like they can't even say hello. . . . They make me feel like an animal." Some visitors and volunteers are "stuffy," and they act like, "'Move the other way! The Professor is here.' Some people bring that and you feel it, and you feel inferior to it." Because I did not give Solo that feeling, she said of my study, "I just want it to be a success. And I want to be a part of it, so wherever I am, I can say I was part of something that was a success."

Because I invited women to share their life stories during their individual interviews, they sometimes engaged in deep and emotional reflection about their experiences, almost as if they were speaking with a counselor; some of these women noted that they "had never talked like this with anyone before." I made it clear that I have no training in counseling, but I occasionally shared thoughts or reflections that seemed especially relevant to what women were saying. On one such occasion, when Solo was recounting a painful story about a childhood shame that she "just can't get past," I offered some thoughts about the struggle for external validation and possibilities for recognizing one's own worth. Solo expressed gratitude for my reflections, suggesting that I was offering them from a more neutral position than if I were a prison counselor: "You're doing it because you don't have a vested interest in it. I'm just someone you're meeting. You're doing a research paper as opposed to say a therapist here. It's more pure. And you even said you're challenged with this issue." At the conclusion of the study, Solo told me that her "best time" with me was "that very first day when I was emotional," and she explained that she has not "had that sense of hurt since that day." As in this instance, prisoners often seemed to want someone to listen attentively and nonjudgmentally to their story.

Most of all, women seemed to want human connection, a recognition of their dignity and humanity in an environment that can feel—in Solo's words—like "trying to live in a grave." On a few occasions, women directly expressed their desire to see their reflection in my eyes. At the conclusion of our final discussion, Genevieve asked, "From the beginning up to now, what do you think of like, me? From the beginning, like from the first time you interviewed me?" On other occasions, women seemed to find it helpful to tell a willing listener about times when others had failed to recognize their humanity. For instance, Jacqueline arrived at her first interview just after being insulted by an officer. She was barely able to speak and began quietly sobbing as she told me what had happened. I listened sympathetically, offering supportive words and tissues, and then the two of us sat quietly for about a minute, looking directly at each other. At the end of her interview, Jacqueline started crying again and said that she was at the end of her rope in terms of treatment by various officers. We talked about ways for her to hold on to her own sense of dignity and worth as a human being even when officers are acting out their fears, insecurities, anger, or frustrations. When I met with her the following morning, Jacqueline seemed very calm and centered, and she said, "You don't know what you've done for me." With books serving as the impetus and vehicle for connection, simple acts of witnessing helped women to regain their sense of dignity in moments when they were feeling erased.

"Did You Learn Anything from Us?"

"I want to ask you a question. Did you learn anything from us?" Over the course of writing this book, I have realized how difficult it is to formulate an adequate response to this question that Mocha posed during her group's final discussion. When I first reviewed the transcript that contains Mocha's question, I cringed in anticipation of reading my response. Here is what I said:

> That's why I'm writing this book is to say what I've learned. I mean, everything from, I didn't even know what an urban book was and you know, I didn't know about Joyce Meyer. I didn't know about Iyanla Vanzant. But I learned, well first of all, I learned some things about who you are and what your lives are like. And for me, that's such a huge part of being able to tell people on the outside—sort of like what I was saying about Patrice Gaines—to be able to say you don't know who women in prison are. You know, let me tell about the courage and the strength and the honor of these women and how much you all are trying so hard to do something with your lives and be reflective and change. And a lot of people on the outside, they don't do that themselves, let alone understand that people in prison are doing that. And so for me it was about learning what your struggles have been, what your hopes are, and how you're going about trying to live your lives and change your lives.

My response to Mocha merely skims the surface of what I want to say about the many things that I have learned from women prisoners. In my efforts to articulate these things, I have struggled to find a voice that merges academic analysis with deeper reflection about what happened to me from spending so much time with women prisoners.

Among myriad lessons about reading, I have learned that recognizing oneself in the pages of a book is a privilege that many women prisoners have not previously enjoyed; whether such recognition feels thrilling, empowering, or frightening, it is almost always a significant experience. I have learned that although books may seem boring, irrelevant, or uninteresting to some readers, they can still spark meaningful and lively dialogue. I have learned, too, that the tactile and aesthetic properties of books can matter a great deal in prisons, where other forms of touch, sensation, and beauty are lacking. Most importantly, I've learned that readers bring a wide range of motivations, needs, and desires to the act of reading and to particular reading situations. Recognizing the strategic, contingent, and context-specific dimensions of reading has enabled me to focus on understanding, rather than judging, different reading practices.

Indeed, conducting this study has taught me a great deal about the fantasies and desires that I bring to the act of reading. Acknowledging the disappointment that I felt when a woman would say, "I read one page. It didn't catch my attention" helped me to recognize my desire to nurture and feed women through books. Given this desire, I sometimes felt at a loss when readers had no appetite for my literary fare. When a woman announced that she "didn't have an epiphany or anything deep from reading," I realized the extent to which I was hoping for epiphanic outcomes for other readers, just as I hope for them for myself. Even though women participated in selecting the books, one woman's comment that "going from abuse to the Holocaust was a bit much" pushed me to recognize my preference for books that facilitate reckoning with personal and collective histories. Given how much pleasure I derive from untangling complex narratives, I was also forced to reckon with the anxiety and incompetence that I felt when faced with a straightforward narrative. Prior to the first group discussion of Jakes's *Woman, Thou Art Loosed!* for instance, I worried that women would have little to say about its familiar plot and themes. In actuality, four different groups discussed the novel with particular intensity and interest, illustrating Elizabeth Long's claim that the quality of a book discussion often has far less to do with "the level of difficulty or quality of the text" than with the extent to which it provides "the pleasures of deep emotional involvement" or "illumination of [readers'] experience."[14]

My involvement in this study has pushed me, moreover, to recognize my blind spots about reading practices that are less familiar to me. I felt an affinity with Denise's reading practice because, in some ways, it resembles my own. She enters and inhabits stories in an intense way, and she makes links between her personal experiences and larger structures. I have had greater difficulty knowing how to discuss reading practices that foreground "lightweight fantasy" or escape because such approaches are less familiar to me. Furthermore, given my desire for women to view their own lives as open-ended narratives that can always accommodate further expansion and change, I felt uncomfortable with the kinds of closure that some urban books propagate. In fact, with one group of women who never wanted to read anything but urban fiction, I found myself enacting something like the "two-book system" that early-twentieth-century public librarians adopted in order to curb readers' engagement with popular fiction. Whereas public librarians allowed patrons to check out two books only if one was nonfiction, I asked the women to pair Danielle Santiago's *Grindin'* with Harper Lee's 1960 novel, *To Kill a Mockingbird*. In my own way, I was encouraging prisoners—as Austin MacCormick advocated in 1931—to "climb" up the "inclined plane" of literary taste by indicating the "hand-holds" above their heads.[15] I wanted women to experience another kind of book that, in my view, offers a nuanced exploration of some of the issues that urban books raise. When we gathered for the discussion, however, Kaye was the only woman who had read all of *To Kill a Mockingbird*, although Nez had started and planned to finish it. One reader said that she did not remember me distributing or talking about the book, and others simply did not open it. We therefore spent the session having an animated conversation about *Grindin'*. In addition to highlighting my bibliotherapeutic instinct, this incident helped me to accept that for women such as Kaye, reading often entails moving toward a new destination, while for some other women, reading often entails staying in a comfortable place.[16]

Ultimately, I stopped trying to identify the limitations of our respective reading practices and tried, instead, to identify the divergent motivations, needs, and desires that fuel various kinds of reading. I found it helpful to focus on the question, "What is she/what am I reading *for*?" As Leah Price argues, readers often have a repertoire of reading styles that they can switch on and off at will.[17] As I do, imprisoned women read strategically, for different purposes at different times. For example, in our discussion of Pearl Cleage's *What Looks Like Crazy on an Ordinary Day*—which I discuss in Chapter 5—I was reading to assess the book's depictions of criminals, while women in the group were reading to find inspiration and models for change. Because I did not recognize this difference, my attempts to expose the novel's narratives of erasure actually threatened to erase incarcerated women's efforts to author their own lives. Through that discussion and numerous others, I have learned that survival takes many, many forms. At times, it entails embracing the most streamlined or strategic story about oneself while holding more complex possibilities in reserve. Survival can also entail embracing seemingly contradictory forms of knowledge; some women, for instance, know that healing is an ongoing process *and* that healing requires feeling over and done with pain.

I have learned, too, that reading is fundamentally an intersubjective process. For women who feel an urgent desire to change but a deep uncertainty about their ability to do so, encountering a character or another reader who inspires them, serves as a model to emulate, or demonstrates an ability to change can seem vitally important. I have gained deeper understanding of the ways in which books can assume tremendous importance—serving as life-breath—for women who are trying to re-create themselves with few resources and little help from the world around them. I have learned, moreover, that helping oneself goes hand in hand, for many prisoners, with supporting and teaching others.

After spending so many hours in women's prisons, I found that the distinction between the worlds inside and outside the prison began to "fra[y] at the seams," and I developed greater understanding of the daily realities and indignities of prison life.[18] Each time that I had to ask for permission to use the restroom, each time that I sustained petty and resentful treatment by some officers who were intent on exercising their power, and each time that I worried about crossing or annoying staff members on whom I had to rely for many things, I gained a tiny sense of the infantilizing and dehumanizing nature of incarceration. In other small ways—from eating prison food to hearing women voice pleasure upon seeing my brightly colored clothing—I developed a deeper awareness of the relentless monotony of institutional life.

Finally, I have learned that one should never underestimate the importance—for women themselves and for the wider culture—of witnessing to women prisoners' experiences. On days when I wondered about the value of conducting this study, I was buoyed by the realization that it meant a great deal, to some women, to be greeted by a friendly face who cared about them and considered their thoughts and stories important enough to record. One day during my research, all activity at the prison was shut down when men dressed in riot gear stormed the grounds for a security exercise. I was in the library waiting for the grounds to reopen, along with a group of women who had just arrived at the prison and were in the midst of their orientation. As time went by and no one explained anything to these women, one woman asked me if the officers had forgotten about them, and another woman expressed alarm about how cold and hungry they were beginning to feel. After I found an officer who explained the situation, I returned to the library and reassured the women that they had not been forgotten. The woman who had asked me about the officers smiled at me in a way that I will never forget; it was a fleeting connection—what Kathleen Stewart might call an "intensit[y]"—but our moment of connection continues to remind me of how important it is to let prisoners know that we have not forgotten them. Although one book can do precious little to witness to the experiences of women prisoners, I understand now, in a way that I did not before, how crucial it is to share what I have learned about the struggles and hopes of these women, and about who they have been and who they aspire to be.[19]

As my study progressed, I realized that talking to people about my research constitutes another ripple of the encounters that this project has fostered. When I rented an apartment to conduct research in Ohio, I learned from conversations with my landlady that she had "never thought about women in prison before," did not realize that so many prisoners had experienced victimization, and pictured prison as "a country club type atmosphere, with free cable, exercise equipment, movies, and free medical care." The Harvard undergraduate who served as my research assistant knew nothing about prison issues when she started working with me. Yet shortly thereafter, she was sharing what she was learning with her roommates, reflecting on the divergences between her own reading practices and those of women prisoners, and applying for a summer internship that focused on juvenile justice issues. My transcriptionist also entered the lives of the imprisoned readers from spending hours immersed in their words. She told me that she sometimes cried as she was transcribing women's interviews, and she began asking me about particular women, commenting on what she liked about each one and expressing her hope that those who will be released will never return to prison. As the transcriptionist recorded women's lives and thoughts, the women assumed complexity in her mind, and she is now rooting for them as they make their way in the world. I shared with her, in return, what an impact it made on some women to encounter themselves through their transcripts.

IN WANTING to know each other, women prisoners and I have wanted many things, and the weight of our collective desires remains heavy. I am aware that this book represents my own versions of women's stories—my cullings and juxtapositions, my framings, my snapshots and partial remembrances. I have inevitably foreclosed important lines of inquiry in privileging particular reading practices, readers, and themes. Nonetheless, through our "awkward, messy, unequal, unstable, surprising," and hopeful "interconnection across difference," women prisoners and I have made forays into each other's worlds, worlds that—respectively—are typically off-limits to us.[20] In *Unmarked: The Politics of Performance*, Peggy Phelan offers a powerful image for conceptualizing these forays: "It is in the attempt to walk (and live) on the rickety bridge between self and other—and not the attempt to arrive at one or the other—that we discover real hope." As Anne Anlin Cheng suggests, putting oneself on that rickety bridge entails both a responsibility to enter "the space of the other" and a deep awareness of "the limits of that ingress." Aware of the limits of my ingress, yet grateful for the ways in which I have been changed through my interactions with incarcerated women, I am hopeful that our encounters will make a little more room for new stories to emerge about reading and about women prisoners.[21]

This Really Isn't a Rehabilitation Place

POLICY CONSIDERATIONS

> We're failing as a society as a whole. It ain't the prison!
> It's society!—PATTY, North Carolina Correctional Insti-
> tution for Women

STARR, a forty-one-year-old African American woman, offered the following reflections in describing "what it's like to grow up in prison":

> Prison has been a learning experience for me. I grew up here. I have ma-
> tured to the woman I am today. I learned how to process things differently,
> and now I understand my self-worth. Is it too cynical to say they saved my
> life? I wouldn't have learned these things otherwise. I saw no way out. I
> couldn't read or write. All I had was my physical being and that was shal-
> low. Some women say they were saved here. I wouldn't say that, but I un-
> derstand and respect what they say. But it's a pendulum. I also learned the
> tricks of the trade here. I've talked to a lot of boosters and learned how they
> do it. Now I think, why couldn't I have been in that field instead of selling
> my body? And I've stole a lot of food here. So prison goes both ways.

Starr's personal history is as familiar as it is tragic. She was raised in South
Philadelphia by her mother, a drug dealer who offered her little guidance or
protection. Starr's uncles and cousins began molesting her when she was in
kindergarten, and the abuse continued for several years. At age ten or eleven,
Starr began her involvement with drugs and alcohol during parties hosted by
her mother. She went to school only through ninth grade and then turned to the

streets, where she survived by working as a prostitute. By the time Starr entered prison, she had already attempted suicide twice. In claiming that she "saw no way out" of the life that she was living and that imprisonment enabled her to "grow up," Starr highlights the gaping holes in our social safety net and the depth of our social problems, including poverty, addiction, and sexual violence. Indeed, Starr's reflections highlight the extent to which imprisonment has become our primary means of managing social problems in the contemporary United States.

The fact that Starr has matured and learned to "process" things, learned to read and write, and gained a sense of self-worth during her incarceration is a testament to her determination, resilience, and creativity; it is *not* a testament to the health of the prison system. Yet as Starr's reflections highlight, by acknowledging that women manage to transform themselves in prisons, one can inadvertently attribute a salvific agency to prisons. In fact, insofar as I focus on the roles that reading plays in women's efforts to change their lives and ways of thinking, a danger exists that this book will perpetuate an overemphasis on the rehabilitative power of the prison. In order to thwart such danger, I conclude by situating my study within a broader policy argument about rehabilitation, reading, and education in U.S. penal contexts.

Starr's claim that prison is "a pendulum" that "goes both ways" articulates a central premise embraced by scholars involved in the International Conference on Penal Abolition (ICOPA) and in Critical Resistance (CR). Scholars from both of these movements argue that prisons themselves can be "criminogenic": imprisoning people makes them more likely to commit additional crimes. Further alienation from society, abuse and humiliation by other prisoners and staff, dehumanizing and infantilizing conditions, and significant barriers to work, housing, and citizenship upon release are some of the factors that make prison a damaging place. Ruth Morris, a founding member of ICOPA, describes the effects of incarceration in these terms:

[We take a person] with a lower than average self-image, and we put that person into prison: take away almost all opportunities to contribute creatively, make their own decisions, learn positive skills and even to maintain whatever positive social skills and ties they had. We further limit contact with the few faithful family who try to keep the ties alive, humiliate those family members when they try to visit, subject the prisoner to blind and random harassment, humiliation, and punishment, enrage them while keeping them helpless. We subject them to sensory deprivation and prevent them from keeping up with rapid social change in the outside world. . . . In this situation, would you expect the person to fit into society positively?

Morris and others acknowledge that for some prisoners, treatment or an educational program will "cause more positive life change" than "destructive institutionalizing effects. For the vast majority, however, the many destructive effects of the revenge system overwhelm any petty gains from reforms."[1]

Furthermore, if rehabilitation entails offering a prisoner "tools and positive resources so she or he can and will choose honest paths," most penal systems provide grossly inadequate rehabilitative services.[2] Monique underscores this inadequacy in reflecting on her experience in prison:

> If you have a lot of people that are returning back to prison, then you need to rethink about the prison system. Like this really isn't a rehabilitation place. . . . A friend of mine, she just went home two days ago, and they gave her six months. She was a heroin addict, and she was petrified to come home. She was asking for help all while she was here, but they never offered her any. So whenever they released her, they released her right back to what she knew. And she didn't want to go there, and she was scared, but you know, you can't stay here. . . . Everybody ought to be coming here and leaving out with something that they didn't come in here with. You know, it's about gaining knowledge or experience and stuff like that. But they don't have a lot of things they offer for people to try to learn to get their life on track.

Considering the inadequate resources that prisons provide for "gaining knowledge or experience" and for helping prisoners "to get their life on track," the extent to which Monique, Starr, and other women prisoners manage to grow and transform themselves seems all the more remarkable.

Perhaps the most damaging aspect of the penal system is that it "underwrites the social problems that it purports to solve" by siphoning off resources that should be used, instead, to address the profound social problems that fuel crime in the first place. The growth of imprisonment "as an almost reflexive response to social problems affects our priorities for public life." Rather than recognizing the extent to which our society "is itself in need of radical transformation," we have adopted a law-and-order approach that entails locking up the human evidence of our social failures.[3]

Because the prison pendulum swings so far toward the negative, current scholarship about prisons tends to emphasize the need to abolish the existing penal system and to create alternatives to incarceration. Toward these ends, scholars involved in CR—the antiprison movement that is currently most prominent in humanities circles in the United States—have generated crucial macrolevel analyses of the economic and political underpinnings, as well as the consequences, of the prison-industrial complex. However, given that the goal of CR "is not to improve the system" but "to shrink the system into non-existence," the movement tends to underaddress the needs of people currently in prison. Furthermore, given the risk of promoting an individualizing and pathologizing framework for understanding crime, CR scholars tend to eschew analysis of prisoners' efforts to change themselves and to come to terms with the interpersonal, emotional, and psychological issues that played a role in their crimes.[4]

I have attempted to address these lacunae by offering a ground-level analysis of the daily ways in which women prisoners engage with books. I remain cognizant, however, that my emphasis on prisoners' efforts to transform themselves through reading and education risks shifting attention away from the institutions and social structures that must be changed. Kevin Warner, head of the Prison Education Service in Ireland, cautions that overemphasizing the rehabilitative function of prison educational programs occludes the criminogenic nature of prisons themselves, and it diverts attention both from the social factors that create a pipeline to prisons and from the social supports that are necessary to keep people from returning to prison. Moreover, the current tendency to discuss penal education within the context of recidivism impoverishes the idea of education. As we have seen in the Ohio penal context—where "reentry" materials focus on skills such as résumé writing, where college courses must now be called "advanced job training," and where literature courses have been deemed too impractical—many penal institutions are eliminating educational programs that do not "directly address criminogenic factors." Although it is important for prisons to offer classes that address issues such as substance abuse, parenting, and anger management, Warner cautions that prison education should not focus exclusively on "deficit models" that "over-concentrate on what is deemed to be wrong or missing." An "over-focus" on rehabilitation invites us to see prisoners "one-dimensionally, only as offenders. . . . Other aspects of their lives and personalities, their complexities, their problems and their qualities (aspects of the whole person, in other words) are screened out."[5]

In an effort to counter such limited notions of penal education, Warner outlines an approach that I find highly instructive because it recognizes the fundamentally damaging nature of imprisonment while simultaneously offering suggestions for addressing the needs of incarcerated men and women. Warner's philosophy of penal education draws on the Council of Europe Report from 1989, which states that prison education should "aim to develop the whole person bearing in mind his or her social, economic and cultural context." According to the report, the education of prisoners should "be brought as close as possible to the best adult education in society outside," and it should seek ways "to link prisoners with the outside community and to enable both groups to interact with each other as fully and as constructively as possible." The Council of Europe Report also identifies three main purposes of prison education: (1) "to limit the damage done to men and women through imprisonment"; (2) to offer "special support" for redressing the "educational disadvantage" that "a high proportion of prisoners" have incurred through their "very limited and negative past educational experience"; and (3) "to encourage and help those who try to turn away from crime." Warner contends that conceptions of adult literacy should be applied in penal contexts as well. Imprisoned learners should "have the right to explore their needs and interests, set their own goals and decide how they wish to learn," and they should have opportunities "to reflect on their situation, explore new possibilities and initiate change." Furthermore, in accordance with the European Prison Rules adopted by the Council of Europe in 1987, Warner argues that prison educators' central aims should be to "treat people with dignity," minimize "the detrimental effects of imprisonment," and help prisoners to sustain and strengthen their "links with family and the larger society outside." In short, Warner's conception of penal education entails "recognition of people's full humanity, their individuality, autonomy and potential, and acceptance of them as full members of the larger society."[6]

I wholeheartedly agree with such a conception of prison education and hope that my study has fostered such aims. By organizing my chapters around issues of victimization, crime, self-repair, and healing, I do not mean to position women prisoners in ways that diminish their "whole person," nor do I mean to suggest that such focal points are necessarily or exclusively appropriate for discussing women prisoners' reading practices. Indeed, a sequel to this work might focus on issues such as motherhood, pleasure, friendship, or fantasy in discussing women prisoners' engagements with books. Nonetheless, the themes around which I structured this book emerged more clearly than any others, not only in terms of the contents of the most popular books, but also in terms of the participants' broadly shared efforts to grapple with victimization, crime, and healing. Through their complex processes of affiliating and disaffiliating themselves with the personae and situations featured in books, the women involved in my study use reading, on one level, as a means to entertain themselves and experience a sense of escape, and to stay connected—in actual or imaginary ways—to realities that exist beyond the confines of the prison. On another level, women use reading as a means to educate themselves and make meaning from their experiences, to reckon with previously unauthorized or suppressed emotions, to find inspiring models and unconditionally supportive mentors and guides, and to become authors of their own lives. As the study progressed, I became increasingly aware of the ways in which women prisoners create a self-in-relation through their individual and group engagements with books. In concert with other readers, they use books to create and maintain social bonds, to broaden their perspectives and understandings of others, to witness to their own and others' experiences, and to claim their place in the multiple communities to which they belong.

If prison libraries were suddenly filled with a vast and varied array of reading materials, such a change would not advance us far toward "a truly transformative justice system." Furthermore, no matter how much women prisoners transform themselves through their reading practices, their efforts will not diminish the economic and political centrality of prisons, decriminalize drug use, or eliminate violence against women. Nonetheless, at a moment when the Supreme Court has construed the *denial* of reading as a form of rehabilitation in prisons, it is crucial to recognize the ways in which some women prisoners "habilitate"—meaning empower and enable—themselves through reading. In the lexicon that Warner highlights, women use reading as a means to minimize the detrimental effects of imprisonment, redress their educational disadvantage, foster their self-reflection and self-creation, turn away from crime, and maintain a sense of dialogue and connection with their fellow citizens on both sides of the prison fence.[7]

Because "autobiographical narratives are also always stories about our shared social world," women prisoners' efforts to restory their lives draw attention to our pressing need to "renarrativize society," to imagine—on the way toward creating—a world in which social justice, rather than imprisonment, will serve as the foundation of social health. Writing this book has deepened my sense of how crucial it is to illuminate prisoners' "availability for compassion, connection, and learning," and to foster their participation in conversations that typically proceed without them. Moreover, it has deepened my conviction that challenging the hegemony of the prison requires honoring prisoners' efforts to develop self-knowledge and a sense of agency, while at the same time elucidating how those efforts relate to larger social and structural concerns.[8]

As I anticipate this book finding its way into readers' hands, my hope is that the stories that it contains and the lives that it chronicles may in some way deepen its readers' understandings of the women who fill our nation's prisons. For it is by entering the stories of these women—by taking a step toward prisoners on that rickety bridge—that each of us can begin to recognize the role that we play in current imprisonment practices. If we allow ourselves to hear these women's stories, they urgently beckon us to chart a new course for achieving communal safety and well-being.

Appendix

STUDY-RELATED MATERIALS

Study Participants

TABLE 1 Participants from the North Carolina Correctional
Institution for Women

Pseudonym	Age	Racial Self-Identification
Arlene	47	black
Audrey	43	black
Candace	25	black
Eleanor	42	black
Gladys	35	black
Grace	27	black
Jill	40	Caucasian
Karen	32	white
Maria	23	white and Indian
Melissa	27	Indian
Nicole	22	black
Patty	37	American Indian (Cherokee)
Rae	41	white
Sakina	35	African American
Shelly	33	black
Sue	31	white and a tad bit Indian
Tamia	24	black
Tanya	31	black

TABLE 2 Participants from the Northeast Pre-Release Center

Pseudonym	Age	Racial Self-Identification
Barbara	33	white
Bobbie	42	black
Cassandra	39	black
Daisey	38	white
Darlene	35	Nubian black American queen
Denise	46	black
Deven	36	white
Ellen	43	black
Genevieve	40	black
Jacqueline	41	black
Lakesha	27	black or African
Lara	23	African American
Marlena	24	white
Miekal	40	black
Mildred	42	African American
Mocha	28	black
Monique	29	African American
Natasha	34	African American
Nellie	42	white
Olivia	27	Caucasian
Peggy	50	Caucasian
Raylene	38	black
Rhonda	52	black
Ronnie	38	black American
Rose	24	biracial
Ruth	77	Irish
Shantell	30	white
Sissy	46	African American
Solo	56	African American
Tyra	46	white
Valhalla	29	Caucasian
Wendy	28	African American

TABLE 3   Participants from the State Correctional
          Institution at Muncy

Pseudonym	Age	Racial Self-Identification
Alice	58	Caucasian
Amy	62	white
Angel	22	white
Angelique	27	white
Boo	46	black
Breeanna	33	white
Caesar	66	black
Candi	36	white
Candy	38	white
Charell	45	black and Indian
Charmaine	27	black
Cherise	26	African American
Christine	27	Caucasian
Connie	20	African American
Darcie	43	white
Debbie	26	white
Dee-dee	49	African American
Donna	45	Caucasian
Drea	36	white
Gracie	31	white
Gypsy Rose	48	white
Heidi	37	white
Helen	47	Caucasian
Karimah	33	black
Kate	51	white
Kaye	26	black
Kerrie	40	white
Kimmie	31	white
Kristin	47	white
Lefty	26	African American
Liz	25	white
Maisey	50	white
Marian	52	Polish American
Marisa	46	Hispanic
Monalisa	56	Hungarian
Nena	29	Hispanic

TABLE 3 Participants from the State Correctional
Institution at Muncy (*continued*)

Pseudonym	Age	Racial Self-Identification
Nez	42	black
Omega	46	black or African American
Sahara	46	white
Sky	39	Caucasian
Soso	48	Indian and black
Starr	41	black
Touché	43	black
Trey	25	black

Recruitment Method

I solicited participants by asking prison administrators to post fliers advertising my study in each living area and common area, in the educational programming area, and in the library. In the Pennsylvania prison, my study was also advertised on the television channel that broadcasts news within the institution. I invited women with at least an eighth-grade reading level to participate in interviews and book discussions related to women, crime, punishment, and/or healing; although I did not formally assess the reading levels of the women, their self-assessments and actual ability to complete the readings sufficed for regulating their involvement in the study. On the flier, I stated that I wanted to learn about books that are popular in prison, the role that reading plays in the lives of women prisoners, and prisoners' ideas about crime, punishment, and healing. At each facility, I held a meeting for all interested participants in which I explained the aims and methods of my study, discussed the consent form, and answered questions. Women who decided to participate signed a consent form at the conclusion of the meeting.

Settings for the Interviews and Discussions

In the North Carolina and Ohio prisons, I conducted interviews with individual women in a classroom or photocopy room in which only the two of us were present. We kept the door to these rooms closed, creating as private a space as possible in a crowded prison. Our group discussions took place in similar settings; the participants and I were alone with the door closed, and we arranged our chairs in a circle. Due to penal authorities' security concerns, the setting for both the individual interviews and group discussions was less private in the Pennsylvania prison. I conducted the individual interviews in a corner section of the library that was off-limits to other library patrons and prison personnel. Although the interviewees sat with their backs toward all others in the library, they had to be visible by prison personnel at all times; consequently, these interviews seemed less intimate and less intense than many of my interviews with women in North Carolina and Ohio. For the group discussions in Pennsylvania, we sat around a rectangular table in the same corner of the library. Other patrons and staff were not permitted to enter the discussion area but were sometimes within earshot, which also lent our conversations a less intimate quality than those that took place in other prisons.

Eighteen women, divided into two discussion groups, participated in my research at the North Carolina prison. Thirty-two women, divided into three discussion groups, participated at the Ohio prison. Forty-four women, divided into five discussion groups, participated at the Pennsylvania prison. The actual size of the discussion groups varied depending on the number of women who could attend on a particular day. The largest session included nine women and the smallest included two; the average size of the groups was five women.

In North Carolina and Ohio, I tried to compose discussion groups that were racially mixed and included women with a range of interaction styles. In Pennsylvania, I tried to accommodate participants' wide range of reading levels and interests by composing groups not only on the basis of race and interaction style, but also on the basis of women's stated preferences for particular kinds of books. In North Carolina and Ohio, women in different discussion groups read many of the same books, but in Pennsylvania, each of the five discussion groups read a unique set of books, with minimal overlap between groups.

In order to accommodate the large number of participants in Pennsylvania, I conducted only one individual interview with each woman, and each discussion group met only four times as opposed to six and seven times, respectively, in the North Carolina and Ohio prisons. As my chapters may indicate, I feel as though I got to know the women in North Carolina and Ohio on a deeper level than women in Pennsylvania, not only because I interviewed a smaller number of women more extensively and in more private settings in the first two sites, but also because I was able to review audio recordings of all of my interactions with those women; my handwritten records of my interactions with women in Pennsylvania did not capture as much texture and detail as the audio recordings in the other two states.

Study Advertisement

Doing Time, Reading Crime
Cultures of Reading in Women's Prisons[1]

- Do you like to read?
- Would you like to be part of a book discussion group?
- Would you like to talk about women, crime, punishment,
  or healing?

If you answered "yes" to ANY of these questions,
you may want to participate in this study.

I'm a professor at University of Michigan, and I'm conducting research about:

- books that are popular in prison
- the role that reading plays in women prisoners' lives
- prisoners' ideas about crime, punishment, and healing

Volunteering for this study will involve:

- participating in 3 tape-recorded, individual interviews
  - one interview will focus on your life experiences
  - two interviews will focus on your reading practices
- reading between 4 and 6 books that we'll select for the group discussions
- participating in 4 to 6 group discussions about those books
- discussing issues relating to women, crime, punishment, and healing

If you choose to participate in this study, your privacy will be protected.
To hear more, please attend the meeting on:
Day, Date
Time
Location

Guiding Questions for Individual Interview #1
(Life History/Narrative)

1. Could you please tell me your age? Race? Marital status? Education level?
2. Can you tell me a little bit about where you were born and the people who raised you?
3. What was family life like for you?
4. What was school like for you?
5. What are some of the joys that you've had in your life?
6. What relationships have been important in your life?
7. Have you helped to raise any children and/or had children of your own?
8. Has violence been a part of your life in any way?
9. Have drugs or alcohol been a part of your life?
10. What was happening in your life around the time that you came to prison?
11. What has it been like for you to be in prison?
12. From your experiences, why do you think that women end up in prison?
13. Do you have any ideas about what society should do to keep more women from coming to prison?

14. What's next for you?

15. Are there other parts of your life story that you would like to share?

Guiding Questions for Individual Interview #2
(General Reading Practices)

1. How would you describe yourself as a reader?

2. What sorts of books do you like to read?

3. How do you decide which books to read?

4. Where do you get the books that you read?

5. How often, and when, do you read?

6. What is your favorite setting for reading?

7. What role, if any, did reading play in your life before you came to prison?

8. What role does reading play in your life now that you're in prison?

9. What role, if any, does the prison library play in your life?

10. Why do you read? What do you get out of reading?

11. What's your favorite thing about reading?

12. Do you ever like to read books that make you think about your own life?

13. Do you ever like to read books as a form of escape from the "real world"?

14. Do you ever talk with friends or family about what you're reading or have read?

15. Have you read anything lately that you've really liked or disliked?

16. Does it matter to you whether or not you feel like you've learned something from reading a book?

17. What kinds of things, if any, do you like to learn from reading books?

18. Do you have a favorite type of book? If so, what do you like about that kind of book?

19. Do you have a favorite book and/or author? If so, what do you like about that book or author?

20. If you could have greater access to any type of book or to particular books, what would you most like to read?

21. Has any book ever made a big impression on you, changed your life in some way, or changed the way you think about yourself or the world?

22. Do you ever read legal materials now that you're in prison?

23. What else would you like to tell me about the role that books and reading play in your life?

Individual Interview #3 (Specific Reading Practices)

The trajectory of this interview was determined by the particular reading practices of each participant. I asked each participant to come ready to discuss one or two books that she has read, and I allowed her to guide the conversation. My aim in leaving this interview open-ended was to allow participants, as much as possible, to frame their experiences of reading in their own terms.

Books Used for Group Discussions

I purchased sets of books through grant money and donated all of the books to the prison libraries upon completion of my study. The following lists specify the books that served as the basis for group discussions in each prison.

North Carolina Correctional Facility for Women

- Pearl Cleage, *What Looks Like Crazy on an Ordinary Day*
- Barbara Davis, *Precious Angels*
- Maria Eftimiades, *Sins of the Mother*
- Clark Howard, *Love's Blood*
- Gayl Jones, *Eva's Man*
- Dolores Kennedy, *On a Killing Day: The Bizarre Story of Convicted Murderer Aileen Lee Wuornos*
- Michael Reynolds, *Dead Ends*

Northeast Pre-Release Center

- Dorothy Allison, *Bastard out of Carolina*
- Pearl Cleage, *What Looks Like Crazy on an Ordinary Day*
- Patrice Gaines, *Laughing in the Dark: From Colored Girl to Woman of Color— A Journey from Prison to Power*
- Zora Neale Hurston, *Their Eyes Were Watching God*
- Harriet Jacobs, *Incidents in the Life of a Slave Girl*
- T. D. Jakes, *Woman Thou Art Loosed!*
- Joyce Meyer, *Battlefield of the Mind: Winning the Battle in Your Mind*
- Joyce Meyer, *The Confident Woman: Start Today Living Boldly and without Fear*
- Sue Russell, *Lethal Intent*
- Sister Souljah, *The Coldest Winter Ever*
- Iyanla Vanzant, *Yesterday I Cried: Celebrating the Lessons of Living And Loving*
- Jeannette Walls, *The Glass Castle*
- Tu-Shonda Whitaker, *Flip Side of the Game*
- Tu-Shonda Whitaker, *Game Over*

State Correctional Institution at Muncy

- Ray Bradbury, *Fahrenheit 451*
- Anne Frank, *The Diary of a Young Girl*
- Ernest J. Gaines, *A Lesson before Dying*
- Shannon Holmes, *Bad Girlz*

- Khaled Hosseini, *A Thousand Splendid Suns*
- Harper Lee, *To Kill a Mockingbird*
- Joyce Meyer, *The Confident Woman: Start Today Living Boldly and without Fear*
- Toni Morrison, *Beloved*
- James Patterson and Howard Roughan, *You've Been Warned*
- Danielle Santiago, *Grindin'*
- Alice Sebold, *The Lovely Bones*
- Jeannette Walls, *The Glass Castle*
- Tu-Shonda Whitaker, *Flip Side of the Game*
- Tu-Shonda Whitaker, *Game Over*

Guiding Questions for Book Discussions

1. What was it like for you to read this book? What did you like and/or dislike about it?
2. How does this book compare to the kinds of books that you usually like to read?
3. From your perspective, what topics seem important to discuss in relation to this book?
4. Take a minute to flip through the book. Do any particular passages seem especially interesting, important, confusing, or surprising to you? Do you especially like or dislike any particular passages or sections of the book?
5. What purpose do you think the author had in mind when writing this book?
6. What audience or audiences do you think the author had in mind when writing this book?
7. When you were reading, did you ever feel like you could relate to any particular characters, situations, or ideas?
8. How do you interpret the ending of this book?
9. If you were going to write a sequel to this book, what would happen next?
10. Would you recommend this book to anyone else? Why or why not?
11. If you could change anything about this book, what would you like to change, and why?

Guiding Questions for Individual Interviews with Prison Librarians

1. How long have you been doing library work with the department?
2. What do you see as the rewards of your job?
3. What do you see as the challenges of your job?
4. Can you tell me anything about the history of library services in the department?
5. Can you tell me anything about the history of library services at this facility?
6. Over the past forty years, librarians, prison administrators, politicians, and the general public have expressed a range of views about the role that prison libraries should play. What is your sense of these debates?

7. How do you envision the role of the prison library? What particular aims or purposes should it serve?
8. From your perspective, what roles do library services and reading play in the everyday lives of imprisoned women?
9. What kinds of programs and services does the library offer?
10. How much reader's guidance do prisoners receive at the library?
11. Are you familiar with bibliotherapy? What role, if any, have you seen bibliotherapy play in the history of the department's library services?
12. From your perspective, who uses the prison library, and for what purposes do they use it?
13. From your perspective, what kinds of books are most popular among incarcerated women readers? Why do you think these particular kinds of books are popular?
14. What kinds of requests for reading materials do incarcerated women make?
15. From your experience, can you make any comparisons between the reading interests and habits of incarcerated women and incarcerated men?
16. What kinds of shifts or changes, if any, have you seen in prisoners' reading interests or reading habits over the years that you've been involved in this facility's library services? How do you understand these changes?
17. What kinds of shifts or changes, if any, have you seen in the department's overall approach to library services for incarcerated women and/or men? How do you understand these changes?
18. What is the book acquisition policy of this library? If the library accepts donations, what kinds of books tend to be donated and by whom?
19. What do you see as the strengths of the department's library policies and services?
20. If you could make any changes to the department's current library policies, or to services at this facility, what changes would you like to make and why?
21. What are the department's policies about library services for prisoners in segregation or under disciplinary restrictions?
22. Is there anything else that you'd like to tell me about your work relating to library services for incarcerated readers?

Organizations That Gather Books for Prisoners:
A Representative Sample

The Appalachian Prison Book Project
P.O. Box 601
Morgantown, WV 26506
appalachianpbp@gmail.com

Asheville Prison Books Program
67 N. Lexington Ave.
Asheville, NC 28801
http://www.main.nc.us/prisonbooks/
  who.html

Book 'Em
P.O. Box 71357
Pittsburgh, PA 15213
www.thomasmertoncenter.org/
  bookem/index.html

Books Through Bars
4722 Baltimore Ave.
Philadelphia, PA 19143
(215) 727-8170
www.booksthroughbars.org

Books Through Bars—Ithaca
c/o Autumn Leaves Bookstore
115 The Commons, 2nd Floor
Ithaca, NY 14850
(607) 645-0250

Books Through Bars—NYC
c/o Bluestockings Bookstore
172 Allen St
New York, NY 10002
(212) 254-3697, ext. 322
www.abcnorio.org/affiliated/btb.html

Books to Prisoners
c/o Left Bank Books
92 Pike St., Box A
Seattle, WA 98101
www.bookstoprisoners.net

Chicago Books to Women in Prison
c/o Beyondmedia Education
4001 N. Ravenswood Ave #204C
Chicago, IL 60613
http://www.chicagobwp.org

Cleveland Books to Prisoners
4241 Lorain Ave.
Cleveland, OH 44012
clevelandbooks2prisoners
  @hotmail.com

The DC Books to Prisons Project
Quixote Center
P.O. Box 5206
Hyattsville, MD 20782
http://www.quixote.org/ej/
  bookstoprisons/

Gainesville Books for Prisoners
P.O. Box 12164
Gainesville, FL 32604
http://www.civicmediacenter.org/
  links/2003/11/01/13.29.05.htm

Inside Books Project
c/o 12th St. Books
827 West 12th Street
Austin, TX 78701
www.insidebooksproject.com

Internationalist Prison Books Collective
405 West Franklin St.
Chapel Hill, NC 27514
www.prisonbooks.info

Midwest Books to Prisoners
c/o Quimby's Bookstore
1573 North Milwaukee Ave. PMB #460
Chicago, IL 60622
www.freewebs.com/mwbtp

The Midwest Pages to Prisoners Project
c/o Boxcar Books and Community
    Center, Inc.
118 S. Rogers, Suite #2
Bloomington, IN 47404
http://www.pagestoprisoners.org/

Oregon Books to Prisoners
1112 NE Morton St.
Portland, OR 97211
http://www.bookstooregonprisoners.org

Prison Book Program
c/o Lucy Parsons Bookstore
1306 Hancock Street, Suite 100
Quincy, MA 02169
(617) 423-3298
info@prisonbookprogram.org

Prison Book Project
c/o Food for Thought Books
P.O. Box 396
Amherst, MA 01004
prisonbookproject@riseup.net

The Prison Library Project
915 W. Foothill Blvd., PMB #128
Claremont, CA 91711
http://www.inmate.com/prislibr.htm

Women's Prison Book Project
c/o Arise Bookstore
2441 Lyndale Avenue South
Minneapolis, Minnesota 55405
http://www.wpbp.org/pages/about.html

NOTES

Introduction

1. Each of the incarcerated women has chosen her own pseudonym to protect her privacy.

2. Throughout this book, I interchangeably use the terms "women prisoners," "incarcerated women," and "imprisoned women." According to prisoner Willy London, the terms "prisoner," "convict," and "inmate" carry vastly different political charges. A "prisoner" is "a positive thinker, always thinking freedom, held against his will, respected, honorable, a leader among prisoners, . . . viewed as a 'smart-ass' and potential problem by prison officials and guards, political." A "convict," by contrast, "has a con mentality of trying to get over on anyone in any way possible" and is "guilty but considers himself to be a 'victim of the system,'" while an "inmate" "has no individual will or resistance, acts as a snitch or a house mouse (informer)" (qtd. in Sabo, Krupers, and London, *Prison Masculinities*, 9). Although women involved in my study most commonly refer to themselves as inmates, I prefer to use the term "prisoner" for the reasons that London invokes. I also use the terms "imprisoned women" and "incarcerated women" because they foreground prisoners' status as women and denote their physical confinement without conferring on them an existential or fixed identity as criminals.

3. Qtd. in Zahm, *Last Graduation*; Davis, "From the Convict," 73; Rhodes, *Total Confinement*, 60.

4. Breyer, *Beard v. Banks*, 8 (quotes), 11.

5. Dodge, *"Whores and Thieves,"* 266; Carlen, "Why Study?," 136; Sullivan, *Prison Reform*, 2; Rodríguez, *Forced Passages*, 85, 185 (emphasis in original); Wideman introduction, xxx.

6. Rhodes, *Total Confinement*, 5; Morris, *Penal Abolition*, 26; Rodríguez, *Forced Passages*, 211. The 1996 welfare reform act—a little-known stipulation in Section 15 of the Personal Responsibility and Work Opportunity Reconciliation Act of 1996, Pub. L. No. 104-193—confers a lifetime ban on receiving cash assistance and food stamps for people convicted of a state or federal felony involving the use or sale of drugs. This act essentially guarantees that the racial and economic disenfranchisement that so many women face before incarceration will continue upon their release from prison. Forty-two states currently enforce the ban in full or in part, and 48 percent of the women affected are African American or Latina. See Allard, "Life Sentences."

7. Davis, *Are Prisons Obsolete?*, 103; Rodríguez, *Forced Passages*, 201.

8. Sabol, Couture, and Harrison, "Prisoners in 2006," 3. At year-end 2006, a total of 1,570,861 prisoners were held under state or federal jurisdiction. Of those prisoners, 1,458,363 were men. See ibid.

9. In 2007, the total student population of Ohio State University was 52,568 and of the

Pennsylvania State University was 57,560. The combined total of these numbers is 110,128, which is 2,370 fewer than the number of women in prison.

10. Frost, Greene, and Pranis, "Hard Hit," 7; Sabol, Couture, and Harrison, "Prisoners in 2006," 3. During 2006, the number of men in prison increased by 2.7 percent. From 2000 through 2005, the average annual growth rate of the prison population was 2.9 percent. See Sabol, Couture, and Harrison, "Prisoners in 2006," 3.

11. Sabol, Couture, and Harrison, "Prisoners in 2006," 6, 8. Since 2000, the percentage of white women among sentenced female prisoners has increased from 40 percent to 48 percent, while the percentage of black women has declined from 38 percent to 28 percent. Since 2001, the rate of incarceration for black women has also decreased while increasing for white and Latina women. The incarceration rate for black women declined from 175 per 100,000 at year-end 2000 to 148 per 100,000 at year-end 2006. The rate for white women increased from 33 per 100,000 to 48 per 100,000, and the rate for Latina women increased from 78 per 100,000 to 81 per 100,000. Vis-à-vis white women, the rate of incarceration for both black and Latina women has declined. In 2000, black women were 5.3 times more likely than white women to be incarcerated, and Latinas were 2.4 times more likely. These groups are now, respectively, 3.1 and 1.7 times more likely than white women to be incarcerated. See Sabol, Couture, and Harrison, "Prisoners in 2006," 8. Some African American prisoners have noted the relative increase in the incarceration rate for white women. According to Rhonda, black women used to outnumber white women at the Ohio prison, but you can now count the number of black women "on one hand." "Black people got their act together," Rhonda argues, and now "white people need to get their act together, too."

12. Liptak, "1 in 100 U.S. Adults." The Pew Center's study calculates the incarceration rate by using the adult population as the denominator, whereas the Bureau of Justice Statistics uses the total population as the denominator.

13. Scholars who foreground the experiences of incarcerated women of color include Beth Richie, Kimberlé Williams Crenshaw, Angela Davis, Joy James, Avery Gordon, Cassandra Shaylor, Ellen Berry, Karlene Faith, Joanne Belknap, Juanita Diaz-Cotto, Luana Ross, Adrien Wing, Nancy Kurshan, Laura Whitehorn, and Marilyn Buck. See, for example, Crenshaw, "Mapping the Margins"; Richie, Compelled to Crime; Davis, Are Prisons Obsolete?; James, States of Confinement; and Gordon, Keeping Good Time. Since its inception in 2000, Incite! Women of Color against Violence has sponsored a yearly conference and numerous initiatives designed to end violence against women of color and their communities.

14. Wilson, "Crime and Public Policy," 507; Daniels, "Between Fathers and Fetuses," 583.

15. For a historical discussion of reading in the British penal context, see Fyfe, Books behind Bars.

16. The Changing Lives Through Literature (CLTL) Program began in Massachusetts in 1991. Robert Waxler, a professor of English at the University of Massachusetts, Dartmouth; Judge Robert Kane, who was then a Massachusetts district court justice; and Wayne St. Pierre, a New Bedford district court probation officer, initiated the program for men at the University of Massachusetts, Dartmouth. In 1992, Jean Trounstine, a professor of humanities at Middlesex Community College, started a women's CLTL program. CLTL programs have since been adopted in Texas, Arizona, Kansas, New York, Rhode Island, Florida, Indiana, and California. The seminars—which are conducted separately for men and women—typically involve ten sessions during which the lawbreakers, a facilitator, a judge, and a parole officer discuss designated works of literature. Those who complete the program attend a graduation ceremony in the same courtroom in which they were sentenced.

17. In her 1995 study, *Black Women as Cultural Readers*, Jacqueline Bobo very briefly discusses black women's engagements with one highly popular novel, Terry McMillan's *Waiting to Exhale*. The majority of Bobo's analysis, however, focuses on black women's responses to films.

18. Burke, "Literature as an Equipment for Living," 10. Burke argues that narratives can serve as "a strategic naming" of "a pattern of experience that is sufficiently representative of our social structure . . . for people to 'need a word for it'" (ibid., 12). Jean Marie Goulemot argues that "to read is to constitute a meaning, not to reconstitute one" (qtd. in Price, "Reading," 311).

19. Smith and Watson introduction, 14; Long, *Book Clubs*, 170, 111, 188 (quote).

20. Qtd. in Booth, *Company We Keep*, 13.

21. Frow, "'Reproducibles,'" 1629, 1631, 1633; qtd. in Dimock, "Introduction," 1383; Frow, "'Reproducibles,'" 1632, 1633.

22. Smith and Watson introduction, 14.

23. Romance novels are also highly popular in women's prisons, but I chose not to focus on them because they have received so much scholarly attention in other contexts.

24. Smith and Watson introduction, 11.

25. As of January 2008, the facility held 308 white women, 268 African American women, 2 Hispanic women, and 1 "Other."

26. The state of Ohio experienced a 7.2 percent growth in its prison population during 2006, and it is one of three states, including California and Georgia, that had the largest absolute increase in the number of prisoners during 2006: 3,312 prisoners. The state of Pennsylvania experienced a 4.8 percent growth in its prison population during 2006. See Sabol, Couture, and Harrison, "Prisoners in 2006," 14.

27. Greenberg, Dunleavy, and Kutner, *Literacy behind Bars*, 38.

28. I conducted two rounds of research in Ohio, from September 2006 through July 2007, and one round of research in Pennsylvania, from July through December 2007. See the Appendix for information about my recruitment method, the settings for the individual interviews and groups discussions, the guiding questions that I used during interviews and discussions, and the books that each group discussed.

29. The North Carolina and Ohio prisons permitted me to audio-record all of my interactions, so I was able to provide women with a complete transcript of their interviews and discussions. Because the Pennsylvania prison allowed me to take only handwritten notes, I could not provide a complete transcript of women's participation; I did, however, give them typed copies of all of the notes that I took during their interviews and discussions. Deborah Brandt argues that researchers often hear and inscribe nonstandard aspects of the most stigmatized dialects in making transcripts, yet "the speech of the nonstigmatized is not so closely scrutinized for its deviations from the accepted standard" (*Literacy*, 14). In accordance with Brandt's call for greater "evenhandedness," the transcripts of incarcerated women's speech do not reflect clipped word endings (i.e., "goin'") or colloquial pronunciations (i.e., "libary," "ten dollar," or "they mother"). Furthermore, I have minimized the prevalence of "you know" when women's statements lose too much clarity from overuse of the phrase. However, I have included women's nonstandard uses of grammar in order to preserve the flavor of their speech (i.e., "it don't matter" or "I done did it").

30. Qtd. in Fontana and Frey, "Interview," 664; Brandt, *Literacy*, 11.

31. Benwell and Allington, "Reading the Reading Experience," 2–3 (emphasis in original).

32. Ibid., 11, 17.

33. Qtd. in Tedlock, "Ethnography and Ethnographic Representation," 467.

34. Holloway, *BookMarks*, 77, 88.

35. Sandra Harding, qtd. in Behar, *Vulnerable Observer*, 29.

36. Warner, "Uncritical Reading," 15, 19. Warner's notion of an "ethical project"—which "has as its end a particular conception of the human being"—reflects Foucault's later emphasis on the ethics of self-creation (ibid., 18).

37. Scott, *Domination*, 183, 201 (emphasis in original).

Chapter 1

1. For a detailed discussion of the case, see Sweeney, *"Beard v. Banks."*

2. Qtd. in Breyer, *Beard v. Banks*, 2, 8. Justice Stephen Breyer wrote the majority opinion, which was signed by Justices John Roberts, Anthony Kennedy, and David Souter. Justice Clarence Thomas wrote a concurring opinion signed by Justice Antonin Scalia. Justice Samuel Alito abstained because he had voted in support of the prison policy as a judge in the Third Circuit Court of Appeals.

3. Ibid., 11, 3.

4. Stevens, *Beard v. Banks*, 6, 12. Writing in 2003, Angela Davis argues, "No one—not even the most ardent defenders of the supermax—would try to argue today that absolute segregation . . . is restorative and healing" (*Are Prisons Obsolete?*, 50). Yet the majority decision in *Beard v. Banks* rests on such a claim in justifying the Pennsylvania prison's deprivation policy as an "incentiv[e] for inmate growth."

5. Shapiro et al., *Brief*, 11; Davis, *Are Prisons Obsolete?*, 49.

6. Davis, *Are Prisons Obsolete?*, 26, 51. U.S. penal history can be roughly divided into four episodes: (1) the origin of prisons to the establishment of the penitentiary system in the 1820s, (2) the 1820s to the beginning of Progressive Era penology in the 1870s, (3) the 1870s to the end of treatment penology in the 1970s, and (4) the late 1970s to the present, which is characterized by a retreat from rehabilitation and the adoption of draconian policies. See Sullivan, "Between," 26.

7. Price, "Reading," 310; Prendergast, *Literacy and Racial Justice*, 37, 7.

8. Qtd. in Rafter, *Partial Justice*, 29; Bashore, "Behind Adobe Walls," 239. Ten years later, all prisons in the northern states had libraries, each of which held an average of 1,535 books; see Sullivan and Vogel, "Reachin' behind Bars," 117. Larry Sullivan notes, "The very fact that social scientists found the numbers important enough to count testifies to the conceptual force of libraries as powerful reformative tools" (Sullivan, "Least," 57).

9. Qtd. in Sullivan and Vogel, "Reachin' behind Bars," 117; qtd. in Coyle, *Libraries in Prisons*, 26; qtd. in Sullivan, "Literature," 5.

10. Davis, *Are Prisons Obsolete?*, 45.

11. Franklin introduction, 4. The convict lease system assumed various forms in the South, but in its purest form, a corporation paid a fixed sum to the state for the labor of its convicts and assumed full responsibility for the convicts' care; in exchange, the corporation reaped all of the profit from the convicts' labor. See Mancini, *One Dies*, 14–15. Because many southern prisons were destroyed during the Civil War, male and female prisoners in the post–Civil War South were often sent directly to coal mines, cotton and sugar plantations, turpentine farms, brickyards and sawmills, phosphate beds, and railroad construction sites. Black women also served as domestics and prostitutes at local road camps and jails, dug the campus of Georgia State College, manufactured shoes in South Carolina and prison garments in Alabama, and did farming, canning, laundry, and sewing

on state-owned prison plantations. See Oshinsky, "Worse Than Slavery," 170, 172; Franklin introduction, 5; Mancini, One Dies, 208; Rafter, Partial Justice, 97.

12. Qtd. in Oshinsky, "Worse Than Slavery," 94. A majority of convict laborers lacked basic literacy skills. For instance, of 64 black women serving sentences in Louisiana between 1866 and 1872, only 5 could read, and of those 5, only 1 could write. Of 25 black women serving sentences in Arkansas between 1874 and 1885, 16 were completely illiterate. See Butler, Gendered, 105.

13. Pre–Civil War statutes in Alabama, Georgia, Missouri, South Carolina, and Virginia prohibited teaching both enslaved and free black people, whereas statutes in Louisiana, Mississippi, and North Carolina prohibited teaching slaves. Maryland, Arkansas, and Florida specifically legislated that white masters were obliged to provide some education to white apprentices but had no obligation toward free black apprentices. See Williams, Self-Taught, 216.

14. Williams et al., Records, n.p.; "Phyllis Wheatley Club," 15; Williams et al., Records, n.p.; qtd. in McHenry, Forgotten Readers, 190.

15. Mancini, One Dies, 221. Chain gangs were actually on the rise as the lease system waned, and the chain gang camps of the 1930s and 1940s seemed virtually indistinguishable from their leasing predecessors. The lease system's decline stemmed from a range of factors, including pressure from labor unions, revelations about harms to white convict laborers, declines in profit due to the rising costs of convict-produced commodities and convict labor, and political motivation. See Mancini, One Dies, 221–22, 225; Sullivan, Prison Reform, 13; Oshinsky, "Worse Than Slavery," 69, 75.

16. MacCormick, Education of Adult Prisoners, 39, 45, 251.

17. Women housed at Auburn Penitentiary, for instance, spent their days without supervision, work, religious instruction, or opportunities for exercise, and so many went mad that prison workers complained about their shrieking. See Dodge, "Whores and Thieves," 14. Despite such appalling conditions, facilities such as Auburn were considered an improvement, since female prisoners were often housed in the same room with male prisoners who were deemed too vulnerable to be housed with other men but were nonetheless prone to sexually exploiting female prisoners. Throughout the nineteenth century, most women were still imprisoned in men's facilities—often in an attic, annex, cellar, or upper floor—and they remained subject to sexual exploitation, especially when working alongside men. See Zedner, "Wayward," 332; Rafter, Partial Justice, 9; Mancini, One Dies, 72. Only New York, Indiana, and Massachusetts established totally separate prisons for women during the nineteenth century.

18. Rafter, Partial Justice, xxxi; Dodge, "Whores and Thieves," 12. Because "proper" women were assigned the cultural role of moral guardian, women who committed crimes were viewed as having violated fundamental principles of womanhood; see Rafter, Partial Justice, 13; Davis, Are Prisons Obsolete?, 70. The neglect of imprisoned women also stems from the fact that they often comprised less than 10 percent of a prison's population; see Rafter, Partial Justice, 10. Nonetheless, an 1840 survey reveals that twelve of fifteen state penitentiaries housed female prisoners.

19. Hill-Collins, Black Feminist Thought, 71; Dodge, "Whores and Thieves," 13.

20. Rathbone, World Apart, 70; Sullivan and Vogel, "Reachin' behind Bars," 115; Kirby, Years of Experience, 193.

21. Qtd. in Levy, Unsettling the West, 12; qtd. in Rafter, Partial Justice, 18.

22. Qtd. in Levy, Unsettling the West, 7; qtd. in Sullivan and Vogel, "Reachin' behind Bars," 115; qtd. in Rathbone, World Apart, 71; Sullivan, Prison Reform, 15.

23. Qtd. in Rafter, *Partial Justice*, 26. Most reformatories were established in the Northeast and Midwest, including Connecticut, Maine, Rhode Island, Massachusetts, New York, New Jersey, Pennsylvania, Ohio, Indiana, Illinois, Michigan, Iowa, Kansas, Minnesota, Nebraska, and California. When black women were admitted to reformatories, they were more likely to be classified as low functioning and placed in tracked educational programs, and white staff members sometimes actively discouraged them from participating in the more meaningful vocational programs; see Rafter, *Partial Justice*, 154; Dodge, "Whores and Thieves," 211. Black clubwomen sought to rectify the lack of reformatory options for African American women by establishing their own detention homes; see Johnson, *Southern Ladies*. The reformatory movement died by 1935 due to the fiscal crisis of the Great Depression and the fact that women's prison populations gradually shifted to greater proportions of felons; see Rafter, *Partial Justice*, xxix.

24. The Massachusetts Reformatory for Women provides a glimpse of reading activities over time; attitudes about reading shifted dramatically depending on the perspective of the superintendent. See Rathbone, *World Apart*.

25. Jones, *Prison Library Handbook*, 111, 110.

26. MacCormick, *Education of Adult Prisoners*, 303; Rafter, *Partial Justice*, 27; Freedman, *Their Sisters' Keepers*, 57; Jones, *Prison Library Handbook*, 112. Historical records suggest that the education level of women in reformatories was low. According to a 1914 study conducted at the Massachusetts Reformatory for Women, 21.1 percent of 400 women had not progressed beyond the primary grades, and 96.3 percent stopped their education during grammar school. Historical records also highlight a serious lack of funding for libraries in women's reformatories; see Curtis, "Libraries of the American State," 23.

27. Dodge, "Whores and Thieves," 84; MacCormick, *Education of Adult Prisoners*, 306. Books and education were more available to men than to women in custodial prisons. For instance, although the Illinois penitentiary at Joliet established a library and prison school in 1873, these services were available only to male convicts; from 1859 to 1896, Illinois prison officials expressed no interest in rehabilitating women. See Dodge, "Whores and Thieves," 6.

28. The earliest manual, the *Catalogue and Rules for Prison Libraries to Aid in the Selection and Maintenance of Reading Matter in the Prisons and Jails*, was published in 1877 by the New York Prison Association. In 1916, the New York State Library published "List of Books for Prison Libraries," pt. 1, and the ALA published its first *Manual for Institution Libraries*. Well-known librarian Florence Rising Curtis published her own influential study in 1918, "The Libraries of the American State and National Institutions for Defectives, Dependents, and Delinquents." MacCormick published *The Education of Adult Prisoners* in 1931. Three other manuals were produced through the cooperation of the APA and the ALA: *The Prison Library Handbook* in 1932, followed by two supplements, *2500 Books for the Prison Library* in 1933 and *1000 Books for Prison Libraries, 1936–1939*.

29. Jones, *Prison Library Handbook*, 113, 114.

30. Ibid., 114.

31. Ibid., 108, 109.

32. Holloway, *BookMarks*, 42.

33. Brown, *Bibliotherapy*, 13.

34. In the Philadelphia system, prisoners remained in individual cells day and night. They served as leased laborers, performing cobblery and harness-making in their cells, and they were forbidden to speak or make eye contact with one another. In the Auburn system, prisoners worked together during the day in complete silence, performing leased

labor for private contractors, and they slept in individual cells at night. The Auburn system ultimately superseded the Philadelphia system because allowing prisoners to perform labor outside their cells was more financially profitable than confining them to in-cell labor. See Rafter, *Partial Justice*, 3; American Correctional Association, *Manual of Correctional Standards*, 11; Sullivan, *Prison Reform*, 10.

35. Qtd. in Cummins, *Rise and Fall*, 5; qtd. in Brown, *Bibliotherapy*, 13.

36. Sullivan, *Prison Reform*, 13.

37. Sullivan and Vogel, "Reachin' behind Bars," 125; Rubin, *Breaking In*, 496; Bashore, "Behind Adobe Walls," 239, 245.

38. Sullivan, "Between," 28; qtd. in Coyle, *Libraries in Prisons*, 18. In his 1844 account of his experiences in the New York City jail known as "the Tombs," George Wilkes describes stumbling upon "a collection of stupid volumes" that calls itself a library yet consists "only of sectarian works" (qtd. in Sullivan, "Reading in American Prisons," 115).

39. Davis, "Race and Criminalization," 36.

40. Garrison, *Apostles of Culture*, 40 (quote), 46, 71–72. Debates about the "fiction question" fill hundreds of pages of the *Library Journal* between 1876 and 1900. In 1881, the ALA attempted to produce a standardized list of the most objectionable best-selling fiction, and the list included several authors who depict criminals as important and sympathetic characters. For instance, books by Edmund Yates depict adulterers, scoundrels, dissipated noblemen, and gamblers; novels by Mary Braddon and Mrs. Ellen Price Wood feature women who commit adultery, bigamy, and murder; and the "Newgate Novels" of Edward Bulwer-Lytton, William Harrison Ainsworth, and G. W. M. Reynolds glorify criminals and liberally feature violence and sex. See Geller, *Forbidden Books*, 36; Garrison, *Apostles of Culture*, 84.

41. Qtd. in Garrison, *Apostles of Culture*, 97.

42. Coyle, *Libraries in Prisons*, 27.

43. Jones, *Prison Library Handbook*, 112; Kirby, *Years of Experience*, 196. With the expansion of prison populations during the 1920s, not all prisoners could be gainfully employed, and prison officials nationwide turned to educational, vocational, and recreational programs to supplement labor as a disciplinary tool; see Dodge, "Whores and Thieves," 144.

44. Curtis, "Libraries of the American State," 42, 27; MacCormick, *Education of Adult Prisoners*, 166, 174.

45. *Catalogue and Rules*, 5; Jones, *Prison Library Handbook*, 98, 79, 78, 99, 85.

46. Scott, *Manual for Institution Libraries*, 7; MacCormick, *Education of Adult Prisoners*, 176, 174, 175; Jones, *Prison Library Handbook*, 14. Ironically, *2500 Books for Prison Libraries*, which was the accompaniment to the 1932 *Handbook*, includes three nonfiction books that detail their authors' radical philosophies of penal reform: Thomas Mott Osborne's *Prisons and Common Sense* (1924), Clarence Darrow's *Crime: Its Cause and Treatment* (1931), and Lewis Edward Lawes's *Twenty Thousand Years in Sing Sing* (1932). Penal authorities may have regarded these nonfiction texts as less likely than crime fiction to fuel prisoners' criminal desires. The inclusion of such texts seems surprising, nonetheless, because it suggests that prisoners have the capacity to reflect critically on social issues that affect their daily lives.

47. New York State Library, "List of Books," 8.

48. Ibid., 47, 48, 49. By reconfirming women's place in the domestic sphere, these novels seem to offer a direct challenge to "the New Woman" who appeared on the political and fictional scene in the early twentieth century. The New Woman flouted accepted notions of femininity because she was typically educated, financially independent, unmarried yet

open about sexuality, knowledgeable about politics, suited to city living, and actively involved in the public sphere.

49. Methven, *1000 Books for Prison Libraries*, 8, 10, 13, 14.

50. Curtis, "Libraries of the American State," 20, 22.

51. Delaney, "Place of Bibliotherapy," 53; Association of Specialized and Cooperative Library Agencies, *Library Standards* (1992), 5. The term "bibliotherapy" actually emerged in a satirical context, in Samuel McChord Crothers's 1916 *Atlantic Monthly* essay, "A Literary Clinic." Crothers's essay describes a "Bibliopathic Institute" that offers "bibliotherapy," or "Book Treatment by Competent Specialists." The bibliotherapist declares that the "true function" of a literary critic is "not to pass judgment on the book, but to diagnose the condition of the person who has read it. What was his state of mind before reading and after reading? Was he better or worse for his experience?" (295, 291, 292–93). Crothers's satirical discussion of the curative powers of books echoes the medicalized discourse about reading evident in turn-of-the-century constructions of public libraries and in reading guides such as *Books and Reading or What Books Shall I Read and How Shall I Read Them?* (1891).

52. Bibliotherapy had been practiced since the nineteenth century at McLean Hospital for the Feeble-Minded in Massachusetts. It began to gain legitimacy in the 1930s with the publication of two important studies. In 1937, the medical bulletin of the Veterans' Administration published Elizabeth Pomeroy's study of 1,538 case reports about bibliotherapy. Later in 1937, Dr. William Menninger published an article about the five-year bibliotherapy program that he and his brother had been conducting in their Kansas clinic. The ALA formed its first Bibliotherapy Committee in 1939, and "bibliotherapy" appeared in *Dorland's Illustrated Medical Dictionary* in 1941. *Webster's Dictionary* first included the term in 1961.

53. Delaney, "Time's Telling," 462; Delaney, "Place of Bibliotherapy," 53; Delaney, "Speech," 5.

54. McHenry, *Forgotten Readers*, 3.

55. Delaney, "Place of Bibliotherapy," 54; Delaney, "Library Activities," 169, 165.

56. As if she anticipated being erased from the historical record, Delaney worked tirelessly to share articles that had been written about her and to inform others of her awards and honors. She was actually being erased from the record even during her lifetime, since the Alabama Library Association repeatedly refused her membership on the basis of race.

57. Cantrell, "Sadie P. Delaney," 105; Teets letter.

58. Freedman, *Library Manual*, vii, 4, 60.

59. Qtd. in Cummins, *Rise and Fall*, 23.

60. Floch, "Correctional Treatment," 454, 453, 454; Floch, "Bibliotherapy," 59.

61. English professor John Erskine invented the Great Books program at Columbia University in 1919, when he asked students to discuss one classic literary text every week.

62. Spector, *Library Program*, 8; Cummins, *Rise and Fall*, 28. California's 1944 Prison Reorganization Act defined each prisoner as "an individual in need of treatment" and mandated that each receive treatment "in accordance with his specific needs" (Spector, *Library Program*, 3). This treatment model was based on an indeterminate sentencing policy that required inmates to prove their successful reform before release. Prison librarians became integral players in this system because their records about prisoners' reading accomplishments often influenced the parole board's determinations. See Cummins, *Rise and Fall*, 10.

63. Cummins, *Rise and Fall*, 17.

64. Freedman, *Library Manual*, 17, 15–16, 106–7; Association of Hospital and Institution Libraries, *Bibliotherapy Methods* 13, 19.

65. Brown, *Bibliotherapy*, 324, 328, 326, 167.

66. Sullivan and Vogel, "Reachin' behind Bars," 121, 121 (quote). As evident in the 1950 *Library Manual for Correctional Institutions*, law books were considered contraband in prisons as late as the 1950s. Congress authorized federal funds for prison law libraries in 1971, and in 1977, the U.S. Supreme Court mandated that prisoners be provided "adequate, effective, and meaningful" access to the courts, either through a prison law library or through free "assistance from persons trained in the law" (qtd. in Vogel, *Down for the Count*, 116, 120).

67. In 1972, the Social Responsibilities Round Table of the ALA urged ALA members to inform themselves about the state of libraries in jails and prisons, and in 1974, an ALA subcommittee produced *Jails Need Libraries, Too*. In 1976, the ALA's Health and Rehabilitative Library Services Division established a section on Library Service to Prisoners, and the ALA passed a resolution stating that prisoners confined within a public library's taxing district must be served by that library. Three library journals also devoted entire issues to prison library service during the 1970s: *Illinois Libraries* (1974), *Wilson Library Bulletin* (1977), and *Library Trends* (1977). At the state level, a 1971 Ohio legal case, *Jones v. Wittenberg*, required a county jail to provide library services to prisoners, prohibited censorship except for pornography, and required that sufficient reading light be provided in each cell. A 1972 California legal case, *Brenneman v. Madigan*, stipulated that tax-supported library services available to those who can post bond must also be available to those in pretrial detention. See Stout and Turitz, "Outside . . . Looking In," 500, 504.

68. Stout and Turitz, "Outside . . . Looking In," 504; Gruensfelder, "Law Enforcers," 511.

69. Qtd. in Cummins, *Rise and Fall*, 78; Stout and Turitz, "Outside . . . Looking In," 499; Sullivan, "Prison Libraries," 512.

70. Jackson, *Soledad Brother*, 60, 87, 158, 223, 228. Jackson intended to learn Spanish, Swahili, Arabic, and Chinese so that he could "communicate with three-fourths of the people on earth." He also regularly read books for developing his vocabulary, since "it is by words that we convey our thoughts, and bend people to our will" (112, 142). After his books were confiscated in 1970, Jackson specifically requested Fanon's *A Dying Colonialism*, *The Wretched of the Earth*, and *Black Face, White Mask*; Malcolm X's *Autobiography* and *Malcolm Speaks*; and Ardrey's *African Genesis: A Personal Investigation into the Animal Origins and Nature of Man* and *Territorial Imperative*.

71. Qtd. in James, *New Abolitionists*, 304.

72. Irwin, *Felon*, 53; qtd. in Sullivan, *Prison Reform*, 111.

73. Qtd. in James, *New Abolitionists*, 305.

74. Cummins, *Rise and Fall*, 238. As the California Department of Corrections became cognizant of the unintended effects of bibliotherapy, it abandoned support for reading-centered initiatives. When Herman Spector retired from San Quentin in 1967, he was replaced not by another librarian but by a prison guard, and the prison administration destroyed Spector's three decades of records about prisoners' reading and writing habits. See ibid., 29.

75. Gilbert, "Attica," 314; Ngo, "'You Have to Be Intimate,'" 251; Levasseur, "Trouble Coming Every Day," 49.

76. Schlosser, "Prison-Industrial Complex"; Davis, *Are Prisons Obsolete?*, 92; Sullivan, *Prison Reform*, 125–26. According to Schlosser, California's 1976 law also amended the section of the state's penal code that declared the ultimate goals of imprisonment: the word "rehabilitation" was replaced by the word "punishment." For additional information

about the development of the prison-industrial complex, see Davis, *Are Prisons Obsolete?*; Schlosser, "Prison-Industrial Complex"; Gilmore, *Golden Gulag*; and Parenti, *Lockdown America*.

77. Davis, *Are Prisons Obsolete?*, 90–91; Schlosser, "Prison-Industrial Complex." At year-end 2006, a total of 113,791 state and federal prisoners were held in privately operated facilities, a number that represents a 5.4 percent increase since the previous year; see Bureau of Justice Statistics, *Prisoners in 2006*.

78. Hartz, Kimmel, and Hartz, *Prison Librarianship*, 42, 9 (quote).

79. Hallinan, *Going up the River*, 81. According to the chief librarian of the Ohio Department of Rehabilitation and Correction, private prisons in Ohio "have to convince the state and the legislature that they are doing the same job for less money," so "they're not doing as much for their libraries. They're not portioning out their Industrial and Entertainment funds like they should."

80. Coyle, *Libraries in Prisons*, viii (quote), 65 (quote), 2.

81. Association of Specialized and Cooperative Library Agencies, *Library Standards* (1981), 7, 8; ALA, qtd. in Association of Specialized and Cooperative Library Agencies, *Library Standards* (1992), 28. These ACA standards seem to be written not with the aim of providing the best library service for prisoners but with the aim of protecting penal authorities from lawsuits about prisoners' access to books; see Sullivan and Vogel, "Reachin' behind Bars," 123.

82. Association of Specialized and Cooperative Library Agencies, *Library Standards* (1981), 8; Coyle, *Libraries in Prisons*, 78, 80, 81, 48, 97.

83. Suvak, "'Throw the Book,'" 32, 33; Vogel, *Down for the Count*, 22.

84. ALA and the Association of American Publishers, qtd. in Association of Specialized and Cooperative Library Agencies, *Library Standards* (1992), 31–33. The "Library Bill of Rights" states that libraries should "challenge censorship" and "cooperate with all persons and groups concerned with resisting abridgement of free expression and free access to ideas" (27). The "Resolution on Prisoners' Right to Read" advocates granting prisoners the right to read all books "except those which describe the making of any weapon, explosive, poison or destructive device" (28). The "Policy on Confidentiality of Library Records" recommends that each library ensure the confidentiality of its circulation records and records of library users, allowing access only for legal discovery procedures or legislative investigation (29). The "Freedom to View" statement calls for "the broadest possible access" to films and audiovisual materials (34).

85. Qtd. in Plettenberg, "User Needs"; Chepesiuk, "S.C.," 502 (quote), 501–2.

86. Morrison letter; Morrison, *Paradise*, 154, 206.

87. "Texan Klan Mailings," 3; Vogel, *Down for the Count*, 17. Although the Texas DCJ has allowed mailings from Klan groups outside the state since 1980, the decision marked the first time that Texas Klan groups have been granted such permission. Prison spokesperson David Nunnelee explained that the Ku Klux Klan of Waco is a registered sales agent in Texas and therefore has the right to distribute materials. Furthermore, the DCJ cannot simply ban unpopular viewpoints, but if any of the material advocates violence against blacks or Jews, they will "have to look at it" ("Texan Klan Mailings," 3).

88. Holloway, *BookMarks*, 7. Angelou's autobiography has been on the list of banned books "because they say it's about child rape," says Ohio's chief librarian, but as she notes, the rape "is a very small part of the autobiography."

89. Qtd. in Goodstein, "Prisons Purging Books"; qtd. in Goodstein, "Critics Right and Left." Scholars across the religious spectrum have noted significant "eccentricities and

omissions" in the lists of approved materials, including a preponderance of titles from the same publishing houses; see Goodstein, "Prisons Purging Books."

90. Qtd. in Rodríguez, *Forced Passages*, 88.

91. MacCormick, *Education of Adult Prisoners*, 28, 7, 15, 16.

92. Ibid., 9, 11, 7, 9, 92, 93, 56, 6. In discussing education for women prisoners, however, MacCormick radically contracts his expansive claim that education should offer "knowledge of what the world of thought has to offer." Arguing that many female prisoners are of "low" and "limited" intelligence, he recommends that penal officials carefully calculate "the exact knowledge of reading, writing, and arithmetic necessary" for women "as a supplement to specific vocational skills." They should ask, "How much English or arithmetic does the waitress need? the family cook? . . . the power machine operator? the beauty culturist? . . . How much ability to read? to write?" (303, 309, 302).

93. Buntman, *Robben Island*, 70, 276, 277, 7.

94. Evans, Rosenberg, and Whitehorn, "Dykes and Fags Want to Know," 262; Ngo, "'You Have to Be Intimate,'" 251.

95. Rodríguez, *Forced Passages*, 110.

96. Ibid., 93, 89, 87, 96.

97. Harlow, *Barred*, 23; Rodríguez, *Forced Passages*, 93, 92, 100, 101.

98. Taylor, "Pell Grants," 107.

99. Worth, "Model Prison," 42, 38 (quote); qtd. in Zahm, "*Last Graduation.*"

100. Rodríguez, *Forced Passages*, 41; Davis, "Race and Criminalization," 44.

101. Wicker foreword, xiii; James, *New Abolitionists*, 316; Davis, *Are Prisons Obsolete?*, 56. According to a 1996 Educational Testing Service report, at least half of all state correctional institutions had cut their educational programs during the previous five years. Prior to 1998, the federal government required states to spend no less than 10 percent of their Basic State Grant for Adult Education in correctional institutions; the law now requires them to spend no more than 10 percent. See Coley and Barton, *Locked Up and Locked Out*, 17.

102. Davis, "Race and Criminalization," 35.

103. Rhodes, *Total Confinement*, 223.

104. As I mention in the Introduction, the Changing Lives through Literature Program adopts such a model in sentencing nonviolent lawbreakers to a literature seminar rather than jail. The "Literature n' Living" class, which has been part of the Youthful Offender Program at California's Orange County Jail since 1995, also endorses a therapeutic model of reading. The program's participants are boys between the ages of fourteen and seventeen who are awaiting sentencing; about 85 percent of these boys get sentenced to adult prisons. The "Literature n' Living" class is discussion-based, and authors frequently participate in sessions that focus on their works. See Smith, "For Violent and Lost Boys."

Chapter 2

1. Burke, "Literature as an Equipment for Living," 10.

2. The libraries in the Ohio, Pennsylvania, and North Carolina prisons are staffed with a professional librarian and prisoners trained as library clerks. In Ohio, I conducted interviews with the chief librarian of the Ohio Department of Rehabilitation and Correction, the general librarian at the Ohio Reformatory for Women, and the general librarian and chaplain librarian at the Northeast Pre-Release Center. At the State Correctional Institution in Pennsylvania, I conducted interviews with the two general librarians and the chaplain librarian. Because my research in North Carolina was more narrowly focused than my

subsequent research, I did not obtain detailed information about the policies and holdings of the library at the North Carolina Correctional Institution for Women.

3. When women first arrive at the Pennsylvania prison, they are on a restricted status that does not include library privileges. Many women emphasize the difficulty of having such little access to books during that period, which can last as long as a year.

4. Association of Specialized and Cooperative Library Agencies, *Library Standards* (1981), 14.

5. All of the following constituents rely on funding from the IGWF: the general library; the chaplain's library; the activities department; the Alcohol or Drug Program; the Beautification Program, which is responsible for gardening on prison grounds; CORE, a jobs and reentry program; the Daily Program, which offers services for those with mental disabilities; Family Resources; the Greenhouse Program; Guitar and Music Theory; Major Purchases, which funds items such as DVD players for the housing units; the Prison Pup Program, which trains seeing-eye dogs; the STEP program for elderly inmates; the visiting room; visual arts; and the Young Offenders Association.

6. For fiscal year 2007, the Pennsylvania library received $24,000. Other constituents received the following amounts of IGWF funding during fiscal year 2006: chaplain's library, $2,000; Activities Department, $32,000; and Alcohol or Drug Program, $1,000. The library lists 10,543 items in its general catalog, including multiple copies of books, tapes, and books on tape.

7. Solo argues that books about starting your own business do not represent "a realistic approach. These books are designed for people who have the capital and the wherewithal to go do it. . . . We're a whole 'nother segment." The prison needs to have "realistic" books about "how to get out and stay out," Solo insists, beyond books about writing résumés and cover letters.

8. Canfield, Hansen, and Lagana, *Chicken Soup*, 347.

9. Noting the arbitrary nature of the prohibition on sexually explicit content, one librarian wryly acknowledged, "How much sex is too much sex? Danielle Steel is OK but Zane is not." Both the Ohio and Pennsylvania prisons have banned African American erotica written by Zane, yet both libraries include huge collections of Danielle Steel's sexually explicit romance novels.

10. According to one librarian, the Publication Review Committees in some Pennsylvania prisons are removing art books, *National Geographic* magazines, and even books about breast cancer because they include pictures of bare breasts.

11. The library in the North Carolina Correctional Institution for Women includes the following sections of books: Romances, Cops & Crime, Suspense, Almanacs, Humor/Comedy, Large Print, Poetry, Easy Reading, GED, Government/Political, Health, Psychology, Writing, Literature, World History, Mythology, and Business Management. My research did not focus on the library's specific holdings.

12. While legal materials occupy several shelves in the Ohio library, the Pennsylvania library's legal collection is largely computer-based.

13. The "Ten American Classics" list includes *Huckleberry Finn*, *The Scarlet Letter*, *To Kill a Mockingbird*, *The Red Badge of Courage*, *The Great Gatsby*, *Grapes of Wrath*, *Call of the Wild*, *Invisible Man*, *A Farewell to Arms*, and *Fahrenheit 451*. At the Ohio Reformatory for Women, which I briefly visited when conducting research at NEPRC, the "classics" are placed out of reach on high shelves, and no sign signals their presence. The books are extremely dusty and get very little use.

14. The library's nonfiction collection includes Dawn Maria Daniels and Candace Sandy's

inspirational book, *Soul of My Sisters: Black Women Break their Silence, Tell their Stories, Heal their Spirits*; Booker T. Washington's *Up from Slavery*; bell hooks's *Bone Black: Memories of Girlhood*; a few books about the history of slavery and Martin Luther King Jr.; and a six-volume set of the *Encyclopedia of African American Culture and History: The Black Experience in the Americas*.

15. The lawsuit, *Fussel v. Wilkinson*, was settled in 2005.

16. By contrast, the main library at the Ohio Reformatory for Women has fifteen shelves of Christian fiction and eight shelves of Christian ministry books. The librarian argues that there is nowhere else to store these books because the chapel library is full.

17. In addition to the general and chaplain's libraries, the housing units in all three prisons have tiny collections of five to fifteen books. These books, which have been weeded out of the general library due to their worn condition or lack of use, are rotated among the units and discarded when replacements arrive. Women in the restricted housing unit, the infirmary, or the mental health unit can request delivery of specific books, or they can choose from the selection of books that the librarian delivers once a week.

18. The loan period for books in Pennsylvania is two weeks. Prisoners face financial penalties for returning books late. In Pennsylvania, for instance, the late fee is ten cents per day. Although the librarians rarely enforce the penalty, women cannot be released from prison if they have not paid for their overdue books. The business office will deduct any unpaid fines from prisoners' accounts.

19. An additional complication with purchasing books is the fact that women are only permitted to keep a limited number of books in their cells. In Pennsylvania, they are permitted to keep ten books plus one religious book. A similar rule exists in the Ohio prison, but it is less strictly enforced. If an officer finds more than ten books in a prisoner's cell, the prisoner must send some of the books home or donate them to the prison library. Miekal, for instance, eventually had to ship some of her books home.

20. The average wage that women earn in the Ohio prison is $22 per month; many women earn only $18 per month. In the Pennsylvania prison, women earn between 19 and 42 cents per hour for employment, and full-time students earn 25 cents per hour for time spent in class. Women receive a raise every sixty days if they remain in the same job.

21. Women are employed in a variety of capacities at the three prisons. They serve as educational tutors, classroom assistants, library and legal clerks, phone bank operators, mentors in therapeutic programs, or quartermasters (responsible for distributing prison-issued goods to new prisoners), and they work as part of the kitchen, laundry, groundskeeping, housekeeping, or maintenance crews.

22. Qtd. in Baxter et al., "Live from the Panopticon," 214.

23. Rodríguez, *Forced Passages*, 213; Saadawi, *Memoirs*, 99.

24. Rodríguez, *Forced Passages*, 214.

25. Prison librarians tend to stock more hardback books than paperbacks because they are more durable and readers are less likely to tear out individual pages. Reflecting on the importance of touch, which is largely forbidden among prisoners, prisoner Dan Pens writes, "Touch is life. It is vitality. It is the music of the skin. . . . To be deprived of touch can wreak devastation on the psyche. To touch is to be human" ("Skin Blind," 151).

26. Saadawi, *Memoirs*, 102.

27. In "Reading: The State of the Discipline," Leah Price notes that classical medical works include reading as a healthful form of exercise; because Roman volumes had to be held with both hands, the body participated as much as the voice in the act of reading. However, with the emergence of the public library, readers have been taught to efface their

own bodies. As Price explains, "The proper thing to put on tables is books, not feet; pages must not be touched with dirty hands or gummy fingers" (309).

28. Davis, *Society and Culture*, 192.

29. Bearing titles such as *Sins of the Mother*, *Cruel Sacrifice*, and *Precious Angels*, true crime books typically take the form of a clearly defined battle between noble law enforcement agents and an evil criminal protagonist, most often a male serial killer or an "All-American housewife" who kills her husband or children for selfish ends. White, middle-class women are the primary readers of these books, and the genre relies on a racist distinction between the presumed criminality of black and brown people and the "exceptional" and thus newsworthy acts of its white, middle-class protagonists. Because true crime books insufficiently acknowledge how race, class, and gender inequalities factor into the "true" stories of women's crimes, women involved in my study often try to complicate, modify, or supplement the books' reductive accounts. "To disidentify," José Muñoz argues, "is to read oneself and one's own life narrative in a moment, object, or subject that is not culturally coded to 'connect' with the disidentifying subject" (*Disidentifications*, 12). Highlighting how she and other prisoners disidentify with true crime books in order to render them more useful, Tamia explains, "It's all how you read into it." For further discussion of women prisoners' true crime reading practices, see Sweeney, "Living to Read True Crime."

30. Harlow, *Barred*, 201; Mathiesen, "Towards the 21st Century," 342.

31. Price, "Reading," 310.

32. Ibid., 305.

Chapter 3

1. Illouz, *Saving the Modern Soul*, 181, 182.

2. O'Neill, "Misery Lit." The sequels to *A Child Called "It"* are titled *The Lost Boy: A Foster Child's Search for the Love of a Family* (1997) and *A Man Named Dave: A Story of Triumph and Forgiveness* (2000).

3. O'Neill, "Misery Lit." See, for instance, Sykes, *Nation of Victims*; Dershowitz, *Abuse Excuse*; Wilson, *Moral Judgment*; and Sommers and Satel, *One Nation under Therapy*.

4. Kaminer, *I'm Dysfunctional*, 155; Armstrong, qtd. in Showalter, *Hystories*, 147.

5. I am aware of feminist debate about the term "victimization." Two concerns about using the term seem most salient to me: (1) it can suggest that women must show severe harm or psychological damage in order for their experiences to count, and (2) labeling some experiences as victimization can allow coercive elements of heterosexual sex to remain unexamined; see Gavey, "'I Wasn't Raped,'" 77. In adopting the term "victimization," I am referring to a spectrum of harmful and abusive experiences that produce a range of responses from different subjects. In my usage, the term is not yoked to a notion of women as eternal victims; if one sustains an experience of victimization, one does not assume a fixed position as the inevitable object of harm. As Judith Shklar argues, victimization "happens to us, it is not a quality" (*Ordinary Vices*, 17). Although the term "survivor" emphasizes women's agency and capacity for resistance, it also suggests that experiences of unwanted sexuality are necessarily life-threatening, and it can encourage either an increased sense of victimization or a sense of guilty fraudulence among those who claim the term but did not feel deeply damaged or traumatized by their experiences. For further discussion of these debates, see Lamb, "Constructing the Victim," and Gavey, "'I Wasn't Raped.'"

6. Alcoff and Gray-Rosendale, "Survivor Discourse," 199, 213, 212, 213, 217.

7. Brown, "Freedom's Silences," 84, 91, 94 (Levi quote; emphasis in original), 94. Brown

presented "Freedom's Silences" at a conference about censorship, sponsored by the Getty Research Institute. She delivered the paper first as part of a panel titled "Silencing Women: Feminism(s), Censorship, and Difference" and then as part of a plenary session titled "Censorship and Silencing: Practices of Cultural Regulation." Brown makes related arguments in her influential 1993 essay, "Wounded Attachments," and in her 2001 monograph, *Politics out of History*.

8. Greenfeld and Snell, *Women Offenders*.

9. Of eighty-five women polled, 11.8 percent reported no experiences of victimization, 41.2 percent reported sustaining physical abuse or severe emotional abuse, 41.2 percent reported sustaining sexual abuse or rape, 44.7 percent reported sustaining domestic violence, and 89.4 percent reported sustaining one or more of these forms of victimization.

10. Sommers and Satel, *One Nation under Therapy*, 7.

11. The North Carolina prison offers an intensive Drug and Alcohol Recovery Treatment program (DART) and a program called Mothers and Their Children (MATCH), which includes parenting skills classes and fosters bonding between incarcerated women and their children. The Ohio prison offers a ninety-day Intensive Program Prison course (IPP) that provides a range of classes and specialized treatment services. When women complete an IPP, their sentences are reduced to the amount of time already served and they are released on supervision. The Ohio facility also offers shorter courses such as "Beyond Trauma," "Family Relations," "Anger Management," "Victim Awareness," and "Attitudes and Self-Sabotage." The Pennsylvania prison offers parenting skills courses, an intensive drug rehabilitation program called "Wings of Life," and "House of Hope," an intensive program that focuses on recovery from physical and sexual abuse.

12. Rhodes, *Total Confinement*, 155.

13. Brown, "Freedom's Silences," 94.

14. One group read Jones's *Eva's Man*, four groups read Jakes's *Woman, Thou Art Loosed!*, three groups read Vanzant's *Yesterday, I Cried*, three groups read Walls's *The Glass Castle*, and two groups read Lamb's edited collection. Various groups also discussed three other narratives of victimization that I do not discuss in this chapter: Dorothy Allison's *Bastard out of Carolina* (1992), Khaled Hosseini's *A Thousand Splendid Suns* (2007), and Patrice Gaines's *Laughing in the Dark: From Colored Girl to Woman of Color—A Journey from Prison to Power* (1994).

15. Alcoff and Gray-Rosendale, "Survivor Discourse," 217.

16. Gordon, *Ghostly Matters*, 4.

17. Heberle is building on Sharon Marcus's argument that "the need to define rape and to assert its existence can distract us from plotting its vanishing point" ("Fighting Bodies," 399). Sharon Lamb illustrates the kind of stance that Heberle wants to avoid in arguing that feminists should emphasize that male violence is "endemic in our culture" and that "women can't go through life expecting not to be abused without some change in society" ("Constructing the Victim," 133).

18. Heberle, "Deconstructive Strategies," 63, 68.

19. Rich, "Twenty-One Love Poems."

20. Brown, "Freedom's Silences," 93, 97.

21. Jones, *Eva's Man*, 45.

22. Dixon, "Singing a Deep Song," 246, 254.

23. Wilcox, "Resistant Silence," 80.

24. Brown, "Freedom's Silences," 93, 94, 96. As a final caveat, Brown argues that "it would be a mistake" to value silence "too highly" as a political goal because it is "a strategy

for negotiating domination, rather than a sign of emancipation from it," a "place of 'freedom from' that is not yet freedom to make the world" (97).

25. Ibid., 94, 93, 84, 93, 95.

26. Ibid., 94, 85, 94, 95.

27. Ibid., 94, 95. Brown makes all of her arguments through rhetorical questioning, which may be an attempt to lessen the normative nature of her claims.

28. Ibid., 96, 94.

29. Jones, *Eva's Man*, 153.

30. T. D. Jakes is a well-known televangelist with a daily television show, *The Potter's Touch*, and a weekly broadcast, *The Potter's House*. Jakes is founder and pastor of The Potter's House and CEO for T. D. Jakes Ministries in Dallas, Texas. He has also authored numerous best-selling books, including a business bestseller, *Maximize the Moment: God's Action Plan for Your Life*, and several books that foreground women's experiences, such as *God's Leading Lady*; *The Lady, Her Lover, and Her Lord*; *His Lady: Sacred Promises for God's Woman*; and *Daddy Loves His Girls*. Several women have seen the film version of *Woman, Thou Art Loosed!* and most assert that the novel is better than the film because it delves into the issues more deeply.

31. Brown, "Freedom's Silences," 94.

32. Maso, *Defiance*, 125; Brown, "Freedom's Silences," 94. In Carole Maso's *Defiance*, the protagonist writes, "How to purge the horror. Not possible. At best to give it shape and name" (125).

33. Kaminer, *I'm Dysfunctional*, 153; Showalter, *Hystories*, 150.

34. Rafter and Heidensohn, *International Feminist Perspectives*, 7; Daly and Maher, *Criminology at the Crossroads*, 9. Psychologist Evelyn K. Sommers's *Voices from Within: Women Who Have Broken the Law* illustrates the infantilization that can result from inadequate theorizations of women prisoners' agency. Insisting that none of her interviewees intended "to act out in a way that would hurt anyone," Sommers argues that "women as a group are engulfed in fear and abuse, restricted to inadequate and irrelevant modes of expression, blindly trained towards cultural images of success, and stunted by notions of character and growth that reflect nothing of their reality" (126, 122). She not only constructs all women as fearful, restricted, duped, and stunted; Sommers also precludes recognition of the strength, anger, resilience, rebellion, insight, and creativity that lawbreaking women manifest through their efforts—however ineffective—to make their way in the world.

35. See Pearson, *When She Was Bad*, which continues a disturbing trend of trying to achieve equality by making punishment levels for women as harsh as those for men.

36. Dershowitz, *Abuse Excuse*, 4.

37. Abandoned by her mother and estranged from her father, who hanged himself while imprisoned for child molestation, Wuornos was raised by her alcoholic grandmother and sexually and physically abusive grandfather. After she was raped and impregnated by a stranger at age twelve, Wuornos was sent to a home for unwed mothers and gave her child up for adoption. During her first year on her own—at age fourteen—Wuornos was beaten and raped by at least six men. She eventually became a homeless highway prostitute whose clients often didn't pay her.

38. *Wuornos v. State*, 1012. By implying that the distinction between "strictly legal issues" and "social awareness" is an inherent feature of the law, Justice Kogan disavows the ways in which legal ideology itself structures certain discourses of victimhood. In the realm of civil law, for instance, existing legal structures essentially force African Americans to articulate themselves as perfect victims against a perfect discriminator in order to prove discrimina-

tion. See Crenshaw, "Color Blindness," 287; Bumiller, *Civil Rights Society*, 62. Likewise, Justice Kogan disavows the fact that determinist legal doctrines such as "duress doctrine" and "provocation doctrine" evaluate criminal incidents in view of the broad social context in which they occur; see Armour, "Just Deserts." Kogan's statement is symptomatic of the significant shift away from "social awareness" that has occurred in criminal litigation since the end of the Warren Court era in the late 1960s; see Minow, "Surviving Victim Talk," 1415.

39. Jordan, "All about Eva," 37.

40. Three of the interviewees were involved in the death of an abusive spouse or sexually violent acquaintance, and five have seriously injured their partners during episodes of abuse.

41. Jones, *Eva's Man*, 120.

42. With its concluding scene of a sexual encounter between Eva and her cellmate—in which her cellmate says, "Tell me when it feels sweet, Eva," and Eva responds, "Now" (Jones, *Eva's Man*, 177)—*Eva's Man* suggests that Eva's ability to speak her own sexual pleasure demonstrates her availability to a future that will not be wholly circumscribed by her experiences of victimization. As Sue said, "Where before it was like, just lay down, spread my legs and let him do it, I think this time Eva actually had a chance to voice what she thought. It was giving her a chance to experience and find something she liked." See Franke, "Theorizing Yes," for further discussion of the ways in which feminist legal arguments about violence against women fail to acknowledge women's rights to enjoy their own bodies.

43. During an interview with Claudia Tate, Jones emphasizes Eva's strategic elusiveness: "The question the listener would continually hear would be: how much of Eva's story is true, and how much is deliberately not true, that is, how much of a game is she playing with her listeners, psychiatrists, and others?" (Jones, "Gayl Jones," 91).

44. Karimah, a thirty-three-year-old African American woman, describes a similar process through which she learned to understand her own experiences: "It started as anger about what happened to other women. Then I learned that I was worth being angry about what happened to me." Karimah began to work through her own experiences—including the extensive sexual violence that both she and her daughter sustained—only after several months of hearing other women witness to their experiences through the prison's House of Hope program. She was asked to leave the program after the first ten months because she was too afraid to speak. When she enrolled a second time, she listened to others' stories for four to five months and was finally able to articulate her own experiences.

45. Lamb, *Couldn't Keep It to Myself*, 9.

46. Sidonie Smith argues that the dominant Western autobiographical tradition is characterized by "the unfolding or the development, the reenactment or the discovery, of an individual's unique historical identity" (qtd. in Warhol and Michie, "Twelve-Step Teleology," 334).

47. Alcoff and Gray-Rosendale, "Survivor Discourse," 214.

48. Lamb, "Constructing the Victim," 133; Gavey, "'I Wasn't Raped,'" 75; Marcus, "Fighting Bodies," 397; Heberle, "Deconstructive Strategies," n.p.

49. Shelly's inability to classify Eva calls to mind the closing line of June Jordan's review of *Eva's Man*—"Who is she?"—as well as Carter's question to Eva, "Who are you? Where did you come from?" (Jordan, "All about Eva," 37; Jones, *Eva's Man*, 20).

50. Minow, "Surviving Victim Talk," 1424.

51. Human Rights Watch Women's Rights Project, *All Too Familiar*, 2; qtd. in Davis, *Are Prisons Obsolete?*, 80.

52. Human Rights Watch Women's Rights Project, *All Too Familiar*, 2; Davis, *Are Prisons Obsolete?*, 81, 77–78.

53. Marcus, "Fighting Bodies," 397, 396, 392.

54. Ibid., 393, 399.

55. By invoking slavery, Sakina draws attention both to the prison-industrial complex, in which prisoners earn "pennies for pay" while corporations "make millions," and to the ways in which prison serves to keep black people disenfranchised. "They are setting us up in here to make us naive," she argues. "They are trying to keep us in bondage because they're trying to keep us blind. But I refuse! I refuse that this is gonna happen to me!"

56. Davis, *Are Prisons Obsolete?*, 77.

57. Five of Vanzant's books have appeared on the *New York Times* bestseller list, including *In the Meantime: Finding Yourself and the Love You Want* (1998) and *Yesterday, I Cried*, which received the thirty-first NAACP Image Award for Outstanding Literary Work, Non-Fiction. As the chief executive officer of Inner Visions Worldwide, Inc., Spiritual Life Maintenance Center, Vanzant conducts workshops and classes and coordinates a correspondence prison ministry with more than 3,500 U.S. prisoners. She hosted a television series called *Iyanla* from 2001 to 2002, and from 2004 to 2006 she participated as a "life coach" on a reality television show called *Starting Over*.

58. Vanzant, *Yesterday, I Cried*, 117, 25, 19, 18, 25, 28, 26, 27 (emphasis in original), 314. Kate, who is "writing a book to reach other women that are hurting," felt inspired by *Yesterday, I Cried* to "enrich" her book and "write it in a way that people will understand where I'm coming from. I need to change the wording and dissect the characters so they understand." Heidi said that *Yesterday, I Cried* made her realize that "now is the time" for her to write her own story, which she had been postponing.

59. Sommers and Satel, *One Nation under Therapy*, 136. Some women prisoners also articulate resistance to normative claims about how to grieve. Deven comments about the stages of grief: "Everybody grieves differently. Everybody does stages of grief differently. You know, they always say it goes this, this, this. But you could do it ass backwards if you wanted to. It just depends on who you are." Deven and other prisoners do not, however, deny the importance of grieving and of having one's grief recognized by others.

60. Campbell, "Being Dismissed"; Illouz, *Saving the Modern Soul*, 18, 142.

61. Howard, *Publishing the Family*, 245; Sánchez-Eppler, "Bodily Bonds," 36–37.

62. Smith, qtd. in Howard, *Publishing the Family*, 225; Travis, "'It Will Change the World,'" 1030.

63. Brown, "Freedom's Silences," 85; Vanzant, *Yesterday, I Cried*, 92, 107, 184, 72.

64. Vanzant, *Yesterday, I Cried*, 152, 185. Vanzant reckons with her painful past by discussing herself as two distinct personalities—Rhonda and Iyanla—but she eventually reaches a point where she must "merge what I used to be with what I could be. Rhonda and Iyanla had to become one." She therefore writes a letter to Rhonda to release her and symbolically buries her by burying the letter and some photos. Now, when interviewers wonder why Vanzant "brush[es] over the details of her past," she insists that "those incidents have nothing to do with me. That history is not mine. It is not Iyanla's." Although she recognizes that she is who she is because of her past, Vanzant argues, "I no longer have the need or even the ability to promote that pain" (*Yesterday, I Cried*, 34, 312).

65. I later discovered that Jacqueline skipped two meetings with her psychiatrist—which conflicted with our book discussions—because she found our discussions of Vanzant's and Jakes's books more useful.

66. Gordon, *Keeping Good Time*, 200.

67. Vanzant, *Yesterday, I Cried*, 313, 191. Starr's belief in the importance of telling one's story is evident in her current efforts to "help others to tell their stories," which she conceptualizes as watching people "grow into a beautiful butterfly" rather than remaining "an injured caterpillar inching along." Because Starr has done a lot of writing while imprisoned, she has learned to "process [her] emotions" more than some other women. "I'm okay with my story. Others aren't," she explains. "If they were given a way to tell their stories, it will help them spiritually and help them move towards recovery." Starr's desire to help other women serves as a moving illustration of the ways in which some women try to make their freedom "usable" for others, so that it is "not simply a private possession" (Gordon, *Keeping Good Time*, 204). Starr's comments suggest that freedom entails the "interdependence of connected individuals," and that struggling for others' freedom is the precondition for one's own (Hames-García, *Fugitive Thought*, 96).

68. Vanzant, *Yesterday, I Cried*, 302.

69. Smith and Watson introduction, 14.

70. Illouz, *Saving the Modern Soul*, 18. Walls's memoir won a Christopher Award, a Books for a Better Life Award, the *Elle* Readers Prize, and the American Library Association Alex Award.

71. Peck, "Mediated Talking Cure," 135.

72. Ibid., 141.

73. Howard, *Publishing the Family*, 251. At the other end of the spectrum, a few readers disliked evidence of craft in Walls's narrative style, which seems more apparent than in genres such as urban fiction. Christine argued that the lessons that Walls learns seemed "scripted." Donna concurred, adding that "when something f'ed up happened, she always had a philosophical statement. . . . It seemed kinda too neat." Because she recognized how Walls's narrative is crafted, Christine ultimately concluded, "I think the writer wrote to capitalize on the market. . . . I'm waiting for it to turn out [to] be false, like *A Million Little Pieces*." Unlike the seemingly raw and unmediated content of urban fiction, which readers do not recognize as crafted or as catering to the market, Walls's literary craft may signal inauthenticity to some readers because "recognizably 'packaged' feelings remind us of the socially constructed nature of emotion," and "evidence that emotion is not only conventionalized but circulates through the commodity system on a vast scale can be downright distasteful" (Howard, *Publishing the Family*, 239).

74. Walls, *Glass Castle*, 28.

75. In their efforts to make meaning from Walls's narrative, some women also sought to classify the behaviors of Walls's parents in terms that circulate widely in penal contexts. Walls does not name her parents' behaviors in clinical or psychological terms; she simply describes them through anecdotes and events. Nonetheless, reflecting long-standing criminological debates about whether lawbreakers are "mad" or "bad," women involved in my study debated whether the parents' behavior stemmed from being "mentally unstable" or from being selfish, irresponsible, and childish. Readers debated whether Walls's mother was codependent, manic depressive, a sugar addict, or merely self-centered. They also debated whether Walls's father was "a paranoid schizophrenic alcoholic," whether his paranoia and alcoholism stemmed from being sexually molested by his mother, and whether he merely pretended to be paranoid because it provided an expedient excuse.

76. Illouz, *Saving the Modern Soul*, 18.

77. Alcoff and Gray-Rosendale, "Survivor Discourse," 208, 207, 214; Brown, "Freedom's Silences," 92; Alcoff and Gray-Rosendale, "Survivor Discourse," 215.

78. Alcoff and Gray-Rosendale, "Survivor Discourse," 220, 212. Disclosing to other sur-

vivors undermines the assumption that a mediator must derive interpretive authority from abstract knowledge rather than personal experience; see ibid., 213.

79. Peck, "Mediated Talking Cure," 136.

80. Alcoff and Gray-Rosendale, "Survivor Discourse," 216.

81. Gordon, *Ghostly Matters*, 203.

82. Throughout her participation in my study, Nena was involved in a "total immersion" therapeutic program designed for women with particularly acute addiction problems. During a six-month period, women involved in this program live in a separate wing of the prison and regularly participate in group therapy, individual counseling, and mini-courses that address issues such as relationship violence and problem solving. Her discussions of books often reflected concepts and approaches that she was learning in that setting.

83. Brown, "Freedom's Silences," 91; Illouz, *Saving the Modern Soul*, 185; hooks, qtd. in Alcoff and Gray-Rosendale, "Survivor Discourse," 216.

84. Lamb, "Constructing the Victim," 113.

85. Gavey, "'I Wasn't Raped,'" 73.

86. Morrison, "Nobel," 16.

Interlude 1

1. Access to books was highly racialized in Denise's town. When she was first sent to a formerly all-white school, the school library made a huge impression on her. "I'll never forget 'cause I'd never seen a library before," she recounts. "I'd never seen a new book. . . . And it was just beautiful, you know. Everybody got on the bus that evening, and that's all everybody was talking about, the library and the books, how pages in the books was clean. We didn't have that." I learned from Solo, an African American woman who is roughly the same age as Denise, that she, too, read the Sears catalog as a child and used it as the basis for "fabricating stories." "The Sears & Roebucks catalog that my grandmother had sent me at the age of seven became my template for everything I thought was good," Solo explained. "They used to mail these catalogs to people, and I would steal them off their porch [laughter] . . . and I would come home, and I would cut families out. Of course, all the families were white, and I would cut out furniture, and I would put it in sections, and I would play like that for hours and hours. . . . I would get the Kenmore washers. I would get a daddy 'cause there was no father figure in the house, and everything came out of this catalog." Solo would also knock on wealthy people's doors in the hope of seeing catalog items that her own family could not afford.

2. Denise's own suggestion for overcoming her shoplifting habit involves "deprogramming" herself: "Maybe I could go into theft prevention if the stores would allow me. Like to go in and give back all my theft secrets, to consult with their theft department just to kind of deprogram myself. . . . With that way, I'm getting both of the things that I need: I'm still at the mall, but I'm deprogramming myself, too."

3. Long, *Book Clubs*, 22, 153.

4. Vanzant, *Yesterday, I Cried*, 225, 224, 45–46.

5. Although Joyce Meyer acknowledges that experiences of abuse can fuel addictive behaviors, she argues that addictions ultimately stem from the devil "controlling [our] thoughts" (*Battlefield of the Mind*, 65). In her 2005 book, *Approval Addiction: Overcoming Your Need to Please Everyone*, Meyer counsels readers "to replace all other addictions with one addiction. I want you to become addicted to Jesus! You should need Him more than you need anything else" (116).

6. Vanzant, *Yesterday, I Cried*, 33.

7. Ibid., 216.

8. Long, *Book Clubs*, 154.

9. Ibid., 22.

Chapter 4

1. Iceberg Slim and Donald Goines were both incarcerated several times, and both drew on their personal experiences with poverty, racism, and crime in writing their novels about ghetto life. They sold many of their earliest works through black-owned drugstores, mail-order catalogs, and street vendors.

2. For instance, Teri Woods wrote *True to the Game* while working as a legal secretary. After twelve major publishers rejected the book, Woods self-published 500 copies and started selling them on playgrounds in West Philadelphia, at basketball games, and from the trunk of her car on Harlem streets. Within three years, she sold more than 1 million copies and earned enough to start Teri Woods Publishing. Woods's company has published twelve best-selling urban books, and Woods recently signed a multimillion-dollar deal with Hatchette Books, which will reprint *True to the Game* and publish its sequel, *True to the Game II*; see Teri Woods Publishing, ⟨http://www.teriwoodspublishing.com/authors.htm⟩. Major presses such as the following now publish urban fiction: Atria Books (Simon and Schuster), One World Books (Random House), Hatchette Books (Warner Books), Griffin (St. Martin's Press), and Urban Books (Kensington).

3. Triple Crown's founder, Vickie Stringer, chooses to publish prisoners' books—despite the difficulties involved—because she knows "that no one else will do it" (qtd. in Bronner, "Queen Behind Triple Crown").

4. In these respects, urban books overlap with African American urban erotica written by Zane. Zane's extremely popular books—also banned in prisons—focus on women's sexual pleasure and on the widespread problem of male violence against women. Penal authorities and some prisoners characterize Zane as an urban fiction writer, but her works differ from the larger body of urban fiction because they do not focus on characters' involvement in criminal activity. As a reader named Darlene explains, "Zane, she's different from most of the urban books. You're not gonna find like too much gangster stuff in her books. Some of them get violent . . . but it's different, Zane's is different. Hers is more on sexuality."

5. Noire, *Candy Licker*, 289; Turner, *Project Chick*, 257, 200.

6. Chiles, "Their Eyes Were Reading Smut"; Southgate, "Writers Like Me." Percival Everett's 2001 novel *Erasure* draws attention to some writers' and critics' anxieties about the kinds of representations of African Americans that publishers and the reading public endorse. The protagonist of *Erasure*, Thelonious Monk Ellison, is an African American novelist whose latest work has been rejected by numerous publishers on the grounds that it is "too difficult for the market" and "not black enough." When Ellison hears of the instant success of a novel titled *We's Lives in Da Ghetto*, he writes a satirical novel titled *My Pafology* as an indictment of the ghetto novel. To Ellison's great dismay, his satirical novel garners tremendous praise from the literary establishment and the public; in fact, it wins "The Book Award" sponsored by the National Book Association. In articulating their reasons for celebrating *My Pafology*, the reviewers unanimously note how "real" it is. As one reviewer remarks, "This is the truest novel I ever read. It could only have been written by someone who has done hard time. It's the real thing" (*Erasure*, 42, 43, 223, 260).

7. Banned urban books—many of which have been read by women involved in my

study—include Teri Woods's *Dutch* and *Dutch II*, Teri Woods's *Deadly Reigns*, Noire's *Thong on Fire: An Urban Erotic Tale*, Deja King's *Bitch*, T. N. Baker's *Sheisty*, Darrell Debrew's *Keisha*, Chunichi's *Married to the Game*, Nurit Folkes's *Triangle of Sins*, Cole Riley's *Guilty as Sin*, Damon Amin Meadows and Jason Poole's *Convict's Candy*, 50 Cent and K Elliott's *Ski Mask*, 50 Cent and Nikki Turner's *Death before Dishonor*, 50 Cent and Noire's *Baby Brother*, Mike Sanders's *Hustlin' Backwards*, Michael Covington's *Chances*, and Erik S. Gray's *It's Like Candy*.

8. Patterson's novels seem to be so popular not only because they are readily available, but also because they are highly accessible and easy to read. As prisoners frequently note, the books have very short chapters (sometimes two pages long), familiar vocabulary, and likeable characters who appear in several books. Many women first learn about Patterson through film versions of his books. I facilitated a group discussion of Patterson's most recent novel, *You've Been Warned*, but the participants strongly disliked it because it was cowritten with Howard Roughan and represents a sharp departure from Patterson's usual style. Several women found the novel too difficult to read because of its nonlinear time structure and its focus on the protagonist's thought processes rather than on fast-moving action.

9. Prisoners can watch all of the Crime Scene Investigation shows (*CSI Las Vegas*, *CSI Miami*, and *CSI New York*), *Criminal Minds*, *Law and Order*, *Law and Order: Special Victims Unit*, and *Law and Order: Criminal Intent*. Whereas urban books often emphasize characters' flouting of legal authority, these television shows emphasize the successful apprehension of criminals.

10. Lakesha found Elaine Brown's *A Taste of Power: A Black Woman's Story* (1993) in the library, but she ordered Assata Shakur's *Assata: An Autobiography* (1987) and Waset's *The Power Journal: Chronicles of a Revolutionary Black Woman in White America* (2004).

11. I took Lakesha's anxiety very seriously and spoke with the penal authorities supervising my study about possible repercussions of my research. I resumed my research only after feeling reassured that the study would not lead to further restrictions on, or deleterious scrutiny of, incarcerated women's reading practices.

12. For further discussion of historical anxieties about women's reading practices, see Garrison, *Apostles of Culture*; Geller, *Forbidden Books*; and Gere, *Intimate Practices*.

13. Franklin, "Can the Penitentiary?," 648; Jameson, *Prison-House of Language*, n.p.

14. Three groups discussed *The Coldest Winter Ever*, three groups discussed *Flip Side of the Game* and *Game Over*, two groups discussed *Bad Girlz*, and one group discussed *Grindin'*. I have focused primarily on female-authored books because more women than men write urban fiction, and female-authored books are more popular in women's prisons. An important exception is male author Shannon Holmes.

15. Women sometimes differ in delimiting what counts as an urban book, yet all agree that the genre's core books "get down and dirty" more than other books by contemporary African American writers such as Carl Weber, Eric Jerome Dickey, E. Lynn Harris, and Michael Baisden.

16. Many authors of urban fiction also defend their novels on the basis of their realism. Some books include prefatory documents or afterwords—such as a lengthy acknowledgments section, an introductory poem, or a note for the reader—that function like the authenticating prefaces in slave narratives: they assure readers of the veracity of the story and justify inclusion of materials that may seem shocking or offensive. For instance, Noire opens *Candy Licker: An Urban Erotic Tale* with a rap-style poem that introduces the novel as "an urban erotic tale / Real life, straight, unscripted / Which 4 some of us is hell." Estab-

lishing a distinction between "Folx chillin in the suburbs / Sucking on a silver spoon" and "urban soldiers living on / the front lines every day," the poem concludes by promising the reader a more truthful and realistic portrait of urban life than is available on CNN:

I speak your truth and sing your song
Cuz real's the only way
So this here ain't no romance
I'ma say it once again
It's an urban erotic tale
Not no bullshyt CNN. (n.p.)

In a May 2007 interview, Noire embraces one reviewer's comment that Noire must "be straight off the streets and must have lived that kind of dirty life" in order to write her books. "I really do know the life I write about," she asserts, "and my readers can see that from the first page." Despite this claim to authenticity, evidence suggests that Noire is actually a mother of five children who lives and writes in Hawaii; see Koerner, "*Candy Licker*."

17. In *Pretty Woman*, a 1990 film starring Richard Gere and Julia Roberts, a wealthy businessman hires a lower-class sex worker to play the role of girlfriend. He provides her with a lavish new wardrobe and hotel suite, and the two eventually fall in love. The Huxtable family is the upper middle-class black family featured on *The Cosby Show*, a television program that ran from 1984 to 1992.

18. Tate, *Domestic Allegories*, 8, 6. In *American Realism*, Eric Sundquist discusses nineteenth-century realism in ways that resonate with the urban fiction phenomenon. Drawing on Alfred Kazin's claim that realism in America "grew out of the bewilderment, and thrived on the simple grimness, of a generation suddenly brought face to face with the pervasive materialism of industrial capitalism," Sundquist argues that the "age of realism in America is the age of the *romance of money*—money not in any simple sense but in the complex alterations of human value that it brings into being by its own capacities for reproduction." The hero of the realist novel is often a financial wizard who "does not reject [debased] society but masters it," and the realist novelist represents "the hero not as different from us but rather very much, too much like us" (5, 19–20 [emphasis in original]).

19. Discussing her crimes of shoplifting, pickpocketing, and grand larceny, Touché explains, "I used materialistic things to mask how I felt about my molestation. If I looked good, had a nice house, car, clothes, [and] fancy jewelry, society would think I'm doing good. But I was dying inside." Touché also draws attention to the pragmatic dimensions of her moneymaking crimes when she says that she does not "foresee any need to commit more crimes," given her financial success as an author.

20. Kaplan, *Social Construction of American Realism*, 160.

21. In *Thelma and Louise*, a 1991 film starring Susan Sarandon and Geena Davis, Louise shoots a man who was trying to rape Thelma, and the two women take to the road to flee from the police. Before driving off a cliff to their deaths, Thelma and Louise engage in a series of criminal acts, including robbery and locking a police officer in the trunk of his car.

22. Santiago, *Grindin'*, 161, 221.

23. In the appendix of *The Coldest Winter Ever*, Sister Souljah argues that one of her aims in writing her book was "to recapture the black male identity," and she offers the ultimate "symbol of the black man" through the character of Midnight, a midnight-black immigrant from Sudan who eventually leaves the game and becomes an upstanding family man. Through Midnight, Sister Souljah claims, she is delivering "the strongest and most relevant

message to black men ever delivered in the form of literature. For men he is a goal and a standard. For women he is a dream and destination. . . . Without a man like him in each and every home, there is an absence so deep it stains the face of our women, steals the chastity of our daughters, and ensures an early burial for our sons" (468, 431, 494). Midnight serves as the prime example of "a man rescuing his own soul," Sister Souljah argues, because he was raped by some other men in prison, which caused him to question his sexuality and "detracted from his sexual identity." Asserting that the confusion that Midnight experienced as a result of his rape relates to the current condition of "black men worldwide," Sister Souljah draws a homophobic connection between racial and economic emasculation and the "unnatural" state of male homosexuality: "So many men, in a subconscious response to the various and continual pressures of American rule, capitalism, and racism, have lost control over their sexual and gender identity. Some men, in an attempt to adapt and avoid the pressures, become other than their natural selves" (509). Midnight could have surrendered to "the pressure that threatens to redefine" who we "were born to be," but he "rescue[d] his soul" by reaffirming that "he is a man, the original black man made to love, protect, and provide for women and children" (510). Sister Souljah then calls all black men to learn from Midnight's example and "return to your original purpose" as head of the black family. As she states in the appendix, another of her central aims in writing *The Coldest Winter Ever* was "to put the black family back together again" and "have readers fall in love with the idea of family" (469, 470). Indeed, Sister Souljah promotes a homophobic vision of the male-governed family as the salvation of black America.

24. Ibid., 201 (emphasis in original), 118, 354.

25. Santiago, *Grindin'*, 178.

26. Ibid., 27, 101 (emphasis in original).

27. Nez's and Soso's comments seem to reflect the legacy of African Americans' resistance to scientific and medical discourse that pathologized black people as poorly prepared for civilization, predisposed to mania, and equipped with a nervous system less developed than that of whites. Ironically, however, their comments echo earlier medical claims that civilized people were more prone to mental illness and insanity because primitives had more rudimentary psychological needs.

28. Other urban books gesture toward the importance of education, but it rarely figures prominently in their plots. For instance, Noire's *G-Spot* emphasizes education as a way out for Gino, its male protagonist. Gino earned a degree in architecture from Stanford University—which his father denigrates as a "white-boy college"—and he rejects his father's criminal empire, arguing, "I'm about building my people up, not about having my sisters selling their ass to buy dope." Juicy, the female protagonist, is enrolled at Fordham University, but her abusive partner regularly thwarts her education and refuses to let her minor in political science because "that would only make [her] sound like one of those smart-mouth bitches who needed their tongues cut out." By the end of the novel, however, Juicy is in a relationship with Gino and simply wants to design clothing and "have me some babies." The novel makes no more mention of her unfinished college education (260, 157, 10–11, 301).

29. Two books written by Noire—*G-Spot* and *Candy Licker*—perhaps best illustrate this tendency.

30. Williams, "Implications of Womanist Theory," 306.

31. A "wifey" is a woman with whom a man shares his house. He may have several mistresses and children by other women, but everyone knows that wifey occupies the primary position in terms of his financial priorities.

32. Sister Souljah, *Coldest Winter Ever*, 290.

33. Santiago, *Grindin'*, 128.

34. Muñoz, *Disidentifications*, 12.

35. Noire, "Author Interview"; Stringer, *Let That Be the Reason*, 243, 244. According to Michael Davitt Bell, in the late nineteenth and early twentieth centuries, naming oneself as a realist writer was a "means for neutralizing anxieties about the writer's status in a culture still intensely suspicious or contemptuous of 'art' and the 'artistic.'" To proclaim oneself a realist was "to claim for literature the status of a 'real'—that is, socially normal—activity, to define literature . . . in the terms sanctioned by an abidingly anti-'literary' cultural orthodoxy." In parallel fashion, some contemporary urban fiction writers emphasize the "realness" of their novels in order to deflect potential charges that they are selling out by joining the mainstream literary establishment. To proclaim oneself an urban fiction author is to claim "the cultural authority both to possess and to dispense access to the real" (Bell, *Problem of American Realism*, 6, 8, 13). Indeed, urban fiction writers sometimes manifest what Kenneth Burke calls a "competitive desire to outstrip other writers by being 'more realistic' than they" (Burke, "Literature as an Equipment for Living," 12).

36. Nikki Turner's second novel, *A Project Chick*, was also published by Triple Crown Publications, and it, too, is full of grammatical errors, misspellings, and misuses of words. Her subsequent books, such as *The Glamorous Life* (2005) and *Riding Dirty on I-95* (2006), were published by One World Books and manifest far more professional editing.

37. Touché received a personal reply from Stringer and a letter with a stamped signature from Woods.

38. Frow, "'Reproducibles,'" 1631, 1632.

39. Qtd. in Brackett, "Facework Strategies," 349.

40. Holmes, *Bad Girlz*, 170.

41. Gordon, *Keeping Good Time*, 60, 61; Knox, *Murder*, 17 (emphasis in original).

42. Santiago, *Grindin'*, 221.

Chapter 5

1. Schaffer and Smith, *Human Rights and Narrated Lives*, 171.

2. Illouz, *Saving the Modern Soul*, 6, 184.

3. For instance, since 2004, the only programming and educational opportunities offered in two Florida state facilities known as "faith and character" prisons—Lawtey Correctional Facility for men and Hillsborough Correctional Facility for women—have been provided by volunteers supervised by a nondenominational Christian church. Moreover, the InnerChange Freedom Initiative (IFI), a Christian reentry program sponsored by the evangelical organization Prison Fellowship Ministries, operates entire wings of prisons in Arkansas, Iowa, Kansas, Minnesota, Missouri, and Texas. Although IFI programs require prisoners to convert to evangelical Christianity in order to participate, they received state funding until December 2007, when a federal appeals panel ruled that an IFI program in Iowa fostered religious indoctrination and violated the constitutional separation of church and state. IFI was the only reentry program offered at the Iowa prison, and its participants were allowed privileges unavailable to other prisoners, including family visits, increased opportunities for substance abuse treatment, free computer programming, guaranteed space in work-release programs, and help with finding housing and jobs upon release. As a result of the Iowa lawsuit, IFI's nine programs are now privately financed. See Erzen, "Testimonial," 1007, 1008; Banerjee, "Court Bars Effort."

4. The following books have also been helpful to particular prisoners: Juanita Bynum's *No More Sheets: The Truth about Sex* (2000), Rick Warren's *The Purpose Driven Life: What on Earth Am I Here For?* (2000), Neil Anderson's *Victory over Darkness: Realizing the Power of Your Identity in Christ* (1990), Ron Lee Davis's *A Forgiving God in an Unforgiving World* (1984), and Kay Arthur's *Our Covenant God: Living in the Security of His Unfailing Love* (2003).

5. Meyer's ministry, which began as a St. Louis radio show in 1983, has grown into a multimillion-dollar empire. Her *Enjoying Everyday Life* program is broadcast on more than 630 television stations and on hundreds of radio stations around the world, several of her books have been international bestsellers, and she hosts about fifteen national and international conferences each year. A prisoner from Zambia told me that before she came to the United States, she used to watch Meyer's television program.

6. Joyce Meyer Ministries, ⟨http://www.joycemeyer.org⟩.

7. Critics have assailed Meyer for her aggressive fundraising and marketing of her products, and for accruing enormous personal wealth through her ministry. She has also been embroiled in various tax evasion scandals. The Meyer family has been under investigation for privately benefiting from the tax-free money that the ministry raises. See Tuft and Smith, "From Fenton to Fame."

8. Peck, "Mediated Talking Cure," 143; Erzen, "Testimonial," 1007; Sommers and Satel, *One Nation under Therapy*, 5; Kaminer, *I'm Dysfunctional*, 149.

9. Illouz, *Saving the Modern Soul*, 246, 173; Rodríguez, *Forced Passages*, 115.

10. As I have demonstrated in previous chapters, however, women prisoners sometimes generate more structural critiques of racism, gender inequality, jurisprudence, criminality, and incarceration through their engagements with other kinds of books.

11. Women frequently emphasize how accessible Meyer makes her books by defining words along the way, offering summaries every few pages, and suggesting that readers review particular chapters to refresh their memories about important points. "She's basically telling you the same thing repetitively over and over again," says Monique, "but she gives you the hardcore facts."

12. Stewart, *Ordinary Affects*, 16.

13. Illouz, *Saving the Modern Soul*, 20 (emphasis in original); Rhodes, *Total Confinement*, 68.

14. Sommers and Satel, *One Nation under Therapy*, 6, 5; Illouz, *Saving the Modern Soul*, 184, 185–86.

15. Price, "Reading," 310.

16. Matthew 4:4 emphasizes God's word as spiritual sustenance: "It is written: 'Man does not live on bread alone, but on every word that comes from the mouth of God'" (*Quest Study Bible*, 1336).

17. Foucault, *Discipline and Punish*, 305, 18, 252; Foucault, "Prison Talk," 47.

18. Foucault, "Technologies of the Self," 18, 21, 31.

19. Foucault, "Ethics of the Concern for Self," 288; Foucault, "What Is Enlightenment?," 312.

20. Foucault, "Michel Foucault," 131; Foucault, "Ethics of the Concern for Self," 282.

21. Foucault, "What Is Enlightenment?," 315, 319.

22. Foucault, "Ethics of the Concern for Self," 292; Vanzant, *Yesterday, I Cried*, 222; Foucault, "Sex, Power, and Politics of Identity," 166; Augé, *Oblivion*, 51.

23. Foucault, "Technologies of the Self," 18; Foucault, "Ethics of the Concern for Self," 287.

24. Foucault, "What Is Enlightenment," 315; Gordon, *Keeping Good Time*, 66.

25. Rodríguez, *Forced Passages*, 85; Meyer, *Beauty for Ashes*, 217.

26. Price, "Reading," 317, 318.

27. Meyer, *Battlefield of the Mind*, 54.

28. Meyer, *Beauty for Ashes*, 11. Meyer subsequently earned a Ph.D. in theology from Life Christian University, an honorary doctorate in divinity from Oral Roberts University, and an honorary doctorate in sacred theology from Grand Canyon University.

29. Meyer, *Beauty for Ashes*, 48, 49, 48, 46, 81, 220.

30. Nena specifically mentioned reading the following books by Joyce Meyer: *Me and My Big Mouth: Your Answer Is Right under Your Nose*; *Approval Addiction: Overcoming Your Need to Please Everyone*; *If Not for the Grace of God*; *Seven Things That Steal Your Joy*; *Eight Ways to Keep the Devil under Your Feet*; *The Confident Woman*; *Life without Strife*; and *Having an Intimate Relationship with God*.

31. Kaminer, *I'm Dysfunctional*, 164–65.

32. Ibid., 165.

33. From my own perspective, Meyer's *The Confident Woman* offers helpful strategies for women to make the most of failure, overcome fear, and develop confidence. At the same time, however, the book relies on a neocolonial, partial, and skewed representation of feminism. For instance, adopting a post–September 11 anti-Muslim perspective, Meyer argues that the "degradation of women" is "at its worst in parts of the world that have no Christian heritage," and she asserts that "much of that injustice [against women] has been corrected in the Western world" but "there are still many cultures in the world where women are terribly mistreated" (21, vii). Furthermore, her representation of feminist history focuses solely on two groups: the "five white women" who began the struggle for suffrage at Seneca Falls in 1848 and the "radical feminists" who "hate" men, have "a bitter, vengeful attitude," and try "to correct a real problem in an extremist way that creates more problems than it solves" (22, 19). In discussing the differences between women and men, Meyer also offers socially constructed stereotypes as factual distinctions: "Women want to be loved, respected, valued, complimented, listened to, trusted and sometimes, just to be held. Men want tickets for the World Series. Women want affection, men want sex. . . . Women are simply more emotional than men. Men are very logical. . . . Women are sensitive to the needs of others. . . . Women are experts in bringing comfort" (128–29, 227).

34. Stewart, *Ordinary Affects*, 84. Women prisoners' resistance to dehumanizing treatment by correctional officers surfaced as a topic in several group discussions. In one group's conversation about Jakes's *Woman, Thou Art Loosed!* a woman described how an officer routinely made jokes about her weight and told her that she looked "like a walking Q-tip" because of her hairstyle. Yet when she would make comments back to the officer, he threatened to lock her up "for disrespect." In her essay, "Resisting the Ordinary," political prisoner Laura Whitehorn describes "haphazard, unspectacular cruelties delivered daily to people who are viewed by administrators, staff, and guards as simply not worthy of decent treatment" (276).

35. Kaminer, *I'm Dysfunctional*, 163; Meyer, *Beauty for Ashes*, 60; Meyer, *Battlefield of the Mind*, 19, 21.

36. Meyer, *Confident Woman*, ix, 25.

37. Berger, "Undefeated Despair." Berger coined the phrase "undefeated despair" in describing how Palestinians manage living in Ramallah.

38. Prisoners can make very few outgoing calls, and phone companies in many states charge higher rates for phone calls to and from prisons. Furthermore, prisoners are often incarcerated several hours away from family members, sometimes in rural areas that are difficult to access.

39. Highlighting the social dimensions of reading, Helen recounted that when she read Khaled Hosseini's 2003 novel, *The Kite Runner*, she wrote to family members and friends to tell them about it because it "encompasses what unconditional love is about. It's amazing to take that concept and put it in print. You could feel that as you read."

40. Vanzant, *Yesterday, I Cried*, 278; Gordon, *Keeping Good Time*, 67.

41. Meyer, *Confident Woman*, 6; Meyer, *Battlefield of the Mind*, 257, 171; Meyer, *Beauty for Ashes*, 127, 192.

42. Fisher and Belli, "Preacher Who Doesn't." Meyer especially angers some Christian conservatives for claiming, "All I was ever taught to say was, 'I'm a poor, miserable sinner.' I am not poor, I am not miserable and I am not a sinner. That is a lie from the pits of hell. That is what I was and if I still am then Jesus died in vain" (qtd. in ibid.).

43. Rhodes, *Total Confinement*, 112.

44. Vanzant, *Yesterday, I Cried*, 278; Meyer, *Beauty for Ashes*, 12, 211, 10, 177, 215.

45. Meyer, *Battlefield of the Mind*, 16, 24; Illouz, *Saving the Modern Soul*, 177.

46. Meyer, *Confident Woman*, vii, 24, 106.

47. Meyer, *Battlefield of the Mind*, 36, 35, 278, 35, 34, 35, 244. Meyer's battle and computer programming metaphors resonate with Kenneth Burke's description of literature as "designed to organize and command the army of one's thoughts and images." Through reading, Burke argues, one "seeks to 'direct the larger movements and operations' in one's campaign of living. One 'manoeuvres,' and the manoeuvring is an 'art.'" One tries to develop a "strategy" for winning, and most of all, for "fight[ing] on [one's] own terms" ("Literature as an Equipment for Living," 11).

48. Meyer, *Confident Woman*, 42; Meyer, *Battlefield of the Mind*, 87.

49. Illouz, *Saving the Modern Soul*, 185, 184, 186.

50. Cleage, *What Looks Like Crazy*, 131.

51. Ibid., 36, 180, 179, 178. At one point in the novel, Eddie offers to kill Frank and Tyrone because sending them to juvenile jail "buys time but it doesn't solve the problem," and he wants "solutions" (178, 180).

52. Currie, *Crime and Punishment in America*, 112; Rhodes, *Total Confinement*, 84.

53. *The Secret* was released on the Internet in March 2006. It soon came out on DVD, and after being featured twice on *Larry King Live*, the film was made into a book. Within hours of being featured on Oprah's show, *The Secret* became the best-selling book in the United States (Whitney, "Review"). As of March 2007, 3.75 million copies of the book had been printed in the United States alone (Kelly, "Sshh!"), and one year later, *The Secret* remained the number one "advice book" on the *New York Times* bestseller list.

54. Byrne, *The Secret*, 130, 17, 96, 97. Vanzant's *Yesterday, I Cried* sometimes promotes similar magical thinking about money. At one point, a voice in Vanzant's head directs her to write a check for money that she does not have. Soon after she does so, the radio station calls and asks her to fill in for someone, so she requests her pay in advance to cover the check. At another point, Vanzant puts her request for a car "into the universe" and once again writes a check for money that she does not have. When she comes home with the purchased car, she finds a check in the mail that is larger than the cost of the car; the check is for a speaking engagement that will occur two months hence (257, 258).

55. Both Meyer's and Byrne's books share an affinity with the New Thought religions that developed in the United States during the late nineteenth and early twentieth centuries. The New Thought tradition emphasized "the power of thought to alter material reality," and it became associated with the attainment of prosperity through desire (Travis, "'It Will Change the World,'" 1018). At times, Meyer's emphasis on positive thinking conflicts with

other aspects of her argument. *Beauty for Ashes*, for instance, manifests an unresolved tension between her claim that one must go back through the "doorways of pain" to get to the other side, and her argument that "talking about the abuse and the person who caused it is equal to picking off a scab. . . . If you want to get over a problem, stop talking about it." Although she qualifies that readers can reveal their abuse "to those to whom it is needful or necessary," Meyer insists that "unless revealing our problem has some godly purpose, we must discipline ourselves to bear it silently." Meyer's ultimate argument in *Beauty for Ashes* is that readers must "shake off" everything negative and "just get over it, and go on" (57, 144–45, 143, 246). This injunction to "shake it off" makes it difficult to understand what it means to go back through the "doorways of pain" in order to get to the other side. Furthermore, Meyer's call to "bear [abuse] silently" makes it difficult to discern when it might be legitimate to complain about or challenge harmful actions.

56. Meyer, *Approval Addiction*, 197, 198.

57. Meyer, *Battlefield of the Mind*, 69, 46, 233.

58. Meyer, *Beauty for Ashes*, 117 (emphasis in original); Meyer, *Confident Woman*, 6–7, 157; Meyer, *Battlefield of the Mind*, 199. Wendy Kaminer argues that in twelve-step recovery programs, "individual freedom of action and thought" is jeopardized by the requirement that participants surrender their will to a higher power (*I'm Dysfunctional*, 129). During an individual interview, a woman named Christine expressed fears about this issue in discussing her participation in a twelve-step program. "I can't buy into the God concept," she argued. "I believe I'm still in control of my destiny. . . . It seems weak-minded to believe in God. . . . Religion is demeaning. It diminishes the power that humans have." At the same time, however, Christine now believes that "self-reliance and self-contentedness" are "character defects" that set her up for relapse, and she feels ready—as a result of participating in the twelve-step program—to adopt a "spiritual foundation" and "turn [her] will over to something."

59. Meyer, *Confident Woman*, 191.

60. Meyer, *Battlefield of the Mind*, 19.

61. Ibid., 24, 18, 21, 18, 20; Peck, "Mediated Talking Cure," 152.

62. Kaminer, *I'm Dysfunctional*, 152, 163; Ellis and Bochner, "Autoethnography," 746.

63. Vanzant, *Yesterday, I Cried*, 242.

64. Foucault, "What Is Enlightenment?," 315.

65. Smith and Watson introduction, 16. As Jimmy Santiaga Baca writes in "Coming into Language," "Through language I was free. . . . I was launched on an endless journey without boundaries or rules, in which I could salvage the floating fragments of my past, or be born anew in the spontaneous ignition of understanding some heretofore concealed aspect of myself" (103).

66. Illouz, *Saving the Modern Soul*, 142.

67. Stewart, *Ordinary Affects*, 117, 19.

68. Illouz, *Saving the Modern Soul*, 184; Meyer, *Battlefield of the Mind*, 171.

69. Vanzant, *Yesterday, I Cried*, 240, 171, 38; Meyer, *Beauty for Ashes*, 217, 221.

70. Rodríguez, *Forced Passages*, 85, 197.

71. Meyer, *Battlefield of the Mind*, 113.

72. Solo published an essay in a Muslim publication about what it was like to be a Muslim on September 11 in a maximum-security state prison, and she published an article called "Islam: The Good, the Bad, and the Ugly" in the *Cleveland Post*. In a prisoner-authored publication called *Angola Speaks*, she published a tribute to a fellow prisoner who started the prison's first AIDS awareness program before she died of AIDS. Solo titled her tribute "Cell

Count" because her friend was always talking about her blood cell count, and because prisoners are counted in their cells four times per day. "I thought it was really ironic that we stand up for cell count, and then her life ended up just being nothing except a cell count," Solo explained.

73. Vanzant, *Yesterday, I Cried,* 222. Solo dwells in what Avery Gordon calls "abolitionist time" by participating in "the ongoing work of emancipation, a work whose success is not measured by legalistic pronouncements, a work which perforce must take place while you're still enslaved" (*Keeping Good Time,* 198).

74. Meyer, *Beauty for Ashes,* 217; Meyer, *Battlefield of the Mind,* 113; Berger, "Undefeated Despair"; Foucault, "What Is Enlightenment?," 319.

Interlude 2

1. A "kite" is an official request, such as a request to participate in a particular program or class. When I returned to the prison six months after completing my research, Monique had completed college courses in communication, psychology, economics, and economic geography, and she was planning to take courses in health, English, science, and sociology.

2. In discussing the "little things that [Stewart] did that people take for granted when they're in the free world," Monique told a story about her incarcerated cousin, who experienced a great deal of joy from inheriting a pair of red earmuffs from an "old timer" who had received them as a gift fifteen years earlier. "The little things that you take for granted are big things that make our whole week," Monique said.

3. Greene, *48 Laws,* xxii, 1, 8, 16, 44, 56, 89, 101, 107, 145. Greene's *48 Laws of Power* seems to illustrate Eva Illouz's contention that therapeutic discourse has become prevalent in the corporate sphere. According to Illouz, the corporate sphere has produced a new form of selfhood in which "strategic self-interest and emotional reflexivity are seamlessly interconnected." A reflexive self internalizes "strong mechanisms of self-control to maintain its self-interest, not through the blatant display of selfish competitiveness, but through the art of mastering social relations" (*Saving the Modern Soul,* 239, 93).

4. Monique reencountered such an ethic of ruthless self-interest in Machiavelli's *The Prince,* which she started reading while awaiting sentencing at another facility. Although she only read about one-quarter of *The Prince,* she ascertained that it focuses on "your personal position and what you do with it. Either you're going to lose it or you're going to gain everything. But what do you sacrifice in between? Do you lose yourself to gain something, or do you lose others to gain something?"

5. Byrne, *The Secret,* 28.

6. Ibid., 109. Byrne's suggestions for harnessing the power of positive thinking pertain almost exclusively to the attainment of personal wealth. "That spirits can spiral upward and remain tied to the bottom line is a singular premise of American capitalism" (Kaminer, *I'm Dysfunctional,* 107).

7. "The Secret can give you whatever you want," Byrne asserts. "Your job is to declare what you would like to have from the catalogue of the Universe." If you request a huge influx of cash, she argues, "it is not your job to work out 'how' the money will come to you. It is your job to ask, to believe you are receiving, and feel happy now. Leave the details to the Universe on how it will bring it about" (*The Secret,* xi, 101–2).

8. Monique also plans to order Muhammad Ibn Bashir's 2004 book, *Raw Law: A Hip-Hop Guide to Criminal Justice.* "It's basically everything that we need to know from the prisoner's

viewpoint," she explains, and it highlights "a lot of ways you can handle the justice system. . . . If the attorney isn't with you, if you can't understand them, don't do it. Because they're supposed to work for us."

9. A "pet program" offers prisoners opportunities to care for neglected animals and to participate in the training of seeing-eye dogs.

Chapter 6

1. Augé, *Oblivion*, 44–45; Stewart, *Ordinary Affects*, 128; Long, *Book Clubs*, 22.

2. Stewart, *Ordinary Affects*, 79.

3. Two texts that I do not discuss in this chapter also sparked interesting dialogue in the group discussions. Ray Bradbury's *Fahrenheit 451* generated a conversation about the differences between reading and watching television, and Alice Sebold's *The Lovely Bones* prompted this beautiful reflection from Candy: "Tragedy can be magnificent. A lot of times major things that happened got people to where they are. . . . A lot happened that wouldn't have happened if she didn't die. All tragedy blooms tears and laughter, or we'd all be crazy."

4. Although it also features abuse, Wally Lamb's novel *She's Come Undone* seems far more palatable to Kate than *A Thousand Splendid Suns* because it depicts "more normalcy in the girl's life." Whereas women in *A Thousand Splendid Suns* "didn't have any good days," Kate said of *She's Come Undone*, "I liked it because it was about an ugly side of life but it was encouraging and kept you rooting for her, and it had a good ending. It left me with a good feeling."

5. As we were discussing Jacobs's *Incidents in the Life of a Slave Girl*, Rhonda used her new insight about the narrative to deepen her understanding of the film version of Toni Morrison's *Beloved*. Referencing our discussion of what would have been permissible for Jacobs to articulate in her narrative, Rhonda reflected, "I was just thinking about how you said they didn't have a voice. They could only say so much about the mistress, the white man's wife. In the movie *Beloved* when she said they stole her milk, I couldn't understand why she was vocalizing like that, and then she started saying about having a tree on my back. You know, she didn't vocalize exactly what was happening. I didn't understand that, but now I understand it."

6. Booth, *Company We Keep*, 138 (emphasis in original), 485. In *Proust and the Squid*, Maryanne Wolf explains that Proust viewed reading as a sanctuary where humans can access thousands of different realities that they otherwise might not encounter or understand. Wolf writes, "While reading, we can leave our own consciousness, and pass over into the consciousness of another person, another age, another culture. 'Passing over,' a term used by the theologian John Dunne, describes the process through which reading enables us to try on, identify with, and ultimately enter for a brief time the wholly different perspective of another person's consciousness" (7).

7. Developing good discussion patterns and developing a sense of community takes time, and I spent less time with women in the Pennsylvania prison. Even during the relatively short span of my research, however, members of the discussion groups were getting to know women whom they did not previously know and seemed to be developing a sense of shared purpose and common endeavor.

8. Kate's complex racial self-positioning became even more evident during a one-on-one conversation in which she defined herself as nonracist while protesting what she calls "reverse racism." "My family fought for civil rights," she argued. "We were not allowed to use

the 'n' word or 'wop' or 'spic.' My people also came over on a boat. We were 'mics.' That's as bad as the 'n' word." Kate then explained that she is "appalled at the amount of prejudice" in the prison, recounting how black women call her "a white cracker bitch." When she was part of a therapeutic group, African American women in the group would say, "You don't understand." In Kate's view, these women "were setting themselves as separate rather than a part of things," so she insisted on undermining the significance of race by emphasizing that "different socioeconomic levels follow the same lifestyle, and so do different areas of the country." Kate also defended her love of Joel Chandler Harris's *The Tales of Uncle Remus*, which she read as a child and has read aloud to her prison roommate, by arguing, "It was criticized as racist, but it's a classic. They're classic tales. It was written in a time when that's how people spoke."

9. Madriz, "Focus Groups," 839.

10. As my study progressed, participants from both the Ohio and Pennsylvania prisons informed me that several other women were interested in participating. I actually did a second round of the study in Ohio, and by the time it was finished, women in the group said that they knew of "forty to fifty" other women who wanted to participate in a third round. Women in Pennsylvania were equally eager to participate in the study, but I did not have time to conduct further research at that site.

11. Hartley, *Reading Groups*, 127.

12. Illouz, *Saving the Modern Soul*, 18. In documenting the work that some women prisoners perform through their reading practices, I do not want to speculate about whether or not those practices will exert a lasting influence over the lives of women who may one day leave prison. Indeed, I want to resist any notion that reading might serve as a permanent cure for, or antidote to, unethical or unlawful behavior. Such a notion not only seems deeply flawed; it also seems dangerous, given that bibliotherapy has served normalizing and coercive ends in penal contexts. My far more modest aim has been to illuminate how some incarcerated women use reading to gain greater insight into their lives and to navigate their circumstances.

13. Qtd. in Tedlock, "Ethnography and Ethnographic Representation," 467.

14. Long, *Book Clubs*, 126, 130.

15. MacCormick, *Education of Adult Prisoners*, 166.

16. In our one-on-one conversation about *To Kill a Mockingbird*, Kaye explained that she would have never read the novel if I hadn't suggested it, but "I like what I got out of it. It was stuff I didn't already know from urban books. With those books, I've been there, done that. . . . I never learn from urban books. There are things I could learn about from them, but I don't want to." Among her many interesting comments about *To Kill a Mockingbird*, Kaye said, "It makes me think about the kind of parent I want to be" and "It gives me hope that not everyone is prejudiced. I'm a black woman with a felony but it made me hopeful that there might be another Atticus out there." Although Nez did not finish *To Kill a Mockingbird*, she made an astute connection between the novel and Robert Greene's *48 Laws of Power* during our group discussion. According to Nez, Scout's experience on the first day of school illustrates Greene's precept that one should "never outshine the master" (1).

17. Price, "Reading," 318.

18. Gordon, *Keeping Good Time*, 64.

19. Stewart, *Ordinary Affects*, 128.

20. Ibid., 128.

21. Phelan, *Unmarked*, 174; Cheng, *Melancholy of Race*, 191.

Conclusion

1. Warner, "Against the Narrowing of Perspectives," 173; Morris, *Penal Abolition*, 52. ICOPA was founded in 1983 by the Quaker Committee on Jails and Justice. ICOPA has hosted conferences every other year in a total of ten countries: Canada, the Netherlands, Poland, the United States, Costa Rica, Spain, New Zealand, Nigeria, Tasmania, and England. CR was formed in 1997 by U.S. scholars and activists interested in challenging the growth and centrality of the prison-industrial complex. CR has hosted an annual conference every year since 1998.

2. Morris, *Penal Abolition*, 26.

3. Davis and Dent, "Prison as a Border," 1238; Rhodes, *Total Confinement*, xiii; Escobar, "Art of Liberation," 310.

4. Critical Resistance, "Our Vision."

5. Warner, "Against the Narrowing of Perspectives," 180, 179, 172, 181, 180.

6. Warner, "Against the Narrowing of Perspectives," quotes from 172, 171–72, and 174; 176; 175 (quote); 179, 181.

7. Morris, *Penal Abolition*, 94. The Latin word "habilitare" means "to empower" and "to enable" (West and Morris, *Case for Penal Abolition*, 313).

8. Peck, "Mediated Talking Cure," 153; Gordon, *Keeping Good Time*, 61–62; Rhodes, *Total Confinement*, 218.

Appendix

1. The name of the study reflects a former title of my project.

BIBLIOGRAPHY

Abrams, Kathryn. "From Autonomy to Agency: Feminist Perspectives on Self-Direction." *William and Mary Law Review* 40 (1999): 805–46.

———. "Sex Wars Redux: Agency and Coercion in Feminist Legal Theory." *Columbia Law Review* 95 (Mar. 1995): 304–76.

Abu-Jamal, Mumia. *Live from Death Row*. New York: Addison-Wesley, 1995.

Alcoff, Linda Martin, and Laura Gray-Rosendale. "Survivor Discourse: Transgression or Recuperation?" In *Getting a Life: Everyday Uses of Autobiography*, edited by Sidonie Smith and Julia Watson, 198–225. Minneapolis: University of Minnesota Press, 1996.

Allard, Patricia. "Life Sentences: Denying Welfare Benefits to Women Convicted of Drug Offenses." Feb. 2002, ⟨www.sentencingproject.org⟩. 30 June 2006.

Allison, Dorothy. *Bastard out of Carolina*. New York: Plume, 1992.

American Correctional Association. *Manual of Correctional Standards*. College Park, Md.: American Correctional Association, 1966.

———. *Religion in Corrections: Self-Instructional Course*. Lanham, Md.: American Correctional Association, 2000.

———. *Standards for Adult Correctional Institutions*. 4th ed. Lanham, Md.: American Correctional Association, 2003.

Ammons, Elizabeth. "Expanding the Canon of American Realism." In *The Cambridge Companion to American Realism and Naturalism*, edited by Donald Pizer, 95–114. Cambridge: Cambridge University Press, 1995.

Ammons, Linda. "Mules, Madonnas, Babies, Bathwater, Racial Imagery and Stereotypes: The African-American Woman and the Battered Woman Syndrome." *Wisconsin Law Review* 5 (1995): 1003–80.

Angrosino, Michael, and Kimberly A. Mays De Pérez. "Rethinking Observation: From Method to Context." In *Handbook of Qualitative Research*, 2nd ed., edited by Norman K. Denzin and Yvonna S. Lincoln, 673–702. Thousand Oaks, Calif.: Sage, 2000.

Armour, Jody. "Just Deserts: Narrative, Perspective, Choice, and Blame." *Pittsburgh Law Review* 57 (1996): 525–48.

Association of Hospital and Institution Libraries. *Bibliotherapy Methods and Materials*. Chicago: American Library Association, 1971.

Association of Specialized and Cooperative Library Agencies. *Library Standards for Adult Correctional Institutions*. Chicago: American Library Association, 1981.

———. *Library Standards for Adult Correctional Institutions*. Chicago: American Library Association, 1992.

———. *Survey of Library Service in Local Correctional Facilities.* Chicago: American Library Association, 1980.

Augé, Marc. *Oblivion.* Trans. Marjolin De Jager. Minneapolis: University of Minnesota Press, 2004.

Augst, Thomas. "Introduction: American Libraries and Agencies of Culture." *American Studies* 42, no. 3 (Fall 2001): 5–22.

Augst, Thomas, and Wayne Wiegand, eds. *Libraries as Agencies of Culture.* Madison: University of Wisconsin Press, 2003.

Baca, Jimmy Santiago. "Coming into Language." In *Doing Time: Twenty-Five Years of Prison Writing,* edited by Bell Gale Chevigny, 100–106. New York: Arcade, 1999.

Banerjee, Neela. "Court Bars Effort Using Faith in Prisons." *New York Times,* 4 Dec. 2007.

Barone, Richard M. "De-Programming Prison Libraries." *Special Libraries* 68 (1977): 294.

Bashir, Muhammad Ibn. *Raw Law: A Hip-Hop Guide to Criminal Justice.* Newark, N.J.: Vandy Publishing, 2004.

Bashore, Melvin L. "Behind Adobe Walls and Iron Bars: The Utah Territorial Penitentiary Library." *Libraries and Culture* 38, no. 3 (Summer 2003): 236–49.

Baun, N., and B. Brooke. *Trading Books for Bars.* N.p.: Center for Juvenile and Criminal Justice, 1994.

Baxter, Charles, Wayne Brown, Tony Chatman-Bey, H. B. Johnson Jr., Mark Medley, Donald Thompson, Selvyn Tillett, and John Woodland Jr. (with Drew Leder). "Live from the Panopticon: Architecture and Power Revisited." In *The New Abolitionists: (Neo)Slave Narratives and Contemporary Prison Writings,* edited by Joy James, 207–15. Albany: State University of New York Press, 2005.

Beatty, William K. "A Historical Review of Bibliotherapy." In *Bibliotherapy,* edited by Ruth M. Tews. Special issue of *Library Trends* 11, no. 2 (Oct. 1962): 106–17.

Behar, Ruth. *The Vulnerable Observer: Anthropology That Breaks Your Heart.* Boston: Beacon, 1996.

Bell, Michael Davitt. *The Problem of American Realism: Studies in the Cultural History of a Literary Idea.* Chicago: University of Chicago Press, 1993.

Benson, Heidi. "Read Two Chapters, Call Me in the Morning." *San Francisco Chronicle,* 19 Oct. 2003, ⟨http://www.sfgate.com/cgi-bin/article.cgi?f=/chronicle/archive/2003/10/19/RV239329.DTL⟩. 13 June 2007.

Benwell, Bethan, and Daniel Allington. "Reading the Reading Experience: 'Booktalk' and Discursive Psychology." 2008. Unpublished essay.

Berger, John. "Undefeated Despair." *OpenDemocracy.* 13 Jan. 2006, ⟨http://www.opendemocracy.net/globalization-debate_97/palestine_3176.jsp⟩. 2 Apr. 2008.

Berlant, Lauren. *The Female Complaint: The Unfinished Business of Sentimentality in American Culture.* Durham, N.C.: Duke University Press, 2008.

———. *The Queen of America Goes to Washington City: Essays on Sex and Citizenship.* Durham, N.C.: Duke University Press, 1997.

Bhattacharjee, Anannya. "Private Fists and Public Force: Race, Gender, and Surveillance." In *Policing the National Body: Race, Gender, and Criminalization,* edited by Jael Silliman and Anannya Bhattacharjee, 1–54. Cambridge, Mass.: South End, 2002.

"Bibliotherapy: A New Word for Your Vocabulary." *Cape Times,* 15 Jan. 1938, 3.

Bobo, Jacqueline. *Black Women as Cultural Readers.* New York: Columbia University Press, 1995.

Bole, William. "Novel Approach to Sentencing Has Criminals Hitting the Books." Ameri-

can News Service, 1997, ⟨http://www.villagelife.org/news/archives/novelapproach
.html⟩. 23 July 2006.

Booth, Wayne. *The Company We Keep: An Ethics of Fiction*. Berkeley: University of
California Press, 1988.

Brackett, Kim Pettigrew. "Facework Strategies among Romance Fiction Readers." *Social
Science Journal* 37, no. 3 (2000): 347–60.

Brandt, Deborah. *Literacy in American Lives*. Cambridge: Cambridge University Press,
2001.

Breyer, Stephen. Majority opinion. *Beard, Secretary, Pennsylvania Department of Corrections
v. Banks*. No. 04-1739. Supreme Court of the United States. 28 June 2006.

Bronner, Angela. "The Queen behind Triple Crown: BV's '5 Questions' for Author Vickie
Stringer." AOL Black Voices, Apr. 2006, ⟨http://www.triplecrownpublications.com/
data/publicity14.doc⟩. 15 Dec. 2007.

Brown, Eleanor Frances. *Bibliotherapy and Its Widening Application*. Metuchen, N.J.:
Scarecrow, 1975.

Brown, Lesley. *The New Shorter Oxford English Dictionary*. Oxford: Clarendon, 1993.

Brown, Wendy. "Freedom's Silences." In *Edgework: Critical Essays on Knowledge and
Politics*, 83–97. Princeton: Princeton University Press, 2005.

———. "Injury, Identity, Politics." In *Mapping Multi-Culturalism*, edited by Avery Gordon
and Christopher Newfield, 149–66. Minneapolis: University of Minnesota Press,
1996.

———. *Politics out of History*. Princeton: Princeton University Press, 2001.

———. "Wounded Attachments." *Political Theory* 21 (1993): 290–410.

Buck, Marilyn. "The Effects of Repression on Women in Prison." In *Warfare in the
American Homeland: Policing and Prison in a Penal Democracy*, edited by Joy James,
238–49. Durham, N.C.: Duke University Press, 2007.

Bumiller, Kristin. *The Civil Rights Society: The Social Construction of Victims*. Baltimore:
Johns Hopkins University Press, 1988.

Buntman, Fran Lisa. *Robben Island and Prisoner Resistance to Apartheid*. Cambridge:
Cambridge University Press, 2003.

Bureau of Justice Statistics. *Prisoners in 2006*. 5 Dec. 2007, ⟨http://www.ojp.usdoj.gov/bjs/
abstract/po6.htm⟩. 22 July 2008.

Burke, Kenneth. "Literature as an Equipment for Living." *Direction* 1, no. 4 (Apr. 1938):
10–13.

Butler, Anne E. *Gendered Justice in the American West: Women Prisoners in Men's
Penitentiaries*. Urbana: University of Illinois Press, 1997.

———. "Still in Chains: Black Women in Western Prisons, 1865–1910." In *We Specialize in
the Wholly Impossible: A Reader in Black Women's History*, edited by Darlene Clark Hine,
Wilma King, and Linda Reed, 321–34. Brooklyn: Carlson Publishing, 1995.

Butterfield, Fox. "Tight Budgets Force States to Reconsider Crime and Penalties." *New
York Times*, 21 Jan. 2002, A1.

Byrne, Rhonda. *The Secret*. New York: Atria, 2006.

Campbell, Sue. "Being Dismissed: The Politics of Emotional Expression." *Hypatia: A
Journal of Feminist Philosophy* 9, no. 3 (Summer 1994): 46–65.

Canfield, Jack, Mark Victor Hansen, and Tom Lagana, eds. *Chicken Soup for the Prisoner's
Soul*. Deerfield Beach, Fla.: Health Communications, 2000.

Cantrell, Clyde H. "Sadie P. Delaney: Bibliotherapist and Librarian." *Southeastern
Librarian* 6, no. 3 (Fall 1956): 105–9.

Carlen, Pat. "Why Study Women's Imprisonment? or Anyone Else's? An Indefinite Article." *British Journal of Criminology* 34 (1994): 131–40.

Casarjian, Robin. *Houses of Healing: A Prisoner's Guide to Inner Power and Healing.* Boston: Lionheart Foundation, 1995.

Catalogue and Rules for Prison Libraries to Aid in the Selection and Maintenance of Reading Matter in the Prisons and Jails. Albany, N.Y.: Argus Company, 1877.

Cheng, Anne Anlin. *The Melancholy of Race: Psychoanalysis, Assimilation, and Hidden Grief.* New York: Oxford University Press, 2001.

Chepesiuk, Ron. "S.C. Scraps Innovative Prison Library System." *American Libraries* 26, no. 6 (1995): 501–2.

Chesler, Phyllis. "A Woman's Right to Self-Defense: The Case of Aileen Carol Wuornos." *St. John's Law Review* 66, no. 4 (1993): 933–77.

Chevigny, Belle Gale, ed. *Doing Time: 25 Years of Prison Writing.* New York: Arcade, 1999.

Chiles, Nick. "Their Eyes Were Reading Smut." *New York Times,* 4 Jan. 2006, ⟨http://www .nytimes.com/2006/01/04/opinion/04chiles.html⟩. 25 Jan. 2008.

Chrisler, Joan C., and Heather M. Ulsh. "Feminist Bibliotherapy: Report on a Survey of Feminist Therapists." *Women and Therapy* 23, no. 4 (2001): 71–84.

Chunichi. *A Gangster's Tale.* New York: Urban Books, 2004.

Clark, Sheila, and Bobbie Patrick. "Choose Freedom Read: Book Talks behind Bars." *American Libraries* 30, no. 7 (1999): 63–65.

Clark, Wahida. *Thugs and the Women Who Love Them.* New York: Kensington Books, 2005.

Cleage, Pearl. *What Looks Like Crazy on an Ordinary Day.* New York: Avon, 1997.

Cole, Alyson M. *The Cult of True Victimhood: From the War on Welfare to the War on Terror.* Stanford: Stanford University Press, 2007.

Coley, Richard J., and Paul E. Barton. *Locked Up and Locked Out: An Educational Perspective on the U.S. Prison Population.* Princeton: Educational Testing Service, 2006.

Coyle, William J. *Libraries in Prisons: A Blending of Institutions.* New York: Greenwood, 1987.

Crenshaw, Kimberlé Williams. "Color Blindness, History, and the Law." In *The House That Race Built,* edited by Wahneema Lubiano, 280–88. New York: Vintage, 1998.

———. "Mapping the Margins: Intersectionality, Identity Politics, and Violence against Women of Color." In *Critical Race Theory: The Key Writings That Formed the Movement,* edited by Kimberlé Crenshaw, Neil Gotanda, Gary Peller, and Kendall Thomas, 357–83. New York: New York Press, 1995.

Critical Resistance. "Our Vision." 2008, ⟨http://www.criticalresistance.org/article .php?id=51⟩. 27 Aug. 2008.

Crothers, Samuel McChord. "A Literary Clinic." *Atlantic Monthly,* Aug. 1916, 291–301.

Cummins, Eric. *The Rise and Fall of California's Radical Prison Movement.* Stanford: Stanford University Press, 1994.

Currie, Elliot. *Crime and Punishment in America: Why the Solutions to America's Most Stubborn Social Crises Have Not Worked and What Will.* New York: Henry Holt, 1998.

Curtis, Florence Rising. "The Libraries of the American State and National Institutions for Defectives, Dependents, and Delinquents." *University of Minnesota: Studies in the Social Sciences* 13 (Sept. 1918): 1–56.

Daly, Kathleen, and Lisa Maher, eds. *Criminology at the Crossroads: Feminist Readings in Crime and Justice.* New York: Oxford University Press, 1998.

Daniell, Beth. *A Communion of Friendship: Literacy, Spiritual Practice, and Women in Recovery.* Carbondale: Southern Illinois University Press, 2003.

Daniels, Cynthia. "Between Fathers and Fetuses: The Social Construction of Male

Reproduction and the Politics of Fetal Harm." *Signs: Journal of Women in Culture and Society* 22, no. 3 (Spring 1997): 570–616.

Darby, Lakeshia T. "Libraries in the American Penal System." *Rural Libraries* 24, no. 2 (2004): 7–20.

Darrow, Clarence. "Address to the Prisoners in the Chicago Jail." 1902, ⟨http://www.bopsecrets.org/CF/darrow.htm⟩. 14 June 2006.

Davidson, Cathy M. *Reading in America: Literature and Social History*. Baltimore: Johns Hopkins University Press, 1989.

Davis, Angela Y. *Are Prisons Obsolete?* New York: Seven Stories, 2003.

———. "From the Convict Lease System to the Super-Max Prison." In *States of Confinement: Policing, Detention, and Prisons*, edited by Joy James, 60–74. New York: St. Martin's, 2000.

———. "Public Imprisonment and Private Violence: Reflections on the Hidden Punishment of Women." *New England Journal on Criminal and Civil Confinement* 24 (Summer 1998): 339–51.

———. "Race and Criminalization." In *The House That Race Built*, edited by Wahneema Lubiano, 264–79. New York: Vintage, 1997.

Davis, Angela Y., and Kum-Kum Bhavnani. "Fighting for Her Future: Reflections on Human Rights and Women's Prisons in the Netherlands." *Social Identities Journal for the Study of Race, Nation, and Culture* 3, no. 1 (Feb. 1997): 7–32.

Davis, Angela Y., and Gina Dent. "Prison as a Border: A Conversation on Gender, Globalization, and Punishment." *Signs: Journal of Women in Culture and Society* 26, no. 4 (Summer 2001): 1235–41.

Davis, Angela Y., and Cassandra Shaylor. "Race, Gender, and the Prison Industrial Complex: California and Beyond." *Meridians: feminism, race, transnationalism,* 2, no. 1 (Spring 2001): 1–25.

Davis, Elizabeth Lindsay. *Lifting as They Climb*. New York: G. K. Hall, 1933.

Davis, Natalie. *Society and Culture in Early Modern France*. Stanford: Stanford University Press, 1975.

Delaney, Sadie Peterson. "Commencement Banquet Speech," 1–6. Atlanta University. 5 June 1950.

———. "Library Activities at Tuskegee." *Medical Bulletin of the Veterans' Administration* 17, no. 2 (Oct. 1940): 163–69.

———. "The Negro Veteran and His Books." *Wilson Bulletin for Librarians* 6, no. 10 (June 1932): 684–86.

———. "The Place of Bibliotherapy in a Hospital." *Opportunity: Journal of Negro Life*, Feb. 1938, 53–56.

———. "Time's Telling." *Wilson Library Bulletin* 29, no. 6 (Feb. 1955): 461–63.

———. "U.S.V. Hospital Library No. 91, Tuskegee, Ala." *The Crisis* 29 (Jan. 1925): 116–17.

Denzin, Norman K., and Yvonna S. Lincoln, eds. *Handbook of Qualitative Research*. 2nd ed. Thousand Oaks, Calif.: Sage, 2000.

Department of Management Services. Office of Inspector General. Internal Audit Report Number 2005-61. "Contract Management of Private Correctional Facilities." 30 June 2005, ⟨http://216.239.51.104/search?q=cache:vTw OojjAr4J:www.cadem.org/atf/cf/%257BBF9D7366-E5A7-41C3-8E3FE06FB835FCCE%257D/GEOGroupAuditReport.pdf+%22Correctional+Privatization+Commission%22+Florida+library+service&hl=en&gl=us&ct=clnk&cd=32⟩. 24 June 2006.

Dershowitz, Alan M. *The Abuse Excuse and Other Cop-Outs, Sob Stories, and Evasions of Responsibility*. Boston: Little, Brown, 1994.

Dimock, Wai Chee. "Introduction: Genres as Fields of Knowledge." *PMLA* 122, no. 5 (Oct. 2007): 1377–88.

Dixon, Melvin. "Singing a Deep Song: Language as Evidence in the Novels of Gayl Jones." In *Black Women Writers, 1950–1980: A Critical Evaluation*, edited by Mari Evans, 236–48. Garden City, N.Y.: Anchor, 1984.

Dodge, Mara L. *"Whores and Thieves of the Worst Kind": A Study of Women, Crime, and Prisons, 1835–2000.* DeKalb: Northern Illinois University Press, 2002.

Dubey, Madhu. "'Don't You Explain Me': The Unreadability of *Eva's Man.*" In *Black Women Novelists and the Nationalist Aesthetic*, 89–105. Bloomington: Indiana University Press, 1994.

Dunne, Bill. "Control Unit Prisons: Deceit and Folly in Modern Dungeons." In *The New Abolitionists: (Neo)Slave Narratives and Contemporary Prison Writings*, edited by Joy James, 39–44. Albany: State University of New York Press, 2005.

Ellis, Carolyn, and Arthur Bochner. "Autoethnography, Personal Narrative, Reflexivity: Researcher as Subject." In *Handbook of Qualitative Research*, 2nd ed., edited by Norman K. Denzin and Yvonna S. Lincoln, 733–68. Thousand Oaks, Calif.: Sage, 2000.

Erzen, Tanya. "Testimonial Politics: The Christian Right's Faith-Based Approach to Marriage and Imprisonment." *American Quarterly* 59, no. 3 (Sept. 2007): 991–1015.

Escobar, Elizam. "Art of Liberation: A Vision of Freedom." In *Imprisoned Intellectuals: America's Political Prisoners Write on Life, Liberation, and Rebellion*, edited by Joy James, 295–302. New York: Rowman and Littlefield, 2003.

Evans, Linda, Susan Rosenberg, and Laura Whitehorn. "Dykes and Fags Want to Know: Interview with Lesbian Political Prisoners by the Members of Quisp." In *Imprisoned Intellectuals: America's Political Prisoners Write on Life, Liberation, and Rebellion*, edited by Joy James, 261–78. New York: Rowman and Littlefield, 2003.

Everett, Percival. *Erasure.* New York: Hyperion, 2001.

Farnham, Eliza. *First Report of the Female Department of the Prison Association of New York.* New York: W. Dean, 1845.

Fellner, Jamie. "Out of Sight: Super-Maximum Security Confinement in the United States." In *Human Rights Watch*, edited by Malcolm Smart. Feb. 2000, ⟨http://www.hrw.org/reports/2000/supermax/⟩. 22 Feb. 2008.

Fisher, G. Richard, and Paul R. Belli. "The Preacher Who Doesn't Tell It Like It Is: The Truth Twisting and Tall Tales of Joyce Meyer." Saint Louis, Mo.: Personal Freedom Outreach, 1999. ⟨http://www.pfo.org/preacher.htm⟩. 14 Feb. 2008.

Fleming, G. James, and Christian E. Burckel. "Delaney, Sadie Peterson." *Who's Who in Colored America.* 7th ed. Yonkers-on-Hudson, N.Y.: Christian E. Burckel and Associates, 1950.

Floch, Maurice. "Bibliotherapy and the Library." *Bookmark* 18 (Dec. 1958): 57–59.

———. "Correctional Treatment and the Library." *Wilson Library Bulletin* 26 (Feb. 1952): 452–55.

Fontana, Andrea, and James H. Frey. "The Interview: From Structured Questions to Negotiated Text." In *Handbook of Qualitative Research*, 2nd ed., edited by Norman K. Denzin and Yvonna S. Lincoln, 645–72. Thousand Oaks, Calif.: Sage, 2000.

Foucault, Michel. *Discipline and Punish: The Birth of the Prison.* 1975. New York: Vintage, 1978.

———. "The Ethics of the Concern for Self as a Practice of Freedom." In *Ethics: Subjectivity and Truth*, edited by Paul Rabinow, 282–301. New York: New Press, 1997.

———. "Intellectuals and Power: A Conversation between Michel Foucault and Gilles

Deleuze." In *Language, Counter-Memory, Practice: Selected Essays and Interviews by Michel Foucault*, edited by Donald F. Bouchard, 205–17. Ithaca, N.Y.: Cornell University Press, 1977.

———. "Michel Foucault: An Interview by Stephen Riggins." In *Ethics: Subjectivity and Truth*, edited by Paul Rabinow, 121–33. New York: New Press, 1997.

———. "Prison Talk." *Power/Knowledge*, edited by Colin Gordon, 37–54. New York: Pantheon Books, 1980.

———. "Sex, Power, and Politics of Identity." In *Ethics: Subjectivity and Truth*, edited by Paul Rabinow, 164–73. New York: New Press, 1997.

———. "Technologies of the Self." In *Technologies of the Self: A Seminar with Michel Foucault*, edited by Luther H. Martin, Huck Gutman, and Patrick H. Hutton, 16–49. Amherst: University of Massachusetts Press, 1988.

———. "What Is Enlightenment?" In *Ethics: Subjectivity and Truth*, edited by Paul Rabinow, 303–19. New York: New Press, 1997.

Frank, Anne. *The Diary of a Young Girl*. Edited by Otto H. Frank and Mirjam Pressler. New York: Anchor Books, 1996.

Franke, Katherine M. "Theorizing Yes: An Essay on Feminism, Law, and Desire." *Columbia Law Review* 101 (Jan. 2001): 181–298.

Franklin, H. Bruce. "Can the Penitentiary Teach the Academy How to Read?" *PMLA* 123, no. 3 (May 2008): 643–49.

———. Introduction to *Prison Writing in 20th-Century America*, edited by H. Bruce Franklin, 1–18. New York: Penguin, 1998.

Freedman, Edwin I., ed. *Library Manual for Correctional Institutions: A Handbook of Library Standards and Procedures for Prisons, Reformatories for Men and Women and Other Adult Correctional Institutions*. New York: American Prison Association, 1950.

Freedman, Estelle B. *Their Sisters' Keepers: Women's Prison Reform in America, 1830–1930*. Ann Arbor: University of Michigan Press, 1981.

Freedman, Robert S., and David M. Hovde, eds. *Libraries to the People: Histories of Outreach*. N.p.: McFarland & Co., 2003.

Frow, John. "'Reproducibles, Rubrics, and Everything You Need': Genre Theory Today." *PMLA* 122, no. 5 (Oct. 2007): 1626–34.

Frost, Natasha, Judith Greene, and Kevin Pranis. "Hard Hit: The Growth in the Imprisonment of Women, 1977–2004." Institute on Women & Criminal Justice. 2008, ⟨http://www.wpaonline.org/institute/hardhit/index.htm⟩. 12 Feb. 2008.

Fyfe, Janet. *Books behind Bars: The Role of Books, Reading, and Libraries in British Prison Reform, 1701–1911*. Santa Barbara, Calif.: Greenwood, 1992.

Gaines, Ernest J. *A Lesson before Dying*. New York: Vintage, 1993.

Gaines, Patrice. *Laughing in the Dark: From Colored Girl to Woman of Color—A Journey from Prison to Power*. New York: Doubleday, 1994.

Garrison, Dee. *Apostles of Culture: The Public Librarian and American Society, 1876–1920*. Madison: University of Wisconsin Press, 2003.

Gaughan, T. "Raunchy 'Prison Classics' Pulled from Prison Libraries." *American Libraries* 26, no. 2 (Feb. 1995): 128–29.

Gavey, Nicola. "'I Wasn't Raped, but . . .': Revisiting Definitional Problems in Sexual Victimization." In *New Versions of Victims: Feminists Struggle with the Concept*, edited by Sharon Lamb, 57–81. New York: New York University Press, 1999.

Geary, Mike. "Trends in Prison Library Service." *Bookmobiles and Outreach Services* 6, no. 1 (2003): 79–91.

Geller, Evelyn. *Forbidden Books in American Public Libraries, 1876–1939: A Study in Cultural Change.* Westport, Conn.: Greenwood, 1984.

Gere, Anne Ruggles. *Intimate Practices: Literacy and Cultural Work in U.S. Women's Clubs, 1880–1920.* Urbana: University of Illinois Press, 1997.

Gilbert, David. "Attica—Thirty Years Later." In *The New Abolitionists: (Neo)Slave Narratives and Contemporary Prison Writings,* edited by Joy James, 313–16. Albany: State University of New York Press, 2005.

Gilligan, James. "Reflections from Life behind Bars: Build Colleges, Not Prisons." *Chronicle of Higher Education,* 16 Oct. 1998, B7.

Gilmore, Ruth Wilson. *Golden Gulag: Prisons, Surplus, Crisis, and Opposition in Globalizing California.* Berkeley: University of California Press, 2007.

Glazener, Nancy. *Reading for Realism: The History of a U.S. Literary Institution, 1850–1910.* Durham, N.C.: Duke University Press, 1997.

Gleason, Eliza Atkins. *The Southern Negro and the Public Library: A Study of the Government and Administration of Public Library Service to Negroes in the South.* Chicago: University of Chicago Press, 1941.

Goodstein, Laurie. "Critics Right and Left Protest Book Removals." *New York Times,* 21 Sept. 2007, ⟨http://www.nytimes.com/⟩. 22 Sept. 2007.

———. "Prisons Purging Books on Faith from Libraries." *New York Times,* 10 Sept. 2007, ⟨http://www.nytimes.com/⟩. 12 Sept. 2007.

Gordon, Avery F. *Ghostly Matters: Haunting and the Sociological Imagination.* 2nd ed. Minneapolis: University of Minnesota Press, 2008.

———. *Keeping Good Time: Reflections on Knowledge, Power, and People.* Boulder, Colo.: Paradigm Publishers, 2004.

———. "Methodologies of Imprisonment." *PMLA* 123, no. 3 (May 2008): 651–57.

Greenberg, Elizabeth, Eric Dunleavy, and Mark Kutner. *Literacy behind Bars: Results from the 2003 National Assessment of Adult Literacy Prison Survey.* National Center for Education Statistics. 10 May 2007, ⟨http://nces.ed.gov/PUBSEARCH/pubsinfo .asp?pubid=200747330⟩. Nov. 2007.

Greene, Robert. *The 48 Laws of Power.* New York: Penguin, 1998.

Greenfeld, Lawrence A., and Tracy L. Snell. *Women Offenders: Bureau of Justice Statistics Special Report.* U.S. Department of Justice, 1999, ⟨http://www.ojp.usdoj.gov/bjs/pub/ pdf/wo.pdf⟩. 12 June 2008.

Gruensfelder, Robert C. "The Law Enforcers Lend a Hand." In *Breaking In: Library Service to Prisoners,* edited by Rhea Joyce Rubin. Special issue of *Wilson Library Bulletin* 51, no. 6 (Feb. 1977): 510–13.

Gubert, Betty K. "Sadie Peterson Delaney: Pioneer Bibliotherapist." *American Libraries* 24, no. 2 (Feb. 1993): 124–29.

Gutiérrez-Jones, Carl. *Critical Race Narratives: A Study of Race, Rhetoric, and Injury.* New York: New York University Press, 2001.

Haag, Pamela. "'Putting Your Body on the Line': The Question of Violence, Victims, and the Legacies of Second-Wave Feminism." *Differences* 8, no. 2 (Summer 1996): 23–67.

Hall, Stuart. "Cultural Studies and Its Theoretical Legacies." In *Stuart Hall: Critical Dialogues in Cultural Studies,* edited by David Morley and Kuan-Hsing Chen, 262–75. New York: Routledge, 1996.

Hallinan, Joseph T. *Going up the River: Travels in a Prison Nation.* New York: Random House, 2001.

Hames-García, Michael. *Fugitive Thought: Prison Movements, Race, and the Meaning of Justice*. Minneapolis: University of Minnesota Press, 2004.

Hannigan, Margaret C. "The Librarian in Bibliotherapy: Pharmacist or Bibliotherapist?" In *Bibliotherapy*, edited by Ruth M. Tews. Special issue of *Library Trends* 11, no. 2 (Oct. 1962): 184–98.

Harlow, Barbara. *Barred: Women, Writing, and Political Detention*. Middletown, Conn.: Wesleyan University Press, 1992.

Hartley, Jenny. *Reading Groups: A Survey Conducted in Conjunction with Sarah Turvey*. New York: Oxford University Press, 2001.

Hartz, Fred R., Michael B. Kimmel, and Emile K. Hartz, eds. *Prison Librarianship: A Selective, Annotated, Classified Bibliography, 1945–1985*. Jefferson, N.C.: McFarland, 1987.

Heberle, Renee. "Deconstructive Strategies and the Movement against Sexual Violence." *Hypatia: A Journal of Feminist Philosophy* 11, no. 4 (Fall 1996): 63–76.

Heitzmann, K. A., and W. R. Heitzmann. "The Science of Bibliotherapy: A Critical Review of Research Findings." *Reading Improvement* 12 (1975): 120–24.

Hengehold, Laura. "Remapping the Event: Institutional Discourses and the Trauma of Rape." *Signs: Journal of Women in Culture and Society* 26, no. 1 (Autumn 2000): 189–214.

Hill-Collins, Patricia. *Black Feminist Thought: Knowledge, Consciousness, and the Politics of Empowerment*. New York: Routledge, 1990.

Holloway, Karla F. C. *BookMarks: Reading in Black and White*. New Brunswick, N.J.: Rutgers University Press, 2006.

Holmes, Shannon. *Bad Girlz*. New York: Atria, 2003.

Hosseini, Khaled. *A Thousand Splendid Suns*. New York: Riverhead Books, 2007.

Howard, Clark. *Love's Blood*. New York: St. Martin's, 1993.

Howard, June. *Publishing the Family*. Durham, N.C.: Duke University Press, 2001.

Hull, Gloria T., Patricia Bell Scott, and Barbara Smith, eds. *All the Women Are White, All the Blacks Are Men, but Some of Us Are Brave: Black Women's Studies*. Old Wellsbury, N.Y.: Feminist Press, 1982.

Human Rights Watch Women's Rights Project. *All Too Familiar: Sexual Abuse of Women in U.S. State Prisons*. New York: Human Rights Watch, 1996.

Illouz, Eva. *Saving the Modern Soul: Therapy, Emotions, and the Culture of Self-Help*. Berkeley: University of California Press, 2008.

Inglehart, Babette. "Pluck and Luck: Edna Ferber's Chicago." *Illinois Periodicals Online*. Northern Illinois University Libraries. 3 Dec. 2003, ⟨http://www.lib.niu.edu/ipo/2000/iht720023.html⟩. 15 Aug. 2006.

Inside Prison Libraries. Special issue of *Wilson Library Bulletin* 64, no. 2 (Oct. 1989).

Irwin, John. *The Felon*. Englewood Cliffs, N.J.: Prentice-Hall, 1970.

Jackson, George. *Soledad Brother: The Prison Letters of George Jackson*. New York: Bantam Books, 1970.

Jacobs, Harriet. *Incidents in the Life of a Slave Girl*. Mineola, N.Y.: Dover Publications, 2001.

Jakes, T. D. *Woman, Thou Art Loosed!* New York: Penguin, 2004.

James, Joy, ed. *Imprisoned Intellectuals: America's Political Prisoners Write on Life, Liberation, and Rebellion*. New York: Rowman and Littlefield, 2003.

———, ed. *The New Abolitionists: (Neo)Slave Narratives and Contemporary Prison Writings*. Albany: State University of New York Press, 2005.

———, ed. *States of Confinement: Policing, Detention, and Prisons*. New York: St. Martin's, 2000.

———. *Warfare in the American Homeland: Policing and Prison in a Penal Democracy.* Durham, N.C.: Duke University Press, 2007.

Jameson, Fredric. *The Prison-House of Language.* Princeton: Princeton University Press, 1975.

Jarjoura, Roger G., and Susan T. Krumholz. "Combining Bibliotherapy and Positive Role Modeling as an Alternative to Incarceration." *Journal of Offender Rehabilitation* 28, no. 1–2 (Dec. 1998): 127–39.

Jenkins, Henry. *Textual Poachers: Television Fans and Participatory Culture.* New York: Routledge, 1992.

Johnson, Joan Marie. *Southern Ladies, New Women: Race, Region, and Clubwomen in South Carolina, 1890–1930.* Gainesville: University Press of Florida, 2004.

Johnson, Paula. *Inner Lives: Voices of African American Women in Prison.* New York: New York University Press, 2003.

Jones, Aphrodite. *Cruel Sacrifice.* New York: Windsor Corp., 1994.

Jones, Edith Kathleen, ed. *The Prison Library Handbook.* Chicago: American Library Association, 1932.

Jones, Gayl. *Eva's Man.* Boston: Beacon, 1976.

———. "Gayl Jones." Interview by Claudia Tate in *Black Women Writers at Work*, edited by Claudia Tate, 89–99. New York: Continuum, 1983.

Jones, M. A. "An Overture." In *Doing Time: 25 Years of Prison Writing*, edited by Bell Gale Chevigny, 28–29. New York: Arcade, 1999.

Jones, M. D. "Information Needs of African Americans in the Prison System." In *The Black Librarian in America Revisited*, edited by E. J. Josey, 338–61. Metuchen, N.J.: Scarecrow, 1994.

Jones, Perrie, ed. *2500 Books for the Prison Library.* Minneapolis: Harrison & Smith, 1933.

Jordan, June. "All about Eva." *New York Times Book Review*, 16 May 1976, 37.

Josey, E. J., and Marva L. DeLoach, eds. *Handbook of Black Librarianship.* 2nd ed. Lanham, Md.: Scarecrow, 2000.

Kaestle, Carl F., and Helen Damon-Moore. *Literacy in the United States: Readers and Reading since 1880.* New Haven: Yale University Press, 1991.

Kaminer, Wendy. *I'm Dysfunctional, You're Dysfunctional: The Recovery Movement and Other Self-Help Fashions.* New York: Addison-Wesley, 1992.

Kaplan, Amy. *The Social Construction of American Realism.* Chicago: University of Chicago Press, 1988.

Kelley, Robin D. G. *Race Rebels: Culture, Politics, and the Black Working Class.* New York: Free Press, 1994.

Kelly, Karen. "Sshh! The Secret Is Out." *Sydney Morning Herald*, 14 July 2007, ⟨http:// www.smh.com.au/news/books/sshh-the-secret-is-out/2007/07/12/1183833675545. html⟩. 15 Jan. 2008.

Kirby, Georgiana Bruce. *Years of Experience: An Autobiographical Narrative.* New York: AMS Press, 1971.

Klein, Dorie. "Crime through Gender's Prism: Feminist Criminology in the United States." In *International Feminist Perspectives in Criminology: Engendering a Discipline*, edited by Nicole Hahn Rafter and Frances Heidensohn, 216–40. Philadelphia: Open University Press, 1995.

Knox, Sara L. *Murder: A Tale of Modern American Life.* Durham, N.C.: Duke University Press, 1998.

Koerner, Brendan I. "*Candy Licker*: A Best-Selling Book about Cunnilingus and Thugs." 2 June 2006, ⟨http://www.slate.com/id/2142831/⟩. 15 Feb. 2008.

Kurshan, Nancy. "History and Current Reality." *Women and Imprisonment in the U.S.* 23 June 2006, ⟨http://www.prisonactivist.org/women/women-and-imprisonment.html⟩. 13 Apr. 2008.

Lamb, Sharon. "Constructing the Victim: Popular Images and Lasting Labels." In *New Versions of Victims: Feminists Struggle with the Concept*, edited by Sharon Lamb, 108–38. New York: New York University Press, 1999.

Lamb, Wally. *Couldn't Keep It to Myself: Wally Lamb and the Women of York Correctional Institution*. New York: Regan Books, 2003.

————. *She's Come Undone*. New York: Atria, 1997.

Leder, Drew. *The Soul Knows No Bars: Inmates Reflect on Life, Death, and Hope*. Lanham, Md.: Rowman and Littlefield, 2000.

LeDonne, Marjorie, et al. *Final Report: Survey of Library and Information Problems in Correctional Institutions*. 4 vols. Berkeley: Institute of Library Research, University of California, 1974.

Lee, Harper. *To Kill a Mockingbird*. New York: Lippincott, 1960.

Lehmann, Vibeke. "Planning and Implementing Prison Libraries: Strategies and Resources." World Library and Information Congress: 69th IFLA General Conference and Council. Berlin. Aug. 2003, ⟨http://www.ifla.org/IV/ifla69/papers/175-E_Lehmann.pdf⟩. 2 Aug. 2006.

Lennox, Lisa. *Crack Head*. Columbus, Ohio: Triple Crown, 2005.

Levasseur, Raymond Luc. "Trouble Coming Every Day: ADX—The First Year." In *The New Abolitionists: (Neo)Slave Narratives and Contemporary Prison Writings*, edited by Joy James, 47–55. Albany: State University of New York Press, 2005.

Levy, Joann. *Unsettling the West: Eliza Farnham and Georgiana Bruce Kirby in Frontier California*. Berkeley: Heyday Books, 2004.

Lewis v. Casey. No. 94–1511. United States Court of Appeals for the Ninth Circuit. 24 June 1996, ⟨http://supreme.justia.com/us/518/343/case.html⟩. 27 June 2006.

Leys, Ruth. *Trauma: A Genealogy*. Chicago: University of Chicago Press, 2000.

Liggett, J. M. "Survey of Ohio's Prison Libraries." *Journal of Interlibrary Loan, Document Delivery and Information Supply* 7, no. 1 (1996): 31–45.

Lipscomb, Carolyn E. "Race and Librarianship." Part 2. *Journal of the Medical Library Association* 93, no. 3 (2005): 308–10. ⟨http://www.pubmedcentral.nih.gov/articlerender.fcgi?artid=1175796⟩. 4 June 2006.

Liptak, Adam. "1 in 100 U.S. Adults behind Bars, New Study Says." *New York Times*, 28 Feb. 2008, ⟨http://www.nytimes.com/2008/02/28/us/28cnd-prison.html?_r=1&hp&oref=slogin⟩. 28 Feb. 2008.

"Lockup." *U.S. News and World Report*, 22 Oct. 1990, 22.

Lombroso, Caesar, and William Ferrero. *The Female Offender*. New York: Appleton, 1915.

Long, Elizabeth. *Book Clubs: Women and the Uses of Reading in Everyday Life*. Chicago: University of Chicago Press, 2003.

Lubiano, Wahneema. "Black Ladies, Welfare Queens, and State Minstrels: Ideological War by Narrative Means." In *Race-Ing Justice, En-Gendering Power*, edited by Toni Morrison, 339. London: Chatto & Windus, 1992.

Macallair, Dan, Khaled Taqi-Eddin, and Vincent Schiraldi. *Class Dismissed: Higher Education vs. Corrections during the Wilson Years*. San Francisco: The Justice Policy Institute, 1998.

MacCormick, Austin H. *The Education of Adult Prisoners: A Survey and a Program*. New York: National Society of Penal Information, 1931.

Madriz, Esther. "Focus Groups in Feminist Research." In *Handbook of Qualitative Research*, 2nd ed., edited by Norman K. Denzin and Yvonna S. Lincoln, 835–50. Thousand Oaks, Calif.: Sage, 2000.

Mahoney, Martha R. "Victimization or Oppression? Women's Lives, Violence, and Agency." In *The Public Nature of Private Violence: The Discovery of Domestic Abuse*, edited by Martha Albertson Fineman and Roxanne Mykitiuk, 59–92. New York: Routledge, 1994.

Mancini, Matthew. *One Dies, Get Another: Convict Leasing in the American South, 1866–1928*. Columbia: University of South Carolina Press, 1996.

Marcus, Sharon. "Fighting Bodies, Fighting Words: A Theory and Politics of Rape Prevention." In *Feminists Theorize the Political*, edited by Judith Butler and Joan W. Scott, 385–403. New York: Routledge, 1992.

Martinson, Robert. "What Works? Questions and Answers about Prison Reform." *Public Interest* 22 (1974).

Maso, Carole. *Defiance*. New York: Penguin, 1998.

Mathiesen, Thomas. "Towards the 21st Century: Abolition—An Impossible Dream?" In *The Case for Penal Abolition*, edited by W. Gordon West and Ruth Morris, 333–53. Toronto: Canadian Scholars' Press, 2000.

Mauer, Marc. "The Race to Incarcerate." In *The Case for Penal Abolition*, edited by W. Gordon West and Ruth Morris, 89–99. Toronto: Canadian Scholars' Press, 2000.

McArthur, Benjamin. "The War of the Great Books." *American Heritage Magazine*, Feb. 1989, ⟨http://www.americanheritage.com/articles/magazine/ah/1989/1/1989_1_57.shtml⟩. 26 June 2007.

McHenry, Elizabeth. *Forgotten Readers: Recovering the Lost History of African American Literary Societies*. Durham, N.C.: Duke University Press, 2002.

McMurtry, John. "Caging the Poor: The Case against the Prison System." In *The Case for Penal Abolition*, edited by W. Gordon West and Ruth Morris, 167–86. Toronto: Canadian Scholars' Press, 2000.

Methven, Mildred Louise. *1000 Books for Prison Libraries, 1936–1939*. St. Paul: Dawson-Patterson, 1939.

Meyer, Joyce. *Approval Addiction: Overcoming Your Need to Please Everyone*. New York: Warner Faith, 2005.

———. *Battlefield of the Mind: Winning the Battle in Your Mind*. New York: Warner Faith, 1995.

———. *Beauty for Ashes: Receiving Emotional Healing*. New York: Faith Words, 1994.

———. *The Confident Woman: Start Today Living Boldly and without Fear*. New York: Warner Faith, 2006.

Mezirow, Jack. *Transformative Dimensions of Adult Learning*. San Francisco: Jossey-Bass, 1991.

Miller, D. A. *The Novel and the Police*. Berkeley: University of California Press, 1989.

Minow, Martha. "Surviving Victim Talk." *UCLA Law Review* 40 (1993): 1411–45.

Morris, Ruth. *Penal Abolition: The Practical Choice: A Practical Manual on Penal Abolition*. Toronto: Canadian Scholars' Press, 1995.

Morrison, Toni. "Home." In *The House That Race Built*, edited by Wahneema Lubiano, 3–12. New York: Vintage, 1997.

———. "Interview with Toni Morrison." Interview by Cecil Brown in *Massachusetts Review* 36, no. 3 (Fall 1995): 455.

———. Letter to Wahneema Lubiano. Sept. 1998.

———. "The Nobel Lecture in Literature." The Nobel Foundation. Stockholm. 7 Dec. 1993.

———. *Paradise*. New York: Alfred A. Knopf, 1997.

Muñoz, José Esteban. *Disidentifications: Queers of Color and the Performance of Politics*. Minneapolis: University of Minnesota Press, 1999.

Newman, Anabel P., Warren Lewis, and Caroline Beverstock. *Prison Literacy: Implications for Program and Assessment Policy*. National Center on Adult Literacy and ERIC Clearinghouse on Reading and Communication Skills. Bloomington, Ind. 6 June 2006, ⟨http://www.nald.ca/fulltext/report3/rep28/REP28-10.HTM⟩. 9 Sept. 2007.

New York State Library. "List of Books for Prison Libraries." Part 1. *University of the State of New York Bulletin* 57, no. 620 (1 Aug. 1916): 1–49.

Ngo, Viet Mike, with Dylan Rodriguez. "'You Have to Be Intimate with Your Despair': A Conversation with Viet Mike Ngo (San Quentin State Prison, E21895)." In *The New Abolitionists: (Neo)Slave Narratives and Contemporary Prison Writings*, edited by Joy James, 249–58. Albany: State University of New York Press, 2005.

Noire. "Author Interview." 2008, ⟨http://www.streetfiction.org/author-interviews/noire⟩. 13 Jan. 2008.

———. *Candy Licker: An Urban Erotic Tale*. New York: One World Books, 2005.

———. *G-Spot: An Urban Erotic Tale*. New York: One World Books, 2005.

O'Neill, Brendan. "Misery Lit . . . Read On." *BBC News*, 17 Apr. 2007, ⟨http://news.bbc .co.uk/2/hi/uk_news/magazine/6563529.stm⟩. 26 Apr. 2008.

Oshinsky, David M. *"Worse Than Slavery": Parchman Farm and the Ordeal of Jim Crow Justice*. New York: Free Press, 1996.

Parenti, Christian. *Lockdown America: Police and Prisons in the Age of Crisis*. Rev. and expanded ed. New York: Verso, 2008.

Parker, Alison M. *Purifying America: Women, Cultural Reform, and Pro-Censorship Activism, 1873–1933*. Urbana: University of Illinois Press, 1997.

Patterson, James, and Howard Roughan. *You've Been Warned*. New York: Little, Brown, 2007.

Pearson, Patricia. *When She Was Bad: Violent Women and the Myth of Innocence*. New York: Random House, 1997.

Peck, Janice. "The Mediated Talking Cure: Therapeutic Framing of Autobiography in TV Talk Shows." In *Getting a Life: Everyday Uses of Autobiography*, edited by Sidonie Smith and Julia Watson, 134–55. Minneapolis: University of Minnesota Press, 1996.

Pelzer, Dave. *A Child Called It: One Child's Courage to Survive*. Omaha, Neb.: Omaha Press, 1993.

Pens, Dan. "Skin Blind." In *Prison Masculinities*, edited by Dan Sabo, Terry Krupers, and Willie London, 150–52. Philadelphia: Temple University Press, 2001.

Pens, Dan, and Paul Wright. *The Celling of America: An Inside Look at the U.S. Prison Industry*. Monroe, Maine: Common Courage Press, 1998.

Phelan, Peggy. *Unmarked: The Politics of Performance*. New York: Routledge, 1993.

"The Phyllis Wheatley Club." *Woman's Era* 2 (1895): 14–15.

Pisciotta, Alexander W. *Benevolent Repression: Social Control and the American Reformatory-Prison Movement*. New York: New York University Press, 1994.

Plettenberg, Lynne. "User Needs in the Prison Library." June 2006, ⟨http://www.wam
.umd.edu/~lpletten/prisons.pdf⟩. 9 July 2007.

Pomeroy, Elizabeth. "Bibliotherapy: A Study in Results of Hospital Library Service."
Medical Bulletin of the Veterans' Administration 13 (1937): 360–64.

Preer, Jean L. "'This Year—Richmond!': The 1936 Meeting of the American Library
Association." *Libraries and Culture* 39, no. 2 (Spring 2004): 137–60.

Prendergast, Catherine. *Literacy and Racial Justice: The Politics of Learning after Brown v.
Board of Education.* Carbondale: Southern Illinois University Press, 2003.

Price, Leah. "Reading: The State of the Discipline." In *Book History*, vol. 7, edited by Ezra
Greenspan and Jonathan Rose, 303–20. University Park: Pennsylvania State University
Press, 2004.

Queer Women and Men United in Support of Political Prisoners. "Dykes and Fags Want
to Know: Interview with Lesbian Political Prisoners—Linda Evans, Susan Rosenberg,
and Laura Whitehorn." In *Imprisoned Intellectuals: America's Political Prisoners Write on
Life, Liberation, and Rebellion*, edited by Joy James, 266–78. New York: Rowman and
Littlefield, 2003.

The Quest Study Bible. Grand Rapids, Mich.: Zondervan, 1994.

Quinn, Eithne. *Nuthin' but a "G" Thang: The Culture and Commerce of Gangsta Rap.* New
York: Columbia University Press, 2005.

Radway, Janice A. *A Feeling for Books: The Book-of-the-Month Club, Literary Taste, and
Middle-Class Desire.* Chapel Hill: University of North Carolina Press, 1997.

———. "Reading Is Not Eating: Mass-Produced Literature and the Theoretical, Method-
ological, and Political Consequences of a Metaphor." *Book Research Quarterly* 2 (1986).

———. *Reading the Romance: Women, Patriarchy, and Popular Literature.* Chapel Hill:
University of North Carolina Press, 1991.

Rafter, Nicole Hahn. *Partial Justice: Women, Prisons, and Social Control.* 2nd ed. New
Brunswick, N.J.: Transaction Publishers, 1992.

Rafter, Nicole Hahn, and Frances Heidensohn, eds. *International Feminist Perspectives in
Criminology: Engendering a Discipline.* Philadelphia: Open University Press, 1995.

Rathbone, Cristina. *A World Apart: Women, Prison, and Life behind Bars.* New York:
Random House, 2005.

Rhodes, Lorna. *Total Confinement: Madness and Reason in the Maximum Security Prison.*
Berkeley: University of California Press, 2004.

Rice, Almah LaVon. "The Rise of Street Literature." *Colorlines Magazine* 44 (May/June
2008), ⟨http://www.colorlines.com/article.php?ID=291⟩. 11 Sept. 2008.

Rich, Adrienne. "Twenty-One Love Poems." In *The Dream of a Common Language.* New
York: Norton, 1978. ⟨http://www.sabrinaaiellophotography.com/files/Complete_21_
Love_Poems_by_Adrienne_Rich.htm⟩. 13 July 2008.

Richie, Beth. *Compelled to Crime: The Gender Entrapment of Battered Black Women.* New
York: Routledge, 1996.

Rodríguez, Dylan. *Forced Passages: Imprisoned Radical Intellectuals and the U.S. Prison
Regime.* Minneapolis: University of Minnesota Press, 2006.

Rooney, Kathleen. *Reading with Oprah: The Book Club That Changed America.* Fayetteville:
University of Arkansas Press, 2005.

Rubin, Rhea Joyce, ed. *Breaking In: Library Service to Prisoners.* Special issue of *Wilson
Library Bulletin* 51, no. 6 (Feb. 1977).

Rubin, Rhea Joyce, and Daniel Suvak. *Libraries Inside: A Practical Guide for Prison
Librarians.* Jefferson, N.C.: McFarland, 1995.

Saadawi, Nawal. *Memoirs from the Women's Prison*. Trans. Marilyn Booth. Berkeley: University of California Press, 1994.

Sabo, Dan, Terry Krupers, and Willie London, eds. *Prison Masculinities*. Philadelphia: Temple University Press, 2001.

Sabol, William J., Heather Couture, and Paige M. Harrison. "Prisoners in 2006." Bureau of Justice Statistics Bulletin, ⟨http://www.ojp.usdoj.gov/bjs/abstract/p06.htm⟩. 22 Jan. 2008.

Saleh-Hanna, Viviane. "Taking Too Much for Granted: Studying the Movement and Re-Assessing the Terms." In *The Case for Penal Abolition*, edited by W. Gordon West and Ruth Morris, 43–67. Toronto: Canadian Scholars' Press, 2000.

Sánchez-Eppler, Karen. "Bodily Bonds: The Intersecting Rhetorics of Feminism and Abolition." *Representations* 24 (Fall 1988): 28–59.

Sandoval, Chela. "U.S. Third World Feminism: The Theory and Method of Oppositional Consciousness in the Postmodern World." *Genders* 10 (Spring 1991): 1–24.

Santiago, Danielle. *Grindin'*. New York: Atria, 2006.

Satter, Beryl. *Each Mind a Kingdom*. Berkeley: University of California Press, 1999.

Schaffer, Kay, and Sidonie Smith. *Human Rights and Narrated Lives: The Ethics of Recognition*. New York: Palgrave Macmillan, 2004.

Schlosser, Eric. "The Prison-Industrial Complex." *Atlantic*, Dec. 1998, ⟨http://www.theatlantic.com/doc/199812/prisons⟩. 21 Feb. 2009.

Scott, Carrie Emma. *Manual for Institution Libraries*. Chicago: American Library Association Publishing Board, 1916.

Scott, James C. *Domination and the Arts of Resistance: Hidden Transcripts*. New Haven: Yale University Press, 1990.

Sedgwick, Eve. Introduction to *Novel Gazing: Queer Readings in Fiction*, 1–37. Durham, N.C.: Duke University Press, 1997.

Shakur, Assata. "Women in Prison: How We Are." In *The New Abolitionists: (Neo)Slave Narratives and Contemporary Prison Writings*, edited by Joy James, 79–89. Albany: State University of New York Press, 2005.

Shapiro, Steven R., Jeffrey M. Monks, David C. Fathi, Elizabeth Alexander, Witold J. Walczak, Steven Banks, Elliot M. Mincberg, Deborah Liu, and Charles F. A. Carbone. *Brief of the American Civil Liberties Union, ACLU of Pennsylvania, the Legal Aid Society, People for the American Way Foundation, American Friends Service Committee, and California Prison Focus as Amici Curiae in Beard v. Banks*, 1–43. The American Civil Liberties Union and the ACLU Foundation. 17 Feb. 2006, ⟨http://www.aclu.org/scotus/2005/24193lgl20060217.html⟩. 18 Aug. 2006.

Shklar, Judith. *Ordinary Vices*. New York: Belknap Press, 1984.

Showalter, Elaine. *Hystories: Hysterical Epidemics and Modern Media*. New York: Columbia University Press, 1997.

Simmons, Russell. *Do You! Twelve Laws to Access the Power in You to Achieve Happiness and Success*. New York: Gotham Books, 2007.

Sister Souljah. *The Coldest Winter Ever*. New York: Pocket Star Books, 1999.

Smith, Dinitia. "For Violent and Lost Boys, Crime Stories Offer Hope." *New York Times*, 16 Oct. 2006, ⟨http://www.nytimes.com/2006/10/16/books/16pris.html⟩. 23 Oct. 2006.

Smith, Sidonie, and Julia Watson. Introduction to *Getting a Life: Everyday Uses of Autobiography*, edited by Sidonie Smith and Julia Watson, 1–24. Minneapolis: University of Minnesota Press, 1996.

Sommers, Christina Hoff, and Sally Satel. *One Nation under Therapy: How the Helping Culture Is Eroding Self-Reliance.* New York: St. Martin's, 2005.

Sommers, Evelyn K. *Voices from Within: Women Who Have Broken the Law.* Toronto: University of Toronto Press, 1995.

Southgate, Martha. "Writers Like Me." *New York Times Sunday Book Review*, 1 July 2007, ⟨http://www.nytimes.com/2007/07/01/books/review/Southgate-t.html?_r=1&emc=eta1&oref=slogin⟩. 15 Feb. 2008.

Spector, Herman K. *The Library Program of the California Department of Corrections.* San Quentin: California Department of Corrections, 1957.

Stearns, Robert M. "The Prison Library: An Issue for Corrections, or a Correct Solution for Its Issues?" *Behavioral and Social Sciences Librarian* 23, no. 1 (Aug. 2004): 49–80.

Stevens, John Paul. Dissenting opinion. *Beard, Secretary, Pennsylvania Department of Corrections v. Banks.* No. 04-1739. Supreme Court of the United States. 28 June 2006.

Stevens, T., and B. Usherwood. "The Development of the Prison Library and Its Role within the Models of Rehabilitation." *Howard Journal of Criminal Justice* 34, no. 1 (1995): 45–63.

Stewart, Kathleen. *Ordinary Affects.* Durham, N.C.: Duke University Press, 2007.

Stingl, Jim. "Check Your Guns, Knives, and Your Boscobel Dial." *Milwaukee Journal Sentinel*, 9 Aug. 2000, ⟨http://www.prisoncentral.org/prisoncentral/Supermax/Articles/MJS%20August%209%202000.htm⟩. 30 May 2006.

Stout, Joan A., and Gilda Turitz. "Outside . . . Looking In." In *Breaking In: Library Service to Prisoners*, edited by Rhea Joyce Rubin. Special issue of *Wilson Library Bulletin* 51, no. 6 (Feb. 1977): 499–505.

Street, Brian V. "The Meanings of Literacy." In *Literacy: An International Handbook*, edited by Daniel A. Wagner, Richard L. Venezky, and Brian V. Street, 34–40. Boulder, Colo.: Westview, 1999.

———. *Social Literacies: Critical Approaches to Literacy in Development, Ethnography, and Education.* New York: Longman Group Limited, 1995.

Stringer, Vickie M. *Imagine This.* New York: Atria, 2004.

———. *Let That Be the Reason.* New York: Upstream, 2002.

Sullivan, Larry E. "Between Empty Covers: Prison Libraries in Historical Perspective." *Wilson Library Bulletin* 64, no. 2 (Oct. 1989): 26–28, 143.

———. "The Least of Our Brethren: Library Service to Prisoners." *American Libraries* 31, no. 5 (May 2000): 56–59, ⟨http://proquest.umi.com.proxy.lib.umich.edu/pqdweb?did=54170695&sid=1&Fmt=4&clientId=17822&RQT=309⟩. 2 Aug. 2006.

———. "Literature, Media, and the Construction of Juvenile Delinquency, or Nietzsche in the Nursery." 2006, ⟨http://www.arts.ualberta.ca/igel/IGEL2002/Sullivan.pdf⟩. 5 June 2006. Unpublished essay.

———. "Prison Libraries." In *Encyclopedia of Library History*, edited by Wayne A. Wiegand and Donald E. Davis Jr., 511–13. New York: Garland, 1994.

———. *The Prison Reform Movement: Forlorn Hope.* Boston: Twayne, 1990.

———. "Reading in American Prisons: Structures and Strictures." *Libraries and Culture* 33, no. 1 (Winter 1998): 113–19.

Sullivan, Larry E., and Brenda Vogel. "Reachin' behind Bars: Library Outreach to Prisoners, 1978–2000." In *Libraries to the People: Histories of Outreach*, edited by Robert S. Freeman and David M. Hovde, 113–27. Jefferson, N.C.: McFarland, 2003.

Sundquist, Eric. *American Realism: New Essays.* Baltimore: Johns Hopkins University Press, 1982.

Suvak, Daniel. "'Throw the Book at 'Em': The Change-Based Model for Prison Libraries." In *Inside Prison Libraries*. Special issue of *Wilson Library Bulletin* 64, no. 2 (Oct. 1989): 31–33.

Sweeney, Megan. "*Beard v. Banks*: Deprivation as Rehabilitation." *PMLA* 122, no. 3 (May 2007): 779–83.

———. "Legally Blind: Seeking Alternative Literacies from Prison." *Genre: Forms of Discourse and Culture* 35, no. 3–4 (Fall/Winter 2002): 599–624.

———. "Living to Read True Crime: Theorizations from Prison." *Discourse: Journal for Theoretical Studies in Media and Culture* 25, no. 1–2 (Winter/Spring 2003): 55–89.

Sykes, Charles. *A Nation of Victims: The Decay of the American Character*. New York: St. Martin's, 1992.

Tapia, Ruby C. "Profane Illuminations: The Gendered Problematics of Critical Carceral Visualities." *PMLA* 123, no. 3 (May 2008): 684–87.

Tate, Claudia. *Domestic Allegories of Political Desire: The Black Heroine's Text at the Turn of the Century*. New York: Oxford University Press, 1992.

Taylor, Jon Marc. "Pell Grants for Prisoners." In *Doing Time: 25 Years of Prison Writing*, edited by Bell Gale Chevigny, 107–12. New York: Arcade, 1999.

Tedlock, Barbara. "Ethnography and Ethnographic Representation." In *Handbook of Qualitative Research*, 2nd ed., edited by Norman K. Denzin and Yvonna S. Lincoln, 455–86. Thousand Oaks, Calif.: Sage, 2000.

Teets, H. O. Letter to Dr. Sadie T. Delaney. 21 Feb. 1957.

Teri Woods Publishing. "Teri Woods." 28 Feb. 2008, ⟨http://www.teriwoodspublishing.com/authors.htm⟩. 28 Feb. 2008.

"Texan Klan Mailings to Prisons Approved." *Corrections Digest*, 3 Sept. 1990, 3.

Travis, Trysh. "'It Will Change the World if Everybody Reads This Book': New Thought Religion in Oprah's Book Club." *American Quarterly* 59, no. 3 (Sept. 2007): 1017–41.

Trounstine, Jean. "Beyond Prison Education." *PMLA* 123, no. 3 (May 2008): 674–77.

———. *Shakespeare behind Bars: The Power of Drama in a Women's Prison*. New York: St. Martin's, 2001.

Trounstine, Jean, and Robert P. Waxler. *Finding a Voice: The Practice of Changing Lives through Literature*. Ann Arbor: University of Michigan Press, 2005.

Trump, Donald J., and Tony Schwartz. *Trump: The Art of the Deal*. New York: Ballantine, 2004.

Tuft, Carolyn. "Jefferson County, Meyer Joust over Tax Exemption." 15 Nov. 2003, ⟨http://www.stltoday.com/stltoday/news/special/joycemeyer.nsf/0/7C0D90DB0AF048E28625DDF00701F8B?OpenDocument⟩. 18 Jan. 2008.

Tuft, Carolyn, and Bill Smith. "From Fenton to Fame." *St. Louis Post Dispatch*, 13 Nov. 2003, ⟨http://www.stltoday.com/stltoday/news/special/joycemeyer.nsf/0/18C14871599F61AC86256DDD0081B42B?Open Document⟩. 18 Jan. 2008.

Turner, Nikki. *Forever a Hustler's Wife*. New York: One World, 2007.

———. *A Hustler's Wife*. Columbus, Ohio: Triple Crown, 2003.

———. *A Project Chick*. Columbus, Ohio: Triple Crown, 2004.

"United States." *Human Rights Watch*, 17 June 2006, ⟨http://www.hrw.org/wr2k/Us.htm⟩. 4 Aug. 2007.

Vanzant, Iyanla. *Yesterday, I Cried: Celebrating the Lessons of Living and Loving*. New York: Simon and Schuster, 1998.

"Veterans' Administration Hospital, Tuskegee, Alabama." *Book Trolly: The Organ of the Guild of Hospital Librarians* (Queen's Gardens, London) 1, no. 17 (Apr. 1938): 346–47.

Vogel, Brenda. *Down for the Count: A Prison Library Handbook*. London: Scarecrow, 1995.

Walls, Jeannette. *The Glass Castle*. New York: Scribner, 2005.

Warhol, Robyn R., and Helena Michie. "Twelve-Step Teleology: Narratives of Recovery/ Recovery as Narrative." In *Getting a Life: Everyday Uses of Autobiography*, edited by Sidonie Smith and Julia Watson, 327–50. Minneapolis: University of Minnesota Press, 1996.

Warner, Kevin. "Against the Narrowing of Perspectives: How Do We See Learning, Prisons, and Prisoners?" *Journal of Correctional Education* 58, no. 2 (June 2007): 170–84.

Warner, Michael. "Uncritical Reading." In *Polemic: Critical or Uncritical*, edited by Jane Gallop, 13–38. New York: Routledge, 2004.

Waxler, Robert P., and Jean R. Trounstine. *Changing Lives through Literature*. Notre Dame, Ind.: University of Notre Dame Press, 1999.

Weeks, Linton. "New Books in the Hood: Street Lit Makes Inroads With Readers and Publishers." *Washington Post*, 31 July 2004, C01.

West, Latoya. "Biography of Public Speaker and Starting Over Coach Iyanla Vanzant." ⟨http://realitytv.about.com/od/startingover/a/IyanlaBio.htm⟩. 19 June 2008.

West, W. Gordon, and Ruth Morris, eds. *The Case for Penal Abolition*. Toronto: Canadian Scholars' Press, 2000.

Whitaker, Tu-Shonda. *Flip Side of the Game*. Columbus, Ohio: Triple Crown, 2004.

———. *Game Over*. Columbus, Ohio: Triple Crown, 2004.

Whitehorn, Laura. "Resisting the Ordinary." In *Warfare in the American Homeland: Policing and Prison in a Penal Democracy*, edited by Joy James. Durham, N.C.: Duke University Press, 2007.

Whitney, Donald S. "A Review of *The Secret* by Rhonda Byrne." 2007, ⟨http://biblicalspirituality.org/secret.html⟩. 12 Feb. 2008.

Wicker, Tom. Foreword to *Prison Writing in 20th-Century America*, edited by H. Bruce Franklin, xi–xv. New York: Penguin, 1998.

Wideman, John Edgar. Introduction to *Live from Death Row*, by Mumia Abu-Jamal. New York: Avon, 1996.

Wiegand, Wayne. "Tunnel Vision and Blind Spots: What the Past Tells Us about the Present. Reflections on the Twentieth-Century History of American Librarianship." *Library Quarterly* 29 (Jan. 1999): 1–32.

Wilcox, Janelle. "Resistant Silence, Resistant Subject: (Re)Reading Gayl Jones's *Eva's Man*." *Genders* 23 (30 June 1996): 72–87.

Williams, Heather Andrea. *Self-Taught: African American Education in Slavery and Freedom*. Chapel Hill: University of North Carolina Press, 2005.

Williams, Lillian, Serece Boehm, and Randolph Boehm, eds. *Records of the National Association of Colored Women's Clubs, 1895–1992*. Bethesda, Md.: University Publications of America, 1993.

Williams, Sherley Anne. "Some Implications of Womanist Theory." *Callaloo* 27 (Spring 1986): 303–8.

Wilson, James Q. "Crime and Public Policy." In *Crime: Twenty-Eight Leading Experts Look at the Most Pressing Problem of Our Time*, edited by James Q. Wilson and Joan Petersilia, 489–510. San Francisco: Institute for Contemporary Studies, 1995.

———. *Moral Judgment: Does the Abuse Excuse Threaten Our Legal System?* New York: Basic Books, 1997.

Wolf, Maryanne. *Proust and the Squid: The Story and Science of the Reading Brain*. New York: HarperCollins, 2007.

Woods, Teri. *Dutch*. New York: Teri Woods Publishing, 2003.

Worth, Robert. "A Model Prison." *Atlantic Monthly*, Nov. 1995, 38–44.

Wright, Paul, ed. "Jail Builder Faces Open Records Suit." *The Razor Wire*. Miami News Herald 2005, ⟨http://www.november.org/razorwire/2005-02/LawLibrary.html⟩. 3 May 2007.

———. *Prison Legal News*. ⟨http://www.prisonlegalnews.org/FAQ.aspx⟩. 24 July 2008.

Wuornos v. State. No. 644 So.2d 1000. Florida. 1994.

Zahm, Barbara, dir. *The Last Graduation*. New York: Deep Dish Television, 1997.

Zedner, Lucia. "Wayward Sisters: The Prison for Women." In *The Oxford History of the Prison: The Practice of Punishment in Western Society*, edited by Norval Morris and David J. Rothman, 329–61. New York: Oxford University Press, 1995.

INDEX

programming, 39, 64–65, 144. See also
 Beard v. Banks; Urban fiction: penal
 officials' banning of
Changing Lives through Literature, 5, 272
 (n. 16)
Charmaine, 153, 182
Cheng, Anne Anlin, 251
Chicken Soup for the Prisoner's Soul, 59, 129,
 174, 182
Christine, 70, 72, 75–76 (ills.), 167, 170–71
Cleage, Pearl, and *What Looks Like Crazy on
 an Ordinary Day*, 198–200, 248
Coldest Winter Ever, The. See Sister Souljah
 and *The Coldest Winter Ever*
Convict lease system, 22–23, 274–75
 (n. 11), 275 (nn. 12, 15)
Counseling and therapeutic programs for
 prisoners, 85–86, 131, 175, 189, 214,
 285 (n. 11), 290 (n. 82). *See also* Meyer,
 Joyce: as mentor for prisoners; Rehabilitation for prisoners; Religion: and
 twelve-step programs; Self-help reading
 practice
Coyle, William J., and *Libraries in Prisons*,
 41–42
Critical Resistance. *See* Prison abolition
 movement
Cummins, Eric, 5, 6
Curtis, Florence Rising, 30, 32

Darlene, 54, 147, 148, 150, 151, 167
Davis, Angela, 3, 5, 48, 110, 112, 175
Deedee, 190
Delaney, Sara Peterson, 33–34, 278 (n. 56).
 See also Bibliotherapy
Denise: on reading, 3, 54, 63, 64, 129, 182,
 247; detailed portrait of, 129–39; on
 The Coldest Winter Ever, 132, 135–36,
 163, 242; on Iyanla Vanzant's *Yesterday,
 I Cried*, 132–33, 136–38; on *Bastard out
 of Carolina*, 133–35; on *Laughing in the
 Dark*, 134, 138; on *Battlefield of the Mind*,
 136, 138–39, 197, 203–4; on the group
 discussions, 138, 236, 238, 239–40, 242;
 on urban fiction, 147–48; on *Their Eyes
 Were Watching God*, 233–35
Deven, 187, 205–7, 233–34, 236–37, 238,
 239–40, 242

Dickey, Eric Jerome, 167
Disidentification, 162, 165, 166, 222, 284
 (n. 29)
Donna, 65, 67, 70, 121, 193
Drea, 191, 196–97, 239

Education, penal: diminishing opportunities for, 1, 2, 51, 281 (n. 101); and
 elimination of Pell Grants for prisoners,
 2, 50, 51; and prisoners' educational
 levels, 11, 157–58, 276 (n. 26); history
 of, 23–24, 25, 46, 47, 276 (n. 27), 277
 (n. 43), 281 (n. 92); and self-education,
 48, 49–50; and courses offered,
 214–15; critical debate about, 255–57.
 See also Urban fiction: depictions of
 education in
Eleanor, 64, 70
Ellen, 173
Evanovich, Janet, 60, 66, 81

Facework, 169
Farnham, Eliza, 24–25
Floch, Maurice, 35
Foucault, Michel, 5, 179–80, 186, 205
Fraden, Rena, 6
Frank, Anne, and *Diary of a Young Girl*, 1,
 228–29
Franklin, H. Bruce, 145

Gaines, Ernest J., and *A Lesson before
 Dying*, 229–30, 237
Gaines, Patrice, and *Laughing in the Dark*,
 135, 136, 138
Gavey, Nicola, 106
Gender. *See* African American women;
 Latina women; Libraries, public; Meyer,
 Joyce: on gender roles; Prisoners,
 female; Prisoners, male; Urban fiction:
 gender and sexuality in; Victimization;
 White women
Genevieve, 121, 191, 207, 239, 240, 241, 245
Genre theory, 8, 168
Ghetto fiction. *See* Urban fiction
Goines, Donald, 42, 43, 44, 140, 144, 145
Gordon, Avery, 88, 190
Grace, 80
Gracie, 238

Ohio prison. *See* Northeast Pre-Release Center

Olivia: book reviews by, 72, 74 (ill.); on John Grisham's books, 78, 79, 118, 119, 163; on self-education, 79; on Joyce Meyer's books, 182, 184–85, 188, 193, 196; on the group discussions, 226, 239, 241

Omega, 148

Oprah, 217, 235; and the *Oprah Winfrey Show*, 60, 66, 221

Patterson, James, 60, 65, 66, 79, 143, 242, 292 (n. 8)

Patty, 99, 199–200, 252

Peck, Janice, 203

Peggy, 67, 79

Pell Grants for Prisoners. *See* Education, penal

Penitentiaries, 20, 21, 22, 27, 28, 274 (n. 6), 276–77 (n. 34)

Pennsylvania prison. *See* State Correctional Institution at Muncy

Phelan, Peggy, 250–51

Price, Leah, 22, 81, 248

Prison abolition movement, 3, 5; and Critical Resistance, 253, 255, 303 (n. 1); and International Conference on Penal Abolition (ICOPA), 253–54, 303 (n. 1)

Prisoners, female: in federal and state prisons, 4; rates of incarceration for, 4, 272 (n. 11); historical neglect of, 22, 24, 275 (nn. 17, 18), 276 (n. 27); and reformatories, 24–25, 27, 276 (nn. 23, 26); and sexualized violence in prisons, 106, 110; "prisoner" as privileged term, 271 (n. 2); and felons' ineligibility for welfare, 271 (n. 6); and prison labor, 283 (nn. 20, 21). *See also* Education, penal; Race; Rehabilitation for prisoners; Victimization

Prisoners, male, 4, 5, 271 (n. 8), 272 (n. 10)

Prisoners, political, 48, 49. *See also* Davis, Angela; Jackson, George; Whitehorn, Laura

Prison-industrial complex, 39–40, 279–80 (n. 76)

Prison Legal News, 48

Prisons, private, 40, 280 (nn. 77, 79)

Punitive individualism, 200

Race: and sentencing trends, 4, 272 (n. 11); study participants' self-identifications of, 9–10, 259–62; and supermaximum prisons, 20; in penal history, 21–24; and prison library holdings, 26–27, 61–62, 282 (nn. 9, 14); in John Grisham's novels, 78; in true crime books, 80; and silence about victimization, 92–93, 94; and resistance to gendered violence, 106–12; and involvement in crime, 133–35; and trends in book publishing, 142–43, 146; as a factor in the group discussions, 236–37, 294 (n. 27). *See also* African American women; Censorship and reading restrictions in prisons; Libraries, public; Literacy; Urban fiction: race in; White women

Rae, 71, 99, 199

Raylene, 67, 71

Readers, non-incarcerated, 6, 7

Reading: scholarship about prisoners and, 5, 145–46; scholarship about women and, 6; cultures of, 6–7, 8, 227; compared to watching television, 8, 65; conceived of as a tool for rehabilitating prisoners, 20, 22, 24, 27–33, 34; therapeutic model of, 21, 27–29, 33–37, 278 (n. 62); disciplinary model of, 21, 28–29, 32, 35, 45; radical model of, 21, 37, 48–50, 52; gendered constructions of, 24–25, 31–32, 276 (n. 24), 277–78 (n. 48); as discussed in prison library manuals, 25, 26–27, 29–32; as a right for prisoners, 38, 41, 42, 43; and book circulation in prisons, 54–55, 64; conditions for, in penal settings, 54–55, 70–71, 79; prisoners' unique preferences for, 66–67, 70, 79; prisoners' personal records of, 72, 73–77 (ills.); and embodiment, 79, 283 (nn. 25, 27); as an intersubjective process, 79–82, 135–39, 243, 249, 301 (n. 6); and fantasy, 129–30, 247; as a catalyst for writing, 153, 167–68, 230, 288 (n. 58); and disidentification, 162, 165, 166, 222, 284 (n. 29); changes in study participants' practices of, 241–42; my discoveries about, 246–49. *See also* Censorship and reading restrictions in prisons; Libraries, prison; Self-help reading practice

Reformatories. *See* Prisoners, female: and reformatories

Rehabilitation for prisoners: critique of the concept, 3–4, 38, 253–57, 302 (n. 12); deprivation theory of, 20; and penal policies about religious reading materials, 20, 24, 27, 28, 36, 45–46, 277 (n. 38); racialized presumptions about, 22; as catalyst for the development of prison libraries, 22, 29, 37; and penal policies about fiction, 29–31, 42, 43, 277 (n. 46). See also *Beard v. Banks*; Bibliotherapy; Counseling and therapeutic programs for prisoners; Education, penal; Reading: conceived of as a tool for rehabilitating prisoners; Religion

Religion: and increase in Christian materials and programs in contemporary prisons, 47, 49, 173–74, 295 (n. 3); prisoners' non-Christian practices of, 70, 193, 299 (n. 72); critical debates about Christian self-help books, 174–75; and twelve-step programs, 299 (n. 58). *See also* Libraries, chaplain's; Meyer, Joyce; Rehabilitation for prisoners: and penal policies about religious reading materials

Research methods, 12–17, 262–68, 273 (n. 29)

Research participants, background information about, 9–11, 243–46

Rhodes, Lorna, 52

Rhonda, 63, 67, 232–33, 272 (n. 11)

Rich, Adrienne, 90, 91

Rodríguez, Dylan, and *Forced Passages*, 3, 49–50, 208

Ronnie, 141, 147

Rose, 72, 121, 167, 171

Rush, Benjamin, 27–28

Sahara, 155

Sakina, 19, 65, 67, 111, 288 (n. 55)

Sánchez-Eppler, Karen, 113

Santiago, Danielle, and *Grindin'*, 154, 155–58, 160–61, 248

Schlosser, Eric, 39, 40

Self-help reading practice: modeled by Denise, 136–39; and predominance of Christian reading materials, 173, 296 (n. 4); and critical debate about self-help books, 174–76; definition of, 176–81; and Foucault's notion of care of the self, 179–81; modeled in prisoners' discussions of Joyce Meyer and her books, 182–85, 187–88, 190–92, 193–97, 200–204, 206–8, 222–23; books as surrogate mentors in, 182–88, 192; intersubjectivity in, 182–88, 215; modeled in prisoners' discussions of Iyanla Vanzant and her books, 185–86, 190, 193–94, 204–5, 207, 208; as a means to reckon with guilt and abandonment, 189–92; as a means to exercise control over one's mind, 193–97; competing conceptions of agency entailed in, 198–204; as a means to (co)author the self, 204–8, 211; the role of autobiographies in, 216–17; modeled by Monique, 216–25

Sentimentality. *See* Victimization: sentimentality and emotion as frameworks for addressing

Sheldon, Sidney, 60, 192

Shelly, 64, 94, 107, 108–10

Silence. *See* Victimization: silence about

Simmons, Russell, and *Do You!*, 217

Sissy: on *Woman, Thou Art Loosed!*, 95; on *Yesterday, I Cried*, 115–16; on *The Coldest Winter Ever*, 162; on *Battlefield of the Mind*, 188, 202; modeling a self-help reading practice, 192; on *Incidents in the Life of a Slave Girl*, 231–32; on the group discussions, 236, 237–38

Sister Souljah and *The Coldest Winter Ever*: depictions of education in, 66, 157; prisoners' written responses to, 68–69 (ills.), 74 (ill.); prisoners' identification with, 80, 132, 135, 160, 162–63, 166–67, 215; thin character portrayals in, 132, 162; as progenitor of urban fiction, 140; use of black vernacular in, 150, 166; depictions of the drug trade in, 155–57;

discussion of women's solidarity in, 160; homophobia and gender politics in, 293–94 (n. 23)

Sky, 231

Solo, 70, 190, 244–45; on reading and prison libraries, 1, 51, 58, 282 (n. 7), 290 (n. 1); modeling a self-help reading practice, 177–78, 185–86, 235, 300 (n. 73); as mentor, 186, 208, 234, 236; writings of, 209–11, 299–300 (n. 72)

Sommers, Christina Hoff, and Sally Satel, 85, 176

Soso, 149, 153–54, 158, 161

Spector, Herman K., 34, 35–36, 279 (n. 74). *See also* Bibliotherapy

Standardized Chapel Library Project. See Libraries, chaplain's

Starr, 4, 70, 116, 118, 148, 252–53, 289 (n. 67)

State Correctional Institution at Muncy (SCI-M), location and population of, 9

Steel, Danielle, 60, 167, 282 (n. 9)

Stewart, Kathleen, 207, 226, 227, 249

Stewart, Martha, 168, 216

Street lit. *See* Urban fiction

Stringer, Vickie, 140, 146, 149; and *Let That Be the Reason*, 164–65. *See also* Triple Crown Publications

Sue, 99

Tamia, 111, 189

Tanya, 107, 111, 123

Television. *See* Censorship and reading restrictions in prisons: compared to availability of television programming; Reading: compared to watching television

Touché, 153, 168, 293 (n. 19)

Trauma. *See* Victimization

Triple Crown Publications, 140–41, 142 (ill.), 143, 144, 167, 240. *See also* Stringer, Vickie

Trounstine, Jean, 5, 6

True crime books: popularity of, in women's prisons and jails, 12, 62, 65, 67, 99, 140, 148; racial dynamics of, 80, 284 (n. 29)

Turner, Nikki, 146, 167, 295 (n. 36)

Tyra, 95, 100, 165, 201, 222, 239

Underground Book Railroad, 54–55

Urban fiction: and penal officials' attitudes about crime fiction, 28, 31, 58, 60, 62, 140, 144, 148; penal officials' criticisms of, 42, 143; penal officials' banning of, 44, 143–44, 146–47, 291–92 (n. 7); prisoners' enthusiasm for, 65, 66, 71, 147, 148–52, 167, 215; as a means to facilitate communication with others, 80, 81, 152, 160; depictions of drug use and the drug trade in, 132, 140, 143, 145, 147, 148, 155–57; prisoners' criticisms of, 132, 147–48, 167, 169–71, 215; history of, 140–41, 291 (nn. 1, 2); class and capitalism in, 141, 145, 149, 152–54, 165–66, 169–70; race in, 141, 145, 151, 152, 157–58; realistic elements of, 141, 147–52, 153, 292 (n. 16), 293 (n. 18), 295 (n. 35); gender and sexuality in, 141–42, 145, 155, 158–61; critical debate about, 141–43, 145–46, 171–72, 248, 291 (n. 6); and trends in book publishing, 142–43, 146; black vernacular speech in, 149–50, 152; fantastic elements of, 150, 151, 153–55; prisoners as authors of, 153, 167–68; depictions of education in, 157–58, 294 (n. 28); prisoners' disidentificatory readings of, 162–64, 165–67. *See also* African American women; Sister Souljah and *The Coldest Winter Ever*; Zane

Valhalla, 66, 81, 144, 152, 156, 182, 239

Vanzant, Iyanla, 81, 288 (nn. 57, 64), 298 (n. 54); and *Yesterday, I Cried* in prisoners' discussions of victimization, 87, 112–13, 114–18; and *Yesterday, I Cried* in prisoners' self-help reading practices, 132–33, 136–38, 176–78, 185–86, 190, 193–94, 204–5, 207, 208

Victimization: theoretical debates about, 83–93, 97, 284 (n. 5), 285 (n. 17), 286–87 (nn. 34, 35, 38); women prisoners' experiences of, 85, 130, 132–33, 285 (n. 9); silence about, 90–96; and race, 92–93, 94, 106–12; and agency in relation to criminal acts, 97–106; and resistance, 106–12, 159; sentimentality and emotion as frameworks for addressing, 112–22; and confession, 122–23; intersubjective dimensions of efforts to reckon with, 122–26; prisoners teaching others about, 126; complicity in, 133; in urban fiction, 158–61; from a cross-cultural perspective, 230–31; in *Incidents in the Life of a Slave Girl*, 231–32. *See also* Brown, Wendy; Heberle, Renee; Meyer, Joyce; Vanzant, Iyanla

Walls, Jeanette, and *The Glass Castle*, 81, 87, 118–22, 120 (ill.), 216–17, 289 (nn. 70, 73, 75)

Warner, Kevin, 255–56, 257

Warner, Michael, on "uncritical reading," 17, 274 (n. 36)

War on Drugs, 39

Wendy, 93, 95, 96, 140, 150, 152, 169, 232–33

Whitaker, Tu-Shonda, and *Flip Side of the Game* and *Game Over*, 163–66

Whitehorn, Laura, 48, 272 (n. 13), 297 (n. 34)

White women, 4, 6, 9, 152, 272 (n. 11). *See also* Race; Urban fiction: race in

Women. *See* Prisoners, female

Woods, Teri, 146, 151, 291 (n. 2)

Wuornos, Aileen, 97, 286 (n. 37)

Zane, 146, 150, 291 (n. 4)